DYNAMICS OF COMPETENCE-BASED COMPETITION

TECHNOLOGY, INNOVATION, ENTREPRENEURSHIP AND
COMPETITIVE STRATEGY SERIES

Series Editors: John McGee and Howard Thomas

Published

STEFFENS
Newgames: Strategic Competition in the PC Revolution

BULL, THOMAS & WILLARD
Entrepreneurship

DAI
Corporate Strategy, Public Policy and New Technologies: Philips and the
European Consumer Electronics Industry

BOGNER
Drugs to Market: Creating Value and Advantage in the Pharmaceutical
Industry

Forthcoming titles

PORAC
The Social Construction of Markets and Industries

MOROSINI
Cross-Cultural Acquisitions and Alliances

Other titles of interest

DAEMS & THOMAS
Strategic Groups, Strategic Moves, and Performance

DENNING
Making Strategic Planning Work in Practice

DOZ
Strategic Management in Multinational Companies

MCNAMEE
Developing Strategies for Competitive Advantage

TSE
Marks and Spencer

Related journals – sample copies available on request

European Management Journal
International Business Review
Journal of Retailing and Consumer Services
Long Range Planning
Scandinavian Journal of Management

DYNAMICS OF COMPETENCE-BASED COMPETITION

THEORY AND PRACTICE IN THE NEW STRATEGIC MANAGEMENT

edited by

Ron Sanchez, Aimé Heene, and Howard Thomas

Pergamon

UK   Elsevier Science Ltd, The Boulevard, Langford Lane, Kidlington, Oxford OX5 1GB, UK

USA   Elsevier Science Inc., 660 White Plains Road, Tarrytown, NY 10591-5153, USA

JAPAN   Elsevier Science (Japan), Tsunashima Building Annex, 3-20-12 Yushima, Bunkyo-ku, Tokyo 133, Japan

Copyright © 1996 Elsevier Science Ltd

First edition 1996

Library of Congress Cataloging-in-Publication Data
Dynamics of competence-based competition: theory and practice in the new strategic management/edited by
Ron Sanchez, Aimé Heene, and Howard Thomas.—1st ed.
p. cm.—(Technology and strategy series)
Includes index.
ISBN 0-08-042585-2 (hardcover)
1. Strategic planning.   2. Industrial efficiency.   3. Competition.
1. Sanchez, Ron.   II. Heene, Aimé.   III. Thomas, Howard, 1943–.
IV. Series.
HD30.28.D93   1996
658.4′012—dc20   95-42283
                                    CIP

British Library Cataloguing in Publication Data
A catalogue record for this title is available from the British Library.

ISBN 0-08-042585-2

Printed and bound in Great Britain by BPC Wheatons Ltd, Exeter

CONTENTS

Contents   vii

EDITORS' PREFACE

The 1990s are witnessing a growing movement in strategic management interested in developing new concepts that more realistically reflect the rapidly evolving nature of business organizations and the changing dynamics of their competitive interactions. Much of this interest has gathered under the banner of the "core competence" perspective. Stimulated by articles and books by Gary Hamel and C. K. Prahalad beginning in the late 1980s, the competence perspective has begun to attract the attention of a growing number of strategy researchers and practitioners.

The chapters which follow aspire to make a significant theoretical contribution to this new perspective on strategic management. Their objectives are ambitious, but straightforward:

1. To begin to lay the foundation for a theory of competence-based competition that can incorporate the dynamic and cognitive aspects of the core competence perspective that promise to reinvigorate the development of strategy theory.
2. To demonstrate through firm and industry studies the practical applicability of the concepts that are key elements in the competence theory proposed here.

This book is the result of efforts by twenty researchers to develop and apply concepts of competence to illuminate its growing importance in competition. It is perhaps unusual among edited volumes in the care which has been taken to define and use a common vocabulary of competence throughout all the papers. This vocabulary is used in both articulating and applying a theory of competence-based competition. As a result, we believe the papers achieve a level of theoretical coherence unusual in an emerging research perspective. This theoretical coherence has allowed the grouping of sixteen papers into true chapters developing several themes essential to building a theory of competence-based competition.

The research included here is part of a growing stream of research and conversation in the strategy field that has had some notable public expressions. A three-day workshop on competence-based competition held in Genk, Belgium, in November 1992 was sponsored by the Strategic Management Society and hosted by the DeVlerick School voor Management. A number of papers from this conference subsequently appeared in a volume on competence-based competition* by Gary Hamel and Aimé Heene in 1994.

A second conference was organized by Howard Thomas, Ron Sanchez, and Aimé Heene at the European Institute for Advanced Studies in Management (EIASM) in Brussels in November 1993. The purpose of the Brussels conference was to discuss firm and industry studies that developed and applied competence concepts. From the stimulating discussions of that conference, the basic elements of a theory of competence-based competition began to emerge and have been developed into the three theoretical chapters in Part One of this book. The generalized conceptions of those chapters would not have been accessible without the grounded studies of firms and industries presented at the Brussels conference and included now in Parts Two to Five.

A final word of gratitude is due to Ms. Gerry Van Dijk and her staff at EIASM for their usual exceptional efficiency and professionalism in hosting the 1993 Brussels conference. Aimé Heene also acknowledges the support provided by Coopers and Lybrand for his work on core competence and competition-based competition, and Ron Sanchez acknowledges support for his research from the Advanced Development Center of Philips Consumer Electronics, Eindhoven, Netherlands.

Ron Sanchez, Aimé Heene, and Howard Thomas
Champaign, Illinois, and Gent, Belgium

Competence-Based Competition, Gary Hamel and Aimé Heene, eds., John Wiley, New York, 1994.

LIST OF CONTRIBUTORS

Luis Araujo is a lecturer in the Department of Marketing at Lancaster University.

David L. Atchison is a Ph.D. candidate at David Eccles School of Business, University of Utah.

Geert Baven is a Ph.D. candidate in strategic management at the Rotterdam School of Business, Erasmus University.

William C. Bogner is an assistant professor in the Department of Management at Georgia State University.

Geoff Easton is Professor and Head of the Department of Marketing at Lancaster University.

Tom Elfring is Associate Professor of Strategic Management and Director of the Ph.D. program at the Rotterdam School of Business, Erasmus University.

Phil Gorman is a doctoral student in strategy at University of Illinois, Champaign, Illinois.

Michael Gregory is a professor in the Manufacturing Group at Cambridge University.

Aimé Heene is professor of strategic management at DeVlerick School voor Management, Gent.

Øystein Jensen is assistant professor in marketing at Bodø Graduate School of Business in Norway.

Michael Lewis is a researcher in the Manufacturing Group at Cambridge University.

Sandra McNabb is a vice-president of AT&T Network Systems in Belgium.

Maurizio Rispoli is a professor in the Dipartimento di Economia e Direzione Aziendale of the Universita degli Studi di Venezia.

Tom Roehl is Assistant Professor of International Business, University of Illinois, at Urbana-Champaign.

Ron Sanchez is Assistant Professor of Policy and Stategy at University of Illinois at Urbana-Champaign.

Stephen Tallman is Associate Professor of Management at David Eccles School of Business, University of Utah.

Howard Thomas is Towey Professor of Strategic Management and Dean of the College of Commerce and Business Administration, University of Illinois, Champaign, Illinois.

Henk W. Volberda is Assistant Professor of Strategic Management and Chairman of the Graduate Program Board at the Rotterdam School of Business, Erasmus University.

Beverly C. Winterscheid holds joint appointments at the Free University of Brussels, the European Institute for Advanced Studies in Management (EIASM), and Baldwin-Wallace College.

Russell W. Wright is Assistant Professor of Policy and Strategy at University of Illinois at Urbana-Champaign.

I

INTRODUCTION: TOWARDS THE THEORY AND PRACTICE OF COMPETENCE-BASED COMPETITION

Ron Sanchez, Aimé Heene, and Howard Thomas

A growing movement in strategic management seeks to use concepts of "competence" or "core competencies" to develop new insights into the nature of interfirm competition and potential sources of competitive advantage. Adapting many concepts developed under the banners of the resource-based view of the firm (Penrose 1959; Lippman and Rumelt 1982; Wernerfelt 1984; Dierickx and Cool 1989; Barney 1991; Grant 1991; Amit and Schoemaker 1993; Peteraf 1993) and dynamic capabilities (Teece, Pisano and Shuen 1990), the emerging competence perspective appears to be striving to build a conceptual framework capable of addressing key dimensions of strategic competition not adequately addressed by those perspectives, useful as they have been in guiding strategic thought to date.

Thinking about competition and management in terms of competences or, especially, "core competencies" (Prahalad and Hamel 1990) has struck a responsive chord in strategy academics and practitioners alike. The competence perspective's new emphasis on intangibles like "technology, skill, and synergy" has found "an immediate and unusually broad resonance within these communities" (Rumelt 1994: xv) as strategy prescriptions derived from concepts of industry structures, portfolio analysis, and the like become increasingly difficult to reconcile with the rapidly evolving nature of strategic competition.

Nevertheless, the core competencies perspective is not without its own limitations. Most of the shortcomings in the current conversation about competence, however, are characteristic of a research perspective still in the process of formation: There is an evident absence of a clearly articulated theory or framework for theory building. Concepts and constructs invoked are often vague and likely to be idiosyncratic to each writer. There is terminological inconsistency across writers. And lacking a well defined theory base, the field has a paucity of empirical studies. In the absence of a shared theoretical framework and a common vocabulary for discussing competence, development of the competence perspective has been stymied by research that is often provocative, but limited in generalizability by the idiosyncratic interpretations of the competence perspective to which individual researchers have had to resort.

The purpose of this book is to take some critical first steps toward building a theoretical foundation for the competence perspective. Our hope is that the theory of competence-based competition we begin to develop and apply in this book will provide a more coherent framework for further development of the competence perspective.

This chapter introduces key ideas previously developed in the competence perspective, explains the ways in which this book extends previous work, and describes this book's intended contribution to furthering development and practical application of a theory of competence-based competition. Thus, this chapter serves as a guide both to the basic ideas which compose a theory of competence-based competition and to the theoretical chapters and industry studies in this book which develop these ideas in more detail. Concluding comments suggest some significant advantages that a theory of competence-based competition can bring to strategy research and practice. We propose some new directions for theory building and research in competence-based competition, and we suggest implications of the theory we develop here for practical applications in strategic management of competence-based competition.

THEMES DEVELOPED IN PREVIOUS RESEARCH ON CORE COMPETENCE

Motivated in large measure by the publication of influential papers by Gary Hamel and C. K. Prahalad (Hamel 1989; Prahalad and Hamel 1990; Hamel 1991; Prahalad and Hamel 1993) in *Harvard Business Review, Strategic Management Journal,* and elsewhere, the November 1992 conference in Genk, Belgium, on competence-based competition sponsored by the Strategic Management Society served as a focal point for assessing the state of the competence perspective in terms of both theory development and applications in practice. The publication in 1994 of the Hamel and Heene edited volume *Competence-Based Competition,* which draws on papers presented at the 1992 Genk conference, provided strategy researchers with the most extensive exposition of the competence perspective to that time. Though not intended as a compendium of all work in the competence area, the Hamel and Heene volume nevertheless serves as a useful benchmark for identifying the "core" of ideas underlying the "core competence" perspective thus far.

Rumelt (1994: xv–xvi) identifies four key components of the concept of core competence:

(1) Core competences are competences that "span" across businesses and products within a corporation. They support several products or businesses.

(2) Competences have "temporal dominance" over products in that they evolve more slowly than the products they make possible.

(3) Competences arise through the "collective learning" of the firm, especially through coordinating diverse production skills and integrating multiple streams of technologies. Such competences are enhanced through use.

(4) The "competitive locus" of competence-based competition is a contest for acquisition of skills. Competition in product markets is "merely a superficial expression" of the underlying competition over competencies.

In essence, the core competence perspective depicts firms as competing by proactively learning-by-doing in order to develop competences that span across business activities and make possible a stream of individual products.

Heene (1994: xxv) identifies several ways in which the core competences perspective complements prior strategy concepts. The core competence perspective, for example, extends the traditional notion of strategy as seeking a "fit" of a firm's capabilities with its environment to the notion that a firm can "stretch" to acquire new competences that can change the competitive environment in its favor. Similarly, the core competence perspective shifts conceptual emphases in strategy from resource allocation decisions to discovering ways to "leverage" resources across businesses and products. The core competences perspective encourages a shift from thinking of the firm as a portfolio of businesses to conceiving of the firm as a portfolio of competences which can be extended across businesses. It also asks managers and researchers alike to think of competition not just as a battle for market share, but as a contest for opportunity share in the industries of the future (Hamel and Prahalad 1994).

The core competence perspective opens the conceptual lens of strategy to admit a more dynamic view of competition in which differences in idiosyncratic firm *capabilities* matter greatly and are the basis for much of the competitive advantage a firm may enjoy in its product markets in the long run. Hamel and Heene (1994) identify several hoped-for improvements in a new theory of strategic management derived from the core competence perspective:

• A new theory of strategy based on competences would yield insights into the ways in which continuous renewals of capabilities by firms determine the dynamics of the changing sources of competitive advantage in evolving product markets. The new strategy theory should clarify the role not just of specific knowledge in a firm's competitive advantage at one point in time, but of processes for "knowledge creation" and "knowledge engineering" (Hamel and Heene 1994: 317) that create, sustain, and extend a firm's competitive advantage.

- A new theory should explicitly integrate the notion of the firm as a "learning organization" that maintains strategic and operational flexibility by thinking and acting systemically, by permanently striving for renewal through continuously rethinking its fundamental sources of competitive advantage(s), by creating an appropriate information infrastructure to promote internal and external information flows, by using self-regulating teams to achieve a flat non-hierarchical organization structure that encourages creativity and initiative, by creating an explicit shared vision of the future to coordinate decisions and actions, and by accepting and using intuition, symbolism, and metaphors in processes for identifying, creating, and renewing competences.
- A new theory would resolve some apparent dilemmas in current strategy theories, such as the dichotomization of cost leadership and product differentiation strategies, by indicating how firms competing in environments that demand both competences simultaneously might organize to reconcile the conflicts that such seemingly opposing competences might create within the firm.
- A new strategy theory would give insights into sources of synergy by identifying the characteristics of a "strategic architecture" and associated "concepts, tools, techniques, and models" (Hamel and Heene 1994: 319) that can help a firm combine resources and capabilities scattered throughout the firm into processes that coherently build and leverage competences.

THIS VOLUME'S RESEARCH ON COMPETENCE-BASED COMPETITION

The research into competence-based competition presented in this volume takes a significant step towards achieving many of the ambitious improvements which Hamel and Heene urge for a new competence-based theory of strategic management. Our approach is straightforward: we hope to begin to compose *a theory of competence-based competition* that makes explicit the premises and elements of the core competence perspective. Then, by clearly articulating and elaborating the premises, concepts, and terminology of a competence perspective and progressively refining them into an integrated and coherent theory of competence-based competition, we hope to suggest how many of the desired improvements in the power of strategy theory identified by Hamel and Heene might actually be realized.

For the purpose of developing a more rigorous theory of competence-based competition, we explicitly choose to set aside for the time being a notion that has thus far had great prominence in the competence perspective—*i.e.,* the notion that some competences of firm are "core," while (by implication) other competences of a firm are not "core." This view of competences has led to much debate within the core competences perspective—and not surprisingly. Since no clear conceptualization of *competence* has yet been put forward in the competence perspective, we believe that efforts to distinguish competences that are "core" from those that are not "core" are likely to fail on grounds of inadequate conceptualization of the underlying notion of competence *per se*. Thus, in this volume our focus is directly on understanding the nature of *competence* and its role in competition.

By deferring the "coreness" issue within the competence perspective, we do not intend to turn our backs on what has been said about "core competencies" to date. On the contrary, many of the ideas about "core competence" advanced by various writers to date are provocative and offer insights fundamental to the work we have undertaken in this volume. For the purpose of theory building, however, we believe the necessary first step is to develop a clear concept of "competence" adequate to serve as the foundation for a theory of competence-based competition. A more developed theoretical base is essential for refining our understanding of how competences are created, used, and obsoleted in competition. As we build a theory of competence-based competition, a more structured picture should emerge of the ways in which competences impact competition and lead to competitive advantages. As the elements of this picture come into place, we will begin to have a more adequate framework for judging the relative importance of alternative kinds of competences. We believe the concepts developed in this volume make considerable progress in providing a theoretical framework for assessing the relative importance of a firm's competences.

EXPECTATIONS OF A THEORY OF COMPETENCE-BASED COMPETITION

Theories try to describe essential aspects of phenomena of interest and to identify and explain causal relationships between phenomena (Hempel 1966; Stinchcombe 1968). As a field of research, strategy undertakes to describe the essential features of competitive interactions between firms and to explain their outcomes. In this endeavor, theory-building in strategy faces several problematic challenges. Strategy theory must try to explain fundamental relationships between many complexly interrelated phenomena. Given the complex subject matter addressed by strategy research, specific relationships which may be isolated theoretically for analysis in the abstract can rarely, if ever, be observed and tested empirically or applied in practice in a comparable degree of isolation. Moreover, those phenomena that are the objects of strategy research and theorizing appear to exist in an environment that is undergoing constant change. Consequently, phenomena which arguably appear to have strong causal relationships at one point in time may appear only weakly related, or even unrelated, in a later—and inevitably different—set of environmental conditions. Further, it is often not at all clear whether some environmental changes are best treated as exogenous or endogenous to the interrelated phenomena we are studying. In strategy, deciding where the boundaries of a theory-building or testing effort lie is often problematic.

Setting boundaries in theory-building efforts in strategy can be likened to trying to find a comfortable balance on a tightwire strung between the horns of an enduring dilemma. On the one hand, placing narrow boundaries on the phenomena to be studied may have the virtue of leading to fairly precise speculations about the nature of the relationships between the phenomena included within the boundaries of the study. Imposing narrow boundaries, however, may allow precise illumination of relationships that may be overwhelmed in a real world setting by the powerful influences of other phenomena not included in the study. On the other hand, casting a wider net to include more interrelated phenomena in a theory-building effort may have the virtue of treating a larger set of phenomena that is more representative of the actual world, but the complexity of the interrelationships between multiple phenomena is likely to frustrate theory-building efforts that try to discover clear causal relationships between specific phenomena.

The emerging focus on *competences* as the conceptual linchpin of theory-building in strategy, however, shows considerable promise of resolving this dilemma. Analyzing competition as a dynamic contest between competences seems to strike a useful balance between a need to encompass the complexity and dynamism of real-world competition, on the one hand, and the need for sensemaking using our limited cognitive capabilities for understanding dynamic complexity, on the other. In essence, taking competences as the unit of analysis in strategy research and theory-building appears to cast the right size conceptual net into the sea of competitive interactions between firms. As the chapters within this volume and elsewhere give evidence, the catch from this conceptual net includes promising new insights into both intrafirm and inter-firm competitive dynamics.

The intended contribution of this volume, as well as the objective of this chapter in summary form, is to propose the essential elements and causal relationships of a theory of competence-based competition and to suggest the implications of this theory for research and practice in strategy. To this end, we first establish an internally consistent vocabulary for identifying and discussing the essential elements in a theory of competence-based competition. We use this vocabulary to advance the theoretical discussions in the chapters in Part One of this volume. This vocabulary is also used throughout the chapters in Parts Two to Five that elaborate specific aspects of competence theory in various industry contexts.

A VOCABULARY FOR DESCRIBING COMPETENCE-BASED COMPETITION

The beginning of wisdom is the definition of terms.

Socrates

To begin building a theory capable of articulating the nature of important relationships in competence-based competition, we adopt a vocabulary for identifying competitive phenomena and describing their relationships as precisely as possible (Camerer 1985). To avoid creating a new and unfamiliar vocabulary for describing competence-based competition, we use a number of terms in current use in the strategy literature. Various researchers, however, have imputed a number of different meanings to many of these terms, with some resulting terminological confusion in the strategy literature on competence. In defining the terms in the following vocabulary, our objective is to develop a vocabulary that is conceptually adequate, internally consistent, and capable of serving as a language for discussing competence-based competition. We use some familiar terms— like *capabilities* and *competences*—for which we have developed specific meanings that may differ in some respects from previous meanings imputed to those terms by others. Since this vocabulary has been adopted in all the chapters in this volume—with, we believe, a resulting benefit of conceptual coherence across these diverse studies—we urge the reader to consider carefully the following definitions of terms and the relationships between these terms that are explicit or implied in these definitions.

Assets are anything tangible or intangible the firm can use in its processes for creating, producing, and/or offering its products (goods or services) to a market. **Tangible assets** are physical, "touchable" objects like machines and buildings. **Intangible assets** are non-physical assets—for example, capabilities (defined below), knowledge (both tacit and non-tacit), information, brand equity, reputation, and intellectual property rights. Assets of strategic importance may be firm-specific or firm-addressable. **Firm-specific assets** are those which a firm owns or tightly controls. **Firm-addressable assets** are those which a firm does not own or tightly control, but which it can arrange to access and use from time to time.

Capabilities are *repeatable patterns of action in the use of assets* to create, produce, and/or offer products to a market. Because capabilities are intangible assets that determine the uses of tangible assets and other kinds of intangible assets, we recognize capabilities as an important special category of assets. Accordingly, in this volume we often refer to "assets *and* capabilities" even though, strictly speaking, *capabilities* are included within the term *assets* in our vocabulary. **Skill** is taken here as a special form of *capability,* with the connotation of a rather specific capability useful in a specialized situation or related to the use of a specialized asset. For example, a firm may have a capability in efficient manufacturing that consists of a number of specific skills in routing flows of work-in-progress, maintaining machine settings, monitoring conformance to specifications, and other specific tasks involved in manufacturing.

Resources are *assets that are available and useful* in detecting and responding to market opportunities or threats. Resources include capabilities, as well as other forms of useful and available assets.

Competence is *an ability to sustain the coordinated deployment of assets* in a way that helps a firm *achieve its goals*. Here we use the word *ability* in the ordinary language meaning of a "power to do something." To be recognized as a competence, a firm activity must meet the three conditions of *organization, intention, and goal attainment*. If a firm's activities result in some form of goal attainment, but the activities lack the element of intention implicit in a *deployment* of assets or the element of organization implicit in *coordinating* a deployment of assets, then the firm's attainment of some goal(s) may be regarded as a matter of luck (Barney 1986), not as a result of its competence. Similarly, if a firm has intention and organization in a coordinated deployment of assets, but its activities do not promise or actually result in some measure of goal attainment, its activities do not constitute a competence.

In a dynamic environment, **maintaining competences** requires continual adaptation to maintain an effective (goal-attaining) coordinated deployment of assets under changing conditions. Even in a stable environment, maintaining competence requires efforts to overcome systemic tendencies to organizational entropy in the form of, for example, gradual declines in coordination capability or in the clarity of the intentions that motivate an on-going deployment of assets.

Competence building is any process by which a firm achieves *qualitative changes* in its existing stocks of assets and capabilities, including new abilities to coordinate and deploy new or existing assets and capabilities in ways that help the firm achieve its goals. Competence building creates, in effect, *new options for future action* for the firm in pursuing its goals. Competence building takes place when a firm acquires qualitatively different assets (for example, a new kind of machine) that it can use more effectively in conjunction with its existing capabilities, but often competence building involves creating or adopting new capabilities (new patterns of action) in the use of new or existing assets.

Competence leveraging is the applying of a firm's existing competences to current or new market opportunities in ways that do not require qualitative changes in the firm's assets or capabilities. Competence leveraging may be carried out using the firm's existing stocks of assets and capabilities or may require *quantitative changes* in stocks of *like-kind assets* similar to those the firm already uses. Competence leveraging, in effect, is the exercise of one or more of a firm's *existing options for action* created by its prior competence building. For example, using existing assets and capabilities to produce and market current products is a form of competence leveraging. Similarly, increasing production by adding a second shift of factory operation meets this definition of competence leveraging, because it is exercising an existing option to use more like-kind assets already being deployed by the firm's existing competences. Increasing production by developing and producing new kinds of products, however, would require competence-building to create new options for action that require qualitatively different assets and capabilities.

Knowledge is the set of beliefs held by an individual about causal relationships among phenomena. To the extent that a group of individuals within a firm have a shared set of beliefs about causality, that set of shared beliefs constitutes **organizational knowledge** (von Krogh, Roos, and Slocum 1994). Since *competence* implies an intention to achieve some desired result (goal) through action, and since action-taking requires some notions of cause and effect, knowledge and the application of knowledge through action are at the foundation of the concepts of skills, capabilities, and (ultimately) competence. The "micro-level" knowledge-in-action of individuals is the source of skills, but the capabilities and competences of firms as organizations arise from a more "macro-level" organizational knowledge about how to coordinate and deploy assets and capabilities.

Goals are the set of interrelated "gap-closing" objectives which motivate a firm's decision making and give direction to its competence-building and competence-leveraging activities. Sanchez and Heene (1996, this volume) characterize a firm as a system for carrying out operations, acquiring tangible and intangible resources, enacting management processes, and forming and acting on a strategic logic. These actions of a firm are motivated by desires of decision makers within the firm to close **strategic gaps** between the perceived and the desired states of any of the firm's **system elements** (operations, tangible assets, intangible assets, management processes, and strategic logic). Sanchez and Thomas (1995, this volume) characterize a firm's goals as *the set of desired states of a firm's system elements* that a firm acts to attain. Thus, a firm's goals at a given point in time will consist of some specific set of gap-closing objectives like achieving targeted profit levels, growth (in terms of revenue, facilities, employees, etc.), developing new technology, creating new products, and improving environmental performance, among many possible objectives.

A firm's goals are interrelated because deploying resources in pursuit of each gap-closing objective of the firm requires allocation of limited resources; an allocation of resources to one objective implies a reduced possibility for resource allocation to another objective, at least in the near term. Because each firm will make specific allocations of resources to gap-closing activities according to its particular set of strategic goals, each firm will engage in a distinctive pattern of competence building and competence leveraging activities in pursuit of its specific set of goals.

Management processes include data gathering and interpreting, decision making about task and resource allocations, communicating decisions, disseminating information, and designing incentive structures intended to carry out the strategic logic of the firm (defined below). Management processes thus determine how evaluations and decisions will be made within the firm. From a firm's management processes emanate the decisions, rules, procedures, norms, values, and other methods of analysis and choice which govern the way a firm obtains and allocates resources to competence building and competence leveraging activities. Management processes design the incentive structures by which the firm allocates rewards (financial compensation, employee benefits, recognition, promotion, etc.) and sanctions (demotions, undesirable transfers, terminations, etc.) to employees and other resource providers.

Strategic logic refers to the rationale(s) employed (explicitly or implicitly) by decision makers in the firm as to how specific deployments of resources are expected to result in an acceptable level of attainment of the firm's goals. All employees within a firm have at least some degree of discretion in the allocation of resources. For example, even the lowest ranking member of a firm will have some discretion to decide the best use of his or her time and effort in performing an assigned task. Thus, the strategic logic of the firm is *not* an exclusive creation of top managers, who are able only to make allocations of resources to broadly defined purposes. Subsequent interpretations by other employees as to how resources should be used for more finely defined purposes within the firm require the adoption by each decision maker of a rationale for deciding the most effective use of resources for a specific purpose. In this sense, the firm's strategic logic for using resources resides at all levels of the firm, and for this reason, a firm's strategic logic may be subject to inconsistencies across the various activities of the firm.

A key management task in competence-based competition is maintaining the effectiveness of the firm's competence building and leveraging processes by achieving consistency of strategic logic throughout the firm. Managers may try to achieve some level of consistency of strategic logic by employing various management processes. Some managers may rely on centralized planning and decision making in a hierarchical organization structure, while others may emphasize corporate culture and values as a unifying force for bringing consistency in strategic logic to a flexible, team-based organization structure.

Competence group is a cluster of firms within an industry that engage in *similar* competence building and/or competence leveraging activities at a given point in time. Firms within a competence group may maintain both competitive and cooperative interactions with each other. The competitive efforts of a firm will most directly impact and be most directly impacted by the actions of other firms in its competence group, because they are likely to be serving more or less the same set of customer needs. Firms in competence groups compete, however, by trying to distinguish themselves in the eyes of their targeted customers through building distinctive competences that allow them to offer differentiated products and/or lower prices.

Converging competence groups arise when some firms that presently have dissimilar competences are following competence building trajectories that suggest those firms will have comparable competences and thus are likely to become competitors in the foreseeable future. **Diverging competence groups** occur when firms with currently similar competences are engaged in different patterns of competence building that suggest they are migrating to different regions in competitive space.

Members of a competence group may also cooperate in various forms of collaborative competence leveraging or competence building. **Competence alliances** are collaborations of firms that have joined together in some way for varying periods of time for the purpose of building or leveraging competences. Competence alliances may include specific forms of inter-firm activities, including project-based partnering, strategic alliances for technology development, establishing supply relationships, and long-term distribution or marketing arrangements. Competence alliances, along with market transactions, are a means by which a firm can access firm-addressable assets and competences. In some contexts, it may also be useful to distinguish between **competence building alliances** and **competence leveraging alliances.**

BASIC CONCEPTUALIZATION OF COMPETENCE-BASED COMPETITION

We now use the vocabulary developed above to articulate a basic conceptualization of competence-based competition. This conceptualization is intentionally dynamic, systemic, cognitive, and holistic. Following this basic statement, we discuss these aspects of this theory of competence-based competition in more detail.

Firms are *open systems* whose actions are motivated by the collective goal-seeking behavior of employees and other stakeholders. Firms pursue *strategic goals* that consist of distinctive sets of objectives (and relative emphases on objectives) for closing gaps between perceived and desired states of the system elements of a firm. Each firm follows a *strategic logic* which is an operative rationale as to how the firm's actions will achieve some acceptable level of goal attainment. That strategic logic is reflected in the *management processes* that determine a firm's use of *resources*—i.e., its available *assets,* including its *capabilities and skills.*

Following its strategic logic for achieving its goals, a firm uses resources in some form of *coordinated deployment* of assets and capabilities to create, produce, and offer products to markets. These coordinated deployments of resources constitute *competences* when they lead to positive market responses that help a firm achieve its goals. Offering products in a market produces flows of financial resources, data about the competitive environments of markets, and other inputs useful to the firm in setting and pursuing its goals. Firms that try to serve market needs through similar competence leveraging and building activities form *competence groups* of firms that compete most directly in markets for input resources and in markets for outputs (products and services).

Because competences take time to develop, firms will usually allocate some resources to *competence building* (creating new assets, capabilities, and modes of coordinating assets and capabilities). Other resources will be used in *competence leveraging* (applying existing competences to markets in ways that do not require qualitative changes in assets or capabilities). Thus, in striking its preferred balance between pursuing long-term and near-term goals, a firm will deploy resources in a distinctive mix of competence building and competence leveraging activities. The strategically important differences between firms, in both the near term and the long term, arise from each firm's distinctive mix of competence building and competence leveraging activities.

As a firm meets success or failure in attaining its goals, it may modify its goals to be more closely aligned with whatever goals it believes it can actually attain in its evolving environment. Goal modification leads to changes in a firm's competence building and competence leveraging activities. Collectively, the competitive dynamics of an industry are driven by changing managerial perceptions and internal processes for goal-setting that lead firms to pursue distinctive patterns of competence leveraging and trajectories of competence-building activities.

The resources useful to a firm in pursuing its goals may reside within the firm (they may be *firm-specific resources*) or they may reside in other firms (they may be *firm-addressable resources*). To have access to resources that are under the control of other firms but that are useful in pursuing its own goals, a firm may bid for use of other firms' competences or resources in market transactions or may enter into *competence alliances* to connect its competences or resources with those of other firms. Thus, interactions between firms to access both resources for inputs and markets for outputs may be both competitive or collaborative, and firms may sometimes maintain simultaneous competitive and collaborative resource relationships with other firms.

ELEMENTS OF A THEORY OF COMPETENCE-BASED COMPETITION

The chapters in this volume develop a theoretical perspective on competitive dynamics that elaborates the foregoing conceptualization of the underlying dynamics of competence-based competition. This perspective essentially views competition as a contest between firms that build and leverage competences in the pursuit of their respective sets of goals. By recognizing the diversity of goals that may motivate firm behaviors, we admit the possibility of a diversity of strategic logics held by different firms about what mix of competence building and competence leveraging will be most helpful to each firm in achieving its specific goals. In pursuit of their goals, firms may have access to and deploy both firm-specific and firm-addressable resources. The goal-seeking behavior of firms may therefore include activities undertaken in concert with other firms, as well as activities that compete with other firms.

As firms try to leverage existing competences into new markets and as they try to build new competences, firms may create new technologies, new organizational forms, and new kinds of product strategies that change the competitive environments of markets. Changes in competitive conditions introduced by one firm's competence leveraging or competence building are likely to provoke competence leveraging or competence building responses from other firms. Thus, from a systems perspective on competence, at least some aspects of the change in a firm's competitive environment may result from a firm's own competence building and leveraging actions.

Certain fundamental properties of firms and their competitive and co-operative interactions in competence-based competition are developed through the following conceptual elements:

- A firm is a *goal-seeking system* of interrelated tangible and intangible assets deployed in pursuit of the firm's goals.
- A firm is an *open system* that requires both (a) other firms and employees to provide resources (materials, skills, knowledge) as inputs to its processes for creating, producing, and offering products, and (b) markets to accept its products and reward the firm with flows of resources (money, market information, reputation, customer relation-ships, etc.) which further help the firm achieve its goals. The firm's prospects for attaining its goals thus depend critically on its ability to manage the *systemic interdependency* of its own internal resources and processes and external resources.
- Firms may try to acquire resources for inputs or markets for its outputs by *competing* against other firms or by *cooperating* with them. Thus, within a firm's strategic logic for achieving its goals, competition and collaboration with firms and customers are not always mutually exclu-sive choices, but rather may be complementary modes of obtaining the flows of resources and the access to markets that a firm needs to attain its goals.
- In a steady-state environment, firms may be expected to engage in stable patterns of competitive actions that promise some acceptable level of goal attainment for each firm. *Competitive dynamics* result, however, when managers in at least one firm change their assessments of the gap between the perceived and desired states of one or more system elements, modify the firm's goals, and begin to take gap-closing actions. Changes in goals may lead managers to undertake new compe-tence leveraging activities that change competitive conditions in the short run, new forms of competence-building that change competition in the long run, or both kinds of activities.
- *Competence leveraging* to close strategic gaps occurs when a firm acquires and deploys more like-kind resources in ways that do not re-

quire the firm to acquire new kinds of competences. *Competence building* occurs when a firm attempts to close strategic gaps by acquiring qualitatively new assets or capabilities or new ways of coordinating its deployments of assets and capabilities.

- Because competence denotes an ability to sustain the coordinated deployment of assets in a way that helps a firm to achieve its goals, in dynamic market environments an essential aspect of maintaining or increasing competence is the flexibility of the firm to acquire and deploy assets in new ways appropriate to changing circumstances. Thus, in dynamic product or resource markets, *strategic flexibility*—the ability to advantageously change assets, capabilities, and coordinated deployments (Sanchez 1993, 1995)—becomes critical to succeeding in competence-based competition.

- Competence-based competition, in which the interactions of firms create dynamic competitive environments as they seek goal attainment through leveraging and building competences, may therefore be likened to a state of *perpetual corporate entrepreneurialism* in which *continuous learning* about how to build new competences and leverage existing competences more effectively becomes a new dominant logic (Prahalad and Bettis 1986; Sanchez 1995) for lending strategic coherence to firm processes.

DEVELOPING A THEORY OF COMPETENCE-BASED COMPETITION

The three chapters in Part One of this volume undertake to build a conceptual foundation for a theory of competence-based competition. These chapters develop a systems view of the firm, examine the strategic goals of firms and their impacts on patterns of firm competence building and leveraging, and investigate resulting industry dynamics.

A Systems View of the Firm

The first chapter in Part One, by Sanchez and Heene (1996, in this volume), develops a construct of the firm as a goal-seeking open system (see Fig. 2.1 in Chapter 2). Sanchez and Heene characterize a firm as a system of *tangible and intangible assets* organized under a *strategic logic* for achieving its goals and using certain *management processes* for guiding its creation, production, and marketing of products. They examine the nature of these system elements when a firm functions as an open system that must constantly replenish its stocks of tangible and intangible assets through its interactions with other firms and markets. Strategic change in the firm as a system is motivated by managers' perceptions of *strategic gaps* between perceived and desired states of each system element. Strategic change occurs as a firm's managers seek to close strategic gaps by changing flows of resources to the asset stocks that make up each system element in the firm. *Learning* is the process through which a firm identifies and seeks to accomplish desirable qualitative changes in its stocks and flows of assets.

This system view of the firm extends prior conceptualizations of strategic competition in several important respects. It extends the resource-based view of the firm as a collection of asset stocks and flows (Dierickx and Cool 1989) by explicitly incorporating (1) *managerial cognition* that affects what kinds of asset stocks and flows the firm will try to achieve, (2) managers' *coordination ability* in deploying resources and managing asset flows, and (3) managers' abilities to *manage knowledge* in processes for building and leveraging competences.

Changes in asset stocks and flows within the firm as a system are accomplished through feedback loops called *control loops* that are subject to increasing *causal ambiguities* as managers try to monitor and change "higher-order" system elements in the firm, like the firm's strategic logic for competing. Because of the causal ambiguities surrounding higher system elements in a firm, strategic management in a dynamic environment can be characterized as including a search by managers for *implied* strategic gaps in the firm's higher system elements. Through this conceptualization, the systems model tries to incorporate both the dynamic uncertainties to be managed in strategic change and the cognitive processes by which managers try to overcome causal ambiguities and make choices that lead to beneficial strategic change.

Sanchez and Heene propose that cognition-based higher system elements are harder to change and thus take a longer time to change than lower system elements (tangible assets and current operations). As a result, higher-order control loops regulating the firm's stocks and flows of intangible assets, management processes, and strategic logic exhibit long dynamic response times as a firm tries to undergo strategic change. The time required to induce change in stocks of higher system elements results in critical *dynamic system effects* that act as a drag on the ability of the firm to adapt in a dynamic environment. Sanchez and Heene suggest that a fundamental means available to managers for managing these system effects is to try to create *strategic flexibility* by acquiring *flexible resources* and a *flexible coordination ability* that can enable the firm to more readily detect and respond to opportunities to redeploy resources to alternative uses.

A systems view of the firm helps to develop further insights into how managers might go about developing "strategy as stretch and leverage" (Prahalad and Hamel 1993). From this systems perspective, "strategy as stretch" suggests that competence-based competition is a *contest between managerial cognitions* about what kinds of assets and capabilities will be most useful in the future—and therefore what kinds of competences the firm should start to build now. "Strategy as leverage" suggests that firms must also compete by leveraging their current competences to greatest possible effect in the present. Achieving strategic flexibility helps managers to pursue both strategy as stretch and strategy as leverage. Acquiring flexible resources that are more likely to be useful in a dynamic and uncertain future than specific-use resources may help managers compensate for their limited cognitive abilities to "stretch" that results from the inability to predict future resource requirements precisely. Flexible resources and coordination abilities also let managers "leverage" the firm's competences broadly and quickly in response to current competitive opportunities and threats.

Strategic Goals

Sanchez and Thomas (1996, in this volume) extend the Sanchez and Heene (1996, in this volume) systems view of the firm by investigating the nature of the strategic goals of a firm. They characterize a firm's strategic goals as the *firm-specific set of desired states of a firm's system elements*. By identifying possible modes of desired change in a firm's system elements, they develop a basic *taxonomy of strategic goal-seeking behaviors* that distinguishes various kinds of competence building and competence leveraging activities.

Sanchez and Thomas develop a perspective on a firm's competence-based competitive behavior that is more *holistic* than the profit-maximizing or rent-seeking motive generally assumed in economic perspectives in strategy research. However, they first place firm goal-seeking behavior in an economic context by showing that the concept of *firm value* in contemporary finance theory recognizes the economic value of both competence leveraging and competence building. They make this argument by characterizing a firm's competence building activities as a process of investing current cash flows and new capital infusions in new competences that create *real options* (Myers 1977) to generate new cash flows in the future. These real options are equivalent to a firm's *strategic options* (Sanchez 1991, 1993, 1995) to develop, produce, and market products in the future. A firm's strategic options, many of which are rooted in human capabilities and cognitions, are shown to be an important component of the firm's market value in dynamic competitive environments.

A firm's competence leveraging activities are then characterized as the exercising of some of the firm's existing strategic options created by prior competence building. Exercising strategic options produces new cash flows that fund further investments by the firm in creating more strategic options, and so on. Sanchez and Thomas thus depict processes of competence building and leveraging as a "virtuous circle" of creating and exercising strategic options.

As firms engage in competence leveraging and competence building, each firm will generate distinctive patterns of resource flows that support the firm's specific processes for creating economic value. A firm engaged primarily in competence leveraging will require flows of like-kind productive resources to exercise its existing strategic options, and exercising existing strategic options will generate current cash flows which are the principal basis for the economic value of the firm. A firm engaged in competence building, on the other hand, will require new flows of qualitatively different kinds of resources (especially intellectual resources) to build competences that give the firm new strategic options. Creating new strategic options does not generate immediate cash flows for the firm, but creates options for the firm to generate cash flows in the future. Financial markets recognize the economic value of the new strategic options a firm creates through competence building in the form of share price appreciation.

The patterns of resource flows that distinguish competence leveraging activities from competence building activities provide the basis for developing a taxonomy of goal-seeking firm behaviors.

Industry Dynamics

The effects of competence-building and competence-leveraging activities of firms on industry structures and dynamics are studied by Gorman, Thomas, and Sanchez (1996, this volume). They first assess the evolution of concepts of strategic groups, from early concepts premised on industry structures to more recent concepts based on managerial cognitions. They propose that competence theory suggests a further evolution of group concepts, and they introduce the concept of *competence groups* consisting of firms engaged in similar competence leveraging and building activities. Because each firm's distinctive set of strategic goals leads it to pursue a distinctive pattern of competence building, competence groups are likely to be dynamic and thus may be transitory. The diversity of firms' competence building activities sometimes brings firms into a cluster of similar competence leveraging activities, but can also lead to disintegration of competence groups as firms seek to build new distinctive competences. Thus, firms may also form converging competence groups or diverging competence groups.

The short-run competitive dynamics of an industry and the long-run evolution of an industry result from the convergences and divergences of firms' competence building activities. Since a firm's efforts to build new competences are guided by managers' cognitions, in the Gorman, Thomas, and Sanchez conceptualization of industry dynamics and evolution, managerial cognitions are the engines of industry change and the precursors of future competitive interactions.

INDUSTRY STUDIES OF COMPETENCE-BASED COMPETITION

The chapters in Parts Two to Five of this volume are studies of firms and industries that amplify many of the elements in the theory of competence-based competition outlined in the theoretical chapters of Part One. We next preview these firm and industry studies, indicating the research subject of each chapter and suggesting what each contributes towards developing the theory of competence-based competition. The studies have been grouped together to offer interrelated perspectives on how competences interact with product markets (Part Two), how firms identify and build new competences (Part Three), how firms leverage competences effectively (Part Four), and how competence building acts as the driver of competitive dynamics and industry evolution (Part Five).

The Market Test for Competence

Competence, as defined in the vocabulary of this chapter, is the ability to sustain the coordinated deployment of assets and capabilities in ways that enable a firm to achieve its goals. Thus, competences must be defined and assessed by the kinds of market responses they are capable of eliciting, including their ability to generate flows of revenues, market information, reputation, and other inputs the firm acquires from the market. The two chapters by Bogner and Thomas and by Rispoli in Part Two explore the interrelationships of competences and product markets in competence-based competition.

Taking a view of products as *bundles of product attributes,* Bogner and Thomas (1996, this volume) propose that the competences required to compete in a given product market can be classified by the competences needed to create specific categories of product attributes. They propose that for any products that comprise a product market, certain product attributes are *threshold attributes* which all products of that type must have to be competitive. Thus, to compete in that product market, a firm must have at least the competence required to provide its products with the essential threshold attributes. However, threshold attributes also have the property that providing more than the minimum level of performance in any threshold attributes will not elicit a better market response to a firm's product. Any capability of a firm to provide threshold attributes in excess of the market threshold cannot be considered a competence, because it would fail the test of eliciting a more favorable market response.

Bogner and Thomas further identify product attributes that are essential in a product category, but for which a higher level of performance beyond some threshold will elicit a better market response. Such attributes are called *central attributes.* In addition, product attributes which are not required to compete in a given product category, but which can nevertheless improve the market's response to a firm's products, are identified as *plus-only attributes.* A firm's capabilities in offering more appropriate central attributes and plus-only attributes are essential to achieving competence in a given product market.

Bogner and Thomas then propose that just as a product can be viewed as a bundle of product attributes, a firm can be understood as a bundle of resources (assets and capabilities) which the firm can deploy to create threshold attributes, central attributes, and/or plus-only attributes in its products. They go on to suggest that competence-based competition within a product market can be characterized by the various competence building and competence leveraging activities firms pursue as they seek to offer products with distinctive combinations of the three kinds of attributes. Achieving a successful combination of threshold attributes, central attributes, and plus-only attributes therefore requires competences based on specific forms of technological and market knowledge needed to produce these attributes. Bogner and Thomas illustrate the main points in their analysis of the market test for competences with examples drawn from the pharmaceutical industry.

Working within the context of competition in services provided by hotels, Rispoli (1996, this volume) develops a related approach to identifying and classifying competences that emphasizes that the attributes of product offerings must often be further distinguished for different market segments. He identifies the "general knowledge and ... appropriate resources" necessary simply to compete in the hotel industry as "general" or "first level" competences (corresponding to competences based on threshold attributes in the Bogner and Thomas [1996, in this volume] framework). Other "second level" competences, however, are needed to offer acceptable products to specific segments of the hotel market. Rispoli then proposes "third level," firm-specific competences that create products with a distinctive appeal within a market segment and therefore that determine how successful a firm will be in eliciting a favorable market response in that segment. Rispoli then describes competition within a sample of the European hotel industry in terms of groups of firms that are similar in their *scope of competences*. These competence groups approach their targeted market segments by leveraging their competences across market segments and by building specific competences that distinguish their product offerings within each segment.

The essential aspects of a theory of competence-based competition recognized and developed in both the Bogner and Thomas and the Rispoli chapters are:

- The assets and capabilities that matter in competition are those that, when deployed by a firm, serve as the basis for creating competences in providing product attributes that attract a favorable response from a targeted market.
- To achieve competence in serving a given market, a firm must have both capabilities to offer products with basic ("threshold" or "first level") attributes in common with products offered by other firms in that market, *and* capabilities to offer central and/or plus-only attributes that make a firm's product offerings distinctive in ways that will attract a favorable market response in its targeted market segment(s).

- Since capabilities to provide distinctive (central or plus-only) attributes are of no use without capabilities to provide essential threshold attributes, competence in an industry must be analyzed in terms of the bundles of both the common and the distinctive capabilities a firm must have to compete. Since both kinds of capabilities are necessary conditions for achieving competence, distinctive capabilities in providing specific product attributes alone will be unlikely to constitute a sufficient basis for competence.

Identifying and Building New Competences

Competitive dynamics within industries result from efforts by firms to create new configurations of assets and capabilities and to find new ways of coordinating deployments of assets and capabilities that will elicit a more favorable market response. The chapters in Part Three examine the competence building processes of identifying, creating, and acquiring new assets and capabilities.

Because of causal ambiguities within firms, often even firms that are currently doing well in their product markets may not know exactly why their products are successful. As a result, relatively few firms are likely to understand clearly what aspects of their competences contribute in exactly what ways to their success. Such knowledge, however, is important in determining what aspects of its competences a firm should improve or acquire in order to maintain or improve its market success. Lewis and Gregory (1996, this volume) propose a process which can be used by both researchers and practitioners to identify the competences which a firm has, or could develop, that enable it to offer products that are effective in a given market segment.

The Lewis and Gregory process elicits and makes explicit the perceptions of a firm's employees about the firm's competences. It then passes those competences through a "competence sieve" to determine which competences of the firm are shared in common with other industry firms, which are specific to the firm, and what each contributes to the firm's ability to compete in its product markets. Lewis and Gregory provide a methodology for identifying the specific firm activities that lead to favorable market responses and thus serve as the basis for firm-specific competences.

The need to build competences, however, will often lead a firm to look for firm-addressable assets and capabilities outside the boundaries of the firm. Three chapters in Part Three investigate efforts of firms to access assets and capabilities of other firms.

Jensen's paper (1996, this volume) investigates the challenges to competence building faced by small tourism service firms in northern Norway. In fundamental respects, these firms are representative of many firms (small and large) in that (1) they operate in a vertically-constrained industry structure which restricts their access to market information and other resources, and (2) they face opportunities for collaborative activities which can improve the attractiveness of each firm's product offerings in a highly competitive market. The ability of tourism service providers in northern Norway to define and develop competences is shown to be constrained by lack of access to critical market information and relationships, since large regional and international tour operators virtually monopolize access to world markets for the firms' services. Because tourist travel to northern Norway is still limited in scale compared to tourism elsewhere in Europe, large tour operators have little incentive support to the efforts of travel service providers in northern Norway to develop and publicize northern Norway's tourist attractions. As a result, these small firms face difficulties in accessing information assets, in developing marketing capabilities, and in creating the critical mass of tourism infrastructure needed to stimulate growth of their local industry.

Jensen investigates the collaborative competence-building activities of those small firms as they seek to identify, develop, and promote the tourist attractions of their locale. Reflecting the market-driven approach to determining competences, he describes the cooperative efforts of those firms and supporting government agencies to identify and develop the essential competences needed to provide basic tourist services, as well as the tourism assets which can make the travel products offered by firms in northern Norway distinctive and attractive in the competitive tourist travel market. Jensen concludes that collaborative competence building by competing firms can create "public goods" that enhance the appeal of the products offered by all firms participating in the competence-building effort. Jensen's study thus adds a useful competence perspective to the study of interfirm collaboration through regional networks (Porac, Thomas, and Baden-Fuller 1989).

Taking an industrial networks approach to competence building and leveraging, Easton and Araujo (1996, this volume) propose that the "boundaries" of a firm are so permeable that they are more a fiction than a real barrier to accessing resources for competence building and leveraging. They argue that individual actors within a firm commonly interact with individuals in other firms in an industry in a multitude of ways. Those interactions make possible exchanges of information and know-how between firms. These exchanges constantly reshape a firm's members' perceptions of their own competences, update their knowledge of useful assets and capabilities, and suggest new ways of organizing and coordinating, all of which contribute to a process of continuous network-based competence building and leveraging. Easton and Araujo propose that strategy researchers and practitioners alike should not be exclusively focused on firm-specific competences, but should recognize the person-to-person networks that link competing firms and facilitate important forms of competence building and leveraging.

The decision to make, buy, or cooperate in competence building is examined by Elfring and Baven (1996, this volume) in the context of the automobile industry. They investigate the competence-building activities of automobile manufacturers in the knowledge-intensive services of providing management information services for dealers and of developing software for computer-integrated manufacturing. Providing effective knowledge-intensive services like these requires both broad and detailed knowledge of the processes of the industry, and improving the effectiveness of services provided therefore requires expanding and deepening the industry-process knowledge base of the service-providing unit. Elfring and Baven describe an evolution of service-providing units through four distinct stages, each with its own distinct possibilities for competence-building.

In the first stage, the service unit only services the internal needs of its firm. Its opportunities for competence building through problem solving and other modes of learning are limited by the learning opportunities arising within their host firm. In the second stage, services are sold to outside firms as well as provided to internal clients. Opportunities for competence building are expanded as the service-providing unit gains exposure to other firms' problems and approaches to problem solving. In addition, second-stage service providers are challenged to improve their capabilities through exposure to market discipline in competing for clients. In the third stage, the service unit is spun off from the firm and interfaces with all its clients through arms-length contracts. In this stage, however, the spun-off firm has an opportunity to learn new interfacing skills that may greatly improve its ability to leverage its problem-solving capabilities across many firms and many kinds of problems. In the fourth stage, the service unit's broadening knowledge base enables it to offer "an integrated package of services" to industry participants. Elfring and Baven suggest that the opportunities in stage four for comprehensive learning-through-problem-solving on behalf of many clients provides rich and diverse opportunities for competence building that ultimately work to the benefit of both the service-providing firm and its clients. Thus, knowledge-intensive service providers may become a critical resource for maintaining and building competences within an industry.

The key contributions to a theory of competence-based competition developed in the Jensen, Easton and Araujo, and Elfring and Baven chapters are elaborations of the basic insight that

- Competence building by a given firm is likely to be carried out in a variety of forms that reach beyond the boundaries of the firm.

These chapters give insights into the mechanics of the open-system process of competence building, and illustrate ways in which competence building may become the driver of industry dynamics.

Leveraging Existing Competences

The theory of competence-based competition developed in this volume also recognizes the strategic importance of effectively leveraging existing competences in the creation, production, and offering of products. Just as a firm must have or gain access to specific assets and capabilities to produce attributes of products appreciated in a given market, it must also have abilities to coordinate and deploy those assets and capabilities in creating and delivering those products. A number of alternative approaches to coordinating and deploying resources may be used by a given firm to provide threshold, central, and plus-only product attributes.

The three chapters in Part Four investigate the efforts of firms to coordinate and deploy assets and capabilities in dynamic competitive markets. The chapter by Volberda (1996, this volume) explores the inevitable tension between competence-building and competence-leveraging. Drawing on his study of Philips' semiconductor division in Holland, Volberda characterizes the challenge of coordinating assets and capabilities in a highly dynamic market environment as a constructive friction or tension between the need to establish routines for deploying existing assets and capabilities, on the one hand, and the need to develop new (potentially disruptive) processes that embody new capabilities required to meet new market opportunities or demands, on the other. He proposes that firms can resolve this paradox by creating *organizational flexibility*, which he defines as the ability and willingness of a firm to configure any of its "managerial capabilities and organizational resources" in any number of ways that facilitate a positive firm response to evolving market opportunities or necessities. Volberda characterizes this dynamic mode of coordinating and deploying assets and capabilities as *entrepreneurial revitalization*. He discusses the kinds of resources and managerial capabilities that appear to provide flexibility in coordinating deployments of resources in Philips' semiconductor operations.

The evolution of technologies and market opportunities in a dynamic product market may call for corresponding changes in a firm's approach to coordinating and deploying assets and capabilities for creating new products. Winterscheid and McNabb (1996, this volume) describe the evolution of AT&T's organizational configurations for developing telecommunications products as AT&T grew from a national to a global company. They describe three evolutionary stages in AT&T's approaches to coordinating and deploying technological and product development capabilities. They characterize the transition to each evolutionary stage as motivated by the need to strike a new balance between maintaining "a tight match between product offerings and customer needs [in different national markets]," on the one hand, and achieving efficiencies in leveraging AT&T's technologies as widely as possible, on the other. They argue that each evolutionary stage demands distinct kinds of organizational structures and coordinating capabilities. They suggest that an organization's ability to evolve from one stage to another is constrained both by delays in managerial recognition of the need to adopt new organizational structures and by the delays and uncertainties of building new coordinating capabilities appropriate to each new organizational structure.

Sanchez (1996, this volume) discusses computer-assisted design and development (CADD) programs and modular product design as coordination technologies that can help a firm leverage its competences more effectively. CADD programs provide standardized communication interfaces and procedural protocols that may let firms connect together in a CADD-based network and work simultaneously on design projects. Analogously, the standardized interfaces between components in a modular product design enable a firm to "quick-connect" with and embed coordination of the activities of many component developers and suppliers, allowing each component developer to work autonomously and concurrently. Sanchez characterizes these product creation technologies as *quick-connect technologies* for embedding coordination of product creation processes. They enable a firm to leverage its competences more broadly by connecting quickly with a potentially large number of providers of firm-addressable competences and resources. Sanchez suggests that firms that are early adopters and effective users of these new coordination technologies may adopt new organizational structures and pursue new kinds of product strategies based on their abilities to coordinate global resource networks. These new coordination mechanisms make possible a new strategic logic in which the product-creating firm may function primarily as a generator of new product ideas and a coordinator of a network of development resources in an electronically mediated product creation environment.

The chapters by Volberda, Winterscheid and McNabb, and Sanchez contribute to the development of competence theory by elaborating ways in which

- The leveragability of a firm's competences depends on the abilities of the firm to *coordinate* its deployments of firm-specific and firm-addressable resources.

In essence, understanding competence-based competition requires understanding the ways in which organization structures and coordination mechanisms facilitate or constrain competence building and leveraging. These studies suggest the need for further studies of the linkages between organization structures, coordination mechanisms, and competence building and leveraging.

Competence-Building as the Driver of Industry Dynamics

Change in a competitive environment results from both competence building and competence leveraging activities of firms. The chapters in Part Five explore ways in which specific forms of causal ambiguity and managerial cognitions affect firms' competence building and thereby shape industry dynamics and the trajectories of industry evolution.

Firms may build competences by innovating new assets and capabilities, or by imitating assets and capabilities innovated by others. Wright (1996, this volume) investigates the impact of the imitability *versus* inimitability of competences on the evolution of the semiconductor industry through several generations of DRAM chips. Wright characterizes knowledge about product and process technologies as being either *tacit* (not articulated) or *non-tacit* (articulated) and either *apprehensible* (comprehensible by an observer) or *not-apprehensible*. Each of these characteristics affects the *transferability of knowledge* between firms. Each can therefore limit the ability of potential new entrants to acquire the basic knowledge needed to create products acceptable to a given market (*i.e.*, to provide the threshold attributes required in a product market).

Similarly, as some firms introduce new generations of products based on advances in product or process technologies achieved through their own innovative competence-building, the imitability of the knowledge underlying that new competence will determine whether firms that are unable to innovate the requisite knowledge on their own will be able to advance to the next generation of product. Wright proposes that identifying the tacit *versus* non-tacit and apprehensible *versus* not-apprehensible characteristics of such knowledge provides a means of assessing the relative imitability of the requisite knowledge—and therefore the likely imitability of the new required competence. Thus, the imitability of knowledge underlying an important new competence may determine which firms will continue on an intergenerational change trajectory and which firms will fail to advance.

Further amplifying the influence of the imitability of competences on industry evolution, Tallman and Atchison (1996, this volume) propose that industry evolution is shaped both by the uncertainty of managers as to the imitability of knowledge and (when imitation is perceived as possible) by the uncertainty of managers about a firm's ability to deploy that knowledge advantageously in its current or potential product markets. Managerial aversion to the perceived risks of such uncertainties leads managers to pursue specific patterns of competence-building. Firms will tend to concentrate on building the assets and capabilities which each firm's managers perceive as having the most acceptable levels of risk resulting from (a) uncertainty about the ability of the firm to sustain knowledge innovation or imitation and (b) uncertainty about the benefits to be derived if a firm tries to use such knowledge.

Although a firm's managers may have diverse perceptions of and preferences for uncertainties that are to some degree distinctive for each manager and firm, perceptions and preferences are also likely to be shared to some degree by managers of other firms with similar technical backgrounds, market experiences, and other demographic characteristics (Hitt and Tyler 1991). Tallman and Atchison propose that similarities in managerial perceptions of and preferences for managing certain kinds of technological and managerial uncertainties result in patterns of similar decision making about investing in competence building. Thus, similarities in the uncertainty preference profiles of an industry's managers lead to strategic configurations of firms with similar competences and competence-building trajectories. Tallman and Atchison thereby provide a key link between managerial cognition, competence building, and competence leveraging activities that helps to illuminate the concept of competence groups (Gorman, Thomas, and Sanchez, 1996, this volume).

Trajectories of industry evolution may also be driven forward by competence building undertaken in response to exogenously induced changes in the competitive environment of a product market. Roehl (1996, this volume) investigates the competence-building responses of Japanese pharmaceutical firms to substantial increases in price pressure resulting from cost reduction efforts by the Japanese government medical insurance system and from price competition precipitated by the entry of foreign drug firms into the Japanese market. Depending on the scope and depth of their existing competences, pharmaceutical firms in Japan pursued one of five patterns of competence building, each characterized by a distinct approach to internationalizing research and development activities. Demonstrating an important competence-based path-dependency effect in managerial decisions about modes of competence building, some Japanese drug firms sought international partners in order to leverage their own proven strengths, others sought to remedy areas of perceived weakness in order to complement perceived strengths, and others sought to reposition within the Japanese market to bring their pursuit of market opportunities into better alignment with existing firm competences.

These chapters amplify the theoretical proposition that industry evolution can be described and explained by the competence building and competence leveraging activities of firms in an industry. They give insights into the role of knowledge in competence building and leveraging and illuminate the role of competence in industry evolution by showing that

- A firm's choices of competence building activities are shaped by the imitability of knowledge underlying a potential competence, by managerial perceptions of uncertainties surrounding the feasibility of imitation and the benefits to be derived from applying imitated competences, and by the perceived compatibility of possible new capabilities with a firm's existing base of competences.

ADVANTAGES OF A THEORY OF COMPETENCE-BASED COMPETITION

The theory of competence-based competition outlined in this volume appears to offer several opportunities for improved explorations of contemporary competition. We summarize below some of the ways in which the competence theory proposed in this volume suggests new possibilities for developing insights into the nature of contemporary competition.

Industry Structures and Change

Competence theory provides a vehicle for understanding how both differences and similarities across firms may arise systemically within an industry from the activities of individual firms seeking to distinguish their products in serving similar customer needs. Recognizing the central role of competence building and leveraging in both firm-level strategies and industry evolution provides a conceptual link between (a) the industry asset structures which both support and constrain competence leveraging and (b) the sources of changes in industry asset structures wrought by competence building. In much prior strategy theory industry structures have been treated as exogenously determined, and dynamics which change industry structures have been ignored.

Competition and Cooperation

By representing firms as open systems that require inputs of resources both from other firms and from markets for their products, competition and cooperation between firms can be approached as closely interrelated and essentially inseparable processes, rather than viewed as dichotomous strategic alternatives to be pursued opportunistically. Further, the open systems view of the firm in competence theory enlarges the notion of competition to include a firm's need to compete for input resources, making clear that firms must compete and cooperate on the resource ("supply") side as well as on the market ("demand") side.

Internal and External Perspectives

The competence theory proposed here makes it clear that resources are of little strategic value unless effectively coordinated and deployed, that coordinated deployments of resources are of little use unless they produce product attributes that meet market needs, and that meeting market needs must produce flows of resources that can be exchanged for resources useful in further coordinated deployments by the firm. Thus, the competence perspective suggests that the internal aspects of strategy (firm competences and resources) and external aspects of strategy (products, markets, and industry environments) are inextricably interrelated and cannot be adequately understood when either is analyzed in isolation from the other.

Critical Role of Coordination

Firms may achieve distinctive competences even in using resources that are similar to those used by other firms, because important differences in competences can arise from firm differences in coordinating the deployments of resources. Conversely, firms with unique resources or superior resources in a key area (*e.g.*, technology) may fail to achieve competence because of failure to achieve effective coordination or appropriate deployments of those resources. The competence view thus makes clear that differences in firms' abilities to integrate skills (Hamel 1994) and other resources are key determinants of competitive outcomes.

Strategic Use of Networks and Alliances

Strategic behaviors of firms in networks can be reinterpreted through the theory of competence-based competition. By linking competences or pooling resources in networks, firms may create competence alliances that increase their strategic flexibility (Sanchez 1993, 1995) by enabling them jointly to realize asset mass efficiencies, achieve the advantages of asset interconnectedness, and overcome time-compression diseconomies (Dierickx and Cool 1989). This perspective on networks suggests a new basis for assessing a firm's success in using networks and alliances in competition. In a dynamic market context, longevity of interfirm alliances is not necessarily an indicator of successful collaboration. A succession of short-term alliances by a firm, for example, may suggest that the firm has a superior ability to learn quickly from its partners, or that it may have superior ability to quickly reconfigure its chain of firm-addressable resources in response to changing competitive and market conditions (Sanchez 1995).

Learning as a Strategic Variable

The competence view suggests that a firm's abilities in learning and in network sourcing of firm-addressable resources may be more important determinants of its competitive success in dynamic markets than the firm's current endowment of unique resources or the industry structure it currently faces. Competitive advantage in the long run is seen to arise from a superior ability in identifying and building competences (Sanchez and Heene 1996, in this volume).

Managerial Cognition and Industry Structures

Competence theory identifies managerial cognition and organizational learning as the engines of strategic change and therefore the ultimate determinants of both resource endowments and industry structures. Managerial cognitions largely determine the resources a firm will seek to accumulate, and accumulations of resources and patterns in uses of resources determine industry structures. Thus, competence theory treats resource endowments and industry structures not simply as determinants of short-run strategic conduct in competence leveraging, but also as outcomes of managerial cognitions and long-run strategic conduct in competence building.

Holistic Strategic Goals

In the theory developed here, the fundamental criterion for assessing firm performance is attainment of a firm's goals. Thus, firm performance must be understood, assessed, and managed holistically—with full regard to the entire set of a firm's goals. In judging firm performance in competence-based competition, many forms of resource uses in competence building and leveraging should be recognized and appraised. Economic parameters of performance that are of primary importance to only a single group of resource providers—*e.g.* returns to providers of financial resources—are inadequate as a basis for judging the viability and sustainability of a firm as a complex, dynamic, human system that requires many forms of inputs from many kinds of stakeholders.

Inseparability of Process and Content

Competence theory helps to overcome the unwarranted dichotomizations in strategy theory of process *versus* content and formulation *versus* implementation. Because a firm's ability to coordinate deployments of assets in a given market (a "process" capability) governs the advantages which can be obtained from use of any specific resources (a "content" variable), process and content are interdependent and thus inseparable in theory and in practice. Similarly, formulation (selection of competence building goals) cannot be viewed as independent of implementation considerations (the firm's relative abilities to leverage potential new competences).

Systemic Interdependency of all a Firm's Competences

The assets, capabilities, and coordination required to create competences are systemically interdependent. Moreover, a firm's own competences are likely to be systemically interrelated to those of other firms whose competences provide key inputs to the firm. These systemic interdependencies suggests that it may often be problematic to determine the relative importance of specific competences. When a large number of systemically interdependent competences are required to achieve success in a market, it may be conceptually impossible to identify only a few competences that are clearly more important than others. Typically, a number of closely interrelated competences may be essential to competing successfully in a market. The theory presented here suggests that the competences of a firm arise from systems of assets and capabilities and therefore must be *managed as a system*. Strategic management focused on developing a few competences judged to be critically important must be careful to recognize that those competences may not be capable of being effectively leveraged if other interrelated competences are not also carefully managed.

NEW DIRECTIONS FOR STRATEGY RESEARCH

The theory of competence-based competition outlined in this volume is intended to provide a framework for further theory development and refinement. It appears to provide a base for further investigation of the four key components of the competence perspective identified by Rumelt (1994: xv–xvi). In addition, the theory development and applications in this volume suggest other aspects of competence-based competition which may be approached through this theoretical framework. We note below several areas of research which seem especially promising.

Knowledge and Learning

The role of knowledge as a foundation of competence invites much more intensive study of knowledge and its creation and use within firms (see for example, Wright 1996, this volume). The current notions of tacit knowledge, "messy learning," and knowledge transfer through human "competence carriers" need to be placed in a more fully elaborated framework of knowledge management. The open systems view of the firm may help to develop a more articulated framework for understanding knowledge that is capable of illuminating the roles of other forms of knowledge, of more structured approaches to learning, and of more formal mechanisms for transferring knowledge within and between organizations. We need better concepts of knowledge, knowledge creation, and knowledge application to guide our research into this fundamentally important area.

Coordination

Similarly, our understanding of actual and potential coordination mechanisms available to firms in building and leveraging competences needs to improve, at both business unit and corporate levels. We need to define more clearly what we mean by *coordination,* we need to understand better how coordination might be achieved, and we need theoretical insights into what the limits of coordination and organization might be. We need a theory of coordination that addresses the competence building and leveraging processes firms must manage in competence-based competition. In particular, in this age of accelerating information technology, we need much better insights into the ways in which computer-based information systems make possible new forms of intrafirm and interfirm coordination.

Network Governance

We need to understand the governance mechanisms that provide underlying structure and order to the dynamics of network sourcing of resources by firms functioning as open systems in competence-based competition. In particular, we need to gain insights into the norms that govern exchanges and linkages of resources when the value of firm-addressable resources cannot be fully assessed, but must be accessed nevertheless in order for firms to build competences in a dynamic environment.

Managerial Cognition

The theoretical framework developed in this volume provides a rudimentary representation of how managerial cognitions are formed and how they affect firm strategies and industry structures. We clearly need better insights into how managers might perceive the need to identify and build new competences in dynamic, uncertain competitive environment. We also need to consider the kinds of competitive environments that would result if strategy research is successful in pointing the way to improved managerial cognition in dynamic competitive environments.

Coherence in Strategic Logic

Many decision makers throughout a firm determine the resource flows that in the aggregate make up the firm's competence building and leveraging activities. If leveraging of competences effectively and broadly is important in competence-based competition, then we need to understand better what mechanisms exist or could be created for achieving coherence across the firm's many decision makers. More fundamentally, we need to understand both the benefits and potential liabilities for the firm as a system of following a single dominant strategic logic *versus* allowing many strategic logics to flourish within the firm. What criteria can be used to judge how much and what forms of cognitive diversity are strategically beneficial to a firm in a dynamic environment?

Strategic Flexibility

Firms as systems must have an adaptive capability to respond appropriately to a changing environment. In what ways can resources and organizations have properties of flexibility, and how do various kinds of flexibilities affect the potential for competence building and leveraging in a dynamic and uncertain competitive environment?

Joining of Process and Content

A systems view of the firm suggests the inseparability of content and process in competence building and leveraging. What potential does the theoretical framework developed here hold for the eventual synthesis of previous strategy research based exclusively or primarily on "content" or "process" concepts?

Joining Reductionist and Systematic Perspectives on the Firm

Currently influential approaches to the scientific study of firms in strategy research are largely reductionist. These approaches, of which the resource-based view is a prime example, try to define firms and explain firm performance in terms of the constituent parts of the firm (*e.g.*, its resource endowments). An alternative approach in science is to explain firms and firm behaviors in terms of the larger system context which firms inhabit and which shape firm composition and actions. This "macro organizational systems" perspective on firms, which has had little prominence in strategy theories since the early attention paid to industry structure, provides an approach to extending the systems view developed here to provide a new basis for classifying strategic types of firms and understanding modes of strategic interactions (McKelvey 1982).

IMPLICATIONS OF COMPETENCE-BASED THEORY FOR PRACTICE

The theory of competence-based competition and its applications developed in this volume also promise some significant contributions to the practice of strategic management. Because this formative competence-based theory of competition is more inclusive, dynamic, and systemic in its characterization of competition than previous strategy theories, it corresponds more closely to the real-world cognitive and decision making environments that managers actually face and in which they must try to function effectively. Thus, competence theory also hopes to offer managers a practical way of thinking about competition that draws on a more "recognizable" set of concepts and constructs than, for example, describing competition only in terms of industry structures or resource accumulation.

The competence theoretical framework developed in this volume also offers an internally consistent vocabulary and related set of concepts for describing and analyzing both traditional and emerging modes of competition. We hope that the vocabulary developed here, in particular, can support a "languaging" process within firms (von Krogh, Roos, and Slocum 1994) that can facilitate the creation of shared meanings among a firm's managers and other employees—and thereby lend coherence to a firm's strategy processes that constitute the bridge from the firm's present to its future.

REFERENCES

Amit, R. and Schoemaker, P. "Strategic Assets and Organizational Rent". *Strategic Management Journal,* Vol. 14, pp. 3 -46, 1993.
Barney, J. "Strategic Factor Markets: Expectations, Luck, and Business Strategy". *Management Science,* Vol. 32, pp. 1231–1241, 1986.

Barney, J. "Firm Resources and Sustained Competitive Advantage". *Journal of Management,* Vol. 17, pp. 99–120, 1991.

Bogner, W. C. and Thomas, H. "From Skills to Competences: The 'Play-out' of Resource Bundles Across Firms". In Sanchez, R., Heene, A. and Thomas, H., eds, *Dynamics of Competence-Based Competition: Theory and Practice in the New Strategic Management.* London: Elsevier, 1996.

Camerer, C. "Redirecting Research in Business Policy and Strategy". *Strategic Management Journal,* Vol. 6, pp. 1–15, 1985.

Dierickx, I. and Cool, K. "Asset Stock Accumulation and Sustainability of Competitive Advantage". *Management Science,* Vol. 35, pp. 1504–1511, 1989.

Easton, G. and Araujo, L. "Characterizing Organizational Competences: Combining Resource Base and Industrial Networks Approaches". In Sanchez, R., Heene, A. and Thomas, H., eds, *Dynamics of Competence-Based Competition: Theory and Practice in the New Strategic Management.* London: Elsevier, 1996.

Elfring, T. and Baven, G. "Spinning-off Capabilities: Competence Development in Knowledge-Intensive Services". In Sanchez, R., Heene, A. and Thomas, H., eds, *Dynamics of Competence-Based Competition: Theory and Practice in the New Strategic Management.* London: Elsevier, 1996.

Gorman, P., Thomas, H. and Sanchez, R. "Industry Dynamics in Competence-Based Competition". In Sanchez, R., Heene, A. and Thomas, H., eds, *Dynamics of Competence-Based Competition: Theory and Practice in the New Strategic Management.* London: Elsevier, 1996.

Grant, R. M. "The Resource-based Theory of Competitive Advantage: Implications for Strategy Formulation". *California Management Review,* pp. 114–135, Spring 1991.

Hamel, G. "Strategic intent". *Harvard Business Review,* Vol. 67, pp. 63–76, 1989.

Hamel, G. "Competence for Competence and Inter-Partner Learning within International Strategic Alliances". *Strategic Management Journal,* Vol. 12, pp. 83–103, 1991.

Hamel, G. "The Concept of Core Competence". In Hamel, G. and Heene, A., eds, *Competence-Based Competition.* New York: Wiley, pp. 11–33, 1994.

Hamel, G. and Heene, A., eds, *Competence-Based Competition,* New York: Wiley, 1994.

Hamel, G. and Heene, A. "Conclusions: Which Theory of Strategic Management do we Need for Tomorrow?" In Hamel, G. and Heene, A., eds, *Competence-Based Competition.* New York: Wiley, pp. 315–320, 1994.

Hamel, G., and Prahalad, C. K., *Competing for the Future*, Boston: Harvard Business School Press, 1994.

Heene, A. "Preface". In Hamel, G. and Heene, A., eds, *Competence-Based Competition.* New York: Wiley, pp. xxv–xxvii, 1994.

Hempel, C. G. *Philosophy of Natural Science*, Englewood Cliffs, NJ: Prentice-Hall, 1966.

Hitt, M. A. and Tyler, B. B. "Strategic Decision Models: Integrating Different Perspectives". *Strategic Management Journal,* Vol. 12, pp. 327–351, 1991.

Lewis, M. A. and Gregory, M. J. "Developing and Applying a Process Approach to Competence Analysis". In Sanchez, R., Heene, A. and Thomas, H., eds, *Dynamics of Competence-Based Competition: Theory and Practice in the New Strategic Management.* London: Elsevier, 1996.

Lippman, S. A. and Rumelt, R. P. "Uncertain Imitability: An Analysis of Interfirm Differences in Efficiency Under Competition". *Bell Journal of Economics,* Vol. 13, pp. 418–438, 1982.

Jensen, Ø. "Competence Development by Small Firms in a Vertically-Constrained Industry Structure". In Sanchez, R., Heene, A. and Thomas, H., eds, *Dynamics of Competence-Based Competition: Theory and Practice in the New Strategic Management.* London: Elsevier, 1996.

McKelvey, B. *Organizational Systematics: Taxonomy, Evolution, and Classification.* Berkeley: University of California Press, 1982.

Myers, S. C. "Determinants of Corporate Borrowing". *Journal of Financial Economics,* Vol. 5, pp. 147–175, 1977.

Penrose, E. *The Theory of the Growth of the Firm.* London: Wiley, 1959.

Peteraf, M. A. "The Cornerstones of Competitive Advantage: A Resource-Based View". *Strategic Management Journal,* Vol. 14, pp. 179–191, 1993.

Porac, J. F., Thomas, H. and Baden-Fuller, C. "Competitive Groups as Cognitive Communities: The Case of the Scottish Knitwear Industry". *Journal of Management Studies,* Vol. 26, pp. 397–416, 1989.

Prahalad, C. K. and Bettis, R. "The Dominant Logic: A New Linkage Between Diversity and Performance". *Strategic Management Journal,* Vol. 7, pp. 485–501, 1986.

Prahalad, C. K. and Hamel, G. "The Core Competence of the Corporation". *Harvard Business Review,* Vol. 68(3), pp. 79–93, 1990.

Prahalad, C. K. and Hamel, G. "Strategy as Stretch and Leverage". *Harvard Business Review,* March–April 1993.

Rispoli, M. "Competitive Analysis and Competence-Based Strategies in the Hotel Industry". In Sanchez, R., Heene, A. and Thomas, H., eds, *Dynamics of Competence-Based Competition: Theory and Practice in the New Strategic Management.* London: Elsevier, 1996.

Roehl, T. "The Role of International R&D in the Competence-Building Strategies of Japanese Pharmaceutical Firms". In Sanchez, R., Heene, A. and Thomas, H., eds, *Dynamics of Competence-Based Competition: Theory and Practice in the New Strategic Management.* London: Elsevier, 1996.

Rumelt, R. P. "Foreword". In Hamel, G. and Heene, A., eds, *Competence-Based Competition.* New York: Wiley, pp. xv–xix, 1994.

Sanchez, R. "Strategic Flexibility, Real Options, and Product-Based Strategy". Ph.D. Dissertation, Cambridge, MA: Massachusetts Institute of Technology, 1991.

Sanchez, R. "Strategic Flexibility, Firm Organization, and Managerial Work in Dynamic Markets: A strategic Options Perspective". *Advances in Strategic Management,* Vol. 9, pp. 251–291, 1993.

Sanchez, R. "Strategic Flexibility in Product Competition". *Strategic Management Journal,* Vol. 16, pp. 135–159, Summer 1995.

Sanchez, R. "Quick-Connect Technologies for Product Creation: Implications for Competence-Based Competition". In Sanchez, R., Heene, A. and Thomas, H., eds, *Dynamics of Competence-Based Competition: Theory and Practice in the New Strategic Management.* London: Elsevier, 1996.

Sanchez, R. and Heene, A. "A Systems View of the Firm in Competence-Based Competition". In Sanchez, R., Heene, A. and Thomas, H., eds, *Dynamics of*

Competence-Based Competition: Theory and Practice in the New Strategic Management. London: Elsevier, 1996.

Sanchez, R., Heene, A. and Thomas, H. "Towards the Theory and Practice of Competence-Based Competition". In Sanchez, R., Heene, A. and Thomas, H., eds, *Dynamics of Competence-Based Competition: Theory and Practice in the New Strategic Management.* London: Elsevier, 1996.

Sanchez, R. and Thomas, H. "Strategic Goals". In Sanchez, R., Heenc, A. and Thomas, H., eds, *Dynamics of Competence-Based Competition: Theory and Practice in the New Strategic Management.* London: Elsevier, 1996.

Stinchcombe, A. L. *Constructing Social Theories.* Chicago: University of Chicago Press, 1968.

Tallman, S. and Atchison, D. L. "Competence-Based Competition and the Evolution of Strategic Groups". In Sanchez, R., Heene, A. and Thomas, H., eds, *Dynamics of Competence-Based Competition: Theory and Practice in the New Strategic Management.* London: Elsevier, 1996.

Teece, D., Pisano, G. and Shuen, A. *Firm Capabilities, Resources, and the Concept of Strategy,* CCC Working Paper No. 90–8, Berkeley: University of California, 1990.

Volberda, H. W. "Flexible Configuration Strategies within Philips Semiconductors: A Strategic Process of Entrepreneurial Revitalization". In Sanchez, R., Heene, A. and Thomas, H., eds, *Dynamics of Competence-Based Competition: Theory and Practice in the New Strategic Management.* London: Elsevier, 1996.

von Krogh, G., Roos, J. and Slocum, K. "An Essay on Corporate Epistemology". *Strategic Management Journal,* Vol. 15, pp. 53-71, 1994.

Wernerfelt, B. "A Resource-Based View of the Firm". *Strategic Management Journal,* Vol. 5, pp. 171–180, 1984.

Winterscheid, B. and McNabb, S. "From National to Global Product Development Competence in the Telecommunications Industry: Structure and Process in Leveraging Competences". In Sanchez, R., Heene, A. and Thomas, H., eds, *Dynamics of Competence-Based Competition: Theory and Practice in the New Strategic Management.* London: Elsevier, 1996.

Wright, R. W. "The Role of Imitable *vs.* Inimitable Competences in the Evolution of the Semiconductor industry". In Sanchez, R., Heene, A. and Thomas, H., eds, *Dynamics of Competence-Based Competition: Theory and Practice in the New Strategic Management.* London: Elsevier, 1996.

PART ONE

ELEMENTS OF A THEORY OF COMPETENCE-BASED COMPETITION

The three chapters in Part One develop basic elements of a theory of competence-based competition. These elements are developed to frame a theory that is explicitly dynamic, systemic, cognitive, and holistic. These chapters develop a view of the firm as an open system whose dynamic system effects affect the ability of a firm to build and leverage competences, examine the ways in which the competence leveraging and building goals of firms lead to distinctive patterns of resource flows and economic value creation, and investigate the ways in which building and leveraging competences shape industry dynamics.

Chapter 2 by Sanchez and Heene develops a construct of the firm as a goal-seeking open system. They identify stocks and flows of different kinds of assets and capabilities that make up the essential elements of the firm as a system. They characterize *strategic change* as a process of adjusting the firm's flows of resources to its system elements and *learning* as a process through which a firm makes qualitative changes in its asset stocks and flows. The systems view of the firm developed by Sanchez and Heene seeks to extend the resource-base views of the firm by explicitly incorporating (1) *managerial cognition*, (2) a firm's ability to *coordinate* resources, and (3) *system effects* that constrain competence building and leveraging.

Chapter 3 by Sanchez and Thomas extends the systems view of the firm by investigating the strategic goals which motivate firm actions. Drawing on the concepts of *firm value* and *real options* in contemporary finance theory, they identify characteristic ways in which competence leveraging and competence building processes create economic value. Competence leveraging and competence building are shown to involve distinctive patterns of resource flows. The distinctive resource allocations associated with each of these two modes of creating economic value are used to develop a taxonomy of goal-seeking firm behaviors and to suggest new parameters for assessing firm performance holistically in competence-based competition.

In Chapter 4, Gorman, Thomas, and Sanchez study the effects of competence-building and competence-leveraging activities of firms on industry dynamics. They survey the evolution of prior concepts of strategic groups and introduce the concept of *competence groups*. Competence building may also lead to converging competence groups or diverging competence groups. Both the short-term dynamics and the long-run evolution of an industry result from converging and diverging competence building by firms. Since managers' cognitive frameworks guide firms' efforts to build new competences, managerial cognitions are viewed as the engines of industry change and the precursors of future competitive interactions.

2

A SYSTEMS VIEW OF THE FIRM IN COMPETENCE-BASED COMPETITION

Ron Sanchez and Aimé Heene

INTRODUCTION

This chapter begins an investigation into the nature of competence-based competition by examining the processes by which managers perceive a need for strategic change and undertake competence building or leveraging actions to improve a firm's competitive situation. To this end, we model the firm as an *open system*. A systems perspective on the firm provides a conceptual base for competence theory that appears capable of integrating into a single dynamic framework several dimensions of firm behavior and competitive environments that are of central importance in competence-based competition.

To concepts about the role of a firm's *resource base* in competition, for example, the system view developed here joins the critical dimension of *managerial cognition* in deciding what kinds of resources a firm should try to develop or access in order to build and leverage competences. Explicitly incorporating cognitive elements in a systems view of the firm makes it possible to recognize that there can be significant *uncertainty* about the strategic value of resources in a dynamic environment. Incorporating the cognitive limits of managers acknowledges that *causal ambiguity is also an internal condition of the firm* and greatly affects a firm's decision processes for selecting, acquiring, and using resources. A firm's decision making can then be seen as a dynamic process driven by the feedback mechanisms or *control loops* through which managers try to monitor a firm's internal condition and external environment, direct and regulate the firm's activities, and adapt to a changing environment. Explicitly incorporating adaptive behavior in a dynamic systems view of the firm provides a conceptual interface with notions of the *strategic flexibility* of a firm to respond advantageously to—or perhaps to instigate—environmental change.

Incorporating cognition, causal ambiguity, control mechanisms, and resource (asset) stocks and flows in an integrative perspective on the firm brings into focus several properties of firms as dynamic systems that seem to have implicitly motivated much discussion about competence-based competition. When considered from a systems view, for example, the observation that competences have "temporal dominance" over products (Rumelt 1994) reflects the longer dynamic response times of higher-order system elements in the firm (*e.g.,* capabilities) in the firm's adaptations. Similarly, the notions of collective learning within the firm and of competition as a contest among firms for the acquisition of skills (Rumelt 1994) can be elaborated in the systems view in terms of changes in stocks and flows of knowledge, coordination abilities, and managerial cognitions. Taking a systems view of learning suggests that competence-based competition is also, in a very fundamental sense, a contest among *managerial cognitions* and a test of adaptive *coordination capabilities* as firms vie to identify and develop those competences of greatest strategic value in dynamic competitive environments.

In the systems perspective on the firm developed in this chapter (see Fig. 2.1), the firm is viewed as a goal-seeking system of *tangible and intangible assets.* The firm's goal-seeking behavior is guided by a *strategic logic,* a term that denotes the rationale operative within the firm as to how it can achieve specific goals by applying available assets and capabilities to perceived market opportunities. A firm's specific uses of its available assets and capabilities are directed by the firm's *management processes,* a term denoting the firm's processes for coordination—*i.e.,* gathering and interpreting data, decision making, communicating of decisions and information, and creating incentive structures to guide behaviors. Sanchez and Thomas (1996, in this volume) discuss strategic goals of firms in more detail and develop a basic taxonomy of goal-seeking firm behaviors. In this chapter we focus on investigating the system effects that arise directly from the functioning of a firm as a goal-seeking system. Although firms may differ greatly in the specific goals they pursue, these system effects impact the strategic behaviors of all firms competing for resources and markets, whatever the specific goals each firm may be pursuing.

When firms compete for limited supplies of input resources and product market positions, they thereby become systemically interrelated. Firms competing in market segments, product markets, and industries can be characterized as competing in progressively larger systems of interacting firms. As the competitive arena of interest narrows from industries to product markets to market segments, a firm's interactions with other firms in competing for resources will generally tend to increase in intensity and in their importance to the near-term survival of the firm.

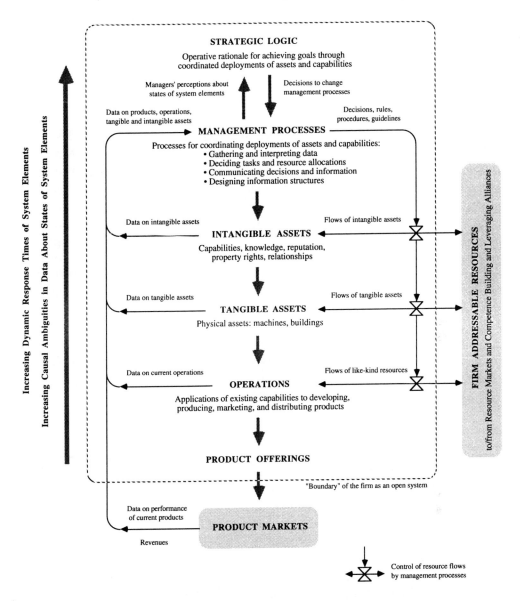

Fig. 2.1. A view of the firm as an open system.

THE SYSTEMS VIEW AS A VEHICLE FOR CONCEPTUAL INTEGRATION

Viewing the firm as an open system provides a conceptual base for developing a theory of competence-based competition that both integrates and extends several important strategy concepts, including new concepts needed to explain more satisfactorily various forms of contemporary competition.

The following discussion first suggests how a systems view of the firm can serve as a vehicle for integrating four key conceptualizations in strategy about the nature of firms and of strategic competition: (i) asset stocks and flows, (ii) causal ambiguity, (iii) adaptation and control, and (iv) strategic flexibility.

Asset Stocks and Flows

The representation of the firm as a system of assets stocks and flows (Dierickx and Cool 1989) can be elaborated to identify different categories of strategically significant assets—which we term *system elements*—of a firm. A firm's system elements include its operations and its stocks of tangible and intangible assets, management processes, strategic logic, and flows of input resources, products, data, information, and decisions. The firm as an open system undergoes *strategic change* when managers seek significant quantitative or qualitative adjustments in the firm's asset stocks or flows. In general, a firm intending to *leverage* its existing competences will seek *quantitative* increases in like-kind asset stocks and flows already deployed by its existing competences. A firm seeking to *build* competences, on the other hand, will seek *qualitative* changes in its asset stocks and flows. Both quantitative and qualitative changes in assets are likely require that the firm obtain resources from external sources as well as through its own internal development efforts, suggesting that asset stocks and flows will exhibit important forms of *systemic interdependencies* with the asset stocks and flows of other firms.

The systems view of the firm extends the resource-base view of the firm as a collection of asset stocks and flows by

- incorporating the dimension of *managerial cognition* in strategic decision making about what kinds of asset stock and flows the firm ought to have (reflected in the concept of a firm's *strategic logic*);
- incorporating the dimension of managers' abilities to *coordinate* efforts to maintain or change a firm's asset stocks and flows (reflected in the concept of *management processes*);
- expanding the scope of strategic analysis of asset stocks and flows to include resources held by other firms (reflected in the *open system* concept of the firm and in the notion of *firm-addressable resources*).

Modeling the firm as an open system provides a vehicle for integrating theoretical perspectives that address the cognitive limits of managers who must initiate and guide strategic change, the abilities of managers to coordinate processes intended to effect strategic changes in asset stocks and flows, and the systemic dependency of the firm on other firms with resources that would be strategically useful to the firm.

Causal Ambiguity

Our approach to studying the systems behavior of a firm models actions to change the states of the firm's system elements as motivated by managers' perceptions of gaps between the *perceived* and *desired* states of system elements. Strategic gaps are those perceived gaps which motivate decisions and actions to undertake change in the firm's asset stocks and flows. A strategic gap is thus an unacceptable shortfall of the perceived state of a system element below its desired state. Managers may perceive strategic gaps in any system element of the firm, and may take various kinds of actions to try to close the gaps they perceive. Sanchez and Thomas (1996, in this volume) suggest that fundamental differences in the strategic behaviors of firms result from differences in the kinds of strategic gaps their managers perceive and in the kinds of actions managers undertake to close strategic gaps. In this chapter, we suggest ways in which differing strategic behaviors of firms may arise from systemic differences across firms in the ways their managers form perceptions of strategic gaps.

In a world with perfect information and without cognitive limitations, a firm's managers would readily detect strategic gaps in any of the firm's system elements. In trying to assess the conditions of system elements in a real firm, however, real managers are likely to encounter significant causal ambiguities (Lippman and Rumelt 1982) with respect to the causal relationships that would suggest what the state of a system element is or ought to be. The internal causal ambiguities about the states of a firm's system elements increase as managers search for strategic gaps in higher-order system elements of the firm like its intangible assets (*e.g.*, its knowledge), management processes, and their own strategic logic.

The problematic nature of assessing higher system elements and making decisions to close perceived gaps under high levels of internal causal ambiguity may lead managers to focus their attention on ostensibly less ambiguous quantified data about stocks and flows of money, products, and tangible assets. In this case, managers will tend to perceive gaps primarily in the firm's lower-order system elements (operations and tangible assets), and their gap-closing actions may become focused on managing changes in those system elements. Overcoming this cognitive bias and resulting tendency to manage lower-order system elements of the firm is likely to require explicit managerial efforts to resolve causal ambiguities about "higher-order" system elements by gathering and interpreting qualitative data about technological and market trends and other aspects of the firm's environment.

By recognizing the existence of causal ambiguities within the firm, a systems view suggests that the concept of causal ambiguity in competition can be enlarged beyond its current role as an isolating mechanism (Lippman and Rumelt 1982) which protects a firm's existing competences from imitation by other firms. In effect, causal ambiguity becomes a fundamental internal condition of the firm-as-a-system which strategic managers must address in their efforts to identify, create, and leverage competences. Managerial efforts to reduce causal ambiguity and minimize cognitive biases, moreover, are seen to be especially critical in managing the firm's system elements most directly impacted by the cognitions of managers themselves: its strategic logic, management processes, and intangible assets. In particular, to perform their function within the firm-as-a-system, strategic managers must be effective in seeking the most effective leveraging of the firm's current stocks of knowledge and in continually assessing and reconstructing the firm's stocks of knowledge. Thus, effective management of processes for creating and applying knowledge poses a central cognitive challenge to strategic managers.

Control and Adaptation

A systems perspective can also help to illuminate the role of feedback flows—which we refer to *control loops*—in firms' strategic adaptations. Control loops are the processes through which a firm monitors and adjusts its stocks and flows of assets. The systems view draws attention to the ways in which higher-order control loops—*i.e.,* those monitoring and adjusting asset stocks and flows in a firm's higher-order system elements of strategic logic, management processes, and intangible assets—affect the adaptive behavior of the firm. Higher-order control loops govern changes in a firm's managerial cognitions that determine its strategic logic, its stock of coordination abilities that determine its management processes, and its stocks of capabilities, skills, and knowledge that constitute its intangible assets. We characterize strategic logic, management processes, and intangible assets as "higher-order system elements" because they guide and direct the firm's efforts to adjust asset stocks and flows in other—thus "lower"—system elements like tangible assets, operations, and products.

Learning is the process by which a firm accomplishes *qualitative changes* in its stocks of assets, especially in its cognition-based higher system elements. Learning may take place at several levels of cognition within a firm, from learning-by-doing that leads to qualitative changes in the firm's knowledge about how to operate its production processes, to learning by strategic managers about alternative models for organizing to compete in a changing environment. Managing a firm's stocks of knowledge at all levels thus becomes a central activity in adaptation and control processes.

We also propose that as a general rule it is generally more difficult—*i.e.,* it takes more time and effort—to change stocks of human cognitions than to change stocks of physical assets. In other words, it takes more time to change the *ideas* in use in a firm than to change the *things* a firm uses. Accordingly, in the system model developed here, cognition-based higher system elements are characterized as having longer *dynamic response times* than lower system elements in effecting changes in their associated asset stocks and flows.

Developing systems concepts of adaptation and control brings into the theoretical foreground several features of higher-order control loops that have substantial impact on competence-based competition:

- Managers must proactively gather and interpret *qualitative* as well as quantitative data about the firm and its environment.
- Adaptation at the strategic level is likely to be driven by a search for *implied* rather than *explicit* strategic gaps in the system elements of the firm, especially with regard to the higher-order system elements. Strategic change in higher order system elements may therefore be motivated by metaphorical thinking, as well as by purely analytic reasoning.
- Dynamic response times vary across system elements, with cognition-based system elements having the longest dynamic response times within the firm as a system.

Thus, incorporating control loops into a theory of competence-based competition provides a means for investigating the perception-forming, direction-setting, decision-making, process-coordinating, and change-inducing activities of decision makers that result in a firm's distinctive patterns of competence building and leveraging over time.

Strategic Flexibility

Strategic flexibility is a concept which characterizes a firm's ability to respond advantageously to a changing environment. A firm's flexibility to respond to change may be thought of as depending jointly on (a) the intrinsic *flexibilities of the resources* available to the firm, and (b) the *coordination flexibilities* of managers in redefining strategies for the use of the firm's available resources and in reconfiguring and redeploying appropriate resource chains in support of those strategies (Sanchez 1995). In the systems view of the firm, the ability of a firm to respond advantageously to change depends on the ability of the firm to detect strategic gaps in the states of its system elements and to take effective actions to close those gaps. The preceding discussions of causal ambiguities and adaptation and control suggest that both cognitive and dynamic system effects constrain the flexibility of a firm to respond quickly and advantageously to changes in a dynamic environment.

Creating *strategic options* that give a firm strategic flexibility to respond to future opportunities or threats has been proposed as a basic approach to managing the irreducible uncertainties and resulting ambiguities of a dynamic environment (Sanchez 1993). Building highly leverageable competences gives a firm a number of strategic options for future competitive actions (Sanchez and Thomas 1996, in this volume). A systems view suggests that building competences that give a firm a range of strategic options for future actions provides managers a means of compensating for their limited cognitive abilities to precisely define strategic gaps in the states of system elements when those elements are subject to significant causal ambiguities that are not reducible in the near term.

In this regard, a systems view of the firm incorporates and extends the concept of strategic flexibility by

- incorporating cognitive and dynamic system effects that constrain a firm's flexibility to respond to change;
- recognizing that acquiring stocks of flexible resources and building up flexible capabilities in coordinating resources can help offset the constraints on adaptation that result from cognitive limitations and dynamic system effects.

Thus, incorporating a strategic flexibility perspective in a systems view of the firm provides dual benefits. Recognizing cognitive and dynamic interdependencies among a firm's resources helps to identify (i) system effects which limit a firm's flexibilities and (ii) properties of resources and coordination abilities that might increase strategic flexibility by overcoming those cognitive and dynamic system effects.

THE FIRM AS AN OPEN SYSTEM

When a firm is viewed as a system, its stocks and flows of assets are seen to be dynamically interrelated and—by virtue of those interrelationships—dynamically constrained. The cognitive limitations and time lags inherent in adjusting stocks and flows of assets illuminate important forms of dynamic interdependencies among assets, whether the assets are within a single firm or shared among firms. Researchers in strategy and other areas have described some aspects of the systems behavior of firms. We combine and extend those concepts in proposing a competence-based systems model. We then consider three properties of firms as systems that result from dynamic interdependencies among asset stocks and flows.

Some Prior System Views of the Firm

The systems behavior of firms has attracted the attention of many researchers, especially those interested in applying concepts from dynamic systems theory to the management of firms in dynamic environments. Ashby (1956), for example, noted the need for a system to be capable of generating the "requisite variety" of responses to a changing environment in order to maintain its internal stability. The industrial dynamics framework of Forrester (1961, 1968) laid important groundwork for the dynamic systems modeling of firms, industries, and macroeconomies. Simon (1969) outlined a number of basic systems perspectives on organizations.

In the strategy literature, Dierickx and Cool (1989) introduce the concept that firm resources can be represented as asset stocks. In their model, flows that adjust levels of asset stocks are subject to *time-compression diseconomies, asset mass efficiencies,* and other system effects. These system effects are used to explain why a firm's current endowments of resources enable the firm to earn economic rents over some time period. When a firm has assets useful in exploiting a market opportunity, it may earn economic rents because competing firms face prohibitive costs in accelerating their build up of stocks of required resources or in building up stocks of complementary assets. In a related argument, Teece, Pisano, and Shuen (1989) maintain that because capabilities are dynamic—*i.e., they take time to develop*—firms with specific capabilities that attract economic rents may continue to enjoy those rents while other firms work to develop comparable rent-generating capabilities.

The Competence-Based Systems View

An expanded systems view of the firm leads to further insights into ways that a firm may earn economic rents or otherwise attain its goals through a superior ability to identify, select, acquire, deploy, and retire resource endowments. As noted above, the systems model of the firm developed here adds three new dimensions to asset stocks and flows. In addition to stocks and flows of tangible assets (physical assets) and intangible assets (capabilities, knowledge), the model includes stocks of *managerial cognitions* embodied in a firm's higher-order system elements of strategic logic and management processes that govern stocks and flows of tangible and intangible assets to lower system elements. In addition, higher system elements are characterized as subject to elevated levels of *causal ambiguity*. Further, different system elements (*i.e.*, different kinds of asset stocks) have different *dynamic response times*. Higher system elements are represented as having longer dynamic response times; change in asset stocks is presumed to take longer to accomplish in higher (cognition-based) system elements. These additional dimensions suggest new ways in which the systemic nature of asset stocks and flows can affect the ability of a firm to build and leverage competences.

Figure 2.1 presents this model of a firm as a system of stocks and flows of tangible assets and intangible assets. Flows of assets are guided by a strategic logic and directed by management processes in developing, producing, distributing, and marketing products through the firm's operations. The firm is viewed as an open system, however, that requires both resource flows of inputs to its operations and other system elements and markets for the outputs (products) which flow from its operations. In this systems model, the firm's operations are treated as a stock of specified activities or organizational routines (Nelson and Winter 1982). The market's responses to the firm's products produce flows of sales revenues and data relating to the sales of the firm's products in the market. Data on the firm's products, operations, and tangible assets are also gathered and flow to the decision making processes within the firm's management processes. The firm may also gather qualitative data internally and externally to be used in assessing the condition of the firm's higher system elements (intangible assets, management processes, and strategic logic).

From the firm's management processes emanate specific decisions, rules, procedures, guidelines, and norms that direct the flows of the firm's financial and other resources. These resources are exchanged internally, within competence alliances, and in resource markets to convert them into flows of desired tangible and intangible resources directed to the firm's operations and other system elements. The arrows to the left of the system diagram remind that data about system elements become increasingly ambiguous and dynamic response times increasingly long as one moves from lower to higher system elements.

The tiered arraying of system elements in Fig. 2.1 is not intended to suggest that the Fig. 2.1 system model presumes that a firm has a hierarchical organization structure. The system model of Fig. 2.1 is not based on any specific set of assumptions, for example, about the form or locus of the firm's strategic logic or management processes. Figure 2.1 could represent a firm whose strategic logic is defined by a detailed strategic plan strictly followed by managers who try to implement that logic through tight control of a centralized system for managing resource flows. Alternatively, it can equally represent a firm whose strategic logic resides largely in a corporate culture whose values and practices are embodied in the staff of a "flat" organization where teams have wide authority to make decisions about resource flows. Figure 2.1 could equally well represent other forms of organization. Whatever the organizational arrangement, Fig. 2.1 suggests that cognitions of decision makers—whom we refer to simply as *managers*—are critical assets and that the strategic logic of the firm determines the approaches to coordinating deployments of resources the firm will develop and carry out through its management processes.

Three System Properties

Three properties of the firm in competence-based competition emerge from this view of the firm as a system:

First, *causal relationships* between system elements essentially flow from top to bottom in Fig. 2.1. The firm's strategic logic is the rationale followed by the firm's decision makers for achieving strategic goals by applying resources to the creation and marketing of products. The firm's strategic logic governs the firm's management processes, which includes its processes for gathering data, its frameworks for interpreting data, its methods for identifying strategic gaps, and its rules, procedures, and incentive structures for allocating resources to gap-closing actions. The firm's management processes thus govern the flow of resources to the firm's intangible assets, tangible assets, and operations and directly determine the level and composition of the firm's asset stocks and flows. The nature of the firm's intangible assets (capabilities and knowledge) determine the uses to which the firm's tangible assets can be applied in its operations. The range of feasible uses of the firm's intangible and tangible assets determines the operating flexibility of the firm and thus the flexibility of the firm to offer products to the market.

Second, *perceptions of managers* about states of the firm's system elements and the need to engage in gap-closing actions are formed from the data gathered and the interpretive framework applied by managers. Data the firm may gather, however, are subject to varying degrees of causal ambiguity. Data are *causally ambiguous* with regard to a specific system element to the extent that those data support alternative interpretations as to whether that system element in its current state is contributing effectively or not to the success of the firm. Some data are relatively unambiguous, like data showing increasing sales, but managers' interpretations could still differ as to what increasing sales data might imply about the state of the firm's operations or other system elements.

Data about the states of system elements are subject to increasing ambiguity as system elements ascend from bottom to top of the array of system elements in Fig. 2.1. To illustrate, data indicating low capacity utilization rates of the firm's tangible production assets might suggest a number of alternative interpretations about the states of the firm's productive assets: inadequate maintenance leading to frequent machine failures, production slowdowns by dissatisfied workers, inept production scheduling by plant managers, or low demand for a plant's products resulting from low quality or inappropriate design of the plant's products. As one moves higher up the array of system variables to the firm's stocks of intangible resources, management processes, and strategic logic, data become increasingly ambiguous. Many forms of ambiguous data may have to be gathered and evaluated in an effort to discover patterns of data that support one interpretation or a limited number of interpretations of the state of a higher system element. For a high-order system element like a firm's strategic logic for competing, it is unlikely that the ambiguities of available data can be definitively resolved no matter how much and how many kinds of data are gathered. Gathering more data may even lead to higher levels of perceived ambiguity. In assessing higher system elements, the best managers may be able to achieve is to develop a reduced set of alternative plausible interpretations of available data.

Third, the *dynamic response times* of system elements increase from bottom to top of Fig. 2.1. By this we are suggesting that in general (though not in all cases) a firm can change its mix of products more readily than it can change its ways of using productive assets (*i.e.*, its mode of operating), its uses of current assets more readily than its stock of tangible assets, its stock of tangible assets more readily than its stock of intangible assets (capabilities, knowledge), and its stock of intangible assets more readily than its management processes and strategic logic. The basic notion behind this ascending array of increasing dynamic response times is that managerial cognitions and managers' approaches to coordinating are harder to change than stocks of intangible resources like knowledge, stocks of tangible resources like machines and buildings, or the firm's operations or products.

Flows of many resources required for lower system elements may be relatively readily obtainable from markets or competence alliances, while sources of resources for changing stocks of managerial cognitions or management processes may be more difficult to identify, evaluate, and obtain. Thus, as one moves from bottom to top of the array of system elements in Fig. 2.1, the ability of the firm to change stocks of system elements in the short-run diminishes. To assure flows of new kinds of resources the firm will need at all levels of system elements in the future, strategic managers therefore have to try to identify and induce desired changes in higher (cognition-based) system elements well *in advance* of future needs.

ADAPTATION THROUGH GAP-CLOSING ACTIONS

A firm's efforts to change the state of one of its system elements will be motivated by managerial perceptions of a *strategic gap* between the desired state of that system element and the perceived state of that element. When managers detect a shortfall of the perceived state of the system element below its desired state, they may decide that the benefits of improving the state of a system element exceed the costs (including opportunity costs) and difficulties of improving the state of the element. Managers may then initiate some form of *gap-closing action* to improve the state of the system element. *Strategic change* occurs when a firm takes actions to close perceived strategic gaps in any of its system elements.

When the gaps the firm wants to close call for changes only in the operations or tangible assets of the firm, the changes in asset stocks sought by the firm are likely to be essentially quantitative (greater output, more capacity, etc.). *Leveraging existing competence* requires gap-closing actions that lead to *quantitative increases* in stocks and flows of like-kind assets. When a firm undertakes to close gaps in its strategic logic, decision processes, or intangible assets, however, the changes in asset stocks sought by the firm will be inherently qualitative in nature (although qualitative changes may entail some quantitative changes as well). *Building new competences* therefore requires gap-closing actions that lead to *qualitative changes* in stocks and flows—i.e., new kinds of assets. Firms' gap-closing actions in competence leveraging are generally the sources of short-run dynamics in competence-based competition, and firms' gap-closing actions in competence building are the sources of long-run dynamics in competence-based competition (Sanchez and Thomas 1996, in this volume).

Important differences in patterns of actions firms undertake to close strategic gaps are likely to arise from differences in the ways managers in different firms perceive strategic gaps. Managers gather and interpret data, make decisions, and initiate gap-closing actions through a firm's control loops. Different managers may respond to the increasing causal ambiguity of data in higher order control loops in different ways, leading to different patterns in the ways firms use control loops to gather and interpret data. These differences, in turn, may lead to significant differences in the kinds of strategic gaps managers perceive and try to close. Control loops gathering data from lower system elements and control loops gathering data on higher system elements are likely to motivate very different kinds of gap-closing actions and will thus have distinctive influences on the asset stocks and flows that lead to changes in the firm's system elements. To illustrate, we consider two polar patterns of gap-closing actions: "bottom up" and "top down" modes of adaptation.

"Bottom-Up" Adaptation Driven By Lower-Order Control Loops

Because human cognitive abilities vary across managers, and because skills in gathering and analyzing data can vary across firms, some managers may be less skillful than others in deciphering suggestive patterns in highly ambiguous data about a firm's higher system elements. As a result, some managers may conclude that it is not useful to spend time gathering data about higher system elements like intangible resources, management processes, or strategic logic. In such cases, managers may direct the firm's data gathering efforts to parameters for which ostensibly unambiguous, "hard" quantified data are available. Quantifiable data are most readily obtained about the firm's products, operations, and tangible assets (buildings and machines). Managers uncomfortable with ambiguity may therefore direct the firm to generate data flows primarily about its products, operations, and tangible assets, with little or no ambiguous qualitative data gathered about higher system elements. As a consequence, management processes may focus on asset stocks and flows directly related to production operations and marketing of current products. This pattern of data gathering and resource allocation is suggested by the predominance of data and resource flows in lower system elements shown in Fig. 2.2(a).

The control loops feeding the firm's operating data to its higher system elements and conveying the decisions made in higher system elements about asset flows to the firm's operations tend to behave like positive feedback loops. Thus, market acceptance of the firm's current products generates data (profitability, revenues, etc.) that managers are likely to interpret in a positive manner, increasing their confidence in the firm's current operations and stocks of tangible and intangible assets, its management processes, and its strategic logic. A period of good market acceptance of the firm's current products may therefore lead to rising levels of confidence in the current states of all the firm's system elements. This confidence may lead managers to expand current operations by increasing stocks of like-kind assets in each system element. If expanding operations

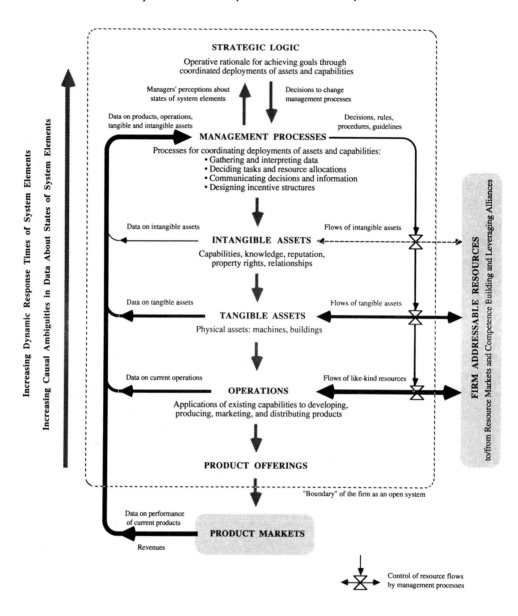

Fig. 2.2(a). Gap-closing actions driven by data on states of products, operations, and tangible assets.

leads to increases in sales and profits, such data may lead managers to have even higher levels of confidence in the firm's system elements, leading to further increases in stocks of like-kind assets, and so on. In this way, success will breed success—as long as the market continues to respond favorably to the firm's current products.

What happens, however, if the market's enthusiasm for the firm's products fades—for example, because competitors begin to offer better products based on new technologies or new product concepts? A decline in the market's acceptance of the firm's products will lead to deterioration in data about the firm's current operations, leading to a decrease in managers' confidence in the firm's operations. If deterioration in operating data continues, managers may begin to lose confidence in the firm's higher system elements, perhaps eventually doubting established management processes and even their own strategic logic. Because changing stocks of assets in higher system elements is more difficult and takes longer than changing asset stocks in lower system elements, however, managers may first try to reverse any deterioration in operating data by making adjustments in asset stocks in lower system elements with relatively short dynamic response times. If adjustments in lower system element asset stocks reverse the deterioration in operating data, managers are unlikely to also seek changes in the asset stocks of higher elements. If closing perceived gaps in lower system elements does not improve operating data, however, managers may eventually try changing the firm's stocks of progressively higher system elements until some gap-closing action appears to reverse the deterioration of operating data.

Driving adaptive change in the firm's system elements from the bottom up—i.e., through lower order control loops driven by operating data—creates two generally intractable problems. First, managers trying to manage a firm's stocks of system elements by responding exclusively or primarily to changes in operating data will generally will not be able to use those data to discover conclusively whether deteriorations in current operating data are evidence of fundamental environmental changes that would call for changes in higher system elements. As a result, when such fundamental changes do occur, managers may waste a great deal of time and misdirected resources trying (to little or no effect) to change lower system elements, while needed changes in higher system elements go undetected. Second, when fundamental change occurs, a firm with deteriorating profitability and revenues may not have sufficient resources or time to make required changes in higher system elements with long dynamic response times.

These inherent limitations of trying to use lower order control loops to drive "bottom-up" adaptation in the firm's higher system elements point to the need for establishing and using higher order control loops.

"Top-Down" Adaptation Driven By Higher-Order Control Loops

To assess the states of a firm's higher system elements, managers have to try to make sense out of the inherently highly ambiguous data about the firm's higher system elements. Managers must usually make explicit efforts

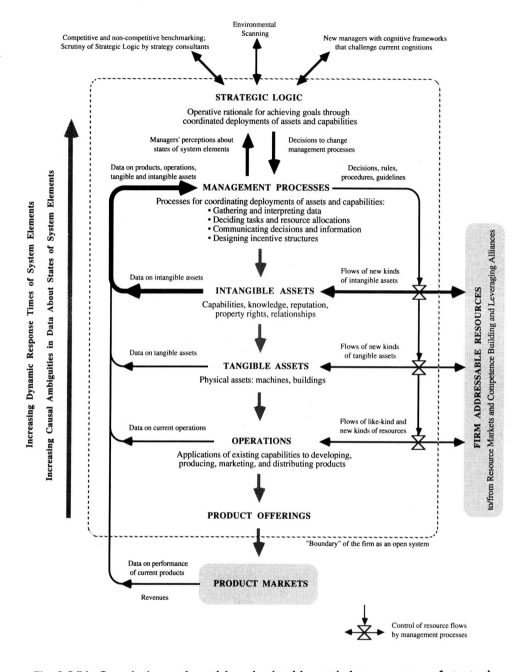

Fig. 2.2(b). Gap-closing actions driven by (ambiguous) data on states of strategic logic, management processes, and intangible assets.

to gather and interpret data relevant to higher system elements, leading to patterns of data gathering and interpreting suggested by the data flows in Fig. 2.2(b). This pattern implies significant processing of ambiguous qualitative data by strategic managers in an effort to discover plausible interpretations about the states of the firm's higher system elements. As Fig. 2.2(b) suggests, higher-order control loops may also behave like positive feedback loops, so that an increase (decrease) in managers' confidence in the firm's strategic logic will lead to increases (decreases) in their confidence in the firm's management processes, intangible assets, and other system elements, which may lead to further increases (decreases) in managers' confidence in the firm's strategic logic, and so on.

Strategic managers must continually challenge their confidence in the firm's strategic logic and other higher system elements. Three approaches to challenging managers' perceptions about the state of the firm's higher system elements and for assessing the firm's long-term competitive position in its environment are suggested at the top of Fig. 2.2(b).

Benchmarking

Various forms of benchmarking (and its more dynamic form, "bench-trending") may be useful in assessing the relative strengths and weaknesses of a firm's strategic logic, management processes, tangible and intangible assets, operations, and current products. To have the greatest chance for usefully challenging the firm's strategic logic, however, benchmarking may have to go well beyond simple comparisons of a firm's aggregate operating data against those of competitors. Managers may have to try to benchmark higher system elements against superior performing firms both inside and outside the firm's industry. Product creation and production processes, technological capabilities, organization structures, incentive plans, information systems, and other aspects of higher-order system elements, including ideas central to the firm's strategic logic for competing, may be compared against their counterparts in best-in-world companies.

As managers discover and analyze differences between specific capabilities of the firm and those of best-in-world companies in any industry, they may begin to perceive explicit or implied gaps in their firm's higher system elements. An *implied strategic gap* might be discovered, for example, when a firm compares well in a specific capability against its direct competitors in its industry, but falls short compared to the capabilities of a superior performing firm with similar kinds of capabilities in another industry. Consistent efforts to discover implied strategic gaps may enable managers to take gap-closing actions in higher-order system elements *before* current products begin to lose market acceptance and current operations begin to deteriorate.

Environmental Scanning

Since the firm's strategic logic is a rationale for applying technological and organizational capabilities to market opportunities, *technological, organizational, and market scanning* are essential means of challenging the appropriateness and durability of the firm's strategic logic. Managers may scan for possible evolutions in the firm's current technology base and for potential new technologies which can be used in current or future businesses. Managers may try to make similar assessments of innovative organizational structures being adopted by some firms or of emerging market trends. Managerial perceptions of possible technological changes or shifts in market preferences may give managers the opportunity to ask how the firm's strategic logic, management processes, knowledge base, or other asset stocks could be changed to be more effective under a variety of future scenarios.

When managers perceive gaps between the firm's current capabilities and knowledge base and ones it might use if technologies or markets change, managers may begin to build new competences that may give the firm options for new kinds of actions in the future. By beginning to build up *qualitatively* new stocks of organizational capabilities and market knowledge in anticipation of possible environmental changes in the future, a firm may be able to significantly shorten its dynamic response time if specific new forms of action in which it is building capabilities are needed in the future. Also, by beginning early to build competences in new areas, managers may be able to resolve some of the causal ambiguities surrounding new technologies, new organizational forms, and new product concepts before competitors develop insights in these areas.

Challenging Cognitive Frameworks

Managers may also try to expose their cognitive frameworks to alternative viewpoints and new conceptual frameworks that directly challenge the appropriateness of their current strategic logic and management processes. Managers may try to overcome the constraints of their cognitive limits by hiring consultants or other advisers to tell them about new models for competing in their industry or in other industries. Managers may seek to hire new managers from other firms or other industries to bring new perspectives that can provide new assessments of the firm's current strategic logic and management processes. In a growing number of cases in the U.S., boards of directors are acting as agents of change by hiring new managers with new cognitive frameworks when current managers are reluctant to let go of inappropriate cognitive frameworks.

Managers may also try to create a pool of different cognitive frameworks within the firm by seeking diversity in its mix of managers. Managers may institute a tradition of confrontation that encourages "no-holds-barred" questioning of the basic assumptions underlying the firm's strategies. Strategic managers may force continual redefinition of the firm's strategic logic and management processes through periodic "zero-based" strategy-making in which the appropriateness of current activities and assets must be argued and affirmed in order to receive further resource allocations.

Any of these three means of challenging managers' strategic logic may help managers to anticipate useful changes in the asset stocks and flows of the firm's higher system elements and to take action in advance of deteriorations in current operating data. An important ability of strategic managers in "top-down" adaptation is skill in using these and other means to discover *implied strategic gaps* in higher-order system elements.

Systemic Differences in Strategic Adaptations

Bottom-up and top-down approaches to managing strategic adaptation lead to significantly different patterns of gap-closing actions because of systemic differences in the kinds of strategic gaps likely to be perceived under the two approaches. Managers focused on closing perceived gaps in products, operations, and tangible assets, as suggested in Fig. 2.2(a), are likely to concentrate on gap-closing actions that do not lead the firm very far from the firm's existing competences. Use of lower order control loops in bottom-up approaches to managing may facilitate a deepening of a firm's current set of capabilities through incremental learning, but may also work to transform the firm's current capabilities into "core rigidities" (Leonard-Barton 1992). Because managers relying on lower order control loops will be focused on managing quantitative changes in like-kind asset stocks and flows useful in leveraging existing competences, they may be unlikely to perceive a need to build new competences in advance of deteriorations in a firm's current operations—and possibly not even after deterioration begins.

Firms relying on lower order control loops may do well in stable environments, achieving considerable success in reducing costs of existing products through established methods of value engineering, standard industrial engineering approaches to improving efficiency, and more efficient utilization of existing production assets. Indeed, achieving current success through such practices is likely to increase the confidence of managers in relying on lower order control loops. Firms managed through lower order control loops, however, will lack an aspect of *organizational intelligence* essential to identifying opportunities to become product innovators, to enter new product markets requiring new technologies, or to adopt new organizational forms requiring new coordination capabilities.

In product markets where managers actively gather and interpret data about higher system elements and pursue gap-closing actions affecting their firm's intangible assets, management processes, and strategic logics, as suggested in Fig. 2.2(b), gap-closing actions are more likely to lead to qualitative changes in these higher system elements. In this case, competence building actions by firms may lead to new ways of competing and cause product markets to become dynamic and much less predictable. In dynamic markets, widespread competence building may result in the continuous emergence of new technologies and new product concepts, firms may pioneer or enter new product markets, and managers may innovate new organizational forms to carry out new kinds of product strategies (Sanchez 1995).

When managers gather and interpret ambiguous data about the states of higher system elements and lead the firm in building new competences in anticipation of possible future needs, the flexibility of the firm as a system to instigate or respond advantageously to environmental change may be increased. Early actions to close implied gaps in higher system elements, however, inevitably constitute a wager that some uncertain future outcomes are more likely than others, because no firm can build all the competences that would be needed in every possible future scenario. Given the inherent limitations of lower-order control loops as drivers of competence building, however, some willingness and ability of managers to undertake top-down adaptation appears essential to firm survival in dynamic markets. Managing strategically in competence-based competition requires a willingness to develop and use higher-order control loops to imagine and pursue competences that may be important in an uncertain future. Top-down managing through higher-order control loops is the essential process through which managers may question the present and propose the future (Hamel and Prahalad 1994).

FLEXIBILITY OF THE FIRM AS A SYSTEM

Managers of firms competing in dynamic environments must continually struggle with the endless conundrum that characterizes strategic management in a dynamic and uncertain environment: Imperfectly predictable changes in the firm's competitive environment may call for rapid changes in a firm's higher system elements, but those elements are characterized by long dynamic response times and high degrees of internal causal ambiguity. How, then, can managers rationally formulate a strategic plan for competing when the data needed to craft such a plan is riven with ambiguity and when assets that may be needed in short order in the future are likely to be those that take substantial time to identify, acquire, and deploy?

Strategic management becomes a more promising pursuit in dynamic environments when we recognize that managers may help their firms-as-systems develop a property of *flexibility* that can mediate (to some degree, if not completely) the constraints on adaptation caused by the causal ambiguities and long dynamic response times of higher system elements. We next discuss a concept of *strategic flexibility* as a property of the firm-as-a-system that improves the ability of the firm to respond to significant shifts in technologies, markets, and other environmental factors. In this concept of strategic flexibility, the flexibility of the firm as a system depends jointly on the *flexibilities of the resources* that make up each system element of the firm and on the *coordination flexibilities* of managers in using the firm's available resources (Sanchez 1993, 1995).

Resource Flexibility

The flexibility of a resource can be defined along three dimensions. Resource flexibility increases as the range of uses to which an asset can be applied effectively increases, as the time required to switch an asset from one use to another decreases, and as the cost of switching from one use to another decreases (Sanchez 1995). In other words, flexible resources—for example, a flexible manufacturing system or broadly applicable technological knowledge—have more than one use and can be switched from one use to another quickly and inexpensively. In contrast, inflexible resources like a dedicated product line or a highly specialized expertise are specific-use resources that either cannot be switched to other uses or may only be switched after significant difficulty and time.

Creating stocks of flexible resources within the firm's system elements may provide at least a partial solution to an otherwise intractable problem of managing strategically in a dynamic and uncertain competitive environment. *Ex ante*, flexible assets help manage the cognitive challenge of choosing assets and capabilities under conditions of high causal ambiguity about which assets and capabilities will be strategically useful in the future. When managers cannot determine conclusively which specific-use assets will be most useful in the future, choosing flexible assets capable of being applied to some set of alternative uses may give the firm a better chance of responding effectively to a larger range of future changes. *Ex post,* once flexible assets are in place, the dynamic response times usually encountered in changing higher system elements may be reduced by the ability of flexible assets the firm already has to be redeployed relatively quickly to alternative uses.

An example may illustrate how resource flexibility can help to mitigate cognitive and dynamic system effects. If a firm invests in acquiring flexible manufacturing systems, it gains some latitude to change its production activities and specific mix of products without having to change its stocks of production resources. Flexible production resources therefore permit short-run changes in the products offered by the firm that would otherwise be delayed and made more costly by the need to make long-run changes in the firm's stock of production resources. From a systems perspective on competence building and leveraging, therefore, flexibility becomes a critically important property of asset stocks, because flexible assets may help overcome the system effects of dynamic response times and may compensate to some extent for managerial cognitive limitations that result from causal ambiguities.

Coordination Flexibility

Because a firm's system elements are interdependent, the flexibility that can actually be realized from a given system element depends on the flexibilities that can be realized from other system elements. Thus, achieving flexibility in the firm as a system requires (i) having some level of flexibility in all the interrelated asset stocks and flows that make up the firm as a system, and (ii) maintaining flexibility in deploying those resources to alternative uses. Coordination flexibility can be defined by the abilities of managers and others in a firm to coordinate new strategic uses for flexible resources by redirecting, reconfiguring, and redeploying the resources available to the firm. Coordination flexibility is therefore essential to using the flexibilities of a firm's resources advantageously in a dynamic environment.

The coordination flexibilities of a firm arise from the flexibilities of the firm's higher system elements—*i.e.*, the firm's abilities to change its strategic logic, management practices, and intangible assets when it becomes strategically advantageous to do so. The interdependencies of a firm's system elements suggest, however, that the inflexibilities of the least flexible system element will act as a bottleneck that limits the overall flexibility of the firm as a system to respond to change (Sanchez 1995). For example, if a firm's computer systems for supporting decision making are designed to gather and process only certain kinds data flows within a specific organizational structure, managers' flexibility to adopt and coordinate new organizational processes will be constrained by the time and cost required to create new information systems appropriate to a new organization structure. On the other hand, if a firm's decision making processes are supported by an information system architecture that can readily reconfigure information flows to suit a variety of organizational forms, managers' flexibilities to imagine and adopt new organizational forms need not be constrained by inflexibilities in the firm's computer-supported decision and control processes.

Given the growing availability of flexible manufacturing systems, flexible information system architectures, and methodologies for creating flexible product designs, a growing concern for strategic management in dynamic environments is the potential inflexibilities in managers' strategic logics and derived management processes that can limit the uses to which increasingly flexible lower system elements might be directed.

CONCLUSIONS: A SYSTEMS VIEW OF STRATEGY AS STRETCH AND LEVERAGE

Strategic managers, through their unique impact on the strategic logic and management processes of a firm, guide the behavior of the firm as an open system. In dynamic product environments, the work of strategic managers

(Sanchez 1993) is *perceiving possibilities* for new competences and new uses for existing competences, leading the firm in *creating* new competences that can bring new strategic options for future actions, and *guiding* the firm's competence leveraging activities to achieve the greatest benefits from the firm's current competences and their associated options for action. Because competence-based competition creates environmental turbulence and uncertainty, the essential dynamic of strategic management in competence-based competition will be a process of *continuous learning* at a conceptual level that leads to qualitative changes in a firm's system elements.

Bottom-up adaptation through lower-order control loops may be essential for making quantitative or incremental qualitative adjustments to whatever operations a firm is already engaged in. Top-down management through higher-order control loops, on the other hand, may be the most effective means of achieving significant qualitative changes in asset stocks and flows of all the firm's system elements.

Given the inherent ambiguity of data about a firm's higher system elements and the long dynamic response times of asset flows in higher system elements, strategic managers' task of inducing adaptive change through higher-order control loops will necessarily be an exercise in "strategy as stretch" (Prahalad and Hamel 1993). Leading the firm to stretch beyond its current capabilities requires the *stretch of managerial imagination* to envision competences that are beyond the reach of the current system elements of the firm. Explicitly working to develop better cognitive capabilities is a fundamental task of strategic managers if they are to improve their abilities to imagine new competences needed to survive in a competitive future that defies precise prediction. Strategic managers in competence-based competition face the never ending challenge of continuously learning how to better manage their own cognitions.

The systems perspective on competence-based competition also suggests that the pursuit of "strategy as leverage" (Prahalad and Hamel 1993) depends on identifying and acquiring the use of flexible resources and flexible coordination abilities that enable a firm to respond broadly to current and future opportunities. Achieving strategic flexibility through developing resource and coordination flexibilities may be the best approach to leveraging the firms existing competences most effectively, both in the firm's current product markets and in the product markets the firm might create or enter in the future.

Within the view of the firm as a cognitively and dynamically constrained system of asset stocks and flows, the notions of strategy as stretch and leverage take on new meaning and importance. The systems view suggested here provides a model for further investigation of strategies for managing the firm-as-a-system to achieve greatest stretch and leverage of its competences.

REFERENCES

Ashby, W. R. *An Introduction to Cybernetics,* London: Chapman and Hall, 1956.

Dierickx, I. and Cool, K. "Asset Stock Accumulation and Sustainability of Competitive Advantage". *Management Science,* Vol. 35, pp. 1504–1511, 1989.

Forrester, J. W. *Industrial Dynamics,* Cambridge, MA: MIT Press, 1961.

Forrester, J. W. *Principles of Systems,* Cambridge, MA: MIT Press, 1968.

Hamel, G. and Prahalad, C. K. *Competing for the Future,* Boston: Harvard Business School Press, 1994.

Leonard-Barton, D. "Core Capabilities and Core Rigidities: A Paradox in Managing New Product Development". *Strategic Management Journal,* Vol. 13, pp. 111–125, 1992.

Lippman, S. A. and Rumelt, R. P. "Uncertain Imitability: An Analysis of Interfirm Differences in Efficiency under Competition". *Bell Journal of Economics,* Vol. 13, pp. 418-438, 1982.

Nelson, R. R. and Winter, S. G. *An Evolutionary Theory of Economic Change,* Cambridge, MA: Harvard University Press, 1982.

Prahalad, C. K. and Hamel, G. "Strategy as Stretch and Leverage". *Harvard Business Review,* March–April 1993.

Rumelt, R. P. "Foreword". In Hamel, G. and Heene, A., eds, *Competence-Based Competition.* New York: Wiley, pp. xv–xix, 1994.

Sanchez, R. "Strategic Flexibility, Firm Organization, and Managerial Work in Dynamic Markets: A Strategic Options Perspective". *Advances in Strategic Management,* Vol. 9, pp. 251–291, 1993.

Sanchez, R. "Strategic Flexibility in Product Competition". *Strategic Management Journal,* Vol. 16, pp. 135–159, Summer 1995.

Sanchez, R. and Thomas, H. "Strategic Goals". In Sanchez, R., Heene, A. and Thomas, H., eds, *Dynamics of Competence-Based Competition: Theory and Practice in the New Strategic Management.* London: Elsevier, 1996.

Simon, H. *The Sciences of the Artificial,* Cambridge, MA: MIT Press, 1969.

Teece, D., Pisano, G. and Shuen, A. *Firm Capabilities, Resources, and the Concept of Strategy,* CCC Working Paper No. 90–8, Berkeley: University of California, 1990.

3

STRATEGIC GOALS

Ron Sanchez and Howard Thomas

INTRODUCTION

This chapter investigates the goals which motivate the strategic competence building and leveraging activities of firms. Extending the view of the firm as an open system (Sanchez and Heene 1996, in this volume), we characterize the goal-seeking behavior of a firm as motivated by desires of managers and others in a firm to improve the states of the firm's system elements. Fundamental differences in the kinds of strategic goals firms pursue result in firms' seeking different forms of quantitative *versus* qualitative changes in the states of their system elements.[1] Following this rationale, a *taxonomy* is developed that identifies basic forms of strategic goal-seeking behavior firms may exhibit in competence-based competition.

We first relate the goal-seeking, competence building and leveraging behavior of firms to economic frameworks for evaluating firm performance. We suggest that profitability measures often used in strategy research for assessing firm performance are both conceptually inadequate and empirically problematic in the context of competence-based competition (Nelson and Gorman 1995). We find a close correspondence, however, between the concept of *firm value* developed in modern finance theory and the concept of the firm as a system for competence building and leveraging in the competence theory developed in this volume. In particular, we propose that there is a close theoretical correspondence between the recognition in modern finance theory that a firm's distinctive abilities may give it *real options* (Myers 1977) to create new sources of firm value, on the one hand, and the characterization of competence building and leveraging as processes for creating and exercising a firm's *strategic options* (Sanchez 1993, 1995) on the other.

This chapter then elaborates the goal-seeking behaviors of firms by investigating patterns of resource flows associated with competence building and leveraging. Distinctive patterns in flows of financial, productive, and intellectual resources are required to carry out competence building *versus* competence leveraging activities. An analysis of those distinctive patterns of resource flows becomes the basis for building a taxonomy of strategic goal-seeking behaviors.

We conclude by considering how the view of strategic goals developed here may be used in strategy research, particularly with regard to improved conceptualizations of firm performance. We also discuss some implications of this view of firm goals for strategic managers.

A COMPETENCE PERSPECTIVE ON FIRM GOALS

Sanchez and Heene (1996, this volume) investigate the dynamic aspects of firm behavior, focusing on the systems effects of asset stocks and flows in a firm's competence building and leveraging activities. In this systems view of the firm, goal-seeking activities are motivated by the desire of a firm's managers to close a gap between the perceived and the desired state of any of the firm's system elements—*i.e.,* its operations, tangible assets, intangible assets, management processes, or strategic logic.

The perspective on the goal-seeking behavior of the firm-as-a-system can be developed further by focusing on the nature of the *strategic goals* that motivate action by a firm. In this discussion, we characterize a firm's strategic goals as originating in managers' perceptions of the set of desired—but unattained—states of a firm's system elements. Of course, not all desires for change of all people within a firm lead to action; for managers and employees alike, some desires simply remain wishes that are never acted on. The criterion of *action* is adopted here to make a distinction between desires that simply remain wishes of managers and others within the firm, and desires that become translated into the strategic goals that motivate firm actions. Thus, in this discussion, only when the gap between managers' desired and perceived states of a firm's system element grows large enough to motivate gap-closing actions will the desired state of that system element be considered a strategic goal of the firm. In essence, *strategic goals* are the desires for change of managers and others in the firm that are strong enough to precipitate some form of action by the firm to attain that desire. Strategic goals may lead to actions intended to change or preserve the *status quo.*

The vocabulary of competence-based competition developed in this volume (Sanchez, Heene, and Thomas 1996) is used in this analysis of strategic goals. *Competence* refers to an ability to sustain the coordinated deployment of assets (both tangible and intangible) in ways that help a firm achieve its goals. *Competence building* is any process by which the firm *qualitatively* changes its assets and capabilities and thereby improves the ability of the firm to coordinate and deploy assets in ways that help the firm achieve its goals. *Competence leveraging* is the use of a firm's existing competences to attain its goals; competence leveraging may involve *non-qualitative—i.e.,* quantitative—expansions of a firm's assets and capabilities used by its current competences.[2] The strategic goals discussed here motivate both competence building and competence leveraging behavior.

Further, our discussion of strategic goals is intended to develop a competence-based perspective on firm behavior that is more holistic than the profit-maximizing motive often assumed in strategy theory and research. There are fundamental theoretical objections to using accounting-based profitability measures as the primary indicators of firm performance. Firms often direct cash flows to important competence building activities that are (inappropriately) treated by traditional accounting methods as expenses that reduce profits. Many uses of financial resources to build and maintain human and organizational assets, for example, are typically treated as wage or overhead expenses that decrease accounting profits, even though such resource allocations may allow the firm to build new competences for competing in the future. Dynamic competitive environments especially may present a firm with many opportunities—or many competitive *necessities*—for competence building that lead to reduced accounting profits in current periods. In such environments, firms that might be judged as high performers in creating new competences may appear to be poor performers if evaluated by measures of current profitability.

Accordingly, this discussion of strategic goals is linked to a more satisfactory economic perspective on firm performance—specifically, to the concept of *firm value* adopted in contemporary finance theory. The finance theory perspective recognizes that various kinds of flows of financial and other resources play an essential role in establishing the value of a firm. That broader perspective on a firm's goal-seeking behavior provides a direct—and more satisfactory—theoretical link between a firm's goals for competence building and leveraging and its financial performance.

FIRM VALUE AND ITS RELATION TO COMPETENCE BUILDING AND LEVERAGING

Much economic theory used to model firm behavior is built on the stipulation that the goal of firm managers is (or ought to be) maximizing profits. Finance theory, on the other hand, stipulates that the proper objective of managers is maximizing the net present value of the firm (*e.g.,* Brealey and Myers 1989). Although ostensibly similar, these two stipulations rest on significantly different views of the tasks managers are presumed to perform. Horowitz (1970: 155–156) points out that neoclassical economic theory presumes that managers can determine the allocation of resources to both variable and fixed cost factors that will maximize the difference between revenues and costs—*i.e.,* firm profits—over a given time horizon. When this theoretical perspective is invoked (either explicitly or, as is more often the case, implicitly) as a framework for judging firm performance, evidence of superior (inferior) profitability relative to other firms over some time period becomes the primary basis for assessing the existence of superior (inferior) firm performance.

Modern finance theory, however, presumes that a firm's investments in factors of production are inherently risky—*i.e.*, that the revenues and costs that may be generated in a given time period by the use of specific productive factors generally cannot be known with certainty. Finance theory therefore ascribes to managers the task of maximizing the *net present value* of the firm, a concept that discounts expected cash flows associated with a firm's use of productive factors for both time and nondiversifiable risk. Finance theory also recognizes that a firm may have specialized assets or capabilities which may give it *opportunities in the future* to invest some of the cash flows from its current uses of productive factors (plus new capital it may attract) in creating new productive factors or new ways of using productive factors that may generate new cash flows at some future time. Thus, in finance theory the value of a firm is taken to consist of the net present value of expected cash flows from the firm's current uses of its productive factors, *plus* the expected present value of opportunities the firm may have in the future to make investments that generate new cash flows.

Like the cash flows from a firm's current operations, the cash flows a firm may generate from future opportunities are uncertain. As the values of its opportunities become more apparent in the future, managers may choose to pursue some opportunities, but not to pursue others. Because the specialized assets and capabilities of the firm may give its managers the option—but not the obligation—to pursue a future opportunity, Myers (1977) introduced the term *real options* to denote a firm's opportunities for making investments in the future that promise to generate new cash flows. The economic value of the firm can then be stated as the sum of the net present value (NPV) of the cash flows expected from its current uses of assets, *plus* the value of the firm's real options to generate new cash flows from new uses of new or existing assets in the future, as stated in Fig. 3.1.

Thus, from a finance theory perspective, the task of managers is to allocate firm resources to *jointly maximize* the NPV of current cash flows and of the firm's real options to create future cash flows.

Both a firm's present and future cash flows result from the firm's strategies for the use of its assets and capabilities in creating, producing, and marketing products. Thus, the real options available to the firm can also be characterized as the firm's *strategic options* to develop, produce, and market products (Sanchez 1991, 1993).[3] To create new strategic options not presently available to the firm, a firm must create or acquire new kinds of assets and capabilities; in other words, it must engage in competence building. Thus, *competence building is the process by which a firm creates its strategic options—i.e.,* its opportunities to generate new cash flows.

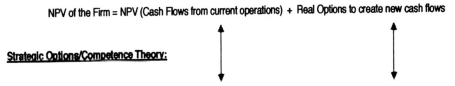

Finance Theory:

NPV of the Firm = NPV (Cash Flows from current operations) + Real Options to create new cash flows

Strategic Options/Competence Theory:

Value of the firm = NPV (Cash Flows from competence leveraging) + Strategic Options created by competence building

Fig. 3.1. Conceptual correspondence between finance theory and strategic options/competence theory.

Similarly, a firm generates its cash flows through its current ways of using its existing assets and capabilities—in other words, through its competence leveraging activities. Therefore *competence leveraging is the process by which the firm exercises its existing strategic options*—and, in so doing, generates current cash flows.

Strategic options are often created during a period of competence building in which the firm has a number of incremental choices (Bowman and Hurry 1993) about how to develop a given set of opportunities. An initial decision to invest in competence building by acquiring a new technological capability, for example, may give the firm a number of strategic options to develop new products based on the new technology. Further investments in developing new product designs would give the firm strategic options to produce and market new products. At any point in time, therefore, the strategic options available to a firm engaged in competence building may include options to acquire new technologies the firm is capable of using, options to develop new products based on the firm's existing technologies, options to put available developed products into production, and options to distribute and market products the firm can currently produce (Sanchez 1991, 1993, 1995).

From the joint perspectives of strategic options and competence building and leveraging, the economic value of the firm consists of the net present value of the cash flows the firm may realize from leveraging its existing competences to exercise some or all of its existing strategic options, *plus* the value of the firm's strategic options to develop, produce, distribute, and market products created by the firm's building of new competences. Figure. 3.1 shows this direct correspondence of the conceptualization of firm value in finance theory with this competence theory conceptualization of the creation of firm value.

Managers seeking to maximize firm value will typically be engaged in a continuous cycle of competence building and leveraging, as suggested by Fig. 3.2. In this process, leveraging a firm's existing competences to exercise some of the firm's existing strategic options generates cash flows, some of which are directed to competence building to create new strategic options.

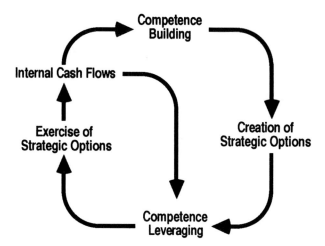

Fig. 3.2. Creating firm value through a "virtuous circle" of competence building and leveraging.

Managers then leverage some of the firm's new and prior competences to exercise new strategic options and generate new cash flows, some of which are directed to creating new competences that bring new strategic options, and so on. This "virtuous circle" of competence building and leveraging in creating and exercising strategic options constitutes the essential dynamic of value creation in competence-based competition. As we will suggest later, this cycle of building and leveraging competences is also the fundamental dynamic of strategic goal-seeking behavior by firms in competence-based competition.

To carry out this dynamic, a firm functions as an open system that must acquire and use resources from many external sources (Sanchez and Heene 1996, in this volume), including markets for financial resources, intellectual resources, and productive resources. Thus, the firm's virtuous circle of competence building and leveraging embeds the firm in a larger system of resource stocks and flows.

RESOURCE FLOWS IN COMPETENCE BUILDING AND LEVERAGING

To build and leverage competences, the firm-as-an-open-system requires inputs of many kinds of resources. In analyzing these resource flows, a basic but useful distinction can be made between financial resources, like-kind productive resources that are qualitatively similar to those already deployed by the firm, and new kinds of intellectual and productive resources that are qualitatively different from those a firm has previously deployed. These resource flows and their relation to a firm's virtuous circle of competence building and leveraging and creation and exercising of strategic options is suggested in Fig. 3.3.

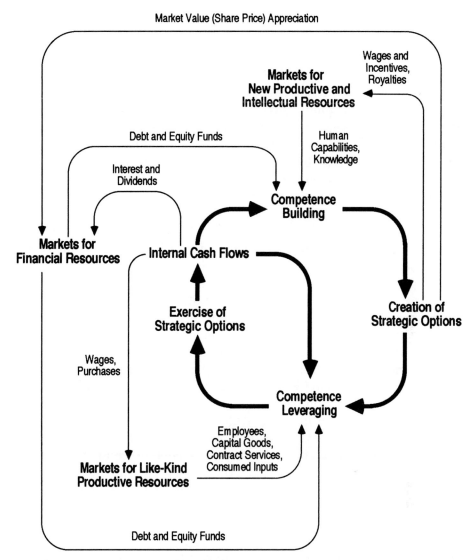

Fig. 3.3. Firm's "virtuous circle" of competence building and leveraging as a system of resource flows.

Within this larger system of resource flows, competence building and competence leveraging generate distinctive patterns of resource flows. The differences in these resource flow patterns suggest that there are important differences in the ways the two forms of goal-seeking behavior create economic value. Recognizing these distinctive patterns of resource flows and modes of value creation leads to the further realization that a firm's performance in competence building and in competence leveraging has to be evaluated by different constructs and measures of performance.

Competence Leveraging

In leveraging competences it has built, a firm will seek to exchange financial resources from its sales revenues for more like-kind resources qualitatively similar to those that it already has experience in coordinating and deploying. Resources for quantitative expansions of a firm's competence leveraging activities may be obtainable directly from external markets for labor, capital goods, contract services, and consumable inputs (materials, supplies). To the extent that a firm uses idiosyncratic firm-specific resources in its competence leveraging, it may have to invest in providing specialized training or in developing customized tangible assets in order to transform resources available from external markets into the additional inputs it needs to expand. If the firm has existing competences in transforming market-sourced inputs, expansion that requires a greater quantity of, but not qualitatively different, transformations of input resources is also a form of competence leveraging.

In its goal-seeking behavior, a competence leveraging firm will seek to survive or grow by exercising whatever strategic options are implicit in its existing competences. The firm may seek to expand production and distribution of existing products, for example, without developing new products or acquiring new marketing capabilities. In such cases, the resources required by the firm will be primarily financial resources and quantitative increases in like-kind productive resources similar to those the firm is already using. Competence leveraging therefore leads to the pattern of resource flows shown in Fig. 3.4(a).

In stable environments in which there are relatively few opportunities for technological change or other forms of competence building, competence leveraging is likely to be the focus of firm goal-seeking behavior and the source of the firm's economic value. When a firm still has unexercised strategic options, firm value will be derived from both the value of its unexercised options for growth and from its cash flows from the options for uses of resources that it has previously exercised. Some part of the firm's cash flows may be paid to capital markets as debt service or dividends. If a firm eventually achieves maximum market penetration with its existing products and has no viable options to develop new products or expand its markets, however, in effect the firm will be fully leveraging its existing competences, having exercised all its strategic options and converted them to current cash flows. In this case, the market value of the firm would be determined by the capital market's assessment of the net present value of the cash flows obtainable from the firm's current competence leveraging activities. Thus, in the special case of a firm that is fully engaged in competence leveraging and whose current competences do not give the firm some special ability to build new competences, current profitability may be a reasonable indicator of firm performance.

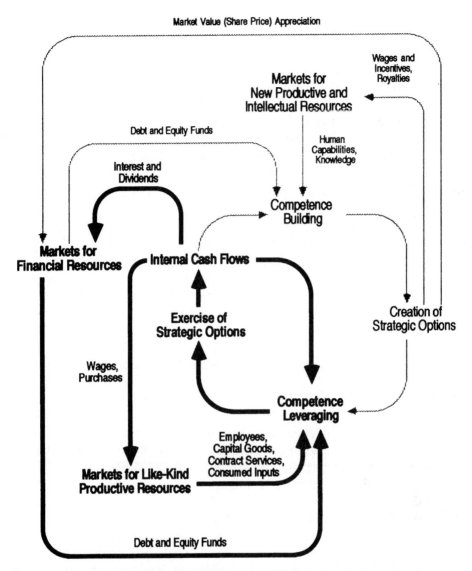

Fig. 3.4(a). Resource flows in competence leveraging and exercising existing strategic options.

Competence Building

To build competences, a firm must have access to flows of financial resources and be able to convert those financial resources into the qualitatively new kinds of resources it needs to build new competences. A firm may obtain financial resources from financial markets (in the form of debt or equity funds) and from its internal cash flows generated by exercising its strategic options. It may then invest its financial resources in its own internal efforts to create qualitatively new intangible assets (*e.g.,* new knowledge) or new tangible assets (*e.g.*, new kinds of production or delivery systems). However, a firm may also have to draw extensively on external sources for qualitatively new kinds of intellectual and productive resources. Firms may obtain new kinds of intellectual resources from markets for human resources with new capabilities or skills, from markets for codified knowledge (licenses for product and process technology), or markets for new cognitive frameworks (consultants or new managers). New kinds of intellectual and productive resources may also be sourced from other firms with competences which the firm can access through competence building alliances.

Especially in dynamic environments, creating new strategic options through competence building may account for a large part of a firm's activities and uses of resources. A significant portion of the firm's cash flows may be directed to investments in recruiting critical human assets, licensing or developing knowledge, creating organizational systems and cultures, and other forms of competence building activities. In the formative stages of a new industry, in particular, firms may direct all their available financial and other resources to competence building. When the basic technology underlying an industry's products is in a state of development or undergoes major change, competence building may become the primary activity of firms for long periods. Competence building has been the dominant activity of most firms in the emerging U.S. biotechnology industry since its inception in the 1970s.

Competence building will require the distinctive pattern of activities and resource flows indicated in Fig. 3.4(b). In dynamic competitive environments in which there are relatively many opportunities for technological change and other forms of competence building, the strategic options at various stages of development within the firm will constitute the major source of firm value. A firm significantly engaged in competence building may therefore provide returns to capital markets primarily (or even exclusively) in the form of share price appreciation, which will occur if enough investors in capital markets believe that the firm is in fact creating valuable strategic options for generating future cash flows. The firm is also likely to invest substantial financial resources (*e.g.*, salaries and incentives like stock options) in retaining and supporting its creative human assets, who are the wellspring of the firm's future competences and strategic options. During intensive competence building, major resource flows may also be directed to creating coordination systems that provide an organizational infrastructure enabling effective responses to emerging opportunities in the firm's competitive environment. Resources may also be directed to other firms that have joined the firm in competence building alliances.

The Firm as a System of Competence Building and Leveraging

Most firms, of course, engage in some mix of competence building and leveraging, as suggested by combined resource flows associated with both

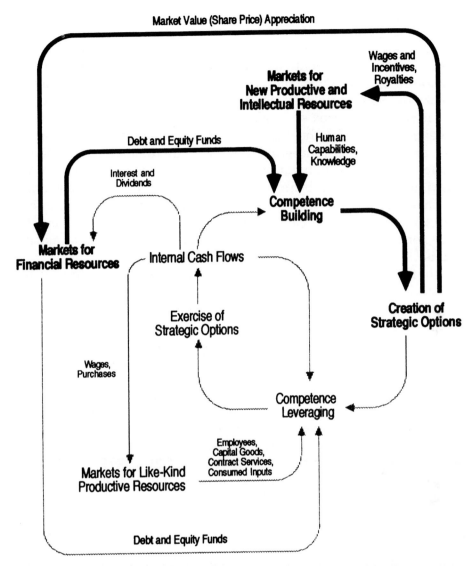

Fig. 3.4(b). Resource flows in competence building and creating strategic options.

competence building and leveraging behaviors shown in Fig. 3.3. The specific set of competence building and leveraging goals pursued by a firm determine the distinctive pattern of asset stocks and flows (Dierickx and Cool 1989) of the firm at any point in time. The specific composition of a firm's asset flows determines the *content* of the firm's own asset stocks[4] and fundamentally constrains the ways in which the firm can coordinate and deploy resources. Thus, a firm's strategic options are determined by the way a firm's goals (and resulting strategic logic and management processes) direct resource flows to specific competence building activities.

From this dynamic perspective, evaluations of firm performance are incomplete if they do not include a firm's activities in acquiring and deploying new assets in ways that enable the firm to create and exercise new strategic options. Conventional performance measures like profitability or market share, while reflecting a firm's success in leveraging competences to exercise its existing strategic options, do not capture the value of a firm's unexercised strategic options or the value of the strategic options being created by the firm's competence building. Such simple measures are therefore conceptually inadequate to assess the actual performance of firms in dynamic competitive environments, where the value-maximizing use of a firm's resources may be intensive competence building that endows the firm with strategic options for future gains. Moreover, value-maximizing competence building may be carried out for protracted periods to the detriment of current accounting profits or market share gains.

Although the dynamic, systemic, holistic perspective on firm value creation developed here may challenge strategy researchers to identify and parameterize new kinds of competence-based performance variables (Sanchez 1995, note 4), the competence perspective offers a necessary corrective to the conceptual inadequacy of simplistic performance measures often used in strategy research. Especially in dynamic competitive environments, researchers need to develop constructs and measures for assessing the effectiveness of resources flows directed to developing the human assets, creating the organizational infrastructures, and strengthening the competence alliances which are essential to creating valuable strategic options. The competence-theoretic view of the firm as a goal-seeking *open system* invites new concepts of firm performance that explicitly recognize the value of strategic options that can only be created through the systemic interactions of many kinds of stakeholders.

A BASIC TAXONOMY OF STRATEGIC GOALS

Competence building and leveraging consists of a number of systemically interrelated processes for gathering and interpreting data, gathering and allocating resources, acquiring and deploying assets and capabilities, and forming and applying a strategic logic and derived management processes (Sanchez and Heene 1996, in this volume). Although these activities are multifaceted and to some extent idiosyncratic within each firm, the competence building and leveraging behaviors of firms will tend to follow fundamental dynamics that generate the distinctive patterns of resource flows we have discussed above. These patterns provide a basis for classifying firm behaviors into some fundamental categories. We next develop a basic *taxonomy of strategic goal-seeking behaviors* based on the distinctive patterns of resource flows which a firm may direct to competence building and leveraging activities.

Figure 3.5 presents a taxonomy of strategic goals derived from the basic forms of quantitative *vs.* qualitative changes—*i.e.,* leveraging or building competences—within each *system element* of the firm-as-an-open-system: its operations, tangible assets, intangible assets, management processes, and strategic logic (see Fig. 2.1 in Sanchez and Heene 1996, in this volume). In the systems view of the firm, goal-seeking behavior is motivated by an "unacceptable" gap between the perceived and desired state of any of the firm's system elements.[5] In this sense, the "acceptability" or "unacceptability" of a strategic gap is not a determination that is necessarily made exclusively by a firm's top managers, since mid-level managers and many other firm members may also be capable of taking actions to close gaps they perceive in the state of a system element over which they have some discretion. Accordingly, our taxonomy of strategic goal-seeking behaviors consists of activities which could improve the state of each of the firm's system elements, not just those with which top managers are usually directly involved. Nevertheless, because managers have a particularly significant impact on the firm's strategic logic and management processes, which in turn usually strongly affects the states of the firm's other system elements, we focus our present discussion on managerial perceptions of unacceptable gaps in a firm's system elements.

The taxonomy makes a basic distinction between strategic goals which motivate competence leveraging activities and those which motivate competence building activities. Competence leveraging activities continue or expand a firm's product development, production, distribution, and marketing operations in ways that do not require the firm to create or acquire qualitatively different assets and capabilities. Goals that motivate competence-building activity, however, require gap closing actions that invite qualitative changes in the assets and capabilities in any of the system elements of the firm. In other words, competence leveraging is motivated by a desire to exercise existing strategic options to make desired changes in operations or asset stocks that are essentially *quantitative* in nature (more machines, more workers, more like-kind inputs). Competence building, on the other hand, is motivated by a desire to create new strategic options to develop, produce, or market products and involves making *qualitative* changes in at least some system element of the firm (machines with greater flexibilities, workers with new skills, managers with new cognitive frameworks).[6]

An example may help to illustrate the importance of this distinction. Suppose that the firm's goal for its operations system element is greater output of an existing product. If output can be expanded by simple quantitative additions to the firm's existing production capacity, using only the *same kinds* of assets and capabilities the firm is already using, then the goal of output expansion motivates a competence-leveraging activity. The firm, in effect, exercises an existing strategic option to expand production without first having to invest in acquiring and learning how to use new kinds of

	System Elements				
	Operations	Tangible Assets	Intangible Assets	Management Practices	Strategic Logic
Competence Leveraging Activities	Product Development: Refine or extend existing product line	Product Development: Expand facilities for R+D with like-kind assets.	Product Development: Expand staff in line with present profile of capabilities and skills.	Changes in the states of these system elements are intrinsically qualitative and constitute competence building.	Redefine the firm's rationale for attaining its strategic goals by offering products to targeted markets:
	Production: Continue or expand output using like-kind assets and capabilities	Production: Expand production facilities using current capabilities	Production: Expand staff in line with present profile of capabilities and skills.		
	Distribution/Marketing: Maintain or extend market penetration of existing products	Distribution/Marketing: Fully utilize existing distribution channels	Distribution/Marketing: Extend distribution through like-kind channels, intensify present marketing approaches		
Competence Building Activities	Product Development: Create new or greatly improved products.	Product Development: Create facilities for new kinds of R+D	Product Development: Develop or acquire new product technologies, new kinds of product designs. R+D staff with new skills	Develop new ways of • creating internal resources • accessing external resources • gathering new data • interpreting data • deciding how to allocate financial and physical resources to projects • coordinating human and information resources (using new kinds of controls and incentives) • managing intellectual assets (human cognitions, knowledge in various forms inside and outside the firm)	• benchmarking or benchtrending against competitors and best in world • scanning for market and technology trends • exposure to alternative cognitive frameworks through consultants, conferences, classes, books
	Production: Adopt new process technology	Production: Create new kinds of production systems to exploit new process technologies	Production: Develop or acquire new process technologies, production staff with new skills		
	Distribution/Marketing: Enter new markets requiring new distribution and marketing capabilities	Distribution/Marketing: Establish new kinds of distribution facilities	Distribution/Marketing: Develop or acquire new kinds of distribution channels, new kinds of marketing capabilities		

Fig. 3.5. A basic taxonomy of strategic goal-seeking behaviors.

assets and capabilities. On the other hand, if to expand production the firm must also invest in developing new kinds of production, distribution, or marketing capabilities to serve new markets for the firm's product, then the goal of expanding output must motivate competence-building activity. In this event, expanding production is not a readily available, pre-existing strategic option, and the firm will have to invest time and resources to create a strategic option to expand production.

The taxonomy in Fig. 3.5 elaborates specific forms of the competence building and leveraging behaviors, *i.e.*, creating and exercising strategic options, shown in Fig. 3.2. The taxonomy identifies basic categories of competence leveraging behavior that cause changes in a firm's operations and in the firm's stocks of tangible and intangible assets. No competence leveraging goals are identified in the taxonomy, however, for the system elements of management processes and strategic logic, because these system elements are essentially intangible intellectual assets of the firm which cannot be expanded quantitatively. The existing strategic logic and management processes of the firm determine both the *content* of the firm's use of tangible and intangible assets in its operations and its *processes* for acquiring and coordinating tangible and intangible assets. In essence, competence leveraging through expansion of lower system elements extends the reach of the firm's strategic logic and management processes, but does not necessarily require a change in their content.[7]

Figure 3.5 also identifies basic categories of competence building behaviors in the system elements of the firm, including flows of resources for acquiring new tangible assets and maintaining current operations. These lower level resource flows, of course, receive considerable attention in management education, in firms, and in strategy research. Flows of *new intellectual resources,* however, are also essential to competence building and eventual competence leveraging, but are only recently beginning to receive serious study. Intellectual resources may be acquired in the form of human resources with new cognitions, capabilities, and skills, or in the form of new knowledge which can be conveyed to or within the firm in codified form.[8] Creating flows of new intellectual resources is the primary means of effecting qualitative changes in a firm's intellectual assets of strategic logic and management processes. Strategic logic, for example, which directs the deployments of the firm's assets and capabilities through the firm's management processes, can only be changed qualitatively through changes in the *cognitions* of top managers. Similarly, achieving changes in a firm's management processes requires new capabilities in gathering and interpreting data and new concepts in coordinating assets and capabilities.

Several chapters in this volume present industry studies of firms pursuing some of the general competence building goals identified in this taxonomy. Examples include defining and creating an infrastructure of public goods that enhance the product offerings of all producers in an emerging product market (Jensen 1996, in this volume), improving the capabilities of knowledge-intensive service functions by providing services to a mix of firms (Elfring and Baven 1996, in this volume), developing organization structures for coordinating national and regional research centers in global product development (Winterscheid and McNabb 1996, in this volume), developing global alliances to improve research and development capabilities (Roehl 1996, in this volume), increasing the flexibility of a semiconductor production system to accommodate greater change and variety (Volberda 1996, in this volume), and developing modular product design capabilities and "quick-connect" computer systems for coordinating product creation networks (Sanchez 1996, in this volume). These studies suggest that improving access to resources outside the firm is a process of fundamental importance in competence building.

Other chapters in this volume give insights into modes of competence leveraging behaviors indicated in the taxonomy of Fig. 3.5. The chapters by Bogner and Thomas (1996) and Rispoli (1996) in this volume suggest that there are also demand-side, market-determined reasons why firms in an industry are likely to exhibit some basic similarities in their patterns of competence leveraging. In particular, there may be technological constraints that lead firms to use similar assets and capabilities in similar ways in order to provide the "threshold" attributes required by consumers of all products in a market. Possibilities for pursuing some alternative technological approaches to leveraging competences to provide the "central" or "plus-only" attributes needed to distinguish products in a marketplace, on the other hand, are likely to result in several groupings of firms that leverage specific assets and capabilities in similar ways. Of course, some specific forms of competence leveraging may be unique to a given firm in a product market and serve to further distinguish a firm's product offerings in the marketplace. To the extent that similarities across firms' patterns of resource use occur in an industry, however, competence groups—*i.e.,* clusters of firms within an industry that engage in similar competence leveraging activities at a given point in time—may arise. Because firms in a dynamically stable competence group require comparable resource flows to support their competence leveraging, they are very likely to compete head-to-head for input resources, as well as for markets for outputs.

The competence leveraging behaviors in the taxonomy of Fig. 3.5 are a menu of the primary forms of short-run competitive interactions between firms within a competence group. These interactions between firms in a competence group and, to a lesser extent, between competence groups define the short-run competitive dynamics of an industry (Gorman, Thomas, and Sanchez 1996, in this volume). The competence building behaviors in the taxonomy, however, the dynamics that drive industry evolution. Differences in the specific sets of strategic goals of firms lead to differences in competence building behaviors across firms, and these differences create dynamics of convergence and divergence in the competence leveraging activities of firms. High levels of competence building in an industry are therefore likely to result in a turbulent environment in which competence groups may rapidly converge and diverge and in which individual firms may migrate across or even span group or industry boundaries. Further research into dynamic patterns of competence building and leveraging may improve our understanding of how the short run competitive interactions of competence leveraging are or could be linked to the long run dynamics of competence building, and how the two dynamics interact in driving the overall evolution of industries.

USE OF THE STRATEGIC GOALS TAXONOMY IN STRATEGY RESEARCH

The basic taxonomy of strategic goal-seeking behaviors in Fig. 3.5 can serve a number of important purposes in strategy research. Both inter- and intra-industry performance studies may use the taxonomy to help identify competence building and competence leveraging activities and to determine the degree to which various forms of each activity are occurring in a sample of firms. Competence building may not only consume significant flows of cash and other resources, but may also obsolete existing firm competences and disrupt positive cash flows that would otherwise be available from leveraging existing competences.[9] Thus, we would expect, for example, that cross-sectional comparisons may show systematically lower current profitability levels across firms and industries with relatively high allocations of resources to competence building activities.

To the extent that capital markets are efficient, individual firms, competence groups, and even entire industries making significant allocations of resources to competence building may generate significant financial returns in the form of appreciation in the market value of firms. In effect, investors should have some ability to look beyond current profitability to the value of the strategic options being created by a firm's competence building. The multi-billion aggregate market valuation of biotechnology firms in the U.S., most of which have yet to post a profit and many of which have yet even to post revenues, is a case in point. The categories of competence building activities in the taxonomy of strategic goals in Fig. 3.5 suggests a number of independent variables for studies of firm performance, using the market value of the firm as the dependent variable.[10]

The taxonomy of strategic goals in Fig. 3.5 also suggests possibilities for extended competence-based groupings of firms within an industry. Firms may be distinguished not only by whether they are engaged mostly in competence building or in competence leveraging, but also by the *kinds* of competence building or competence leveraging goals each is pursuing. Firms could be classified on the basis of resource allocations to specific competence-building or competence-leveraging activities, for example, or on the basis of a firm's current profile of specific skills (Farjoun 1994) used in competence building and leveraging.

The range of activities included in the taxonomy also suggests that aggregated measures of cash flow allocations that do not distinguish allocations to competence building from allocations to competence leveraging are unlikely to capture essential *dynamic* differences between firms. An aggregated figure for cash flows allocated to research and development, for example, may obscure strategically important differences between research intended to create new competences and development intended to enhance the firm's existing competences. Although disaggregated data may be difficult to obtain on most firms, some effort to distinguish competence building from competence leveraging appears to be essential to identifying alternative competence-based strategies and to investigating their impacts on firm performance.

Finally, strategy research must develop new constructs for classifying and measuring intellectual assets. The resources that make up a firm's stocks of cognitions, capabilities, and skills and the codified knowledge a firm acquires may appreciate or depreciate in strategic value in ways that are as yet poorly understood. Moreover, the human resources essential to competence building cannot be "accumulated" in the same manner as intangible assets. In particular, competence theory and research into firm performance must pay attention to the impact of alternative control and incentive structures in attracting, motivating, and retaining the creative human assets essential to the development of new competences and the firm's strategic options for the future.

IMPLICATIONS FOR STRATEGIC MANAGERS

From the managerial perspective, our discussion of strategic goals also suggests a critical difference between competence leveraging and competence building. Compared to pursuit of goals that require only competence leveraging, pursuit of strategic goals that require competence building typically demands greater efforts to develop *managerial insights* into future resource requirements of the firm, a *longer planning horizon* for resource allocations, and a greater ability to *manage the risks* of uncertain future outcomes. In essence, while competence leveraging is goal-seeking behavior that can be carried out in relatively well charted territory using familiar cognitions, capabilities, and assets, competence building is inevitably goal-seeking in relatively uncharted regions. Competence building is likely to challenge managers to continually develop new cognitive abilities and to try to imagine how to use new kinds of assets and capabilities in new ways. It also requires managers to make a sustained effort to interpret highly ambiguous data about the firm's competitive environment in an effort to anticipate possible future changes in technologies and markets. Managing competence building may therefore be a task that is intrinsically different from managing competence leveraging. The two kinds of management tasks may well require managers with distinct intellectual and personality profiles (Hitt and Tyler 1991).

Our discussion also brings to the fore the important role of *intellectual assets* in competence-based competition, especially in processes for competence building in the firm's system elements most directly affected by managers—its strategic logic and management processes. Obtaining flows of intellectual resources that may change a firm's managers' strategic logic and management processes may require relatively insignificant flows of financial resources, but may demand a major effort by managers to engage in sensemaking processes that continually challenge their current cognitive frameworks.

Important changes in the strategic logic of the firm may begin with a cognitive shift in the perceptions of a few managers or even one top manager, a process that may result from executive education programs, discussions with management consultants, conversations with managers of other firms, reading, or other activities requiring intellectual effort but minimal financial resources. Creating new concepts of incentive structures for managers and other employees, for example, may make little or no net demands on the firm's cash flows, but may result in significant changes in patterns of managerial decision making and employee behavior within the firm.

New cognitive frameworks can only create value if they lead to action, but enacting new cognitive frameworks, reinventing organizational processes, and redirecting resource flows may require great organizational resolve. Thus, despite the importance of many forms of competence building that may require substantial financial resources, competence building at the highest levels of the firm may depend most critically on flows of intellectual resources, and on a firm's organizational flexibility to deploy those new resources, in achieving strategic change.

NOTES

1. In essence, we seek to make explicit several critical differences between *qualitative* and *quantitative* changes in the asset stocks and flows (Dierickx and Cool 1989) that determine the states of a firm's system elements.
2. A firm may sometimes leverage its competences by *intensifying its use* of existing assets without expanding its assets quantitatively. People and machines may simply work longer hours. Competence leveraging may also involve using flexible assets in new ways without requiring a significant qualitative change in the asset. A firm may leverage its existing knowledge, for example, by combining its knowledge with the knowledge of other firms in a competence leveraging alliance.
3. A firm may also have important financial options. A firm with unused debt capacity, for example, usually has an option to borrow funds quickly and on favorable terms compared to issuing new stock. Ultimately, however, a firm's financial options arise in conjunction with the firm's pursuit of opportunities to create and sell products (or assets it holds). A financial option to obtain funds at some rate of return has value only if the funds obtained can ultimately be

productively invested to generate a higher rate of return by creating and marketing products.

4. Note that the firm's available resources include firm-addressable resources controlled by other firms but accessible to the firm. The extent to which a firm's own stocks of assets and capabilities are perceived as valuable resources by other firms, however, will often determine the willingness of other firms to make use of their resources available to the firm through competence building or leveraging alliances.

5. We do not address here the possible implications for the strategic goals we identify of (a) moral hazards arising from the agency relationship of managers to the firm (Jensen and Meckling 1976), or (b) the X-inefficiency of managers and other employees (Leibenstein 1980). Also, we do not address the causes or consequences of "goal drift" in which the perceptions of significant gaps leads to a diminution of the desired state of a system element rather than action to improve the state of the system element. Moral hazard, X-inefficiency, and goal drift all deserve further analysis and research to illuminate their impact on the behavior of the firm-as-a-open-system.

6. Any activity of the firm is likely to involve *both* competence building and leveraging to some degree. Hiring more workers, for example, may call for at least some *qualitatively* different skills to coordinate a *quantitatively* larger organization. Conversely, hiring workers with qualitatively new skills may also lead to hiring more workers with old skills that can be used in conjunction with the new skills. Thus, competence building and leveraging are unlikely ever to be strictly separable. We use the term *competence building* to denote activities in which effecting qualitative changes in assets and capabilities is the intended primary nature of the task undertaken by the firm, while *competence leveraging* denotes activities in which effecting qualitative changes in assets and capabilities is not the primary intended nature of the task undertaken.

7. We note that changes in managerial cognition may also arise through competence leveraging. For example, managers may learn by studying the firm's competence leveraging activities. Such managerial learning-by-doing, however, usually requires an intent to learn and thus would imply a manager's desire to build competence in the course of coordinating assets and capabilities in competence leveraging.

8. By *codified knowledge* we mean non-tacit (articulated) apprehensible knowledge which can be conveyed without significant loss of meaning from one person to another or from one organization to another. Examples could include an algorithm for production scheduling or a market research report on the preferences of a market segment.

9. For example, see Conner's (1988) discussion of cannibalizing products and Sanchez' (1995) discussion of product strategies based on accelerating performance improvements in products.

10. To the extent that capital markets are not perfectly efficient, the actual value of the strategic options the firm is creating through competence building may not be fully reflected in the current market value of the firm. To the extent that capital markets are inefficient in valuing strategic (real) options, better means of evaluating current patterns of competence building may enable better prediction of *future* appreciation in the market value of a firm.

REFERENCES

Bogner, W. C. and Thomas, H. "From Skills to Competences: The 'Play-Out' of Resource Bundles Across Firms". In Sanchez, R., Heene, A. and Thomas, H., eds, *Dynamics of Competence-Based Competition: Theory and Practice in the New Strategic Management*. London: Elsevier, 1996.

Bowman, E. H. and Hurry, D. "Strategy Through the Option Lens: An Integrated View of Resource Investments and the Incremental-Choice Process". *Academy of Management Review,* Vol. 18(4), pp. 760–782, 1993.

Brealey, R. A. and Myers, S. C. *Principles of Corporate Finance*, New York: McGraw-Hill, 1989.

Conner, K. R. "Strategies for Product Cannibalism". *Strategic Management Journal,* Vol. 9, pp. 9–26, 1988.

Dierickx, I. and Cool, K. "Asset Stock Accumulation and Sustainability of Competitive Advantage". *Management Science,* Vol. 35, pp. 1504–1511, 1989.

Elfring, T. and Baven, G. "Spinning-off Capabilities: Competence Development in Knowledge-Intensive Services". In Sanchez, R., Heene, A. and Thomas, H., eds, *Dynamics of Competence-Based Competition: Theory and Practice in the New Strategic Management*. London: Elsevier, 1996.

Farjoun, M. "Beyond Industry Boundaries: Human Expertise, Diversification, and Resource-Related Industry Groups". *Organization Science,* Vol.5(2), pp. 185–199, 1994.

Gorman, P., Thomas, H. and Sanchez, R. "Industry Dynamics in Competence-Based Competition". In Sanchez, R., Heene, A. and Thomas, H., eds, *Dynamics of Competence-Based Competition: Theory and Practice in the New Strategic Management*. London: Elsevier, 1996.

Hitt, M. A. and Tyler, B. B. "Strategic Decision Models: Integrating Different Perspectives". *Strategic Management Journal,* Vol. 12, pp. 327–351, 1991.

Horowitz, I. *Decision Making and the Theory of the Firm*, New York: Holt, Rinehart and Winston Inc., 1970.

Jensen, M. C. and Meckling, W. H. "Theory of the Firm: Managerial Behavior, Agency Costs, and Ownership Structure". *Journal of Financial Economics,* pp. 305–360, 1976.

Jensen, Ø. "Competence Development by Small Firms in a Vertically-Constrained Industry Structure". In Sanchez, R., Heene, A. and Thomas, H., eds, *Dynamics of Competence-Based Competition: Theory and Practice in the New Strategic Management*. London: Elsevier, 1996.

Leibenstein, H. *Beyond Economic Man: A New Foundation for Microeconomics*, Cambridge, MA: Harvard University Press, 1980.

Myers, S. C. "Determinants of Corporate Borrowing". *Journal of Financial Economics,* Vol. 5, pp. 147–175, 1977.

Nelson, T. and Gorman, P. "Investigating Performance: A Review and Empirical Test of Indicators Employed in Strategy Research". Working Paper, Department of Business Administration, University of Illinois, Champaign, IL 61820, USA, 1996.

Rispoli, M. "Competitive Analysis and Competence-Based Strategies in the Hotel Industry". In Sanchez, R., Heene, A. and Thomas, H., eds, *Dynamics of Competence-Based Competition: Theory and Practice in the New Strategic Management*. London: Elsevier, 1996.

Roehl, T. "The Role of International R&D in the Competence-Building Strategies of Japanese Pharmaceutical Firms". In Sanchez, R., Heene, A. and Thomas, H., eds, *Dynamics of Competence-Based Competition: Theory and Practice in the New Strategic Management*. London: Elsevier, 1996.

Sanchez, R. "Strategic Flexibility, Real Options, and Product-Based Strategy". Ph.D. Dissertation, MIT, Cambridge, MA 02139, USA, 1991.

Sanchez, R. "Strategic Flexibility, Firm Organization, and Managerial Work in Dynamic Markets: A Strategic Options Perspective". *Advances in Strategic Management*. Greenwich, CT: JAI Press Inc., Vol. 9, pp.251–291, 1993.

Sanchez, R. "Strategic Flexibility in Product Competition". *Strategic Management Journal,* Vol. 16, pp. 135–159, Summer Special Issue 1995.

Sanchez, R. "Quick-Connect Technologies for Product Creation: Implications for Competence-Based Competition". In Sanchez, R., Heene, A. and Thomas, H., eds, *Dynamics of Competence-Based Competition: Theory and Practice in the New Strategic Management*. London: Elsevier, 1996.

Sanchez, R. and Heene, A. "A Systems View of the Firm in Competence-Based Competition". In Sanchez, R., Heene, A. and Thomas, H., eds, *Dynamics of Competence-Based Competition: Theory and Practice in the New Strategic Management*. London: Elsevier, 1996.

Sanchez, R., Heene, A. and Thomas, H. "Towards the Theory and Practice of Competence-Based Competition". In Sanchez, R., Heene, A. and Thomas, H., eds, *Dynamics of Competence-Based Competition: Theory and Practice in the New Strategic Management*. London: Elsevier, 1996.

Volberda, H. W. "Flexible Configuration Strategies within Philips Semiconductors: A Strategic Process of Entrepreneurial Revitalization". In Sanchez, R., Heene, A. and Thomas, H., eds, *Dynamics of Competence-Based Competition: Theory and Practice in the New Strategic Management*. London: Elsevier, 1996.

Winterscheid, B. and McNabb, S. "From National to Global Product Development Competence in the Telecommunications Industry: Structure and Process in Leveraging Core Capabilities". In Sanchez, R., Heene, A. and Thomas, H., eds, *Dynamics of Competence-Based Competition: Theory and Practice in the New Strategic Management*. London: Elsevier, 1996.

4

INDUSTRY DYNAMICS IN COMPETENCE-BASED COMPETITION

Phil Gorman, Howard Thomas, and Ron Sanchez

INTRODUCTION

In this chapter, we analyze industry dynamics in terms of competence building and competence leveraging activities of firms. We discuss the inter-relationships between competence building and leveraging activities, firm strategies, and groupings of firms within and across traditional industry boundaries. We trace the evolution of concepts of strategic groups and suggest their relation to the concepts of competence groups and competence alliances introduced in this volume (Sanchez, Heene, and Thomas 1996).

We discuss ways in which industry dynamics can be better understood by analyzing interactions within and between groups of firms in terms of their competence building and leveraging actions. While prior concepts of groups have typically been based on product market interactions, the competence perspective brings into sharper focus an essential "supply side" of competitive interactions—i.e., firms' transactions in markets for resources that are integral to firms' competence building and leveraging strategies. In addition, recognizing the interdependencies and complementarities of competences that may be held by different firms provides a basis for identifying groupings within industries that may include competence building and leveraging alliances of firms, not just individual firms. The competence perspective thus provides a basis for reformulating prior concepts of groups based on certain aspects of firms' current activities (e.g., firms' currently deployed asset structures or the product markets in which firms currently compete) to incorporate a more dynamic, systemic view of firms within industries.

USING COMPETENCE BUILDING AND LEVERAGING TO IDENTIFY GROUPS

A competence is the ability to sustain the *coordinated deployment of assets* in ways that enable a firm to achieve its goals (Sanchez, Heene and Thomas 1996, in this volume). As firms build and leverage competences in pursuit of their goals, *competence groups* emerge, which we define as groupings of firms that engage in similar competence building or leveraging activities at a given point in time.

Competence building is the source of strategic change at the firm level and of industry evolution at the aggregate level. To the extent that some firms are currently engaged in similar competence leveraging activities, but their competence building activities are directed towards different competence building goals, those firms constitute a *diverging competence group*. Similarly, if some firms are currently engaged in different competence leveraging activities, but share similar competence building objectives, they constitute a *converging competence group*. Firms with similar competence leveraging and similar competence building activities constitute a *dynamically stable competence group* over some time horizon. Figure 4.1 summarizes these categories of competence groups.

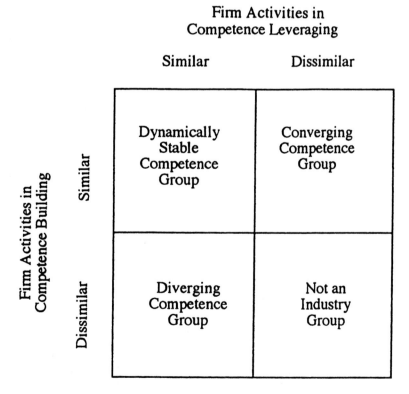

Fig. 4.1. Types of competence groups.

Firms often have much to gain through cooperating, as well as by competing. Competence alliances among firms may therefore arise in response to opportunities to realize mutual gains through cooperation in competence building or leveraging. Thus, both *competence building alliances* and *competence leveraging alliances* may become important in shaping industry dynamics.

A fundamental consideration in competence building is the range of strategic options (*i.e.*, strategic flexibility) a firm can derive from various competences it might create (Sanchez 1993, 1995; Sanchez and Thomas 1996, in this volume). Because alternative opportunities for building competences may lead to very different strategic options, the specific sets of strategic options created by firms' individual competence building choices will determine the forms of competence leveraging each may undertake and thus the ways in which each firm will interact with other firms, both competitively and cooperatively. Competences may also differ in the extent to which they can be upgraded to retain their value in an evolving competitive environment in which competitors actively build new competences. Differences in the potentials of specific competences to be leveraged and to be upgraded over time are thus important determinants of firm heterogeneity and performance over time.

Firm heterogeneity results from diversity in the strategic goals that motivate firm competence building and leveraging. Sanchez and Thomas (1996, this volume) propose a taxonomy of strategic behaviors based on categories of goals for competence building and leveraging. The range of competence building behaviors of firms included in the taxonomy suggest that concepts of strategic groups based only on competence leveraging activities overlook underlying competence building activities that could fundamentally distinguish one firm from another in a dynamic perspective.

PREVIOUS STRATEGIC GROUPS CONCEPTS

Efforts to identify groups of firms pursuing similar strategies rest on some set of assumptions that suggest there is a limited number of ways of competing in a industry. The firms populating these subsets of strategic possibilities are then described as *strategic groups*. While firms may have some mobility to move between groups in the long run, a firm is usually constrained in the near term to a strategy or set of related strategies associated with the region of competitive space it currently occupies. By identifying and studying group formation and firm migration patterns over time, analysts may gain insights into competitive interactions that shape the evolution of an industry. We next summarize prior strategic groups concepts to put into perspective the further insights to be gained from applying competence concepts to the analysis of industry dynamics.

Early industrial organization theory often implicitly assumed homogeneity of capabilities across firms in an industry by explicitly assuming that industry structure alone determines conduct and performance. The concept of strategic groups within an industry was developed by researchers in the early 1970s to investigate apparent differences in firm conduct and performance within the same industry. By looking at industries at a more micro level than that used by traditional industrial organization research, Hunt (1972) showed that the performance of firms may be different from that which would be predicted solely on the basis of the structural characteristics of the industry in which they operate. After initial studies using cross-sectional analyses to group firms in an industry (e.g., Hunt 1972; Newman 1973; Porter 1973; Hatten 1974; Schendel and Patton 1978), later studies used longitudinal analyses that began to shed some light on the dynamics of groups of firms within industries (e.g., Cool and Schendel 1988; Mascarenhas 1989; Fiegenbaum and Thomas 1990, 1994).

Caves and Porter's (1977) concept of mobility barriers provided a construct for studying firms' strategic movements within an industry. The cornerstone of the mobility barriers concept is firms' collective interest in erecting barriers to deter other firms from entering their competitive space. Creating mobility barriers therefore becomes a means for a group of firms to invest in creating a form of limited "public good" by providing group members with some measure of protection from would-be rivals. Incentives for group members to maintain mobility barriers can weaken considerably, however, if rivalry increases between firms. Understanding the nature of incentives for collaboration *versus* rivalry thus becomes critical in studying groups in a dynamic context.

Recent research has applied the mobility barriers concept to study the entry of firms into a new geographic market. Bogner and Thomas' (1994, 1995) studies of foreign firms' entries into the U.S. pharmaceutical market found support for Caves and Porter's proposition that firms lacking developed abilities to compete in an industry or market would try to enter at the point of least competitive resistance. Subsequently, as a new entrant begins to acquire more industry-related experience and capabilities, it is likely to migrate between groups, hurdling mobility barriers one by one until eventually reaching its desired position in the industry. What group a firm may ultimately desire to enter is suggested by Bogner and Thomas' (1994, 1995) hypothesis that the desired destination of a new entrant into a geographic market will be the strategic group in which the firm can most closely replicate the patterns of resource uses it follows in its home country.

Concepts of groups defined by resource bases of firms have been used in longitudinal studies of firm movements across groups and of new entries into an industry. The challenge in this approach to modeling group dynamics is to identify the specific resources that distinguish strategies and thus may serve as predictors of performance. Some theory exists to inform this process (Wernerfelt 1984; Rumelt 1984, Dierickx and Cool 1989; Prahalad and Hamel 1990; Barney 1991; Peteraf 1993). Recent studies using firm resource bases to identify groups of firms and predict migrations of firms between groups (Bogner and Thomas 1994, 1995) suggest a new basis for extending early concepts (Caves and Porter 1977) about mobility barriers.

JOINING OF ECONOMIC AND COGNITIVE PERSPECTIVES

Recent characterizations of strategic groups have sought to join economic and cognitive perspectives on firm behaviors. The economic perspective of the resource-base view of the firm motivates an effort to identify what kinds of strategically significant resources might serve as bases for grouping firms in an industries. Resource criteria are used to define potentially important dimensions of firm heterogeneity and to suggest the nature of mobility barriers that restrict entry to strategic groups.

Cognitive approaches to the study of groups (*e.g.*, Porac, Thomas and Baden-Fuller 1989; Porac and Thomas 1990; Reger and Huff 1993; Tallman and Atchison 1996, in this volume) have sought to develop constructs for identifying groups based on the perceptions and cognitive frameworks of managers. Constructing cognitive maps based on managers' perceptions enables identification of criteria that managers use to define perceived modes of competition and cooperation among firms. Researchers' then use these perceptions to define variables for identifying groups of firms. Comparing the cognitive maps of managers across firms may allow construction of an aggregate cognitive map of an industry at a given point in time. Cognitive maps may then be constructed and compared over time to discover patterns in the evolution of managerial perceptions about interactions between firms. Longitudinal cognitive mappings may identify a number of dimensions on which managers' views begin to diverge or converge, leading to further insights into the dynamics of competition and cooperation.

This most recent development in the strategic groups literature suggests that concepts of groups may serve as essential cognitive reference points (Porac, Thomas and Baden-Fuller 1989; Fiegenbaum and Thomas 1994) for managers trying to make sense of complex and dynamic environments. The cognitive frameworks that managers construct by grouping firms in various ways may then lead to specific modes of competition and cooperation between firms and may be influential in managers' choices of entry modes to a new industry or market (Bogner and Thomas 1994, 1995; Porac, Thomas and Baden-Fuller 1989).

Groups may also serve an important cognitive function by providing managers with a frame of reference for comparing strategies and performance. Cognitive groupings may provide referent firms for benchmarking to indicate to managers how well a firm is performing (Fiegenbaum and Thomas 1994). Managers' appraisals of firm performance acquired through benchmarking against perceived group members may therefore help to identify factors that managers consider important in defining group membership. Defining a referent group of firms within an industry may allow managers to economize in environmental scanning and information-gathering activities (Arrow 1974) by focusing primarily on other firms perceived to be in the firm's own group.

The study by Porac, Thomas and Baden-Fuller (1989) of the Scottish knitwear industry suggests that managers believe that distinct groups exist within their industry and that those beliefs shape managers' strategic decisions—and hence competition in an industry—in important ways. While firms within a strategic group tend to focus on competing directly with one another, and only indirectly against firms in other groups, managers' knowledge of and identification with firms in their own perceived group may suggest opportunities for cooperation that might not arise otherwise. Cognitive studies may therefore uncover important factors promoting cooperation and moderating competition that would be unlikely to be discovered through the use of secondary (archival) data sources. In the Porac, Thomas and Baden-Fuller study, for example, cultural and social factors perceived by managers appeared to be important in managers' choices of the dimensions on which they would compete and of the dimensions on which competition was not "acceptable".

Some researchers (e.g., Barney and Hoskisson 1990; Johnson 1994) have questioned the existence of groups. They point out, for example, that studies that rely strictly on cluster analysis to define groups may generate groups as an artifact of the cluster analysis method. Cognitive studies suggest, however, that managers define their competitive environments in terms of groups of firms and that the decisions managers make are influenced by perceived membership in such groups. Cognitive mapping thus provides a theoretical basis for identifying strategic groups that may serve as a corrective to and check on statistical methods for identifying competitive groupings of firms.

INDUSTRY ANALYSIS USING COMPETENCE THEORY

The resource-base view of firms provides some insights into strategically significant sources of heterogeneity among firms, but provides relatively little theory to explain the dynamics that lead to changes in the distinguishing resources that firms possess. Fiegenbaum and Thomas (1990: 213) address this issue:

> "...strategic groups research is at a cross-roads. To continue with interest-
> ing studies without theoretical insight will no longer be productive. What
> is needed is well-designed, theoretically informed and precise research,
> preferably research that is placed within a comprehensive framework that
> covers initially the stable aspects of group behavior, then moves
> progressively to theory development and testing of dynamic behavior."

Cool and Schendel (1988: 212) also suggested that "the dimensions which define strategic group membership are those strategic *actions* intended to alter competitive advantage" [emphasis added]. Other researchers have offered similar views (Caves 1984; Cool 1985; McGee and Thomas 1986). Patterns in firms' current competitive behaviors are likely to result from responses to near-term pressures, but may not be indicative of firms' long-term strategic objectives. Thus. current competitive interactions may not be adequate indicators of underlying strategies needed to identify stable groupings of firms in a more dynamic context (Cool 1985). Thus, research into strategic groups would benefit from concepts for identifying groups that include firm processes for creating and redeploying resources, rather than just using descriptions of firms' current resource endowments and deployments (Sanchez and Thomas 1996, in this volume).

Competence theory suggest possibilities for joining economic and cognitive perspectives through the concept of *competence groups*. By recognizing that firm strategies consist of both competence building and competence leveraging, which in turn are influenced by both current resource endowments and managerial cognitions, researchers may better able to discover dynamic patterns of competitive interactions that provide a more systemic and holistic view of competitive interactions at any point in time. We suggest, for example, that firms in an industry may be fundamentally distinguished by the relative emphasis their managers place on specific forms of competence building, as well as by current forms of competence leveraging (e.g., presence in product markets).

Competence-based concepts of groups also suggest the need to recognize differences in the ways managers *coordinate* currently available resources, including firm-addressable resources, and *cooperate* with other firms to leverage existing competences and to build new competences that enable a firm to change its resource base, coordination capabilities, and competence leveraging activities. Thus, the competitive space for strategic groups should include competition and cooperation in obtaining inputs of new assets and capabilities, as well as in securing markets for outputs of firms. From the competence perspective, therefore, strategic groups and their associated mobility barriers need to be reconceptualized to include the dynamic, systemic, and cognitive dimensions of both competence building and leveraging. Although defining and measuring competence leveraging and (especially) competence building activities may pose new challenges for researchers, these activities appear to be essential constituents and indicators of firm goals, strategies, and performance in dynamic environments (Sanchez and Thomas 1996, in this volume).

Competence Groups in Stable Environments

In the special case of relatively stable technological and market environments, in which current competence leveraging activities may be the primary focus of firm goals and strategies, traditional strategic group concepts based on current firm resource endowments and current firm participations in product markets may be adequate to identify dynamically stable competence groups. Even in this special case, however, it may still be important to understand managerial cognitions which may underlie the stability of strategic groups. For example, Porac, Thomas and Baden-Fuller (1989) noted that the competences of one group of knitwear manufacturers appear to be imitable by knitwear firms in other strategic groups, but that imitation rarely occurs. Italian manufacturers have long concentrated on styling trends, for example, while Scottish manufacturers have focused on maintaining superior quality of the material used in their traditionally styled garments, even though both groups possess the basic competence to make the kind of knitwear the other group produces. While neither of these groups would be able to fully replicate the other's competences immediately, these groups nevertheless appear stable and well-defined by their respective product offerings in the long term.

Members of strategic groups in stable competitive environments appear unlikely to try to migrate or diversify to another group as long as no major shocks disturb the competitive equilibrium in the industry. The cognitive maps of managers may act, in effect, as mobility barriers that prevent the creation of endogenous shocks—like a major repositioning by a large Scottish knitwear firm to emphasizing styling—that would threaten existing perceptions and competences of groups. When managers share perceptions of an industry as a system in a state of reasonably satisfactory equilibrium, managerial cognitions may focus on established patterns of competence leveraging activities, leading to high levels of stability in competence groups.

External Stimuli for Changes in Groups

In the knitwear industry, stable competence groups with distinctive current competences and patterns of competence leveraging appear to be well defined by cognitive mapping. Neither endogenous shocks (*e.g.*, firm repositionings) nor exogenous shocks (*e.g.*, changes in regulation or technology) seem likely in that industry. Many other industries, however, do not share this level of stability. In many industries, significant technological, market, regulatory, and other changes are occurring, often at a high rate of change. Major environmental changes may greatly reduce the efficacy of established competences and modes of competence leveraging, undermine managers' satisfaction with current conditions, challenge their current cognitive frameworks, and greatly reduce the likelihood that cognitive frameworks will be shared across managers. In dynamic environments, therefore, managers' cognitive frameworks may shift to an emphasis on building new competences that destabilize group structures.

Bogner and Thomas (1994, 1995) studied the effects of regulatory and technological shocks on the pharmaceutical industry. The events studied led to significant changes in the performance of many firms and precipitated realignments of strategic groups within the industry. In both effects, changes in managerial perceptions and interpretations of their environments appear to have played a key role in shaping the ensuing repositionings of firms and realignments of perceived groups. Roehl (1996, in this volume) observes similar effects in realignments of firms in the Japanese pharmaceutical industry.

Regulatory and market changes may also change the competence-basis of competence groups. This effect can also be observed in the pharmaceutical industry. For example, Merck has excelled at rapidly moving its new products through regulatory review processes, while other drug firms often spend years in clearing these hurdles. This key capability of Merck, however, cannot be deployed alone; it must be linked to and coordinated with other product creation, distribution, and marketing capabilities to create a competence that can take advantage of opportunities for introducing new products (Sanchez 1995). Merck's recent acquisition of Medco (and similarly, Eli Lilly's acquisition of PCS) suggests that new distribution capabilities have become critical to achieving and maintaining competence in an industry that is being transformed by rapid changes in the purchasing practices of large customers (HMOs and hospitals).

Thus, exogenous shocks that change the capabilities needed to compete effectively in an industry may lead some firms to migrate to strategic groups where their existing competences may be adequate to survive, while other firms may be motivated to build new competences that redefine the competitive space of an industry and lead to realignments of firms in new competence groups.

Internal Stimuli for Changes in Groups

Firms in an environment with low levels of causal ambiguity and little perceived uncertainty about the future value of specific competences may tend to form stable competence groups based on similarities in competence leveraging specializations and in managerial perceptions about the direction of their group and other industry groups as an evolving system (Sanchez and Heene 1996, in this volume). Technological or market turbulence induced by competence building activities may lead managers to perceive the future value of a firm's current competences as uncertain. When the turbulence of dynamic environments leads managers to perceive the future value of their firm's current competences as highly uncertain, managers in different firms (or even within a single firm) may be less likely to have stable sets of shared perceptions that lead to stable patterns of competence leveraging activities.

Nevertheless, environmental uncertainty may have various impacts on competence building. The difficulty of benchmarking under conditions of significant causal ambiguity and environmental turbulence may prevent emergence of shared managerial perceptions or "industry recipes"

(Spender 1989) for competence building. On the other hand, managers' need for some kind of cognitive framework in a dynamic environment may encourage them to focus on discovering other firms' competence building strategies and activities, leading to benchmarking and cognitive anchoring in competence building activities rather than competence leveraging activities. Examples from three industries illustrate the range of possible impacts of environmental turbulence on competence groups.

Specialty footwear is a highly competitive industry that nevertheless has a dynamically stable group structure based on competence specialization. Industry leader Nike, for example, has selectively internalized only certain capabilities in innovative product design, design-for-manufacture, and marketing, while subcontracting through a network of firm-addressable resources for manufacturing and other capabilities needed to maintain its competence in the specialty shoe market. Nike's recipe for competence building and leveraging is a model for competing that is emulated by major competitors in that industry. Other firms emphasize R&D, production, or marketing to varying degrees, but they tend to make similar choices about what new capabilities to develop internally (e.g., design and marketing) and which capabilities to access through markets (e.g., manufacturing and distribution services). The superior flexibility of Nike's competence configuration to sustain high rates of new product introductions (Sanchez 1995) creates a dynamic competitive environment that limits the feasible choices of competence configurations other firms can make if they intend to compete in the same competitive space as Nike. A narrowed set of feasible competence choices encourages convergence of managerial perceptions, leading in the specialty shoe market to a salient competence grouping that includes most major competitors. The common focus of these firms on building and leveraging competences in design and marketing drives a high rate of competence building along a relatively stable trajectory of evolving competences, creating a dynamically stable competence group.

Personal computers are an example of a product market in which convergences in managerial perceptions of critical relationships between competences appear to be precipitating converging competence groups that are significantly redefining the trajectory of industry evolution. The recent competence building and leveraging alliance between former rivals Apple, IBM, and Motorola appears to be motivated by their managers' shared perception of key interdependencies between the competences of the three firms (Apple in creating user-friendly operating systems, IBM and Motorola in various aspects of semiconductor design and production). Managers of these three firms see the linking of their respective competences as critical to building and leveraging their individual competences more effectively in the emerging market for integrated computing and communications products. Managers of Compaq, Intel, and Microsoft appear to have a similar perception, and they have formed their own alliance. Managers' perceptions of the need to more closely coordinate their firms' complementary competences in dynamic product markets may increasingly lead to the formation of competence groups whose members are competence building and leveraging alliances rather than individual firms.

Further, while software firms, semiconductor designers and manufacturers, and computer firms would be unlikely to be placed in the same strategic group by prior concepts for defining groups, competence-based concepts of groups readily suggest such possibilities. Systemic interdependencies among specialized capabilities may well cross traditional "industry" boundaries as firms engage in collaborative competence building and leveraging. Using competence theory to analyze competitive and cooperative interactions of firms should help researchers to construct better models of industry dynamics that reflect more closely the open-systems behavior of firms, groups of firms, and industries (Sanchez and Heene 1996, in this volume).

Technological shocks that produce environmental turbulence may originate outside an industry or group, but often result from the competence building activities of firms within an industry or group. If the competence building effort of a firm is successful in developing a significant new technology, developing new competences based on the new technology may give the firm important advantages arising not just from being the first firm to have the new technology, but also from gaining superior *understanding* of the potential uses of the technology earlier than competitors. Early managerial recognition of the uses to which a new technology can be applied may precipitate related competence building efforts in market capabilities and other areas. Managers late in recognizing the benefits of building comparable new competences may face significant time compression diseconomies (Dierickx and Cool, 1989) that may force them to reposition their firms to a competence group in which the new competence is not a primary basis for competition. The development of rational drug design techniques and of new uses of biological processes in the pharmaceutical industry, for example, has led to significant realignments of competence groups within the pharmaceutical industry.

CONCLUSIONS

These conceptualizations of competence as a basis for grouping firms suggest three critical issues for practitioners and researchers alike. One is the identification of competences on which to base group classifications, which may be difficult because those assets and capabilities which are most valuable to a firm may be obscured via isolating mechanisms (Rumelt 1984). Further, internal causal ambiguities may exist, and key assets and capabilities essential to achieving or maintaining competence may not be apparent even to the firm's own managers or other employees. A second issue is the fundamental importance of competence building relative to competence leveraging. Competence leveraging results from success in building competences, but the observation of firms' competence leveraging activities may reveal little, if anything, about the critical processes by which an individual firm built up its competences. Third, managers' perceptions of possible actions and reactions, both competitive and cooperative, of present and *potential* future competitors are likely to influence managers' decisions about the direction of a firm's competence building and leveraging activities (Hamel and Prahalad 1994), but these perceptions may only be discoverable through cognitive studies.

Grouping firms by competence building activities as well as by their more readily observable competence leveraging activities may require defining new parameters for measuring competence building activities. The discussion in this chapter suggests some ways in which firm similarities and differences in competence building and leveraging might be identified and provides a preliminary basis for recognizing competence-based groupings of firms within industries. We close by suggesting that competence groupings of firms are empirically feasible and conceptually essential constructs for improving our understanding of both the short-term and long-term dynamics of industries.

REFERENCES

Arrow, K. J. *The Limits of Organization*. New York: W. W. Norton and Company, 1974.

Barney, J. B. "Firm Resources and Sustained Competitive Advantage". *Journal of Management*, Vol. 17, pp. 99–120, 1991.

Barney and Hoskisson. "Strategic Groups: Untested Assertions and Research Proposals". *Managerial and Decision Economics,* Vol. 11, pp. 187–198, 1990.

Bogner, W. C. and Thomas, H. "Core Competence and Competitive Advantage: A Model and Illustrative Evidence from the Pharmaceutical Industry". In Hamel, G. and Heene, A., eds, *Competence-Based Competition*. Chichester: John Wiley, pp. 111–144, 1994.

Bogner, W. C. and Thomas, H. "A Longitudinal Study of the Competitive Positions and Entry Paths of European Firms in the U.S. Pharmaceutical Industry". *Strategic Management Journal*, forthcoming, 1995.

Caves, R. "Economic Analysis and the Quest for Competitive Advantage". *American Economic Review*, pp. 127–132, May 1984.

Caves, R. and Porter, M. "From Entry Barriers to Mobility Barriers". *Quarterly Journal of Economics*, pp. 241–261, May 1977.

Cool, K. "Strategic Group Formation and Strategic Group Shifts: A Longitudinal Analysis of the U.S. Pharmaceutical Industry, 1963-1982". Ph.D. Dissertation, Purdue University, 1985.

Cool, K. and Schendel, D. "Performance Differences Among Strategic Group Members". *Strategic Management Journal*, Vol. 9, pp. 207–223, 1988.

Dierickx, I. and Cool, K. "Asset Stock Accumulation and Sustainability of Competitive Advantage". *Management Science*, Vol. 35(12), pp. 1504–1511, 1989.

Fiegenbaum, A. and Thomas, H. "Strategic Groups and Performance: The U.S. Insurance Industry, 1970-84". *Strategic Management Journal*, Vol. 11, pp. 197–215, 1990.

Fiegenbaum, A. and Thomas, H. "Strategic Groups as Reference Groups: Theory, Modeling and Empirical Examination of Industry and Competitive Strategy". Revised July 1994.

Hamel, G. and Prahalad, C. K. *Competing for the Future*, Boston: Harvard Business School Press, 1994.

Hatten, K. "Strategic Models in the U.S. Brewing Industry". Ph.D. Dissertation, Purdue University, 1974.

Hunt, M. "Competition in the Major Home Appliance Industry," Ph.D. Dissertation, Harvard University, 1972.

Johnson, D. R. "Testing for Intra-Industry Structure: Do Strategic Groups Exist?". Working Paper, Los Angeles: University of California, 1994.

Mascarenhas, R. "Strategic Group Dynamics". *Academy of Management Journal*, Vol. 32, pp. 333–352, 1989.

McGee, J. and Thomas, H. "Strategic Groups: Theory, Research, and Taxonomy". *Strategic Management Journal*, Vol. 7, pp. 141–160, 1986.

Newman, H. "Strategic Groups and the Structure-Performance Relationship: A Study with Respect to the Chemical Process Industries". Ph.D. Dissertation, Harvard University, 1973.

Peteraf, M. A. "The Cornerstones of Competitive Advantage: A Resource-Based View". *Strategic Management Journal*, Vol. 14, pp. 179–191, 1993.

Porac, J. F. and Thomas, H. "Taxonomic Mental Models in Competitor Definition". *Academy of Management Review*, Vol. 15(2), pp. 224–240, 1990.

Porac, J. F., Thomas, H. and Baden-Fuller, C. "Competitive Groups as Cognitive Communities: The Case of Scottish Knitwear Manufacturers". *Journal of Management Studies*, Vol. 26, pp. 397–416, 1989.

Porter, M. "Retailer Power, Manufacturing Strategy, and Performance in Consumer Goods Industries". Ph.D. Dissertation, Harvard University, 1973.

Prahalad, C. K. and Hamel, G. "The Core Competence of the Corporation". *Harvard Business Review*, pp. 79–91, May–June 1990.

Reger, R. K. and Huff, A. S. "Strategic Groups: A Cognitive Perspective". *Strategic Management Journal*, Vol. 14, pp. 103–123, February 1993.

Roehl, T. "The Role of R&D in the Competence Building Strategies of Japanese Pharmaceutical Firms". In Sanchez, R. Heene, A. and Thomas, H., eds, *Dynamics of Competence-Based Competition: Theory and Practice in the New Strategic Management*. London: Elsevier, 1996.

Rumelt, R. "Toward a Strategic Theory of the Firm". In Lamb, R., ed., *Competitive Strategic Management*. Englewood Cliffs, MD: Prentice-Hall, pp. 556–570, 1984.

Sanchez, R. "Strategic Flexibility, Firm Organization, and Managerial Work in Dynamic Markets: A Strategic-Options Perspective". *Advances in Strategic Management*, Vol. 9, pp. 251–291, 1993.

Sanchez, R. "Strategic Flexibility in Product Competition". *Strategic Management Journal*, Vol. 16, pp. 135–159, Summer Special Issue 1995.

Sanchez, R. and Thomas, H. "Strategic Goals". In Sanchez, R., Heene, A. and Thomas, H., eds, *Dynamics of Competence-Based Competition: Theory and Practice in the New Strategic Management*. London: Elsevier, 1996.

Sanchez, R. and Heene, A. "A Systems View of the Firm in Competence-Based Competition". In Sanchez, R., Heene, A. and Thomas, H., eds, *Dynamics of Competence-Based Competition: Theory and Practice in the New Strategic Management*. London: Elsevier, 1996.

Sanchez, R., Heene, A. and Thomas, H. "Towards the Theory and Practice of Competence-Based Competition". In Sanchez, R., Heene, A. and Thomas, H., eds, *Dynamics of Competence-Based Competition: Theory and Practice in the New Strategic Management*. London: Elsevier, 1996.

Schendel, D. and Patton, G. R. "A Simultaneous Equation Model of Corporate Strategy". *Management Science*, Vol. 24, pp. 1611–1621, 1978.

Spender, J. C. *Industry Recipes: An Inquiry into the Nature and Sources of Managerial Judgement*. New York: Basil Blackwell, 1989.

Tallman, S. and Atchison, D. L. "Competence-Based Competition and the Evolution of Strategic Configurations". In Sanchez, R., Heene, A. and Thomas, H., eds, *Dynamics of Competence-Based Competition: Theory and Practice in the New Strategic Management*. London: Elsevier, 1996.

Wernerfelt, B. "A Resource-Based View of the Firm". *Strategic Management Journal*, Vol. 5, pp. 171–180, 1984.

PART TWO

THE MARKET TEST FOR COMPETENCE

If competence is the ability to sustain the coordinated deployment of assets and capabilities in ways that enable a firm to achieve its goals, then competences must be defined and assessed by the kinds of market responses they are capable of eliciting. The two chapters in this section explore this market test for a firm's competences.

In Chapter 5, Bogner and Thomas link the requirements for competence in a given product market to categories of product attributes. Products are characterized as bundles of attributes, including threshold attributes, central attributes, and plus-only attributes. The competence of a firm can then be understood in terms of the bundle of assets and capabilities which enable a firm to create threshold attributes, central attributes, and plus-only attributes in its products. Competence-based competition within a product market consists of building and leveraging competences to offer products with distinctive combinations of the three kinds of attributes. Bogner and Thomas illustrate their analysis of the market test for competence with examples drawn from the pharmaceutical industry.

In Chapter 6, Rispoli develops a related approach to identifying and classifying competence based on the attributes that product offerings must have to be distinguished for different market segments. Analyzing competition among hotels, he identifies "general" or "first level" competences necessary simply to compete in the hotel industry, "second level" competences required to offer acceptable products to specific market segments, and "third level," firm-specific competences that create products with a distinctive appeal within a market segment. Rispoli describes competence-based competition within the European hotel industry in which groups of firms with similar scope of competences compete by leveraging some competences across several market segments, while building other competences that distinguish their product offerings within each segment.

5

FROM SKILLS TO COMPETENCES: THE "PLAY-OUT" OF RESOURCE BUNDLES ACROSS FIRMS

William C. Bogner and Howard Thomas

INTRODUCTION

Although it is often presented as something that lies below the surface of competition, competence is, in fact, a market driven concept. Similarly, the existence of competitive advantage in a market is primarily determined through a process of competition involving many firms' internal skills. The link, therefore, between market-place competitive advantage and internal competence is strong. In this paper we will explore the linkage between patterns of market demand and the internal skills of firms. We will draw upon several established theories that inform strategic management and present a model that captures the complexity of both the supply- and demand-side characteristics that interact when competitive advantage is created. Thus, this paper is an effort at integration of several conversations surrounding the central focus of strategic management—sustained above-average performance.

It has become axiomatic for strategy researchers to state that core competence *leads to* competitive advantage (Prahalad and Hamel, 1990) and to sustained, above-average economic performance (Bogner and Thomas, 1994). Those statements imply that there exists an external competitive process in addition to the internal skill development process that ties competence to desired performance outcomes. Obviously this competitive process takes place with other firms, where each competing firm possesses its own internally developed skills. In this paper we posit how different firms combine their skills. How to align those combined bundles of skills with demand is as important for the firm seeking above-average returns as it is to understand how the skills are developed within each firm. Although recent research has modeled how the internal skills are developed and how they are used to repeatedly provide firms with new, unique assets with which to compete in the longer term (Bogner and Thomas, 1994; Prahalad and Hamel, 1990), demand-side models have not been so detailed and integration has not occurred.

CONCEPTS FOR A MODEL

In presenting a comprehensive view of competitive advantage several different streams of research are accessed. In recent years there has been an attempt to bring together two or more perspectives to explain part of this relationship. For example, in order to gain insights into the supply side of competitive advantage Bogner, Thomas and McGee (1995) combined the resource based view and organizational learning, and Peteraf (1993) combined the resource-based view with Ricardian economics. In this section we will look at the various components that have to be brought to the discussion so that a comprehensive view of the demand side of competitive advantage can emerge.

Sustainable Economic Profits

Economic profits are returns to invested capital that exceed the returns that comparably risky investments receive in the market. While such returns are possible in the short term under a variety of circumstances, market forces hold the potential to quickly eliminate such profit levels in most cases.[1] Indeed, it is those cases when economic profits, or rents, are not quickly eliminated that have attracted the attention of economists in the field of Industrial Organization (IO) economics for some time. More recently such sustained profitability has interested strategic management researchers as they explore a wide range of issues such as competence (Bogner and Thomas, 1994), learning (Spender, 1989), cognition (Barr, Stimpert and Huff, 1992), and competition (Hammel and Prahalad, 1990). While managers seek to develop strategies that sustain economic profits and maximize shareholder returns, among other goals (Sanchez and Thomas 1996, this volume), strategic management research has often sought to identify those managerial actions behind firms that produce sustained economic profits.

Various concepts have been provided to explain how managers can build sustainable economic profits. Porter (1980) initially focused on industry traits. Later, Porter (1985) added his value chain arrow to the analysis. This shifted the manager's attention for sustainable competitive advantage to a mix of industry (5-forces) and firm-specific (value chain) factors. Porter's

(1985) second book, and its more firm-specific focus coincided with a renewed emphasis on the internal "resources-base" of the firm as the basis of sustained economic profits (see Mahoney and Pandian, 1992 for an overview). Wernerfelt (1984) raised ideas that drew on Penrose (1959) and others. (See Wernerfelt, 1995 for comments on how slowly his work was picked up upon in the strategy field). A stream of work from Barney (1986a, 1986b, 1991), Conner, (1991), Peteraf (1993), Amit and Schoemaker (1993), Hall (1992, 1993) and others, sought to provide economic based explanations for how these internal attributes could sustain economic profits. While these views use different language and different points of departure for their analysis, all attempt to show that (a) some firms possesses unique characteristics of some kind, (b) those characteristics are valuable in earning economic profits in otherwise open competition, and (c) for some reason those characteristics are not available to others for a meaningful period of time, thereby giving rise to the perception that the economic profits are sustainable.

Core Competence and Bundles of Attributes

Core competencies have become the primary focus of analyses seeking to identify those characteristics that satisfy the three above requirements (Prahalad and Hammel, 1990; Bogner and Thomas, 1994; Bogner, Thomas and McGee, 1995). Core competencies are things that organizations do distinctively well. When exercising their competencies firms can create unique value in a product or service that is the outcome of that action. Attributes are traits of firms that are perceived by customers (Murray, 1988). The mix of attributes customers perceive determines the tradeoff between price and non-price considerations in the market. These unique attributes that competencies produce are "bundled" with other product attributes prior to selling to intermediaries or end consumers.[2] In these transactions the firm has the potential to capture economic profits for the unique value that they have added if the market is otherwise open and competitive.[3]

The other attributes with which the competence outcome is bundled may be significant additional components of a final product, or simply the marketing and administrative activities that surround the selling of the competence outcome. Importantly, there is no distinctive skill outcome that can be marketed alone, void of *any* other skill provided by the firm. Thus, even a focused producer of a single distinctive component engages in other activities in the conduct of business (e.g., billing, packaging) that are bundled with that component, and, of course, figure in the costs and profits of the firm. It will be argued in this paper that performance of these activities are important considerations in assessing and managing competitive advantage.

The bundling of attributes into a final good or service combines a firm's unique resources and skills with those available in the market to any firm.

Chamberlin's (1933) concept of monopolistic competition emphasizes such a mix of unique and common resources among competing firms. The resulting competition is "partly monopolistic and partly competitive" (Barney, 1986a), reflecting the mix of attributes found in the firms' competitive offerings. It follows that the more significant any firm's unique attributes to the final bundle, the more that firm can act in a monopolist way. It is similarly obvious that no firm will likely be uniquely superior on every attribute for every customer group, with the resulting opportunity for multiple firms to earn persistent economic profit in a market. Firms, therefore, have to decide which combinations of unique attributes and common attributes will give them the best advantage possible given the resources that each has to employ.

Unique attributes underpinned by competence have the potential to change. That is, they are subject to innovation and improvement on several fronts, such as quality and cost. To sustain its uniqueness a firm must remain ahead of competitors that seek to neutralize part of a firm's competitive advantage by copying or surpassing its existing standard. These dynamics are more regular than the occasional revolutionary changes often associated with Schumpeter (1934), but are also often less dramatic than the regular convulsions described by D'Aveni (1994).[4] They represent persistent learning processes that are largely endogenous to the firm (Helleloid and Simonin, 1994) that seek to keep skills ahead of learning competitors (Bogner, Thomas and McGee, 1995). The persistent ability to earn economic profits in monopolistic competition often reflects a firm's ability to sustain unique product attributes through learning. This is not always true and it is important to distinguish persistent profitability in monopolistic competition based on sustaining competence from that based on other traits.

Ricardo (1817) identified other ways besides constant improvement ahead of competitors that will enable firms to compete with unique attributes in monopolistic competition. These are the unique advantages that firms could include in their attribute bundles because they are scarce, i.e., they could not likely be copied or imitated, such as a particular business location. Over time however, most such advantages do lose their strength, either through legal rule (e.g., the expiration of a patent), technological innovation (e.g., in electronic communications) or changing consumer preferences (e.g., certain brand names). Note that if such advantages are underpinned by competencies (e.g., in R&D or identifying prime store locations), then new unique assets can replace those that are lost (e.g., new patents) and replicate those that exist (e.g., new prime locations). Without such under-lying skills the firm's ability to bundle a unique attribute for monopolistic competition will likely be lost over time—and surely it can not grow. Thus, on the supply side, sustaining and growing competitive advantage is linked to sustaining skills underlying attributes—attributes that produce unique outcomes that are bundled into a market product.

A MARKET VIEW OF COMPETITIVE ADVANTAGE

Attributes as the Link to the Demand Side

The supply side just described has been well analyzed and dissected. Most of the concepts just discussed are well developed in the referenced articles. In the strategy literature, however, the same detail of the demand side is missing. Such parallel development, and subsequently its integration with the supply side models, is surprising. Strategy has embraced customer-driven views of markets; the power of customers is one of the five forces of Porter (1980); and differentiation and related diversification are clearly predicated on fragmented demand. Yet all of these topics, along with strategic groups, social constriction of industries, and a host of other strategy topics, focus primarily on the supply side implications of their insights. On the one hand the supply side is where the managerial action is felt. Yet the demand side is equally subtle in its nuances. In this part of the paper we present such an enriched view believing that such an understanding is complementary to and enriching of the supply side view just described.

Abell's (1980) question "What customer needs does a firm satisfy?" is typically answered with a view of a product as a "bundle" of desired attributes. Murray (1988) provides one of the few articles in the strategy-oriented literature to discuss strategy from the demand side. Murray's view is simple but allows for a rich analysis of how the demand side is structured. Product attributes perceived by customers can be weighted and standardized to equal one. From there cost and not-cost attributes can be distinguished and, subsequently, the mixes of non-cost attributes that different customer groups perceive as differentiation in the market. Those attributes, therefor identify the needs that a firm's product satisfies. Following on Murray's perspective, Abell's further question, "what technologies will be used in satisfying those needs?" can be reframed by substituting "skills" for "technologies". Thus, demand-side customer needs are linked to the supply-side resource-base through the skills that produce the attributes of the products. By breaking down perceptions of attributes beyond the extent done by Murray, the way in which those attributes, whether underpinned by competence or otherwise, are bundled can be more precisely described. Hence, how monopolistic competition determines competitive advantage in a market is explained.

Markets for Competitive Advantage

In order to see how attribute bundles compete, the arena in which skills are deployed to seek competitive advantage must be defined. Does it include all firms in an industry, or some sub-portion thereof? In this framework, an industry's customers, like its firms, are presumed not to be homogeneous, but neither are they randomly spread across the competitive landscape. Rather, customers can be grouped according to the combinations of product attributes they most desire. Customer groups so defined provide a mirror to the strategic groups of firms (Porter, 1980; McGee and Thomas, 1986), reflecting similar skill and resource bundles. Thus, competitive advantage is pursued among a group of rival firms who have developed skills and resources in similar ways in the past, and now are deploying those skills and resources in pursuit of groups of customers with similar needs.

In this market oriented perspective, whether or not competitive advantage exists for any firm depends in part on that firm's group of targeted customers. A firm may still earn an above average return in an intensely competitive marketplace if enough customers choose the firm's product over those offered by competitors. A firm's strategic task, therefore, is to assemble skills and other resources in such a manner that, when aggregated, they best reflect targeted customers' preferences and thus have the potential to earn above average returns.[5] In such a competitive context it is important to examine how the customers in a market perceive both product attributes in general and each firm's specific skill in providing each attribute.

Attribute Types and Attribute Perceptions

The attributes that customers demand can be classified in terms of customer perceptions. These perceptual differences determine the contribution that a skill can make to the competitive advantage of an individual product. Consequently, based on conceptualizations developed by Huang (1993a, 1993b) and others, we propose three types of attributes that products have and that customers evaluate. Our framework labels the three types of attributes, which are bundled by the firm into a product offering in order to seek competitive advantage, as "Plus-only Attributes," "Central Attributes," and "Threshold Attributes," which we define momentarily. The customer, in turn, evaluates each firm's skill as providing one of three levels of satisfaction for each attribute: "insufficient," "sufficient," or "distinctive". Thus, for each attribute in the product bundle, both the attribute type and the firm-specific level of satisfaction provided for that attribute determine the extent to which a firm's skill level can lead to competitive advantage. How core competence is translated into competitive advantage, therefore, cannot be understood without examining the different ways in which skills are deployed in markets.

For example, Fig. 5.1 presents idealized product offerings from three competing firms. Each product is composed of six attributes, two derived from each of the three attribute types (Threshold, Central, and Plus-only).

These three types of attributes are distinguished by the different opportunities that they provide for the firm to change consumer decisions and influence evaluations by improving the firm's internal skill level. Each of the three attribute types can be mapped in terms of each of the three potential levels of customer satisfaction with attribute quality and distinctiveness, as shown in Fig. 5.2.

An important level of firm skill is that which raises customer perceptions of attributes above the line between "insufficient" and "sufficient" in Fig. 5.2. Indeed, for *every* attribute provided in a product offering, a firm must be judged as exceeding at least a sufficient skill level in order to compete. The second important level of skill is that which achieves "distinctiveness" for a given attribute. When this level is obtained, a skill has the potential to give a firm competitive advantage (although, as will be explained later, it is possible for a firm to gain competitive advantage without any such skill).

Between the insufficient level and the distinction level lies a level of skill that produces product attributes that, while not distinctive, are sufficient. This customer evaluation suggests that the firm's skill level lies between the attribute threshold and the level of the best competitors. While customers recognize gradations in the level of sufficiency that different firms provide, none of the differences among providers of sufficient attributes reaches the level of distinctiveness. Although the minimum threshold is fixed for all firms by customers' expectations of minimum performance levels for each attribute, the top of the "sufficient" range varies with the relative

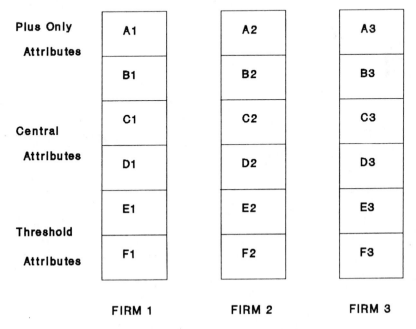

Fig. 5.1. Attribute bundles and types.

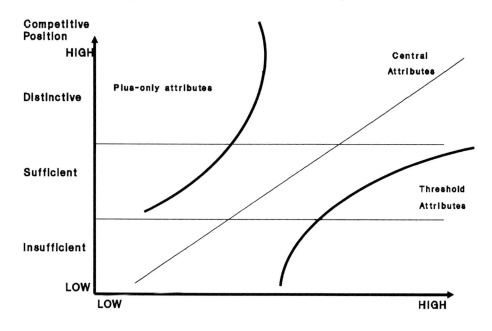

Fig. 5.2. Attribute chart.

skills of each competing firm in the product market at any given time. For attribute leaders, the top of the "sufficient" range is set by the skill levels of "second-best" competitors—the level below which a leader's skill will lose its distinctiveness.

The extent to which consumers are influenced by a firm's skill level depends on how consumers generally perceive a given attribute in general. "Threshold Attributes" are those attributes that a group of targeted customers *require* a firm to provide at least at some minimal level of quality, but that do not have the potential for competitive advantage. Failure of a firm to develop a skill level sufficient to exceed an attribute threshold will be unable to sell its products. However, skill improvement beyond the threshold point provides diminishing marginal contributions to the appeal of a product. Importantly, increased skill levels will not make this attribute a source of "distinctiveness". For example, the ability of an automobile ignition system to "start every time" may well be seen as a threshold attribute in that market. Firms must provide automobiles that start at a high level of reliability. However, that threshold is sufficiently high that further improvements are not likely to be perceived by customers as making one producer's product distinctive in performance.

At the other extreme are "Plus-only Attributes". Here customers do not *require* the attribute at any level, but by acquiring a skill level sufficient to offer satisfaction in this attribute, a firm can achieve some degree of competitive advantage. For example, power seats in an automobile may not be required for some groups of automobile purchasers, but firms that do add this attribute may be able to distinguish their products from others. An absence of the attribute is competitively permissible, but adding the attribute will increase overall product desirability. Only firms with appropriate skills can use this attribute to achieve distinctive products and resulting competitive advantage.

Finally, there are "Central Attributes". These are product attributes for which customers require a threshold level of quality and that can also be a source of competitive advantage if done well. In Fig. 5.2 the line representing Central Attributes crosses all three satisfaction levels. An automobile radio may fall into this category. Few customers will purchase an automobile without one, thereby establishing a threshold skill requirement, but the opportunity remains to turn the radio into a high-performance "entertainment system" to add distinctiveness to an automobile. Thus, central attributes can range from a level of insufficiency (below the threshold) to a potential source of competitive advantage as a firm's skill level allows it to offer a distinctive level of that attribute.

Aggregation of Attributes for Competitive Advantage

Given the different types of attributes and different skill levels of firms in providing each attribute, the building of different types of attributes into products becomes a critical step in moving from competence to competitive advantage. As Fig. 5.1 illustrates, products are combinations of multiple attributes of different types. Competitive advantage springs from the *superior bundling* aggregation of these attributes and, hence, the superior aggregation of the internal skills required to offer a superior bundle. Because firms possess different skills and resources, the aggregation of skills that can be brought to a product will vary from firm to firm. The only mandatory requirement is that all participants in a product market meet the threshold levels of skills for that product's Central and Threshold Attributes. Beyond that, different skill aggregation strategies for gaining competitive advantage are available, as presented in Fig. 5.3.

On one end of Fig. 5.3 is a "narrow focus" strategy. Here firm **A** seeks to gain such a significant competitive advantage in *one attribute* that, in the absence of "insufficiency" of other attributes, the firm offers a product that will be preferred by at least some customers.[6] In this case, the level of contribution by other sufficient attributes is not as relevant as that of the one distinctive attribute and being "the best" in providing that one attribute is the essence of this strategy. For example, the distinction that pharmaceutical houses seek to develop for the US retail market is "drug-of-choice" efficacy. A drug-of-choice is one that has established such

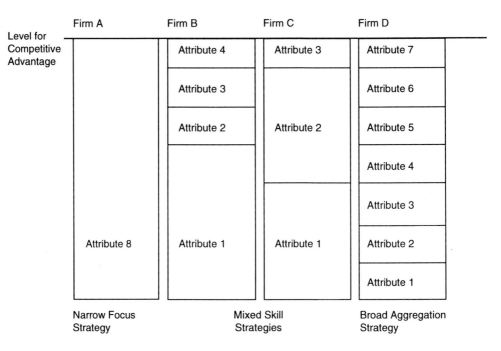

Fig. 5.3. Strategic opportunities for attribute aggregation.

therapeutic distinction that it becomes the preferred choice whenever a particular malady manifests itself. While other attributes, such as price, may be important in most circumstances, the role of physicians in the US as gatekeepers who do not pay for their choices creates the opportunity for this single-attribute focus strategy to succeed. Generally then, this strategy is viable in any market where being "best" on an attribute is so singularly significant to customers or product specifiers that a level of distinctiveness on that attribute alone is sufficient to induce a purchase.

At the other end of Fig. 5.3 is a "broad aggregation" strategy of firm **D**. Here no attribute may be "distinctive" *vis-à-vis* rivals, but, in the aggregate, all of the firm's "sufficient" attributes combine to produce an overall higher need satisfaction for customers relative to any competitors' attribute combinations. Thus, competitive advantage can be obtained without a firm developing distinctive skills in providing even one attribute. For example, in the clinical market for pharmaceuticals in the US there are opportunities for firms without drug-of-choice distinctiveness to compete. In a hospital, along with the efficacy consideration mentioned above, factors such as price, dosing convenience, and nursing requirements are considered. Here the different gradations above the sufficiency threshold (but below distinctiveness) become important. Superiority on any one attribute may not be required if a firm can provide a hospital or clinic with an overall superiority when all attributes are aggregated. Importantly, "broad aggregation" does not require a firm to develop or maintain any internal skill levels that are "distinctive" (other than, perhaps, the managerial skill of combining product attributes effectively, which the strategy suggests can be quite valuable). Acceptable internal levels of skill may be identified through benchmarking competitors (Bogner and Thomas, 1994).

Between the two extremes laid out above exist "mixed skills" strategies that employ combinations of "distinctiveness" on one or more attributes, with various levels of "sufficient" skills on the others. Here, too, different gradations of sufficiency below distinctiveness are important. However, unlike the narrow focus strategy mentioned first, a firm possessing a "distinctive" skill here must rely on contributions above the "sufficiency" threshold from non-distinctive attributes in order to gain competitive advantage. And unlike the broad aggregation strategy mentioned second, the firm here does have the skills necessary to produce a distinctive attribute. In Fig. 5.3 firm **B** combines one distinctive attribute (1) with other sufficient attributes, while firm **C** combines two distinctive attributes (1 and 2) with sufficient attributes. In the pharmaceutical industry, a firm with a distinctive dosing system for drug delivery may not be able to rely on that attribute alone, but that distinctiveness combined with sufficient attributes that are evaluated as "better than some" but not "distinctive" from all others, may nonetheless give the drug a competitive advantage. In this case, if the dosing system was not "distinctive", then the firm's product may not have sufficient overall appeal. If sales could be sustained in the absence of a distinctive dosing system, this becomes the basis for a "broad aggregate" strategy.

An important implication of all of the approaches to competitive advantage discussed thus far is that firms *with* a distinctive level of skill on a particular attribute may not necessarily gain competitive advantage, since competitive advantage is determined by customer evaluations of various offered combinations of all relevant attributes. Combined with the potential for "broad aggregation" strategies, this carries strong implications for internal skill development. Neither the presence of a distinctive skill in any attribute, nor the absence of such a skill level from all attributes, may accurately predict a firm's ability to gain competitive advantage. Skill levels, including distinctive ones, have to be managed in the light of how those skills will "bundle" for the market. Because of the feasibility of pursuing different approaches to skill aggregation, firms with significantly different skills may be strong rivals in spite of their skill differences.

Attributes and Competences in a Pure Commodity Market

A situation that deserves special consideration in our framework is the pure commodity market. This market is of particular interest because among customers for like-grade-and-quality goods, only price matters. Porter's

(1980) low-cost leadership strategy was geared toward such a marketplace. Using our framework there would seem to be no opportunity to "bundle" attributes for competitive advantage in a pure commodity market, yet there would clearly be opportunities for persistent above-average profits through the development of distinctive cost-reduction skills. For example, in retail gasoline sales among a group of street-corner competitors, the firm with the most efficient delivery, distribution, and management systems would tend to be the most profitable if prices are identical for all sellers. Still, the attribute combinations on which the producer must focus are dictated by customer evaluations. Thus, threshold levels (the like-grade-and-quality requirement) still need to be meet on non-price factors. These factors, however, may just be Threshold Attributes; they may all lack the ability to create distinctiveness. If so, then the internal cost-reduction skills become critical for producers.[7] And even here there still remain alternative ways of bundling activities in order to arrive at low-cost advantages. Thus, the mix of potential sources of above average return are all internal cost-reduction skills, as long as product attributes are maintained above the threshold level.

Attribute Bundles in a Dynamic Environment

Changes in competitive patterns and outcomes are driven by both the internal changes in firms' resource bases (e.g., innovations from a firm's R&D efforts) and external changes in the environment (e.g., changes in government regulation). This two pronged impetus for change suggests that the mix of attributes that produce competitive advantage in Fig. 5.3 will change over time in response to supply or demand pressures or both. Customers will demand new attributes in the mix, and the weights and characteristics given to existing attributes will change as well. What was once a Plus-only attribute may become a Central or a Threshold attribute. For example, until recently airbags in automobiles were a Plus-only attribute. The total absence of an airbag did not disqualify a car from purchase. In the future airbags may become a Threshold attribute; no one will be able to sell a car without one, but with them one automobile can not be made distinctive from another.

Dynamic changes in attributes can represent both "competence enhancing" and "competence destroying" changes (Tushman and Anderson, 1987) in how firms compete. The future viability of a given combination of internal skills will be determined by changes in the customer evaluations of the attributes to which skills are directed. On the one hand, competence enhancing changes are those that render leading firms more able to exploit their existing skill base to achieve or strengthen competitive advantages. For example, the attribute or attributes on which a firm already enjoys a "distinctive" level of quality may be *further* distinguished as a result of changes in consumer demand *and* of the leading firm's ability to use existing skills to take advantage of that change. Thus, in change that is competence-enhancing for a given firm, there will be a parallel relationship between the *direction of change* in the marketplace and the *trajectory of skill development* within the firm.

By contrast, competence destroying change represents a change in the weights given to certain attributes in customer evaluations of products, including the addition of new attributes. For example, if the first firm in Fig. 5.1 had achieved competitive advantage through an emphasis on attribute A1, then a shift in customer emphasis to attribute B1 (an attribute on which another firm might possesses a distinctive advantage) would result in competence destroying change. In this case, the underlying *skills* of the first firm will not have been destroyed or even reduced with respect to A1, but they will no longer be able to provide competitive advantage. With no competitive advantage flowing from their application, the development of those skills no longer constitute distinctive competences.

Changes in the category in which customers place a given attribute or in a firm's ability to exploit its skills are often precipitated by the actions of competitors. One such activity that has received significant attention is the degree to which follower firms can copy or imitate the actions of the leaders (Lieberman and Montgomery, 1988). Competences are difficult to imitate (Prahalad and Hamel, 1990). Indeed, without this restraint, any competitive advantage would quickly be eroded. However, as argued earlier, virtually all competences can *eventually* be copied or superseded, and the greater the returns flowing from a competence, the greater the incentive for competitors to try to copy or obsolete that competence.

The dynamics of developing and losing distinctiveness in an attribute are suggested by the typology of attributes shown in Fig. 5.2 and the alternative strategies for building attributes shown in Fig. 5.3. The gain or loss of distinctiveness needs to be understood in terms of the bundle of attributes that is creating competitive advantage for a firm at any point in time. Indeed, our framework of competitive advantage suggests that the persistence of competitive advantage to leading firms is "amplified" by the bundling of distinctive attributes. Multiple distinctive attributes can "amplify" each other, reinforcing an overall satisfaction with a product and resulting in a multi-dimensional source of competitive advantage. This result is what Prahalad and Hamel (1990: 84) referred to as the "complex harmonization of individual technologies and production skills" that lies behind the most persistent market leaders.

DISCUSSION

This paper began by defining competences as skills that enable a firm to achieve competitive advantage, a process that requires both internal skill development and complex skill application in the marketplace. The framework presented here also emphasizes that targeted customers determine what attributes can be advantageously aggregated in a product, as well as their required level (i.e., sufficiency or distinctiveness). This suggests that Hamel and Prahalad's (1993) concept of "stretching and leveraging" skills in order to gain competitive advantage is, in the end, based on a firm's ability to develop alternative combinations of attributes and to anticipate a market's future, relative preferences for new or existing product attributes.

The competitive advantage that can result from aggregating bundles of attributes in a market provides some insight into current forms of competitive behavior as well. For example, although a single product competes in the market, all of the product's attributes need not be provided by one firm. Alliance building strategies provide opportunities for alliance partners to gain competitive advantage for a product through the aggregation of different firms' skills in providing different attributes. In product markets characterized by a multiplicity of attributes in products, the ability to aggregate attributes in a product to satisfy customer needs suggests that alliance building among providers of complementary attributes is a viable strategy for establishing industry leadership. Because market competition is "played out" among skill bundles possessed by different firms, alliances of firms can often aggregate higher levels of quality across all attributes than any firm could individually, and alliance vs. alliance competition emerges (Quinn, 1992).

Similarly, Porter's value-chain "arrow" could be linked to the framework presented here. Just as the arrow identifies different places in which skills can be developed (Porter, 1991), it also identifies the many different opportunities for attribute distinction. The value-chain arrow combines sequential stages of value creation with infrastructure-based activities in diagnosing opportunities for applying value-creating activities to the search for competitive advantage. In our framework, a firm's skills can be directed to providing various aggregations of product attributes in a search for distinctive competence and competitive advantage.

Finally, we believe this framework suggests an important cognitive dimension of competitive strategy. On its face, this framework employs a rational-actor view of the firm. While it does consider the perceptions of the customer, it does not consider impacts of various managerial perceptions. Managers' perceptions of the source of firm-level competence, either in the attributes of their own products or those of competitors, may differ from that of targeted customers (Heene, 1993). Clearly, such perceptions will determine patterns and priorities of resource allocation and skill development (Sanchez and Heene, this volume). Thus, firms in the same industry, facing to the same set of environmental conditions and changes, may have quite different competitive responses because of differences in manager's perceptions and judgements as to how internal skills should be built and aggregated for market competition.

In using this framework to understand competitive advantage careful attention needs to be paid to subtleties of trait combinations and shifts in market demand, as well as to changing skill levels within the firms. This may often make research in this area difficult. It may be hard under such circumstances to collect large samples and avoid reciprocal causation and over-specification. Indeed, given that the competence-based perspective illuminates the uniqueness of each firm and the constant evolution of skill-based competition, use of research methodologies based on statistical analysis may be impossible. More qualitative and contextual case method research (Yin, 1984; Eisenhardt, 1989) may be called for here. Further, competitive analysis needs to address the multiple dimensions upon which firms compete in an industry, and researchers need to consider how each firm competes along those dimensions over time. Such analysis may not only provide a rich view of industry competition, it may also provide a view of how changing competence requirements, and the differing abilities of firms to satisfy those requirements, fundamentally affect competitive outcomes (Teece, 1987; Temin, 1979).

NOTES

1. These concepts can be broadened to include the goals of all organizations by substituting a measure of sustained excellence for economic profits.
2. In this paper the term "product" will be used to refer to products, services and combined offerings of product and service and "customer" refers to the immediate buyer, whether an industrial customer or an end consumer.
3. The economic profits earned in such transactions may be called "composite quasi-rents" (Klein, Crawford and Alchian, 1978), reflecting the increase in value of the product above the next best alternative.
4. Schumpeter is often associated with entrepreneurial action. That begs the question as to whether constant improvement is "entrepreneurial". The point that we wish to raise here is that the sustaining of competence in dynamic and innovative, but not necessarily revolutionary or shocking.
5. The one modification to this task is found in the pure commodity market, discussed below.
6. Clearly not all customers, even within a defined customer group, will evaluate firms and attributes in the same way. A firm with any sales level has created some perception of distinctiveness. Competitive advantage and the resulting above average returns, however, are based on having a sufficiently large number of customers evaluate a particular firm's offerings as superior.
7. Note that cost-reducing advantages in a market where the demand is *not* based solely on price can be reflected in price differences that the market can sustain. For example, US discount retailer Wal-mart's efficient distribution and warehousing system allows the firm to charge lower prices, which contribute to sales of products. But these products are not purchased on price alone. Price differences among competitors may be sustained in such a non-commodity market because of non-price attributes that all competitors, including Wal-Mart, add in different amounts. Competitive advantage and above-average profits require, however, that the "low-price" attribute pursued by Wal-Mart not reduce total revenues beyond

the total savings generated by its internal, cost-reduction skills. Thus, pursuing low-cost positions in a non-commodity market contributes to one attribute (price), which still must be bundled with others for competitive advantage.

REFERENCES

Abell, D. *Defining the Business: The Starting Point of Strategic Planning.* Homewood, IL: Dow-Jones-Irwin, 1980.

Amit, R. and Schoemaker, P. "Strategic Assets and Organizational Rent", *Strategic Management Journal*, Vol. 14, pp. 33–46, 1993.

Andrews, K. *The Concept of Corporate Strategy*, 2nd edn. Homewood, IL: Richard D. Irwin, 1980.

Barney, J. "Types of Composition and the Theory of Strategy: Toward an Integrative Framework", *Academy of Management Journal*, Vol. 11, pp. 791–800, 1986a.

Barney, J. "Strategic Factor Markets: Expectations, Luck, and Business Strategy", *Management Science*, Vol. 42, pp. 1231–1241, 1986b.

Barney, J. "Firm Resources and Sustained Competitive Advantage". *Journal of Management*, Vol. 17 (1), pp. 99–120, 1991.

Barr, P., Stimpert, L. and Huff, A. "Cognitive Change, Strategic Action, and Organizational Renewal", *Strategic Management Journal*, Vol. 13, pp. 15–36, 1992.

Bogner, W. and Thomas, H. "Core Competence and Competitive Advantage: A Model and Illustrative Evidence from the Pharmaceutical Industry". In Hamel, G. and Heene, A., eds, *Competence Based Competition*. London: John Wiley, pp. 111–144, 1994.

Bogner, W., Thomas, H. and McGee, J. "Technological Forces as the Source of Industry Change: An Industry study". In Thomas, H., O'Neal, D. and Kelly, J. eds, *Strategic Renaissance and Business Transformation*. Chichester: John Wiley, pp. 365–387, 1995.

Chamberlin, E. *The Theory of Monopolistic Competition*. Cambridge: Harvard University Press, 1933.

Conner, K. "A Historical Comparison of Resource-Based Theory and Five Schools of Thought within Industrial Organization Economics: Do we have a New Theory of the Firm". *Journal of Management*, Vol. 17, pp. 121–154, 1991.

D'Aveni, R. *Hypercompetition: Managing the Dynamics of Strategic Maneuvering*. New York: Free Press, 1994.

Eisenhardt, K. "Making Fast Decisions in High Velocity Environments". *Academy of Management Journal*, Vol. 31, pp. 246–275, 1989.

Hall, R. "The Strategic Analysis of Intangible Resources", *Strategic Management Journal*, Vol. 13, pp. 135–144, 1992.

Hall, R. "A Framework Linking Intangible Resources and Capabilities to Sustainable Competitive Advantage", *Strategic Management Journal*, Vol. 14, pp. 607–618, 1993.

Hamel, G. and Prahalad, C. "Strategy as Stretch and Leverage". *Harvard Business Review*, pp. 75–84, March–April, 1993.

Heene, A. "Classifications of Competence and their Impact on Defining, Measuring and Developing 'Core Competence' ". Paper presented at the EIASM Workshop on Industry Specific Strategies in Competence Based Competition, Brussels, November 1993.

Helleloid, D. and Simonin, B. "Organizational Learning and a Firm's Core Competence". In Hamel, G. and Heene, A. eds *Competence Based Competition*, Chichester: John Wiley, pp. 213–239, 1994.

Huang, K. "Integrating Vertical and Horizontal Dimensions in a Spatial Framework of Strategic Product Competition: An Application to the U.S. Photocopier Industry". Unpublished Doctoral Dissertation, Cambridge, MA: Harvard University, 1993a.

Huang, K. "Panel on Integrating Technology Strategy and Marketing Strategy in the Product Development Process". 1993 Strategic Management Society Annual Meeting, Chicago, 1993b.

Kline, B., Crawford, R. and Alchian, A. "Vertical Integration, Appropriable Rents and the Competitive Contractin Process", *Journal of Law and Economics*, Vol. 21, pp. 297–326, 1978.

Lieberman, M. and Montgomery, D. "First Mover Advantages". *Strategic Management Journal*, Vol. 9, pp. 41–58, Summer Special Issue 1988.

Mahoney, J. and Pandian, J. "The Resource-Based View within the Conversation of Strategic Management", *Strategic Management Journal*, Vol. 13, pp. 363–380, 1992.

McGee, J. and Thomas, H. "Strategic Groups: Theory, Research and Taxonomy". *Strategic Management Journal*, Vol. 7, pp. 141–160, 1986.

Murray, A. "A Contingency View of Porter's 'Generic Strategies' ", *Academy of Management Review*, Vol. 13, pp. 390–400, 1988.

Peteraf, M. "The Cornerstone of Competitive Advantage: A Resource-Based View", Vol. 14, pp. 179–191, 1993

Porter, M. *Competitive Strategy*. New York: Free Press, 1980.

Porter, M. *Competitive Advantage*. New York: Free Press, 1985.

Porter, M. "Toward a Dynamic Theory of Strategy". *Strategic Management Journal*, Vol. 12, pp. 95–117, Winter Special Issue 1991.

Prahalad, C. and Hamel, G. "The Core Competency of the Corporation". *Harvard Business Review*, pp. 79–91, May–June, 1990.

Quinn, J. "The Intelligent Enterprise: A New Paradigm". *Academy of Management Executive*, Vol. 6, pp. 48–63, 1992.

Sanchez, R., Heene, A. and Thomas, H. "Towards the Theory and Practice of Competence-Based Competition". In Sanchez, R., Heene, A. and Thomas, H., eds, *Dynamics of Competence-Based Competition: Theory and Practice in the New Strategic Management*. London: Elsevier, 1996.

Teece, D. "Capturing Value from Technological Innovation: Integration, Strategic Partnering and Licensing Decisions". In Guile, B. and Brooks, H., eds, *Technology and Global Industry: Companies and Nations in the World Economy*. Washington, DC: National Academy Press, pp. 65–95, 1987.

Temin, P. "Technology, Regulation, and Market Structure in the Modern Pharmaceutical Industry". *The Bell Journal of Economics*, Vol. 10(2), pp. 429–446, 1979.

Tushman, M. and Anderson. P. "Technological Discontinuities and Organizational Environments". In Pettigrew, A., ed., *The Management of Strategic Change*. Oxford: Basil Blackwell, pp. 89–122, 1987.

Wernerfelt, B. "A Resource Based View of the Firm". *Strategic Management Journal*, Vol. 5, pp. 171–180, 1984.

Yin, R. *Case Study Research*. Beverly Hills: Sage, 1984.

6

COMPETITIVE ANALYSIS AND COMPETENCE-BASED STRATEGIES IN THE HOTEL INDUSTRY

Maurizio Rispoli

INTRODUCTION: A THREE-LEVEL APPROACH

Competence-based competition is a powerful concept for understanding both the recent evolution of several industries and the strategic paths of single firms. The increasing complexity of the economic and social world has greatly contributed to the need for organizations to recognize the importance of the development of specific resources, competences, and capabilities.

Generally, researchers adopt a two-level approach in analyzing specific, critical resources and capabilities: the industry level and the single firm level (Barney 1991; Grant 1991; Amit and Schoemaker 1993; Peteraf 1993). In my opinion, it would be useful to analyze competence at **a first level**— i.e., the general knowledge and the appropriate resources (hard and soft) necessary to operate in a given industry. However, critical competences may also be seen at **a second level** as we consider the different segments in a market and the various connected groups of firms competing to stay in each market segment. Obviously at **a third level** there are firm-specific competences which characterize each single firm and enable it to succeed in a given competitive arena.

Therefore, what I propose is **a three-level approach** in studying and achieving a good understanding of the strategic path of individual firms: one focusing on the general competences that are specific to a certain industry—the threshold traits of Bogner and Thomas in this volume—

another focusing on the specific competences that characterize every set of firms competing in the same market segment; the third concerning competition within each group of firms, in the form of the distinctive competences of each firm.

In the search for a better understanding of industry and firm-specific competence-based strategies which have evolved in recent decades, relatively little attention has been paid to firms selling that particular class of products we call services. Obviously, some researchers have already pointed out specific characteristics of services production and their most important implications for strategic moves and operational problems and decisions (Levitt 1972, 1976; Sasser, Olsen and Wyckoff 1978; Thomas 1978; Shostack 1982; Grönroos 1982; Crozier, Normann and Tardy 1982; Lovelock 1983; Normann 1984; Parasuraman, Zeithaml and Berry 1985; Eglier and Langeard 1987; Heskett 1988).

In order to capture some of the key issues in competence-based competition between service firms, it seems desirable to focus attention on the firms of a specific industry in a particular competitive context.

This paper aims to make a concise application of the three-level analysis of competence-based competition in the hospitality industry, examining both exogenous and endogenous constraints that emerge in managing hotel firms in a competitive environment, which is becoming more uncertain and global year by year, (Olsen, Crawford-Welch and Tse 1992: 213–25).

The first part of the paper is devoted to clarifying both endogenous and exogenous aspects of managing hotel firms, focusing on the particular characteristics of hotel operations and consequently on the specific competences that are critical to staying in the market and to competitive success in the hotel business in general.

In the second part of the paper, I will try to define both specific competences necessary to manage different kinds of hotel firms in their particular competitive environments. This study refers mostly to Italian hotels: national chains; hotels of very large foreign chains; small privately-owned chains; single-unit hotel firms affiliated with different forms of consortia; and single-unit unaffiliated hotel firms. For this purpose, I develop several concepts necessary to define the actual competitive arena. Referring to this second aim, I will propose the utilization, alongside the Porterian concept of the five forces of competition (Porter 1979: 88) and Hunt's strategic group (1972), of the concept of **competitive group**, which seems helpful for a better understanding of the current evolution of the competitive environment.

Competitive group (of firms) is a simple concept: it consists of the set of firms that, in a given industry setting and in a certain segment of a specific market, compete against one another for customers with similar preferences. It is the set of firms that virtually every firm will single out to identify its competition in the short and medium term. (Rispoli 1992; 244–7). In defining this concept, we adopt a demand-side approach to competition analysis. To define a competitive group it is not enough to identify firms who have developed resources in similar ways in the past; it is necessary to enlarge the analysis to include traits which customers demand and with which firms try to gain competitive advantage. These product traits should be classified by how they are perceived by the customers (Bogner and Thomas, 1996).

In the third and last part of the paper, I will try to apply the approach suggested here to the case of Jolly Hotels, a quoted Italian chain which has experimented with a sequence of different expansion strategies, from its foundation in 1949 to the present day, and has concentrated particularly on expanding internationally over the last decade.

SPECIFIC CONSTRAINTS AND CAPABILITIES FOR MANAGING FIRMS IN THE HOTEL INDUSTRY

Endogenous Factors Characterizing Hotel Firms Operations

It has recently been stated that in the strictest terms there is no definitive statement of the numbers of hotels in Europe, because there is no pan-European consensus about what constitutes a hotel (Johnson and Slattery 1993). In fact, the variety of forms of hotels and hotel firms in Europe appears greater than that in any other region in the world. For the purposes of this discussion, however, I will stipulate that a hotel is a place (generally a building), where accommodation and ancillary services are produced, offered and provided to people away from home, and a hotel firm is a for-profit organization running one or more units (commercial hotels).

With this generic but, for the moment, sufficient definition in mind we now try to identify the nature of the hotel operations and the factors and constraints characterizing it.

Let us consider first the endogenous side of the issue—i.e., the factors that affect directly and internally the hotel firm's production and provision of service:

(a) end-users need to be physically present to receive the core service (overnight accommodation);

(b) the core service is characterized by a mix of tangible and intangible elements (Hall 1992);

(c) production and provision of the hotel service can only occur simultaneously, therefore end users have a high level of contact and interaction with operations;

(d) interpersonal relationships between the end-user and the producer (front-desk clerks, waiters, housekeepers, barmen and so on) are very important and sometimes may be more important than the core service itself;

(e) hotel service is not only people-based, like services in general, but also, importantly, equipment-based. In certain hotel contexts, end-users interact more with physical facilities than with service personnel;

(f) hotel firms are subject to high fixed costs as a proportion of their total operating costs; as a consequence, their profit performance may be quite variable under unstable demand conditions (Jones and Lockwood 1989, 22);

(g) transactions are typically discrete with individual customers, but much more continual with customers that represent organizations;

(h) contact personnel can influence the quality of service provided, but have little discretion over the type and style of service;

(i) the level of customization in general cannot be very high, but service may be different from one hotel to another depending both on the range of facilities available within the hotel and on the style of management and service;

(j) hotel operations show a high level of rigidity, in various senses:

— the physical plant cannot be modified in the short run to meet the particular requirements of customers;

— the physical plant is characterized by a production capacity—i.c., the total number of rooms and beds cannot be increased with peaks of demand;

— accommodation service cannot be stored if unsold; therefore there is a fall in the rate of capacity utilization in low demand periods (particular days of the week, or specific weeks or months in a year);

— the physical plant is characterized by a particular quality level not changeable in the short run;

— the physical plant occupies a fixed location in a certain geographic area, around which the environment may change and demand may shift to other areas;

— the quantity of human resources cannot be reduced or expanded *ad libitum*, following the quantity of service demanded day by day;

— the quality and skills of human resources cannot actually be improved in the short run.

Exogenous Factors Affecting Hotel Firms Operations

Let us consider now exogenous factors affecting hotel operations that are related to qualitative and quantitative aspects of demand.

From the qualitative point of view, we must recognize that there are three groups of customers (Rispoli and Tamma 1991: 105–7) which are likely to behave in different ways, because of different motivations and expectations, in transactions with hotel firms:

1. end-users (ultimate users of the service) who are also customers when they individually seek, choose and pay for hotel service;

2. organizations (profit and non-profit) operating in the tourism sector which act as intermediaries (i.e. travel agents, local public agencies for the incoming of tourists) or as firms producing a package in which one

component is the hotel service (i.e. tour operators, professional congress organizer);

3. organizations (private and public) operating in any field which seek, select, buy, and pay for hotel service provided to end-users travelling on behalf of the organizations (i.e. firms, foundations, associations, universities, public agencies).

Customers of hotel service (end-users and organizations) cannot generally shift their demand to a different time, because their need for accommodation, both for business travel or in the case of leisure, is related to a specific time in a specific location, and is usually scheduled in advance. Besides the two main demand segments—leisure and business—there is the possibility to segment the market in many other ways on the basis of different variables (geographic, demographic, psychographic, usage, benefit, price, etc.) (Lewis and Chambers 1989: 211–23). Therefore, the managers of hotel firms have a tough task to carry out: matching hotel characteristics and resources with the preferences of specific segments.

Legal constraints, which are different in each country even within the European Union, may also complicate a matching of resources and preferences.

From the quantitative point of view, what we must keep in mind is that demand for hotel services can be particularly volatile. Furthermore, of the three classical components of the demand in relation to time—season, cycle, and trend—in the case of hotel service demand, the first component is the most specific. In fact, in managing hotel firms, the concentration of demand on certain days of the week, on particular holidays, during particular business events (exhibitions, shows, fairs), in some months of the year (summer, winter), and so on, poses significant problems to be overcome (Jones and Lockwood 1989: 71–3).

Competences Necessary to Manage a Hotel Firm

The above mentioned characteristics and constraints of hotel operations are the starting point for determining the most relevant resources and skills necessary to cope with the threats and opportunities arising from the competitive environment. Between the threshold and the level of distinction lies a level of competence which produces product traits which, while not distinctive, are *sufficient* (Bogner and Thomas, 1996).

We may argue that, in general, the most important resources needed to successfully manage a hotel business are a set of managerial capabilities that enable a hotel firm:

(a) to cooperate with other actors within the tourist and travel sector (tour operators, professional congress organizers, travel agencies, airline companies, etc.). This is necessary because in the contemporary hotel business environment, it is increasingly difficult for a hotel firm to sell its service without inserting the hotel offering in a more complex product, made up of different services;

(b) particularly in the case of single-unit unaffiliated hotel firms, to enter some consortia or some other form of collaboration that can compensate for at least some of the weaknesses of the small size of the unit (e.g. through good connections with the market, suppliers, advertising, etc.);

(c) to develop good relations with local public and private organizations in order to build a positive company image, which is necessary to obtain favorable attitudes towards the firm's initiatives, particularly in restyling, restructuring and enlarging the hotel's buildings;

(d) to exploit the wealth (landscape, art, history, business, transport facilities, and so on) of the area where the hotel is located, since the product of a hotel is seen by the end-users as being mixed with the elements of the local environment which may reinforce, but also sometimes weaken, the offering of the hotel firm;

(e) to choose the right booking and selling network, because even for the smaller hotel firms, it is becoming very important to acquire customers from a wide international area in order to expand activity in new markets;

(f) to achieve and maintain the maximum possible level of flexibility in the use of human resources, since an important aspect of the perceived quality of hotel service is both the rapid and appropriate reply to the end-users' requests and the fast solution of queue problems;

(g) to make explicit and identifiable a particular style that must always unify all the components of the hotel product, from the core service— accommodation—to the mere information given by the bell captain, in order to achieve a standard of quality the end-users may appreciate in every aspect of their stay in the hotel.

For a hotel firm, like others, the assets that seem to be relevant are: human, physical, locational, organizational and reputation (Hofer and Schendel 1978: 145–48). Apart from physical assets which in the case of hotel firms mean the characteristics of the hotel unit (buildings, furniture, fittings, decor, equipment, etc.) and those tangible and intangible assets connected with the location of the unit, the three other assets are typically intangible resources and are therefore more difficult to identify and appraise using quantitative measures (Hall 1992).

The capabilities a hotel firm derives from its resources may be identified by functional classifications of firm activities, and by connecting each function with the five resources mentioned above. Consequently:

(a) a hotel firm's capabilities in many activities, like general management, operations, marketing, distribution, personnel management and finance, can be related to specific human and organizational assets present in the firm;

(b)   reputation is a critical input to a firm's marketing capabilities;
(c)   both physical and human assets are the basis for high quality operations;
(d)   locational assets greatly impact hotel attractiveness and its potential product distribution.

Of course all the connections proposed may appear a little schematic; we must be aware that some competences may derive from a single asset, while others may require highly complex interactions involving two or more assets. From this point of view, a key ingredient in the relationship between resources and capabilities is the ability of an organization to achieve cooperation and coordination within teams (Grant 1991: 122). This particular capability may be viewed as an intangible asset, that is difficult to imitate (Winter 1987).

THE DEFINITION OF THE PARTICULAR COMPETITIVE ENVIRONMENT OF SINGLE-HOTEL FIRMS AND THE EMERGENCE OF SPECIFIC COMPETENCES AND CAPABILITIES

In the hotel business, one must take into account the competitive environments defined by the services offered by other hotel firms.

In the previous section we reviewed the characteristic factors affecting a hotel firm and the resources and skills necessary to meet them. In this section the focus will be on more specific competitive situations and on specific forms of hotel firms and competitive arenas.

A first distinction must be made by defining the scope of the potential competitive actions of hotel firms: this distinguishes firms inserted in various ways into a network that enables them to operate in a wide geographic area, and those single-unit hotel firms that are unaffiliated (Rispoli and Tamma 1991: 134–7). The former, usually referred to indiscriminately as *hotel chains*, must be grouped into different categories:

(a)   firms made up of a great number of owned hotel units generally located in various countries (true hotel chains);
(b)   chains composed of a large hotel firm, with well-known brand and image, and many other (small) hotel firms using the same brand as the former, on the basis of franchising or management contracts;
(c)   chains of many different hotel firms, that are relatively homogeneous in terms of quality level, which adopt a particular brand beside their previous name and which join in consortia or other forms of partnerships that carry out important functions like marketing, selling, and supplying for all the firms (Grava 1993).

The latter group of unaffiliated hotel firms operates rather independently or is, at the most, connected with some booking network, but it is still the largest set of hotels in Europe, and particularly in Italy.

The largest hotel chains compete with each other in a market that is global in geographic terms, but also in the sense that each of them operates in the most important market segments: business, conventions, and leisure. In terms of the quality-price level offered, some chains concentrate on only one level (for instance, the luxury level like Four Seasons, Park Hyatt, Forte Exclusive, or Ciga). On the other hand, some adopt a strategy of operating at several quality-price levels of the market, in general using different brands for different quality-price levels (for instance, Holiday Inn, Forte, and Accor, all use different brands for different quality-price levels) (Litteljohn and Roper 1992: 194–212).

In Italy, as in other countries with well-developed tourism, domestic chains compete both with the large multinational chains present in the country and with single-unit hotel firms which are unaffiliated, but which offer substantially the same kind and level of service (mid to first class).

Small hotel firms, which are generally unaffiliated, compete primarily against each other for customers in a particular, limited geographic area (for instance: Adriatic Riviera, Costa del Sol, Tyrol, the Cotswolds), generally in the leisure segment at the mid to economy levels.

This brief analysis simplifies a more complex reality, but gives an idea of the starting point necessary to define the competitive arena of different kinds of hotel firms. It is a demand approach that helps to identify competitors that are trying to attract the same kinds of customers.

Building on this approach, we can now define the concept of *competitive group* as the set of firms that, in a given geographic area and in a specific segment of the hotel market, compete with one another for customers with similar preferences. Thus a competitive group is a broader set of firms than Hunt's and Porter's *strategic groups,* because the inclusion of hotel firms in a competitive group is not limited by supply-side criteria of the same structural characteristics (size, degree of vertical integration, diversification, etc.) and the same strategic path.

With this concept of competitive groups in mind, a hotel firm entrepreneur or general manager, as well as any industry analyst, may single out the specific players in a competitive arena, at least in the short run. However, while this concept is useful for projecting and programming a competitive strategy, particularly in terms of marketing tools to be used in the short run, it needs some further refinement before it can be used to identify the competences shared by hotel firms belonging to the same competitive group.

The starting point for identifying shared competences in a competitive group is their ability to satisfy the requirements of targeted buyers and therefore their skill in providing the characteristics of products offered by firms and bought by targeted buyers. It is these product characteristics that determine the resources and competences that enable a firm to compete in a particular segment of the market. From this point of view, it appears useful to recognize that within a competitive group there will exist competence groupings of firms that share some strategically important competences (Gorman, Thomas and Sanchez, 1996) derived from basic structural, financial, and managerial characteristics that *must be similar*.

We have found it useful to use these constructs of competitive groups and competence groupings in our recent research into the evolution of the structure and organization of the hotel industry and the behaviors of a significative number of individual firms. Turning to some examples, applying these concepts leads us to conclude that what gives the large hotel chains (Hilton International, Forte, Hyatt, Intercontinental, Sofitel, Novotel, to mention only the most important) much of their success in the global market is a specific competence derived from their presence, with their hotels, in many different countries: their creation and operation of a network made up of multiple locations for promotion, selling, booking and production of hotel services. Important intangible assets shared by this competitive grouping of hotel firms are a recognized brand name of the chain and its quality image. Another key asset is the size of the firm, which enables it to develop favorable relations with wholesale and intermediate markets (tour operators, travel agents) as well as with the corporate accounts.

To illustrate the process of identifying competences shared in a set of hotel firms, let us consider another strategic group: the large chains expanding worldwide through franchising and management contracts based on a particular formula of interfirm collaboration developed over many decades. These firms have specific knowledge and know-how in franchising and establishing management contracts. Chains like Holiday Inn, Sheraton, and Ramada are examples. In this grouping of hotel firms other competences are also important, some of which have been discussed in the case of the previous group (the very large network of points of operations, the large size, and the brand image of each firm), but the distinguishing competence of this group is the capability to enlarge the firm's network by franchising or otherwise contracting with lots of single-unit hotel firms or small local chains in many different countries (Bell 1993). Equally critical to the success of this group of hotel firms is their competence to create a remarkable consistency and coherence of products offered by several hundred hotels spread across the continents. In fact, customers choosing this kind of hotel do so precisely because they seek the same atmosphere, facilities, and quality level they have experienced worldwide in hotels with the same brand.

In order to demonstrate the robustness of the competence grouping concept and the scope of its application in the case of hotel industry, let us consider a group of firms that are at the other end of the competitive spectrum from the large multinational chains: the small-size family hotels. These hotels compete with each other in a certain segment of the market in a specific geographic area. Consider, for example, the low segment in terms of quality-price in a holiday resort like Rimini on the Adriatic Sea, and in particular the group of the firms with only one hotel, not located on the sea shore, of the 1 or 2 star-category, run by a family. This kind of hotel firm has certain competences which enable it to stay in the market: flexibility in the use of human resources, the ability to solve the small problems of their guests immediately, real low prices, and a very friendly atmosphere.

Finally, let us consider the competence group made up of the single-unit hotel firms operating in a historical city of art—Venice—offering their services to the high quality-price level segment of leisure tourists (examples: Bauer, Monaco, Londra Palace, Metropole, Gabrielli). Hotels in this group are characterized by the following competences: very high quality standards of personnel behavior, antique furnishing, and decor coupled with up-to-date conveniences and comfort, an ancient and possibly historical building, and a fine view of Venetian canals or lagoon. In this case, however, if we want to identify the actual competitive group in which this competence grouping competes we must include hotels belonging to a chain, a different competence group which offers a service with substantially the same characteristics mentioned above, but with some further characteristics of its own (particularly the network). In this second competence grouping, there is at least one other hotel belonging to Ciga chain: Europa e Regina.

As we have seen in considering a geographically bounded local market, the concept of competence grouping helps to solve some problems of competitive analysis. In the first case—small family hotels of Rimini—there is a substantial coincidence between the competitive group and the competence group, while in the latter case—four-star Venetian hotels—the competitive group consists of at least two competence groupings. Generally speaking, we may argue that when attention is directed to the local characteristics and boundaries of the market, the usefulness of defining the competitive group emerges clearly. This may be particularly true when market segments exist for medium to high quality level offerings, because at this level it is likely that different kinds of hotel firms belonging to different competence groups, will compete directly with one another for the same customers. In other words, competence groupings allow us to recognize that the competences needed to be competitive in satisfying the essential demands are unlikely to be held only by hotel firms with the same resources characteristics and similar strategies. Rather, such threshold competences (Bogner and Thomas 1996) may be also shared by other firms that are different in terms of their history, size, degree of vertical integration, horizontal diversification, and other elements, but compete for the same customer, therefore belonging to a larger set of competitors (competitive group).

DISTINCTIVE COMPETENCES OF THE SINGLE FIRM: THE CASE OF JOLLY HOTELS

The aim of this section is to focus on competences at the level of the single firm in order to clarify the role of competence building and leveraging in

creating and maintaining a competitive advantage and sustained profitability (Grant 1991).

To achieve competitive advantage requires competences that make best
use of each firm's unique assets and capabilities. Of course, the resources
which can lead to a competitive advantage may sometimes be owned jointly
by a set of firms offering similar products (as in the case of franchise hotels
analysed in the previous section), but our aim here is to underline the role
of resources owned and capabilities developed specifically by individual
firms (Reed and De Filippi 1990). We examine the case of Jolly Hotels, an
Italian firm founded in 1949 as the result of a strategic diversification move
of a textile company (Manifattura Lane G. Marzotto & F. SpA). The
new firm was endowed with numerous capabilities in management culture,
skills and tools assimilated from the textile manufacturing context and
experiences.

To illuminate the relations linking the competences and competitive
advantage which have characterized Jolly Hotels, let us now take into
consideration some details of four periods of the company life (1949–61,
1962–74, 1975–79, and 1980–91) corresponding to different realized
strategies that emerged from the dialectical interaction between its
reference environment (not only competitive) and its deliberated strategies
(Mintzberg and Waters 1985). We will attempt to define the competences
of critical importance in building competitive advantages in each of the four
periods into which we have divided the life of Jolly Hotels.

During the **first period** (1949–61), the capabilities of the general
management to conceive and develop an appropriate business idea and to
exploit external financial resources were of crucial importance.

The declared mission of the company was to endow Southern Italy with
a network of hotels. Southern Italy is rich in natural, architectural and
historical attractions, and therefore is supposedly attractive for tourists, but
at the time it was poor in terms of hotels (at the time, 11.3% of the hotels
in Italy compared with 37.6% of the resident population). Tourist hotels had
to be comfortable, but not luxurious, to be suitable for tourism expected to
grow rapidly after the reconstruction of the postwar years. Company's
management selected localities that lacked hotels comparable with those
envisioned by Jolly Hotels, and in just a few years (from 1952 to 1956) 43
hotels were opened.

Financial resources were drawn from three main sources: (1) internal
capital, (2) bank credits, and (3) international and national public aid
(Marshall Plan for the recovery of postwar European economies and Cassa
per il Mezzogiorno for the development of the southern part of Italy).

Occupancy rates in those years were quite high (from 75 to 80%), but
during the first decade the net income was consistently low, perhaps because
the size of most of the company's hotel units was relatively small and unable
to exploit economies of scale, or perhaps because there was something wrong
in Jolly Hotels price policy.

In the **second period** (1962–1974), competences based on managing personnel, product mix, divestment, and investment became the relevant factors of success of Jolly Hotels. The goals in this period were to: (1) increase the capacity of specific hotels by investing new financial resources; (2) acquire a quality standard in all the hotel units in which the product of Jolly Hotels was obtained and delivered to the end-users; (3) enter a substantially new segment of the Italian market: business travel. To accomplish these goals required, at the same time, an increase in the overall production capacity (total number of rooms and beds), rationalization of operations, and expansion into new segments of the market. These actions led to numerous new investments and some divestments at the end of which (1974) the number of rooms was greater than that in 1961, while the number of hotel units dropped to 34 (from 58 in 1961). Also, new hotel units were built or acquired (in Milan, Turin, Florence, Rome, and Taormina) to enter new segments and new geographical markets. At the same time, brand differentiation was developed, and as a result three different groups of hotels were established.

In the **third period** (1975–79) the crucial competences were in organization, control, and accounting functions. There was a general commitment to designing and implementing a deep process of rationalization of the overall production flow. The goals of this action were reducing costs (particularly costs like labour and administrative overhead) and reinforcing the firm's capability in self financing—a strong point throughout the life of the company—in a period of general growth in the prices of inputs and in labor rates.

In the second half of the 1970s, after the oil crises, the base strategy of Jolly Hotels was no longer aimed at continuously shifting towards the higher segments of the market, both in the business segment- with the Jolly Hotels entry into the convention segment—and in leisure tourism. Indeed, during this period three hotels were opened under the Jolly brand (in Naples, Siena, and Milan) and six other smaller units in the south of Italy were divested.

In the **fourth period** of the Jolly Hotels strategic path (1980–91), the critical competences appear to have been the ability to develop contacts in foreign markets and to support the development of both new geographical markets and the upper levels of the business market segment.

Marketing was particularly strong in the selling function. In that period the direct selling network was enlarged with sales and booking points in Milan, Turin, Rome, New York, Brussels, Amsterdam, Paris, London, and Frankfurt.

Financial efforts were aimed at acquiring new capital for investments. In 1981 management decided to increase the share capital of the company to 15,000 million lire and in 1982 managed to have the shares of Jolly Hotels quoted on the Milan Stock Exchange. The company also made good use of all the opportunities under particular laws making financing available at convenient rates and conditions. At the end of the period, in 1990, Jolly Hotels Finance A.V.V. was established in Dutch Antilles with the mission of collecting funds in the international market.

The firm's first innovative strategic move into foreign markets was the establishment of Jolly Hotels Belgio S.A. in 1980, which took on management of the Hotel Atlanta in Brussels. Expansion in foreign markets continued with the foundation of a holding in Luxembourg, the Jolly Hotels Internazionale S.A. (1981), with the objective of supporting the financial aspects of Jolly Hotels' further foreign initiatives. Chronologically, these were:

(a) the creation of Jolly Hotels USA Inc. in 1982, which opened an important promotion and selling point in New York for the American market;

(b) the establishment of Jolly Hotels France S.A. in 1984, which a short time later acquired and began the management of Hotel Lotti, a well-known hotel in Paris;

(c) the establishment of Jolly Hotels Holland B.V. in 1985, followed by the acquisition of the Carlton Hotel in Amsterdam, which was extensively renovated in 1989 to acquire the high quality standard characterizing the chain;

(d) in 1991, the first successful entry of an Italian chain into the U.S. market, with the purchase of the Madison Tower in the heart of Manhattan, with convention spaces and a large number of rooms;

(e) the opening of a second hotel in the center of Brussels in 1991: the Jolly Hotel du Grand Sablon;

(f) the signing of an agreement with the National Academy of the Economy of the (former) Soviet Union for the management of a huge hotel unit under construction in Moscow.

Along with this expansion into foreign markets, other strategic initiatives carried out by management of the chain included:

1. a continuous shifting towards the business travel segment, particularly for conventions, combined with the divestment of the smallest hotel units that were generally located in medium or small towns of Southern Italy. In this period five important units were acquired: Leonardo da Vinci and Midas Palace in Rome, the hotel and convention centre Milanofiori in Milan, the Plaza in Genoa, and the Hotel Ligure in Turin;

2. a progressive up-grading of an enlarged concept of quality, including the characteristics of fixed assets (physical plant, decor, furniture, other equipment), the direct centralized control of most of the inputs of the hotel units, the creation of a new computerized management information system, and a comprehensive training and retraining program for the work-force.

Analysis of Jolly Hotels' competitive environment today helps us obtain further insights into the development of competitive strategies based on competences. Today Jolly Hotels confronts other hotel firms in several different competitive environments. What is needed therefore is, first of all, to take into account the competitive groups in which Jolly's various hotel units compete, because a hotel chain basically competes through each of its units; therefore geographic and locational aspects and issues become relevant.

At the beginning of the 1990s the company had 36 hotel units, of which 31 were in Italy. In order to clarify the current competitive situation of the company, it is useful to remember that, with all its hotel units, the chain offers its products to customers in the medium to high quality-price segment (four stars following the Italian scale). However, there are significant product differentiations within these segments, in terms both of intended use by customers and of the specific locality where each hotel unit operates.

Applying the first of these two criteria, we can place Jolly Hotels in the following market segments: business, convention, leisure, and fitness.

Beginning with the last segment, the company has only one hotel unit offering this kind of product, Grande Albergo delle Terme on the island of Ischia. It would be wrong, however, to limit the competitive analysis in this case to hotels located in the same area. To define the competitive group to which this unit belongs, we must also take into account hotels located far from Ischia island, even outside Italy, but offering substantially the same product in terms of both the level of service quality and the mix of product traits (mud-baths, water therapies, climatic conditions, etc.). On the other hand, the intensity of the competition within this competitive group will be mitigated by the combination of two unique assets: the characteristics of the locality (Ischia is in the center of Mediterranean Sea, well linked to the nearby ports on the continent, including Naples, with charming natural features) and the characteristics of the hotel unit itself. Both of these assets are source of "isolation mechanisms" (Rumelt 1982), which contribute to competence groupings that further distinguish hotel firms and units within competitive groups.

In considering the convention segment, we can adopt a similar approach. Jolly Hotels has seven units in this segment, two of which are in the subsegment of major convention centers (Midas in Rome and Milanofiori in Milan). These last units compete not only with other hotels offering the same equipment and capacity (meeting rooms for over one thousand people) but also with convention centers, run by private or by public organizations that use surrounding hotels for accommodation services. They also compete not just in the area where they are located but in the larger geographic region of destinations which the targeted customers consider suitable for their conventions. Consequently, for the purpose of competitive analysis, each of the two hotel units for major conventions must be included in several competitive groups consisting of hotels and non-hotels in various localities. The identification of competitive groups for the Jolly chain's other hotels in the convention segment is less difficult, because their convention facilities, particularly in terms of the limited size of meeting rooms, implies a great number of potential competitors but limited to the same locality.

In the business segment, the identification of competitive groups for each hotel unit is easier, because people who travel to visit some people for business purposes cannot choose to go to any town. Consequently competitive groupings of hotel units in this segment are typically those located in the same area, although hotels within a competitive group may belong to different competence groupings. As an example, the competitive group to which the units of Jolly Hotels in Turin belong are shown in Table 6.1. Table 6.1 includes nine hotel units thought to be of the same level in terms of quality and business facilities (meeting rooms and other equipment) and located in the center of Turin. Seven larger hotels of the nine belong to Italian hotel chains; two of these are affiliated with the brand chains Spacehotels and Italhotels. Consequently, the competence grouping which applies to the three Jolly Hotels also includes the two units of Atahotels and Starhotels. However competition occurs directly among all nine hotel units in the competitive grouping.

It is likely that the price differences within the competitive group are not meaningful in their impact on customers' choices, but the nine hotels of this competitive group may face price competition from hotels of other competitive groups. For example, the group of "three-star" hotels located in the

Table 6.1. The definition of the competitive group to which the hotel units of Jolly Hotels in Turin belong.

Hotels	Chains	Price (rack-rate for double room)	Rooms
Hotel AMBASCIATORI	Jolly Hotels	320000	199
Hotel PRINCIPI DI PIEMONTE	Jolly Hotels	390000	107
Hotel LIGURE	Jolly Hotels	340000	169
Hotel CONCORD	Atahotels	320000	135
Hotel MAJESTIC	Starhotels	330000	93
Grand Hotel SITEA	Spacehotels	370000	119
TURIN PALACE Hotel	Italhotels	330000	125
Hotel CITY		330000	44
Hotel DIPLOMATIC		350000	129
Total number of rooms			1120
Mean		308000	112
Standard deviation		23863.04	43.97
Min		320000	
Max		390000	

Source: Hotels Yearbook 1993, Azienda di promozione turistica di Torino.

centre of the city offer services whose quality may not be so different from that of the nine "four-star" hotels. Further, other "four-star" hotels are located outside the center, near the motorway exits and on the Turin airport road. The former group (about 30 "three-star" hotels) has a mean price of 145,000 lire (less than half of that of the nine "four star" units), while the latter group (3 hotels with comparable equipment) shows a price range from 235,000 to 275,000 lire, significantly lower then the price range of the competitive group made up of the nine "four-star" hotels in the town center. Clearly, careful analysis of competition in such a case will look beyond the boundaries of a competitive group to include hotels of competitive groups offering substitute products which may pose a real competitive threat.

In the case of the leisure segment, the correspondence of locality to the needs of users of hotel services appears less direct than in the case of business travel, because apart from some special cases ("we want to visit Venice and don't want to go elsewhere"), it is likely that different destinations will be compared before deciding on an itinerary to visit localities or on a resort where to stay for some days. Thus in this segment a hotel unit competes with others not only within the same locality, but sometimes with other hotels located in different and even distant areas. An example from the Jolly Hotels offerings can illustrate it. If the problem is defining the competitive group to which the Hotel Diodoro in Taormina belongs, the analysis must consider all the possible Mediterranean resorts with characteristics similar to those of the Sicilian small town: located on the coast, with outstanding archaeological ruins and a well preserved historical centre, enjoying a dry and warm climate. Thus, other hotels in this competitive group might be found in, for example, Rhodes, Dubrovnik, Nauplion, and Split. The combined attraction of the resort and the hotel must be considered. Thus, the managements of Jolly Hotels and of Hotel Diodoro have to analyse first of all their direct competitors in Taormina, which are other "four-star" hotels belonging to the same competitive group. Subsequently, enlarging the boundaries of this set, a competitive analysis must include, on the one hand, the "three-star" hotels in Taormina that are nearer to the quality standards and product traits of Hotel Diodoro, and on the other, competing hotels in localities with similar attractions to those of Taormina.

SUMMARY AND CONCLUSIONS

In the second section of the paper, we surveyed the specific constraints characterizing the management of hotel firms and the general capabilities necessary to compete in the market for accommodation service and ancillary services. We referred to what Bogner and Thomas call **threshold traits**: "those traits which the group of targeted customers require a firm to provide at a minimal level of quality, but which do not have potential for competitive advantage (Bogner and Thomas 1996). Those elements (constraints) represent the starting point for the definition of the most relevant resources and managerial capabilities needed to cope with the threats and opportunities arising from the competitive environment.

In the third and central section of the paper we have focused on the differences emerging from both the characteristics of four supply-side diversities in types of hotel firms (hotel chains, franchising or management contract hotel chains, brand hotel chains, and unaffiliated hotels) and the demand-side characteristics of specific competitive environments. The aim was twofold: (1) to define **different competences** that each type of hotel firm use in its efforts to be competitive, and (2) to suggest the use of **competitive groups** and **competence groupings** as conceptual tools useful in defining the real dimensions of various competitive arenas.

In the fourth section, the analysis of the previous sections is applied to a single hotel firm to illustrate the context-dependent ways in which competences must vary in different competitive situations to ensure some kind of competitive advantage. In order to support our arguments with empirical evidence, we have used the example of Jolly Hotels, an Italian chain. We have briefly analyzed four periods in this firm's strategic path from its foundation in 1949 to the beginning of the 1990s, with the aim of identifying the competences developed by the firm that were critical in each of the four periods and that distinguish specific hotel units of Jolly Hotels in various competitive arenas today.

At the end of the paper, the main conclusion we propose is that what hotel firms offer to a market segment is more complex than a generic product (mix of services). Although it is important that hotel firms develop strategies that effectively utilize their resources and the specific ones of each hotel unit, we must realize that two sets of resources outside the firm also operate to define the characteristic traits of a product offering.

The first set of resources is represented by environmental traits of the area where the hotel units are located. These traits are probably only marginally under the control of each firm, limited by the extent to which it can contribute directly to their change and improvement, by cooperating with public and private organizations, including those belonging to the hotel industry and to different sectors.

The second set of resources, which also result in the traits of a hotel firm's product offering, is represented by the social, cultural, historical, and natural characteristics of the localities where the hotel units operate and over which firms have no influence at all. If those characteristics are positive, the hotel firms should of course try to make best use of them in their hotel-level strategies and marketing campaigns. Consequently, the initial location decision for each new unit appears particularly important in the process of building distinctive competences in the hotel business.

What we have come to understand is that, if we assume the point of view of the users of the hotel service (demand-side approach), what is considered in the selection process of a hotel is a very complex mix of product traits delivered by tangible and intangible assets that may be characteristic of a specific hotel unit, of a hotel firm, or of the specific locality (outside the control of the hotel firm to varying degrees).

In this sense we may argue that competence is expressed through both distinctive product traits, threshold traits, and important externalities, that depend on the positioning of a product offering in a (in this case, literally) product space.

REFERENCES

Amit, R. and Shoemaker, J. H. "Strategic Assets and Organizational Rent". *Strategic Management Journal*, Vol. 14(1), 1993.

Barney, J. "Firm Resources and Sustained Competitive Advantage". *Journal of Management*, Vol. 17(1), 1991.

Bell, C. A. "Agreements with Chain Hotel Companies". *The Cornell H.R.A. Quarterly*, February 1993.

Bogner, W. C. and Thomas, H. "From Skills to Competences: The Play-out of Resource Bundles Across Firms". In Sanchez, R., Heene, A. and Thomas, H., eds, *Dynamics of Competence-Based Competition*, Oxford: Elsevier Science, 1996.

Crozier, M., Normann, R. and Tardy, G. *L' Innovation dans le Services*. Paris: Mission a l'Innovation, 1982.

Eglier, P. and Langeard, E. *Servuction: Le Marketing des Services*. Paris: McGraw-Hill, 1987.

Gorman, P., Thomas, H. and Sanchez, R. "Industry Dynamics in Competence-Based Competition". In Sanchez, R., Heene, A. and Thomas, H., eds, *Dynamics of Competence-Based Competition*. Oxford: Elsevier Science, 1996.

Grant, R. M. "The Resource-Based Theory of Competitive Advantage: Implications for Strategy Formulation". *California Management Review*, Spring 1991.

Grava, L. "Organizzazione dell'offerta, Concorrenza e Strategie nella Produzione Alberghiera in Italia: Primi Risultati di una Ricerca". Working Paper No. 3, Dipartimento di Economia e Direzione Aziendale, Università di Venezia—Cà Foscari, 1993.

Grönroos, C. "Strategic Management and Marketing in Service Sector". *Svenska Handelshogskolan*. Helsinki, 1982.

Heskett, J. L. *Management in the Service Economy*. Boston: HBS Press, 1986.

Hall, R. "The strategic Analysis of Intangible Resources". *Strategic Management Journal*, Vol. 13, February 1992.

Hunt, M. S. "Competition in the Major Home Appliance Industry 1966-1970". Unpublished Doctoral Thesis, Harvard University, 1972.

Johnson, S. M. and Slattery, P. "Hotel Chains in Europe". *EIU Travel and Tourism Analyst*, No. 1, 1993.

Jones P. and Lockwood, A. *The Management of Hotel Operations*. London: Cassel, 1989.

Levitt, T. "Production-line Approach to the Service". *Harvard Business Review*, September–October 1972.

Levitt, T. "The Industrialization of Service". *Harvard Business Review*, September–October 1976.

Lewis, R. C. "The Positioning Statement for Hotels". *Cornell H.R.A Quarterly*, May 1981.

Lewis, R. C. and Chambers, R. E. *Marketing Leadership in Hospitality*. New York: Van Nostrand Reinhold, 1989.

Litteljohn, D. and Roper, A. "Changes in International Hotel Companies' Strategies". In Teare, R. and Boer, A., eds, *Strategic Hospitality Management*. London: Cassel, 1992.

Lovelock, C. H. "Classifying Services to Gain Strategic Marketing Insight. *Journal of Marketing*, Vol. 47, Summer 1983.

Mintzberg, H. and Waters, J. A. "Of Strategies, Deliberate and Emergent". *Strategic Management Journal*, Vol. 4(3), 1985.

Normann, R. *Service Management: Strategy and Leadership in Service Industry*. New York: John Wiley and Sons, 1984.

Nykiel, R. A. *Marketing in the Hospitality Industry*, New York: Van Nostrand Reinhold, 1989.

Olsen, M., Crawford-Welch, S. and Tse, E. "The Global Hospitality Industry of the 1990s". In Teare, R. and Boer, A., eds, *Strategic Hospitality Management*. London: Cassel, 1992.

Parasuraman, A., Zeithaml, V. A. and Berry, L. "A Conceptual Model of Service Quality and its Implications for Future Research". *Journal of Marketing*, Vol. 49, Fall 1985.

Peteraf, M. A. "The Cornerstones of Competitive Advantage: A Resource-based View". *Strategic Management Journal*, Vol. 14(3), 1993.

Porter, M. "How Competitive Forces Shape Strategy". *Harvard Business Review*, March–April 1979.

Porter, M. *Competitive Advantage. Creating and Sustaining Superior Performance*. New York: Macmillan, 1985.

Reed, R. and De Filippi, R. J. "Causal Ambiguity, Barriers to Imitation, and Sustainable Competitive Advantage". *Academy of Management Review*, Vol. 15(1), 1990.

Rispoli, M. *Appunti per l'Analisi dello Sviluppo della Jolly Hotels s.p.a.* Venezia: Cafoscarina, 1992.

Rispoli, M. "L'Analisi dell'Ambiente Competitivo". In P. Biffis *et al.*, eds, *Il Governo delle Imprese*. Padova: Cedam, 1992.

Rispoli, M. and Tamma, M. *Le Imprese Alberghiere*. Padova: Cedam, 1991.

Rumelt, R. P., "Diversification Strategy and Profitability". *Strategic Management Journal*, No. 3. 1982.

Sasser, E. W., Olsen, P. R. and Wyckoff, D. D. *Management of Service Operations*. Boston: Alleyn and Bacon, 1978.

Shostack, G. I., "How to Design Service". *European Journal of Marketing*, Vol. 1, 1982.

Slattery, P. "Hotel Branding in the 1990s". *EIU Travel and Tourism Analyst*, No. 1, 1991.

Thomas, D. R. E. "Strategy is Different in Service Business". *Harvard Business Review*, July–August 1978.

Winter, S. G. "Knowledge and Competence as Strategic Assets". In Teece, D. J., ed., *The Competitive Challenge*. Cambridge, MA: Bollinger, 1987.

PART THREE

IDENTIFYING AND BUILDING NEW COMPETENCES

Competitive dynamics within industries result from efforts by firms to create new configurations of assets and capabilities and to find new ways of coordinating deployments of assets and capabilities to provoke a more favorable market response. The chapters in this section investigate the competence building processes of identifying, creating, and acquiring new assets and capabilities.

In Chapter 7, Lewis and Gregory propose a process for identifying the competences a firm has or could develop. This process elicits and makes explicit the perceptions of a firm's employees about the firm's competence. Those perceptions are then evaluated through a "competence sieve" that assesses which competences are shared in common with other industry firms, which are specific to the firm, and what each contributes to the firm's ability to compete in its product markets.

Since in building competence a firm will often have to draw on firm-addressable assets and capabilities outside the boundaries of the firm, the remaining three chapters in this section investigate various efforts of firms to build competence by accessing the assets and capabilities of other firms.

In Chapter 8, Jensen investigates the challenges to competence building faced by small tourism service firms in northern Norway. These firms are representative of many firms (small and large) whose industry structure restricts their access to vital market information and other resources. Jensen discusses ways in which collaborative competence building by competing firms can create "public goods" that enhance the appeal of the products offered by all firms.

In Chapter 9, Easton and Araujo apply an industrial networks approach to analyzing competence building and leveraging. They propose that the "boundaries" of a firm are highly permeable and that interactions between individual actors in different firms facilitate informal exchanges of information and know-how between firms. These exchanges constantly reshape a firm's members' perceptions of their own competence, update their knowledge of useful assets and capabilities, and suggest new ways of organizing and coordinating, all of which contribute to a process of continuous network-based competence building and leveraging.

In Chapter 10, the decision to make, buy, or cooperate in competence building is examined by Elfring and Baven. They investigate the competence-building activities of automobile manufacturers in the knowledge-intensive services of providing management information services for dealers and of developing software for computer-integrated manufacturing. Elfring and Baven describe an evolution of service-providing units through stages of being "spun off" by parent firms and suggest how each stage has distinct possibilities for improved competence-building. Once fully spun-off, knowledge-intensive service providers have opportunities for learning through problem solving for many clients that may synergistically work to the benefit of both the service-providing firm and its clients.

7

DEVELOPING AND APPLYING A PROCESS APPROACH TO COMPETENCE ANALYSIS

M. A. Lewis and M. J. Gregory

INTRODUCTION

As a complement to the majority of strategic analyses (e.g. Porter, 1980) the *resource-based* view of the firm is receiving an increasing amount of attention in the strategy literature. This perspective emphasizes the bundle of tangible and intangible resources on which the firm can draw. There are clear reasons for this resurgence of interest in theories whose roots lie in the works of Schumpeter (1947) and Penrose (1959). For example:

- Growing dissatisfaction with the static, equilibrium framework that underpins most strategy literature. The Porter models take insufficient account of the dynamic aspects of competition when viewed as the deployment and development of resources (Wernerfelt 1984; Barney 1986; Dierickx and Cool 1989);
- Increasingly persuasive examples of successful organizations (e.g. Canon, Honda, 3M, Black and Decker) that appear to have developed strategy around their existing and future resources rather than simply market and competitor analysis. (Prahalad and Hamel 1987, 1989, 1990; Meyer and Utterback 1992);
- Growing recognition that management of R&D, product and process development and human resource management requires an emphasis on building resources over long periods of time and as such need new dynamic theories. (Teece, Pisano and Shuen 1992);
- Driving for efficiency (especially in recession) has forced many companies to reduce their resource base—through outsourcing and simple

reduction of asset levels. The fear that this may damage the long-term survival of an organization has led to a closer examination of the strategic importance of resources (Venkatesan 1992).

Given the apparent importance of the resource-based view in addressing the above issues, very little work has been done in converting theoretical concepts into practical tools to assist managers in formulating strategies for competence building and leveraging. This paper outlines the development and initial application of such a tool.

Much of the relevant work has been done in economics, technology management, and human resource management, and as such a lack of focus is common. With the exception of the dynamic capability's approach (Teece, Pisano and Shuen 1992) there has been little cumulative theory building and empirical work has tended to be in the tradition of econometric formulae and data. If one attempts to define exactly 'what competence is', many definitions seem too broadly based. For example, describing competence as the "collective learning in the organisation" (Prahalad and Hamel 1990) forms a useful starting point for discussions, but lacks the specificity necessary for operationalization.

This paper begins with a broad review of the literature and based upon this, working definitions are proposed. These definitions guide the development of a process, which makes explicit managers' perceptions of a firm's strengths and weaknesses. The process reviews the resources that the firm has access to and those it potentially requires. Customers perspectives are also considered. Each of the elements contribute to an original model of the firm which is intended to aid strategic decision making. The first version of the process was tested at 'Advanced Audio Limited' and the perceived value-adding benefits are described. The paper concludes with a discussion of the theoretical implications of the process and directions for its future development.

COMPETENCE AND CAPABILITY?—A LITERATURE REVIEW

This section discusses the areas of literature that have touched upon the ideas of competence and capability.

> "...research in such areas as management of R&D, product and process development, manufacturing and human resources tend to be quite relevant. Because these fields are normally viewed as outside the traditional boundaries of strategy, much of this research has not been well connected with or incorporated into existing strategy research." (Teece *et al.* 1992)

By collecting together this rather divergent literature, it is possible to review both the common themes and the major differences that exist.

The Resource-Based View of the Firm

The resource-based perspective stresses the achievement of competitive advantage through 'fundamental efficiency advantages of various kinds', emphasizing firm-specific capabilities and assets. It is rooted in work carried out by economists such as Schumpeter and Penrose. The seminal work by Penrose, *The theory of the growth of the firm* (1959) is of particular importance. A firm as defined by Penrose has a 'basic position' that consists of its unique collection of internal productive resources;

> "....the emphasis is on the internal resources of a firm—on the productive services available to a firm from its own resources, particularly the productive services available from management with experience within the firm. It is shown not only that the resources with which a particular firm is accustomed to working will shape the productive services its management is capable of rendering, but also that the experience of management will affect the productive services that all its other resources are capable of rendering." (Penrose 1959: 5)

The importance attached to the influence of management experience (perceptions) should be noted. It is only recently that the perspective was first directly applied to the field of strategy[1] (Rumelt 1984; Wernerfelt 1984) but it is now possible to describe a 'growing body of empirical literature that highlights the importance of firm-specific (and not industry wide) factors in explaining performance' (Cool and Schendel 1988; Jacobson 1988; Hanson and Wernerfelt 1989; Rumelt 1991; Teece *et al.* 1992). In developing strategies to exploit these assets, consideration has been given to their idiosyncratic nature, the links between them and the activities that utilize them (Rumelt 1984). Competence and capability have their roots in this bridge between resource and strategy.

Another concept, that of 'core business' provides a useful context (Teece 1984) for explaining current work on competences and capabilities.

> "In the long run the profitability, survival and growth of a firm does not depend so much on the efficiency with which it is able to organise the production of even a widely diversified range of products as it does on the ability of the firm to establish......wide and relatively impregnable "bases" from which it can adapt and extend its operations in an uncertain, changing and competitive world. It is not the scale of production nor even, within limits, the size of the firm, that are the most important considerations, but rather the basic position it is able to establish for itself." (Penrose 1959: 137)

> "It purports to provide a framework to explain corporate coherence and corporate diversification by developing the concept of a firm's "core business", which in turn is the set of competencies that define a firm's distinctive advantage." (Teece 1988: 66)

Envisaging a 'core business' has major consequences for the firm because it implies that there are naturally embedded restrictions to the selection and development of new competences (Lieberman and Montgomery 1988). With this concept, competences not only define the 'inherent strengths' of a firm but also its boundaries (Leonard-Barton 1992a). A good indication of why this perspective has aroused so much interest is given when considering the impact of technological discontinuities (Teece 1976, 1986, 1988; Nelson and Winter 1982; Dosi, Teece and Winter 1986; Lieberman and Montgomery 1988);

> "Suppose however that the firm experiences a discontinuity in its technological regime that makes its skills obsolete. ... In these circumstances, established firms will lack many of the research competencies needed in the new business environment. However downstream competencies, particularly in sales and distribution, may remain relevant to the new technological regime." (Teece 1989: 68)

One of the most influential contributions, the *dynamic capabilities* approach (Teece *et al.* 1992) considers how firm-specific resources transform into competences and capabilities. Many factors[2] are influential in the evolution of competences, but the role of firm-history is highlighted as critical (Nelson and Winter 1982). This clearly suggests that competences must be viewed in dynamic terms and therefore be governed by dynamic capabilities.[3] Their foundations lie in three areas: how the firm learns new skills; the forces both external and internal that constrain and focus the learning process; and the environment in which the firm competes for resources as well as for customers. The dynamic capabilities perspective is especially important for operationalization because of its emphasis upon developing clear definitions.

Manufacturing/Operations Management

Hayes and Wheelwright (1979) defined "Competence" as a patch around the point where the product and process structures intersect on their product-process matrix[4] and described "Distinctive Competence...as a notion that each company should identify and exploit those resources, skills and organisational characteristics that give it a comparative advantage over its competitors." They view competence (Cleveland, Schroeder and Anderson 1989) as being potentially the "elusive...linkage between strategy and production operations" (Skinner 1969).

Corporate Strategic Management

> "The capability of an organisation is its demonstrated and potential ability to accomplish against the opposition of circumstance or competition, whatever it sets out to do. Every organisation has actual and potential strengths and weaknesses; it is important to try and determine what they are and to distinguish one from the other." (Learned *et al.* 1969)

Perhaps the earliest relevant definition describes distinctive competences as sets of unique capabilities and values possessed by certain organizations (Selznick 1949). More recently, literature describing the ideas of competence and capability as a new paradigm has aroused a great deal of interest. Based upon persuasive anecdotal examples,[5] these works (Prahalad and

Hamel 1989, 1990, 1991, 1992; Stalk 1992) attempt to describe the methods that organizations (Canon, Komatsu, Coca-Cola etc.) used to achieve global leadership.

Strategies (and hence the managers that develop them) that can create core competencies, are portrayed as the key to corporate success (Prahalad and Hamel 1991; Ross 1991; LaFrance and Doutriaux 1991). This work introduces the ideas into the arena of corporate strategy, thus providing a vision of their potential for senior management.

> "While ... [Prahalad and Hamel] ... provide no methods to measure their concept[s], nor do they present data, their case illustrations are nonetheless compelling, calling forth firms such as 3M, Black and Decker, Honda, NEC and Canon that sustain world brand recognition by exploiting their respective core competencies." (Meyer and Utterback 1992)

The Management of Technology and Innovation

Problems in the development of new products and processes offer a representation of the larger problems associated with the maintenance, renewal and change of core capabilities (Dorothy Leonard-Barton 1992a). *Core capability* is here defined as the 'knowledge set that distinguishes and provides competitive advantage'. It is given four dimensions: employee knowledge and skills; technical systems; managerial systems and; the firms' values and norms. This fourth dimension re-emphasizes the role of managerial experience and perception first highlighted by Penrose (Winterscheid 1994). An examination of sustained success in new product development (Meyer and Utterback 1992) has led to another definition for core competence—'those skills and assets that exist in a firm that result in actual products and services delivered in chosen markets'.

> "For each product, the product team receives varying degrees of "inputs" in the form of the four components of core competence. ... In the course of developing the product, the team either adds value to these competencies, or creates new competencies in each respective area." (Meyer and Utterback 1992)

Human Resource Management

> "Human resource management can be best conceptualised as the process of analysing an organisation's human resource needs under changing conditions and developing the activities necessary to satisfy these needs." (Sparrow 1992)

Studies of strategic change describe it as a learning process (Whipp 1991; Leonard-Barton 1992b). Others claim that the ability to learn faster than competitors may be the only sustainable advantage (deGeus 1988). The idea that "...the ability of the organisation to reconstruct and adapt its knowledge base (skills, structures and values) should be a key task for managers" (Whipp 1991) strikes a chord with the idea of leveraging resources that is at the heart of competences. In reviewing the various HRM models of competence[6] it becomes apparent that they also suffer from problems of variance in definition.

There is a growing link between the strategy literature that emphasizes *learning*, *competence* and *skills-based competition* and work by HRM practitioners (Sparrow 1992). Corporate skills have been described as strategic combinations of individual (human) competencies, hard organizational factors (such as equipment and facilities) and soft organizational factors (such as culture and organization design) (Klein, Edge and Kass 1991). Methodologies exist that potentially allow HRM competency-based approaches to be integrated into strategy formulation and one such approach, the 'competence life-cycle' perspective (Sparrow 1992) reinforces the importance of considering the dynamic nature of competencies.

Implications for the Operational Process

Five main conclusions can be drawn from this brief review of the relevant literature:

1. Competence (and capability) clearly have their theoretical roots in the bridge between resources (defined very broadly) and strategy. They are currently being used as ways of explaining firm success, growth, failure etc. and as such might offer great potential for exploitation as practical models to help managers.
2. The importance of considering the dynamic nature of both resources and strategy, dictates that any analysis of competences must also include a time dimension. This is especially true if the impact of "learning through doing" (i.e. routinization) is to be assessed.
3. Any analytical process developed will build upon managers' own perceptions and experiences of the firm. This necessitates consideration of the social psychology of organizations.
4. The diverse sources of the literature has meant that the field lacks cumulative theory building. There is a clear need for a consistent terminology if any operationalization is to be attempted. The table overleaf summarizes the 'key' definitions from the literature and presents a set of working definitions that will form the heart of the analytical process.
5. There is a lack of practical application and empirical evidence to support the theorizing.

   "Further theoretical work is needed to tighten the framework, and empirical research is critical to helping us understand how firms get to be good, how they sometimes stay that way and how they sometimes decline." (Teece *et al.* 1992)

The following section will outline the application of a practical competence

Table 7.1.

Economics -Teece et al. 1992	Competence - when firm-specific assets are assembled into integrated clusters spanning individuals & groups enabling distinctive activities to be performed.	Core competence - those critical to a firms survival. Should be derived with due reference to opportunities & threats facing the firm.	Distinctive competence - the differentiated skills, assets and organisational routines which allow a firm to co-ordinate activies that provide the basis for competitive advantage in particular market (s).	Dynamic Capability - the capacity of a firm to renew, augment and adapt its core competences over time. Capabilities thus reflect the firm's latent competences.
Corporate Strategic Management -Prahalad & Hamel 1990	Competencies - the collective learning in the organisation, especially how to co-ordinate diverse production skills & integrate multiple streams of technology.	Core competencies - 'source of competitive advantage. 3 qualifying tests; Access to wide variety of markets; contributes towards perceived customer benefits; is difficult for competitors to imitate.		
Management of Technology (learning) -Leonard-Barton 1992		Core capability - the *knowledge set* that distinguishes and provides competitive advantage. Identifies 4 dimensions.		
Human Resource Management -Sparrow et al. 1992	Competencies - should be viewed as behavioural repertoires which some people carry out better than others.	Core competences - those that remain important to a firm. It is these competencies that provide continuity.		Transitional Competencies - those not currently important, not implied by the strategic plan, but change may only be implemented through their greater emphasis.
Working definitions	Competence - those activities which a company recognises as containing its *unique* resources	Core competences - those competences that management perceive as of central importance to the company's *goals and strategy*.	Distinctive competences - those competences that are recognised by the market and hence provide the basis for the organisations competitive advantage in a market or markets.	

analysis process, developed with the intention of being both useful to the firm and to further research in this area.

THE COMPETENCE ANALYSIS PROCESS

This section describes a practical approach to competence analysis. Intended to be of use to both practitioners and researchers, it begins by building a graphical model of firm activities and resources. This provides a framework for evaluating and making explicit managerial perceptions of firm competences. The understanding generated is intended to provide the management team with the ability to link considerations of competence into business strategy (i.e. competence building and leveraging). The process is composed of four stages and data are collected using interviews and questionnaires— with regular review sessions to improve validity and avoid obvious omissions.

Development Criteria

In attempting to provide a tool of practical value to managers, it was necessary to use interviews/discussions with managers and consultants, in order to assess best practice and current needs. In addition, the process was developed against the criteria that, in general, a good process should:

- Be definable, repeatable and reliable.
- Be viable—having some self-checking elements and include feedback and control loops for assessment and evolution.
- Be efficient in terms of resources used.
- Be visible, transparent and easily understood.

When developing a practical aid to decision-making, it is important to consider how people process information, consider problems and what will be most effective in aiding these processes. The power of pictures and diagrams to convey multi-dimensional quantitative and qualitative information has been clearly demonstrated (Tufte 1983, 1990). In the management cognition literature several visual techniques are available, although these have all been developed for a specific purpose (Huff and Fletcher 1990; Eden 1990). Huff and Fletcher (1990) suggest clear design steps for a 'cognitive map'; definition of purpose; territory to be covered; features to be included; the data source; and the context. The guidelines were expanded to also include; tidiness (Klein 1993). In developing a model for firm activities and resources, these design criteria have been respected.

There is also an important aspect of cognition that relates more specifically to competence analysis. Penrose (1959) recognized the role of individual perception and experience in shaping the strategic resources of the firm, but since then, the role of the individuals who actually enact strategy has often been ignored (Winterscheid 1994)—this can probably be explained by the normative, economics perspective of most of the relevant works. In developing a process approach, heavily reliant upon managers' own perceptions, the importance of individual cognition is addressed.

In reviewing the application of the process, each phase of the method and its case results will be described separately.

The Research Environment—Advanced Audio Limited

Advanced Audio Ltd[7] is a UK-based, privately owned, low-volume, consumer electronics company. Founded in the 1970's, it began by manufacturing solid-state hi-fi amplifiers to order. The company earned a reputation for offering well built, value for money equipment with excellent sound quality. The firm grew steadily and using their experience of the relevant technology and markets, gradually broadened their product range. Today Advanced Audio employs approximately 150 people and has retail sales in excess of £10 million. Over one third of the sales go to export markets. 80% of total sales (and gross profit) comes from amplifiers and compact disc players, but the product range also includes tuners, loudspeakers and an analogue cassette deck. In the UK. 90% of quality hi-fi sales are through independent specialist dealers, and Advanced Audio sells all its products through such intermediaries.

The impact of recession has forced the firm to consider its future plans in a more systematic way than ever before. This has led to a rationalization of its product range, and the introduction of quality and concurrent engineering practices. Given the nature and size of the company, its owner-directors and the management team as a whole, felt that they knew the company and its resources extremely well. Figure 7.1 illustrates the different elements of the process.

Method: Phase I—Activity and Resource Analysis

The first phase of the process, is intended to identify (and model) the firm's activities and constituent resources. Using structured interviews, the goal is to develop a common model of the firm, and in order to do this, the following three distinct elements are addressed:

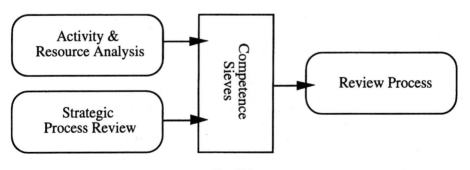

Fig. 7.1.

- Firstly, a picture of the generic (top-level) activities within the firm is drawn—attention is paid to how people perceive activities interacting. These pictures are later amalgamated into an overall representation of the firm.
- Secondly, using further structured interviews, the top-level activities are decomposed into more detail. Each interviewee is asked to compare the activities they have described against the metrics shown in Table 7.2.
- Finally, the resources associated with different activities are examined by asking each interviewee to consider the three categories described in Table 7.3.

This categorization is intended to broaden the interviewees' perception of what might be considered a resource. They are then compared against a further set of metrics (see Table 7.4).

These metrics are intended to describe aspects of resource "uniqueness" and are drawn from the *resource-based* literature (Dierickx and Cool 1989; Grant 1991; Amit and Schoemaker 1993). Early fieldwork[8] revealed that simple discussions of which firm resources were unique proved confusing and did not address issues of strategic relevance. The intention in providing a series of dimensions is to allow people to consider the concept in broader terms. It should be highlighted however that an important research interest in this first application of the process was to investigate the suitability of the different metrics. A brief discussion of this can be found in the conclusions.

Table 7.2.

Activity Metric	Description
Importance	The importance to the firm & the general activity—now & in the future
Performance	The performance of firm & *best practice* competitor—now & in the future
Imitability	The "uniqueness" of an activity—comprising the following:
Transparency	The visibility of an activity to competitors—important for protection
Transferability	Could a competitor buy this activity into his/her business
Replicability	Could a competitor—through investment—develop this activity.

Table 7.3.

Resources	Description
Tangible	i.e. machines, software, hardware etc.
Skill/Knowledge/Experience	human resources, intangible.
Management Routines	reward, supervision systems etc.

Table 7.4.

Resource Metric	Description
Scarcity	The degree to which demand exceeds supply for a particular resource—in particular competitive circumstances a high scarcity measure may make a resource unique, especially if it has a low imitability measure.
Imitability	"Uniqueness" of resource—inc. transparency, transferability, replicability. Clearly if a resource is unique but can be easily identified as so & then easy to acquire/copy, this is potentially less useful in a competitive environment.
Durability	A measure of the useful life of the resource. A resource may be truly unique but if it will only have a short effective life then it is no good making long term strategic plans around it.
Retention	The degree of ownership that the firm can exercise over the resource. Closely linked with the above measure, this is intended to reveal any formal controls that a firm might possess. i.e. patents etc.
Codification	How much is/can be written down?—an indication of "understandability" this is linked to imitability and retention. If a company "understands" a resource this may make it easier to redeploy in different activities.
Embodiment	Identifying who actually embodies the resource (knowledge, skill etc.)? This is important for identifying key personnel and again adjusting strategic plans accordingly.
Importance	The importance to the firm & the activity. Finally after considering all the above measures, each participant is asked to assess importance. This is important in making explicit managerial (mis)perceptions!

The output of phase 1 is a model, based upon a series of charts, that represent firm activities and resources. These charts have two important features:

- A hierarchical structure which denotes 'level of detail'. Level 0 represents the generic, top-level of activity, and the subsequent levels offer increasing detail. This is intended to enable the firm-specific resources identified, to be viewed in the context of the firms activities as a whole.
- A key, based upon the importance and performance of the activity in question and the "uniqueness" of its associated resources. The different elements will be highlighted in phase 3—the competence sieve—to indicate the activities (high importance and high performance) and resources ("unique") that form competences. As an example of the visualization, the Advanced Audio quality activities are illustrated in Fig. 7.2.

It must be stressed that the maps are not intended to prescribe solutions to problems, but rather to promote the processes of articulating and exploring individual and group knowledge (Weick 1990). These diagrams

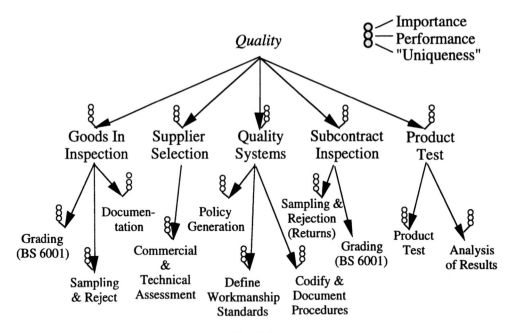

Fig. 7.2.

form the basis for the first review session, where people's concerns over the data could lead to further data collection if necessary.

Case Study Data: Phase 1—Activity and Resource Analysis

At Advanced Audio structured interviews were held with 11 people—the directors, the management team, and staff from service, accounts and personnel. It was remarked that the data appeared quite functionally based—as the production manager pointed out;

> "...we are good at flexibility, that's an important resource, how do you represent that?"

It was argued that such "synergy" should hopefully be revealed in phase 2—the strategic process review. The resource and activity model is not the analysis, but is intended at this stage to act as a framework for 'holding the data', and guiding discussions.

Revealing the unique resources associated with their different activities highlighted the central role played by market knowledge in the company. This represented a tangible representation of what the management had tacitly understood to be their strength. The data set was agreed (with one or two minor omissions highlighted) and the top-level company diagram provided the focus for some extended debate amongst the managers about their internal communications—especially with the service department.

Method: Phase 2—Strategic Process Review

The second phase explores the internal "environment" of the firm. Three different elements are examined: (i) business planning processes, (ii) company goals, and (iii) company strategy for achieving those goals. Two questionnaires are used to collect the data

- The business planning processes questionnaire (Mintzberg 1983; Francis 1989) draws simple conclusions about the type of organization being examined. It requires participants to assess the validity of a series of statements as they relate to their business.
- The strategy and goals are derived using a more 'open-ended' questionnaire, requiring people to provide commentary. This information is backed up by interview in phase 3.

As with the first phase, these results are then subject to review by all the participants.

Case Study Data: Phase 2—Strategic Process Review

At Advanced Audio, the same 11 people completed this stage as had completed the first:

(i)   Business Planning Processes
Despite confusion over the language employed in the first questionnaire, some interesting results emerged. Broadly speaking, Advanced Audio fell into the category of firm known as an Adhocracy.[9]

> "This is a creative, flexible, informal and expert form of organisation. ... Bureaucracy, formalisation, systems and the like are kept to a minimum. There is much emphasis on open communication." (Francis 1989 based on Mintzberg 1983)

This also reinforced the impression that the management team had all expressed informally—namely that although they found themselves needing increasingly to systematize and plan more formally, they wanted to retain the drive, vision and flexibility of a smaller, more entrepreneurial company.

(ii) Goals
The firm has a stated objective, "to be the leading player in the high quality domestic audio electronics business in the UK and Europe". This was fairly well understood across the company—although not always expressed in exactly the same terms. All participants referred to the impact of the recession and talked of the need to temper all their goals with the condition that "the company must always be successful in business terms".

(iii) Strategy
The strategy consistently highlighted was one of continuing to develop

quality product, backed by an effective dealer/service network. The strategy would appear to reflect a relatively good understanding of the needs of their current market, however more time could be spent on the detail of the strategy—especially how it will impact the different areas of the company. This seems particularly important for the operations function, when considering how their growth strategy will affect production volumes, materials flow etc. It also became clear that (not surprisingly) the owner-directors of the company have the greatest responsibility for strategy.

Smaller organizations such as Advanced Audio do not often have a great deal of time to spend on strategy formulation and goal setting. In this context, phase 2 permitted them to articulate and discuss these areas, and then compare perceptions across the management team. This was felt to have been of great value, especially as the managers perceive themselves as increasingly requiring more formal planning procedures.

> "It helped crystallise ideas and objectives which we had realised needed to be done" (Sales Manager)

Method: Phase 3—Competence Sieves

In sieving for competences, the data from the first two phases is used as an input into a series of interviews, both internal and external to the company. The working definitions form the basis for this analysis, giving two criteria for competence;

- the "unique" resource must be active, i.e., form part of an activity within the organization (phase one should highlight this).

  > "Strictly speaking, it is never *resources* themselves that are the 'inputs' in the production process, but only the *services* that the resources can render ... the very word 'service' implying a function, an activity." (Penrose 1959: 25)

- the "uniqueness" should in *some* way be recognized—not necessarily in terms of competences, but perhaps in terms of strengths, special/key elements, differentiators etc.
- A provisional list of *competences* is then be developed.
- This list is compared with the strategy and goals identified earlier. The competences that are perceived by the participants as being of central importance to their *strategic intent* are classified as *core competences*.
- Finally, the company's customers are asked to identify the firms strengths, uniqueness etc. The procedure is the same as for the first competence sieve—except that this time the competences are externally recognized and hence *distinctive*. External perspectives on firm competence will clearly be surrounded by causal ambiguity, but with this consideration in mind, it is still essential that market considerations are used as a "reality check" on the process.

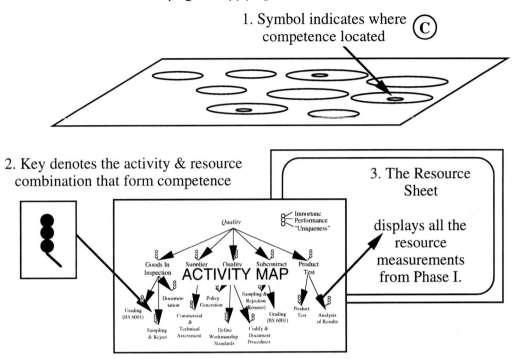

Fig. 7.3. Mapping the competences in the business.

A company competence "map" is drawn by tying together this new data and the activity and resource model drawn in phase 1. Such a map is intended to facilitate both top-level review of the data (i.e. "Where are our competences?") and also any more detailed examination that may be required. An exmaple is given in Figure 7.3.

Case Study Data: Phase 3—Competence Sieves

(i)   Competence

- The competences derived were very close to the lists of "strengths" perceived by the management team. This may simply reflect the generic findings of the organization type questionnaire ("... there is much emphasis on open communication ...") suggesting that in this relatively entrepreneurial organization, the management team is very close to all the activities and resources. Further discussion of these findings can be found in the section describing the Phase 4 review.
- Most of Advanced Audio's unique resources were related in some way to market knowledge and the application of this knowledge in key functions (e.g. design, marketing, materials etc.) This may reflect the *market following* nature of their business. As the design and development manager remarked;

"...we are waiting and watching carefully for the next big digital medium to become apparent ... like with compact disc ... we don't want to jump too soon ... "

(ii)   Core Competence

The issues surrounding *core* competence were more interesting to the firm. It was here that the issues linking strategy and resources became very clear. Identifying and analysing core competence starts to address fundamental questions such as "If we are to enact this strategy—what are the competences that we need to create and/or develop?"

- Advanced Audio has a number of core competences, but none which relate to areas outside of assessing market knowledge. This probably reflects a very good understanding of the differentiators in their current markets.
- In discussion it became clear that if their current growth strategy is to be successful, it will be necessary for the firm to develop other core competences, for example in export sales.

(iii) Distinctive Competence

Finally, interviews were arranged with two of Advanced Audio's dealers (it must be reiterated that all of Advanced Audio's sales are through dealers—hence they are the company's direct customers). The question of distinctive competence is crucial, as it is here that the roots of marketplace advantage can be found. The slightly unusual situation of the dealer-supplier relationships in this industry, may have meant that the results were slightly unrepresentative (and it might have been useful to visit non-Advanced Audio dealers to seek their opinions).

- The results that emerged from the dealers interviews, reinforced those from the internal management interviews. Clearly the information was not as representative, but those elements highlighted by the management team as being distinctive were also those that the dealers selected. Of course, this may also reflect a competence in developing dealer relationships.

The drawing of the competence map produced some of the most interesting results. Based upon the unique resource analysis, it soon became clear that although seemingly a technological company, they had no real competences built simply upon technology. This seemed a little counter-intuitive, but hopefully demonstrates the importance of collecting the detailed data before assessing the competences. If this had not been done, the company's design competences might have been attributed to unique technical resources rather than technological and market knowledge.

Method: Phase 4—The Review Process

The final phase of the process—the review—is split into two stages;

- The first involves a workshop session where all aspects of the project—results, implications, conduct etc. were discussed. This provides essential feedback for the development of the process itself and also in validating the data generated.
- The second stage is potentially the most interesting—both for the company and the researcher. In developing a competence map, we are able to review the data over time and hence establish how it has changed. This may ultimately lead us to an understanding of the dynamics of the company.

Case Study Data: Phase 4—The Review Process

The final review session aimed to bring together all the information collected during the process and offer the results for discussion. The discussion raised many points both about the results and the process itself. Several important issues were raised:

- It was felt that overall the process had been a success. The management expressed interest in both the process elements and the data generated. The stimulation provided by discussing strategy and resources with someone external to the organization was viewed as beneficial.
- Several elements of the process were seen as very interesting. A top-level activity chart, made up from all the individual pictures drawn by the management team in phase 1, was discussed at length. No formal technique was employed, and this may be an issue to be addressed in reviewing the process structure.
- In general, the overall competence results were not seen as very surprising. This is probably because of the size and nature of the company—as one manager observed:

  "... then we are a pretty self aware company anyway, so perhaps this is not surprising."

  However, when the link into strategy was discussed, i.e. what are we going to need to develop, change modify, in order to reach our goals, much interest was aroused. This use of the process, as a type of "gap analysis" may prove to be one of its strongest benefits.
- When discussing the metrics, and their validity, the subject of benchmarking was raised several times. It clearly is very important (in general and specifically for the process) because without an adequate picture of how activities/resources perform relative to competitors, it is difficult to assess them critically.

BENEFITS OF THE PROCESS

The primary goal of this work was to develop an analytical tool that could provide value-adding benefits in the context of strategy formulation. This leads us to ask, just how useful did the process prove to be? The identifiable (explicit) benefits are divided into two categories:

- The first category, **direct** benefits, contain those that were envisaged in developing the competence analysis process.
- The second group, the **indirect** benefits relate to those accrued through the application of some of the research methods in different stages of the process.

The assessment of the benefits is based upon direct observations from the different review sessions during the process and the final workshop. To compliment these observations a post-process questionnaire sought to establish 'before and after' perspectives for the process and its outputs (content).

Direct Benefits—A Process Approach

A process approach to strategic problem solving is arguably more beneficial than traditional "expert" analysis of a business. Some of the important justifications (and hence benefits) of this approach (Schein 1969) are as follows:

1. All that is required for the process to begin is intent on the part of someone in the organization to improve the way things are going.
2. Most organizations can be more effective if they learn to diagnose their own strengths and weaknesses.
3. A researcher could probably not, without exhaustive and time-consuming study, learn enough about the culture of an organization to suggest reliable new courses of action. Therefore, he/she must work jointly with members of the organization.
4. The management team must learn to see a problem for itself, share in the diagnosis, and be actively involved in generating solutions and an important role of the process is to provide new and challenging alternatives to consider. The decision-making about these alternatives must, however, remain in the hands of the management team.

Direct Benefits—The Resource and Competence Analysis

The goal of this ongoing research is to encourage consideration of competence building and competence leveraging during strategy formulation. It was the intention that by adopting a process approach to identifying competences (as described by the working definitions) a clearer understanding of the importance (and complexity) of resources and strategy would emerge. Although difficult to gauge;

"Without controlled testing how can one have confidence that the process is valid?" (Platts 1993)

the post-process questionnaire examined participants' perceptions of the purpose of the process and its actual utility. All respondents identified "examining resources and strategy" as a primary benefit of the process, and all rated the results as "good or very good" (on a scale of one to five, with very good as a five). When asked to assess participation, all respondents rated the process as "worth or well worth doing" (same five point scale).

Direct Benefits—Developing a Unified Model of the Company

The cognition literature argues (Eden 1988; Huff and Fletcher 1990; Weick 1990) that strategic decision making is facilitated through the development and application of external models that to as great an extent as possible reflect the internal cognitive models possessed by the managers (Klein 1993). This is also backed up by the "commonsensical" notion of agreement or "buy-in" to the content of what is being considered. The very nature of the process approach—means that all the models are developed through group discussion of the data.

Direct Benefits—Building/Leveraging Competences for New Products/Markets

Advanced Audio is in the process of developing a new product:

- The firm is aware that the overall audio market is shrinking. It has plans to exploit its knowledge of compact disc data-storage technology by producing a new product and moving into a new market segment. Given the design knowledge of the company, assessing the technological requirements of the new product is relatively simple. However, the analysis indicated that the firms' competence in product development lies in the ability to interpret market information and generate products accordingly.

  "We stock Advanced Audio because it sells ... they know what the customer wants" (Audio dealer)

- Advanced Audio's other competences reinforce this perspective. A distinct market position is maintained through a comprehensive understanding of its segment of the quality audio market. The dealer network may not be able to (or want to) cope with a different product and this could in turn damage the main product range.
- The value of having a picture of the firms competences now becomes clearer. The goal of moving into a new market might be more easily realized if the competence issues highlighted by the analysis are considered in the new product strategy. An understanding of both

resource limitations (e.g. underdeveloped dealer expertise?) and resource advantages (e.g. technological design knowledge) will help strategy formulation and implementation.

Indirect Benefits

These benefits are clearly non-generalizable, but provide an interesting *plus point* for using a process approach. For example at Advanced Audio, the phase 1 descriptions of how different activities interact, revealed the need for better communications with the service department. Subsequent to these discussions, service were brought into the concurrent engineering process. It quickly became known that the service engineer had over the last 3/4 years developed his own database of service returns, analysing faults and repairs information. The immediate impact of this data on the C.E. process was clearly beneficial.

IMPLICATIONS OF THE WORK

So, what implications does this application of a competence analysis process have? Clearly a single case cannot prove or disprove the validity of the process, but the results described can generate interesting hypotheses for both the theory and practice of competence-based strategy.

Implications for Theory

1. The literature review demonstrated that there is a problem in the field with consistency of definitions. This study revealed that in operationalizing the concepts, there appears to be a trade-off between utility/clarity and 'breadth' of definition. The worry that we may not be operationalizing the most important aspects of competence, those that relate to the long-term growth and survival of a firm, is an important debate that needs to be pursued both through further theoretical and empirical study.
2. There is clear evidence of the importance of managerial perceptions/experience in making decisions for the future. It has been suggested that new product development involves primarily, consideration of technical issues—isolated from their potential organizational effects (Winterscheid 1994). Advanced Audio's product development plans revolve almost exclusively around the technical (i.e. design and manufacture) problems of bringing a new product to market, despite the acknowledged importance of broader, non-technical factors to the company (i.e. the nature of their dealer network). Consideration of such cognitive issues must form a central theme in future competence theory.

Implications for Practice

3. The development of working definitions necessitated an examination of what exactly competence is. The concepts are rooted in theory that

attempts to explain corporate coherence, diversification, success, failure, growth etc. In such theory the idea of tying together firm resources and strategy is clearly very important. The Advanced Audio case shows that the concept can also be practically useful/relevant for managers. This proved to be especially true in providing the management team with the ability to add consideration of competence building and leveraging into their strategy formulation process.

Implications for Research

4. Findings from the Advanced Audio case reinforce a research suggestion made by Penrose:

> "A firm is basically a collection of resources ... The effort to discover more about the productive services of a resource may take the form of research into its characteristics or of research into ways of combining its known characteristics with those of other resources." (Penrose 1959: 77)

The characteristics of firm resources are examined in this process by assessing the different dimensions of uniqueness. However the idea of investigating different ways of combining resources (their mobility?) is something that the participants of this study felt would have been of great benefit. In pursuing this idea, the process (and the root definitions) will develop from the concept of resource "uniqueness" towards the idea of a "strategic resource" that assesses potential for recombination.

5. Reviewing the case study helps to indicate what modifications are needed to improve the process. More case studies are needed to refine and improve the process fully, especially in trying to reduce the impact of contingent factors (type of company, culture, industry, facilitator, etc.).

To conclude, it is important to return to the original justifications for developing a practical approach to competence analysis. If we accept the fundamental value and importance attached to the concepts of competence, then practically based work such as this is essential. Managers, seeking to develop strategies to compete in an ever-changing environment need practical tools to help them make complex competence related decisions, and researchers require further empirical evidence to build theoretical work upon.

POSTSCRIPT

Since the completion of this initial case study, five further case studies have been completed in different industrial sectors; automotive and aerospace.[10] Following each of the studies, the process has been developed in order to improve its "usefulness" to both the business under study and the researcher. The "strategic resource" concept (outlined earlier) was formally included and more emphasis placed upon competence building/leveraging issues with the identification of *potential* competences.

NOTES

1. Unfortunately this means that many of the earlier works can seem rather narrow in perspective. Much of the terminology employed may be inaccessible to non-specialists.
2. Porter (1990) argued that differences in local product markets, local factor markets, and institutions play an important role in shaping competitive capabilities.
3. Compare these with the "dynamic routines" as described by Nelson and Winter, 1982.
4. See Hayes, R. H., and Wheelwright, S. C. "Link manufacturing process and product life cycles". *Harvard Business Review*, Vol. 57 (1), pp. 133–142, 1979.
5. This reliance upon anecdotal evidence is potentially a weakness as it seems simply to represent a post-rationalist justification for why some companies have succeeded. For a review of the dangers of post-rationalizing events, see "The Honda Effect", Richard T. Pascale, in Mintzberg, H. and Quinn, J.B., eds, *The Strategy Process—Concepts and Contexts*. Prentice-Hall, pp. 114–123, 1992.
6. Sparrow (1992) provides an excellent review of many of these models.
7. For reasons of confidentiality, the real name of the company cannot be used.
8. A series of interviews and studies were carried out at eight UK manufacturing firms prior to this study. The fieldwork examined the viability of the working definitions and elements of the process.
9. Realistically firms cannot be so neatly categorized, and this is not the intention of the questionnaire. It intends simply to provide focus/provocation for subsequent discussion about the nature of the firm.
10. See Lewis and Gregory (1994).

REFERENCES

Amit, R. and Schoemaker, P. J. H. "Strategic Assets and Organisational Rent". *Strategic Management Journal*, Vol. 14, pp. 33–46, 1993.

Barney, J. B. "Strategic Factor Markets: Expectations, Luck and Business Strategy". *Management Science*, pp. 1231–1241, October 1986.

Cleveland, G., Schroeder, R. G. and Anderson, J. C. "A Theory of Production Competence". *Decision Sciences*, Vol. 20, pp. 655–668, 1989.

Cool, K. and Schendel, D. "Performance Differences among Strategic Group Members". *Strategic Management Journal*, No. 9, pp. 207–224, 1988.

deGeus, A. "Planning as Learning". *Harvard Business Review*, pp. 70–74, March–April 1988.

Dierickx, I. and Cool, K. "Asset Stock Accumulation and Sustainability of Competitive Advantage". *Management Science*, pp. 1504–1511, December 1989.

Eden, C. "Strategic Thinking with Computers". *Long Range Planning*, Vol. 23(6), pp. 35–43, 1990.

Francis, D. *50 Activities for Unblocking Organisational Communications*. Gower Publishing Ltd, 1989.

Grant, R. M. "The Resource Based Theory of Competitive Advantage: Implications for Strategy Formulation". *California Management Review*, pp. 114–135, Spring 1991.

Hansen, G. S. and Wernerfelt, B. "Determinants of Firm Performance: The Relative

Importance of Economic and Organizational Factors". *Strategic Management Journal*, No. 10, pp. 399–411, 1989.

Hayes, R. H. and Wheelwright, S. C. "Link Manufacturing Processes and Product Life-Cycles". *Harvard Business Review*, pp. 133–142, January–February 1979.

Hayes, R. H, Wheelwright, S. C. and Clark, K. *Dynamic Manufacturing: Creating the Learning Organization*. New York: Free Press, 1988.

Hitt, M. A. and Ireland, R. D. "Relationships Among Corporate Level Distinctive Competences, Diversification Strategy, Corporate Structure and Performance". *Journal of Management Studies*, Vol. 23(4), pp. 401–415, 1986.

Huff, A. S. and Fletcher, K. E. "Conclusion: Key Mapping Decisions". In Huff A. S., ed., *Mapping Strategic Thought*. Chicester: Wiley, 1990.

Itami, H. and Roehl, T. *Mobilizing Invisible Assets*. Cambridge, MA: Harvard University Press, 1987.

Jacobson, R. "The Persistence of Abnormal Returns". *Strategic Management Journal*, No. 9, pp. 41–58, 1988.

Klein, J. H. "Cognitive Science and Development of Decision-Aiding Methods". Working Paper Presented at EIASM Workshop on Managerial Cognition, Belgium, May 1993.

Klein, J., Edge, G. and Kass, T. "Skill-Based Competition". *Journal of General Management*, Vol. 16(4), pp. 1–15, 1991.

Lafrance, M. and Doutriaux, J. "Sustained Success Through the Management of Core Competencies: An Empirical Analysis". Conference proceedings, PICMET, pp. 141–144, 1991.

Learned, E. C., Christensen, C., Andrewa, K. and Guth, W. *Business Policy: Text and Cases*. Homewood, IL: R. Irwin, 1969.

Leonard-Barton, D. "The Factory as a Learning Laboratory". Working Paper No. 92–023, *Harvard Business School*, 1992a.

Leonard-Barton, D. "Core Capabilities and Core Rigidities: A Paradox in Managing New Product Development". *Strategic Management Journal*, No. 13, pp. 111–125, 1992b.

Lewis, M. A. and Gregory, M. J. "Developing a Practical Procedure for Competence Analysis". Working Papers in Manufacturing, Nos 94–02, Cambridge University, 1994.

Lieberman, M. and Montgomery, D. B. "First-Mover Advantages". *Strategic Management Journal*, No. 9, pp. 41–58, Summer 1988.

Meyer, H. and Utterback, J. "Core Competencies, Product Families and Sustained Business Success". Working Paper No. 3410-92, *Sloan School of Management*, February 1992.

Mintzberg, H. *Structuring in Fives, Designing Effective Organisations*. Englewood Cliffs: Prentice-Hall, 1983.

Nelson, R. and Winter, S. *An Evolutionary Theory of Economic Change*. Cambridge, MA: Harvard University Press, 1982.

Penrose, E. T. *Theory of the Growth of the Firm*. London: Basil Blackwell, 1959.

Platts, K. W. "A Process Approach to Researching Manufacturing Strategy". *International Journal of Operations Management*, Vol. 14(8), 1993.

Porter, M. E. *Competitive Strategy*. New York: Free Press, 1980.

Prahalad, C. K. and Hamel, G. "Strategic Intent". *Harvard Business Review*, pp. 63–76 (Reprint No. 89308), May–June 1989.

Prahalad, C. K. and Hamel, G. "The Core Competence of the Corporation". *Harvard Business Review,* pp. 79–91 (Reprint No. 90311), May–June 1990.

Ross, B. N. "Managing R&D as an Opportunity Centre", Conference Proceedings, PICMET, pp. 149-152, 1991.

Rumelt, R. P. "Towards a Strategic Theory of the Firm". In Lamb, R. B., ed., *Competitive Strategic Management.* Englewood Cliffs, NJ: Prentice-Hall, pp. 566–570, 1984.

Rumelt, R. P. "How Much Does Industry Matter?". *Strategic Management Journal,* No. 12, pp. 167–185, 1991.

Schein, E. H. *Process Consultation,* Reading, MA: Addison-Wesley, 1969.

Schoemaker, P. J. H. "Strategic Decisions in Organizations: Rational and Behavioural Views". *Journal of Management Studies,* Vol. 30(1), pp. 107–129, January 1993.

Schumpeter, J. A. *Capitalism, Socialism and Democracy,* New York: Harper, 1942.

Selznick, P. *Leadership in Administration: A Sociological Interpretation.* New York: Harper and Row, 1957.

Skinner, W. "Manufacturing-Missing Link in Corporate Strategy". *Harvard Business Review,* pp. 136–145, May-June 1969.

Sparrow, P. "Building Human Resource Strategies around Competencies: A Life Cycle Model". Working Paper No. 235, *Manchester Business School,* August 1992.

Stalk, G., Evans, P. and Shulman, L. "Competing on Capabilities: The New Rules of Corporate Strategy". *Harvard Business Review,* pp. 57–69 (Reprint No. 92209), March–April 1992.

Teece, D. J. *The Multinational Corporation and the Resource Cost of International Technology Transfer.* Cambridge MA: Ballinger, 1976.

Teece, D. J. "Economic Analysis and Strategic Management". *California Management Review,* pp. 87–110, Spring 1984.

Teece, D. J. "Profiting from Technological Innovation". *Research Policy,* December 1986.

Teece, D. J. "Technological Change and the Nature of the Firm". In Dosi, G. *et al.,* eds, *Technical Change and Economic Theory.* London: Pinter, pp. 256–281, 1988.

Teece, D. J., Pisano, G. and Shuen, A. "Dynamic Capabilities and Strategic Management". Working Paper, University of California, Berkeley, August 1992.

Tufte, E. R. *The Visual Display of Quantitative Information,* Cheshire, CT: Graphics Press, 1983.

Tufte, E. R. *Envisioning Information,* Cheshire, CT: Graphics Press, 1990.

Tushman, M. L. and Anderson, P. "Technological Discontinuities and Organizational Environments". *Administrative Science Quarterly,* No. 31, pp. 439–465, 1986.

Venkatesan, R. "Strategic Sourcing: To Make or Not to Make". *Harvard Business Review,* November–December 1992.

Weick, K. E. "Introduction: Cartographic Myths in Organizations". In Huff, A. S., ed., *Mapping Strategic Thought.* Chichester: John Wiley, 1990.

Whipp, R. "Human Resource Management, Strategic Choice and Competition: The Role of Learning", *International Journal of HRM,* No. 2, pp. 165–191, 1991.

Winterscheid, B. "Building Capability from Within: The Insiders' View of Care Competence". In Hamel, G. and Heene, A., eds., *Competence-Based Competition.* Chichester: John Wiley, 1994.

8

COMPETENCE DEVELOPMENT BY SMALL FIRMS IN A VERTICALLY-CONSTRAINED INDUSTRY STRUCTURE

Øystein Jensen

INTRODUCTION

For many small businesses, there are severe limits on strategic conduct because of limited availability of resources. This may be observed within many industries, such as the tourism industry. The tourism industry in several countries has the feature of being fragmented, with many small firms operating in a limited portion of the industry value chain. This study, which studies the tourism service providers in the fragmented tourism market of northern Norway, uses a competence-based approach to investigate one way that such firms can go about building competitive advantage. This study identifies the creation of regional networks as a significant tool for overcoming market structure constraints. We suggest ways in which a network strategy may give small firms opportunities for competence building that may create a positive competitive edge.

We first present some conceptual elements based on the competence-based approach and some restrictions that industry structure places on organizational strategy. Second, we discuss the opportunities that cooperation within networks gives for creating competitive advantage in the tourism industry. We also present the northern Norway tourism industry as an illustration of a setting where such networks may prosper.

SOME MAIN CONCEPTUAL ELEMENTS

The identification of specific assets that may be used for pursuing market opportunities frequently represents a basic problem for most firms. The use of scarce assets with rent generating potentials may offer competitive advantages for a firm if it is able to deploy them effectively (Grant, 1991). Effective deployment of assets is the basis of competence-based competition (Sanchez, Heene and Thomas, 1996, in this volume). If other companies are not able to imitate a firms competence by buying comparable or substitute assets, such assets controlled and deployed by the firm may be characterized as *"strategic assets"* (Amit and Shoemaker, 1993). Grant (1991) cites geographical immobility as one of the sources of imperfections in the transferability of resources and capabilities between firms. The localization of firms is of obvious importance as a potential source of strategic assets and competitive advantage in the tourism industry.

The ability to own or control assets or resources will normally be more restricted for small firms than for large firms. Still, a small firm may have possibilities for getting access to needed assets outside the firm—*i.e.* for arranging to use firm-addressable assets. Small tourism firms within a specific geographical region, for example, may be able to access assets within and outside a region by cooperating with other small firms. The ability of small firms in a local tourism industry to access related assets may be extended to a regional level or beyond through a network of cooperative initiatives. Increased access by small local firms to regional assets that may have value for non-local firms, might improve the abilities of such small firms to arrange access to important complementary assets outside their own region—for example, the reservation systems and promotional capabilities of global tourism firms.

Lacking such cooperative arrangements, many small firms will experience competitive disadvantages resulting from the *"asset mass efficiencies"* and *"interconnectedness of asset stock"* (Dierickx and Cool, 1989) enjoyed by larger, more vertically integrated firms.

Asset mass efficiencies results when specific know how can be combined synergistically with a larger stock of knowledge developed within a firm to create new abilities and to increase the firm's existing stock of knowledge. Firms will normally need to reach a *critical mass of know how* to enjoy asset mass efficiencies. This critical mass may be hard to reach for small single firms. Small local tourism firms therefore have to find cooperative ways of achieving a critical mass of knowledge shared with other small firms.

Interconnectedness of asset stocks results when the level of one asset stock is conditioned by the level of other asset stocks. A firm's stock of "brand name" asset may, for example, depend on having a superior stock of marketing channels. For a local tourism firm, connectedness with other small firms with complementary assets in the destination where it is located represents *one* opportunity for achieving the benefits of interconnectedness of asset stocks.

In the next chapter we will indicate some of the difficulties of small tourism firms in deploying competence that results from a fragmented industry structure. As will be seen, barriers in vertical linkages between the local firm and the market for its services may represent a major problem that must be overcome to realize the full potential of a firm's or region's strategic assets.

LIMITATIONS IMPOSED ON SMALL FIRMS BY THE INDUSTRY STRUCTURE

The relations between atomistic actors (buyers or sellers) and oligopolies or oligopsonies occur as an important topic in micro-economics (cf. Clarkson and Miller, 1982). Porter (1980, 1985) describes competitive strategies within different industry structures, like concentrated or fragmented industries. Fragmented suppliers tend to have weak negotiating positions relative to buyers. Buyers who are in powerful bargaining positions relative to suppliers, may capture rents available from suppliers' unique resources and may even be able to control the way those resources are deployed. The most extreme forms of buyer power results in monopsonies (Wernerfelt, 1984).

Porter (*op cit*) claims that small independent firms often fail to have the strategic discipline needed to band together the fight against monopsonies. Suppliers in service industries, like small firms providing hotel accommodations, are frequent examples of situations with many sellers who have great difficulties in maintaining prices above a competitive level because of their inability to cooperate (Clarkson and Miller, 1982).

Some of the strategic steps recommended to small firms in such cases (Porter, *op cit*) are stronger coordination among the independent units, adding more service value to products, specialization and differentiation of products, and concentration on specific market segments. This strategy is similar to a concentrated market segmentation strategy (Kotler, 1991) or a niche-strategy (Mintzberg, 1988). Many small firms may maintain their positions in specific market niches, when these markets are unattractively small for bigger companies or when a competition in a niche does not depend importantly on larger companies' sources of competitive advantage (Grant, 1991).

The perceived disadvantages of small firms vs large firms often seem to outweigh the perceived advantages of small firms. Limited possibilities of economies of scale, for example, give small firms cost disadvantages. Small firms also suffer from limited management resources. Small, single firms within fragmented industries will rarely have a R&D department, a marketing department for developing a national or international profile, well controlled distribution channels, or the financial strength to launch long-term programs. Small firms are often affected by a wider range of environmental factors and environmental changes than larger firms. On the other hand, many small firms may have favorable positions in local markets or in specific market niches.

Among researchers in small business, small firms are not considered simply to be "smaller copies of big ones" and there is a recognized need for concepts of strategic management that address the special characteristics and situations of small firms (Dandridge, 1979; Borch, 1993). Flexibility to adapt quickly to environmental changes, for example, is often cited as an important advantage of smaller firms. Nonetheless, small producers within industries that are dependent on long and complex marketing channels will normally have considerable difficulties trying to make their own way downstream in the distribution system.

From a marketing point of view, all firms—including small local firms— should keep a strategic perspective which reaches to end-user markets (Stern and El-Ansary, 1992). *"..as a firm plans for the future, it is only sensible to consciously select target market(s)"* (Bowersox and McCarthy, 1970: 52). Many small firms, however, find themselves in positions in which larger intermediary firms are the only firms that come in direct contact with end-user markets (e.g. Bonaccorsi, 1993). Lack of contact with end-user markets creates barriers that prevent market information from reaching small firms, and it puts larger intermediary firms in a powerful position based on superior information and expertise (French and Raven, 1959; Stern and El-Ansary, *op cit*). Since good market information is essential for identifying future opportunities and for the creation of competence, small firms can often benefit greatly from finding ways to overcome this problem.

Small firms may achieve some of advantages of large firms by "quasi-integration" (Jarillo, 1988; Heide and John, 1992) achieved through strategic alliances and networks. This form of cooperation may offer the small firm access to complementary capabilities and assets it could not otherwise obtain. The identification of a firm's own competences is a first step towards identifying cooperative arrangements that can link the complementary competences of small firms and expand goals for future achievements. Horizontal quasi-integration may also be one means of obtaining a more favourable bargaining position in a vertical industry structure. As will be suggested in the next section, local networks represent *one* possibility for quasi-integration.

Teece (1992) suggests that various forms of cooperation exist and are important within **fragmented** industries. Complex cooperative forms with tight linkages and feedback mechanisms promote abilities to operate quickly and efficiently. In such settings, managing small firms effectively requires the ability to manage potentially many interfirm relationships and alliances. New competitive conditions often call for new hybrid organizational arrangements based on cooperation that links firms with complementary capabilities and capacities (*ibid*).

VERTICAL QUASI-INTEGRATION, STRATEGIC ALLIANCES, AND LOCAL NETWORKS

Strategic Alliances and Local Networks

The development of alliances among firms is often seen from a strategic perspective, although such alliances in their nature have many dimensions (e.g. Johannisson 1986). Granovetter (1994) presents different perspectives and aspects of research on alliances in various forms of "business groups". He uses the term alliances quite broadly (from a sociological perspective) and investigates several types of alliances in business group constellations in different countries. He offers examples of alliances between large firms, between (one) large and several small firms, and between mainly small firms.

Following Jarillo (1988) and James (1985), a strategic alliance may be described as *"a purposeful and binding cooperative agreement between autonomous firms, of which the objective is to improve competitive advantage and long-term profitable value creation for all cooperating parties"* (Borch, 1992: 2). A strategic alliance often consists of a dyadic relationship between two parties, and strategic networks can then be seen a system of several strategic alliances.

As developed by Johanson and Mattsson (1987), network theory is based upon a resource control perspective (Pfeffer and Salancik, 1978). Actors generally control activities and/or resources (Håkansson and Johanson, 1992), and actors may achieve indirect control over and access to resources through the network. A strategic alliance frequently seems to be based upon personal relationships and to achieve a condition of mutual trust between parties (ref. Macneil, 1980; Heide and John, 1992).

A Geographical Perspective on Networks and Resources

The distinction between functional and territorial integration suggested by Friedmann and Weaver (1979) indicates two basic dimensions in the growth of small firms. Territorial integration or quasi-integration focuses on the *geographical dimension* of strategic alliances and networks. By combining territorial integration and "opportunity management" (Johannisson, 1991) entrepreneurs may use alliances to achieve "economies of overview". Such alliances may allow pooling of various real-world experience which *"facilitates the identification and subsequent exploitation of opportunities"* (Johannisson, 1991: 35). In contrast to "internal growth" obtained by extension through ownership, Johannisson (*op cit*) suggests that small firms can experience "external growth" through the access to target resources achieved by cooperative means.

Brown and Butler (1993) distinguish between *regional* and *external* networks, and Johannisson (1986) recognizes both *local* and *global* networks.

Effective regional networks may help to develop competitiveness in wider national and international markets (Brown and Butler, 1993). Johannisson emphasizes that *"..dense local networks of firms provide a favourable learning environment for entrepreneurs"* (Johannisson, 1991: 38). Through "qualitative growth" in network environments, entrepreneurs can enhance their learning capacities as well as extend their reach in the marketplace. Porter (1990) also stresses that industry-specific networks of competences developed in geographic zones may create real competitive advantages for firms that belong to such networks.

The capacity for learning should be regarded as a basic condition for the development of competence. Dense local networks may have a positive effect on the awareness and utilization of market information by local firms. Brown and Butler (1993) find empirical support for hypotheses proposing that development of regional networks has a positive influence on the creation of external networks reaching broader markets. Regional networks may in some cases create new potential for direct horizontal competition between firms within an industry. Some firms also worry about losing know how and competence to competing enterprises (Borch, 1992) through network activities. Nevertheless, in districts with extended regional cooperation among firms, *"Generally, interorganizational links occur because firms in specific regions see their counterparts as allies rather than as competitors"* (Brown and Butler, 1993: 103). In this case, the *aggregate business* in a region is regarded as a basis of the strategic assets of each firm and as a source of a critical mass of related competences. *"The network metaphor creates a bridge between, on the one hand, local agglomerations of small entrepreneurial firms which jointly and simultaneously nurture and exploit a favourable local business setting, and, on the other the large corporation promoting an entrepreneurial culture"* (Johannisson, 1991: 41–42).

Johannisson and Gustavsson (1984) illuminates the role of local identity in the creation of local (regional) networks and of further global networks. *Local identity* is here described as the connection between the distinctive characteristics of a local community and common properties of its firm or firm leaders (Johannisson, 1986). The local community itself may thus be regarded as an "organising context" (Johannisson, 1991) that facilitates development of capabilities and competences.

Porter's (1990) environmental framework for analyzing the sources of the competitive advantage of nations may also be utilized on a regional level (Porter, 1991). *"The environment shapes how activities are configured, which resources can be assembled uniquely, and what commitments can be made successfully"* (Porter, 1991: 111). On a regional level, Italian textile and footwear industries are often cited as examples of how industrial specialization and regional cooperation between smaller, independent firms can create a competitive regional industry (Grannovetter, 1994; Porter, 1990; Piore and Sabel, 1984; Nilsen, 1991). Such firms of *flexible specialization* (Piore and Sabel, 1984) may result when small local firms cooperate within a region characterized by local traditions and tight local networks. In such cases, the activities of the business networks become integrated into the life of the local community.

LOCAL FIRMS IN A TOURISM INDUSTRY

Some General Characteristics of the Organized Tourism Industry and Destinations

The tourism industry can be described as a very complex pattern of heterogeneous parties trying to serve diverse peoples' demands for travelling and for visiting specific destinations. Purposes for travelling also vary greatly and may be motivated by recreation/pleasure, private matters, business, conferences, etc.

The types of intermediaries involved in tourism activities between different national markets and indigenous service suppliers vary considerable. Within the business of *organized tours* (inclusive tours), the **tour operators** represent the primary link between markets and destinations.

Tour operators are producers and/or wholesalers who assemble various product components and offer bundles of services directly to end-users, to travel agents, or to other types of retailers or intermediaries in tourism distribution channels (Middleton, 1988; Holloway, 1991). By packing and marketing different product elements in an inclusive tour, tour operators may create "new" products for target markets. Tour operators primarily target consumer markets for leisure-trips (especially short or long holidays), but incentive-tours and special arrangements for business traveller groups may also be marketed. Frequently, the tour operator's brand name and image are the main focus of marketing, and a specific destination's profile will be presented in a way that fits into the operator's profile (Goodall and Bergsma, 1990).

Holiday travel may be organized mainly as resort holidays (only one place) or "round-trips" (with visits to many places). The part of the tourism industry located at the travel destinations may be described as *local* producers or suppliers in the sense that they are stationary, like hotels and restaurants. In a tourism region there will probably be more than one local tourist firm providing services to the same tour operator. In many tourist destinations, single local firms bargain with operators separately, as independent units. Local or regional tourist organizations, however, sometimes play some kind of coordinating role vis-à-vis tour operators.

The "tourist destination product" may be divided into three main component elements: attractions (natural and/or man made), facilities, and accessibility (Medlik and Middleton, 1973; Wahab *et al.*, 1975). A region's natural and cultural attractions and other unique characteristics lure visitors to an area. Facilities provide food, accommodation, and comfort.

Accessibility is the condition for entering the area and getting in contact with various local tourism products. Image may also be regarded as an element of the destination product.

It is assumed among most researchers in tourism that a *complementary relationship* exists between the various product elements within a destination. Krippendorf (1980) states that the needs of a tourist visiting a destination cannot be satisfied only by the product elements offered by one single firm, but by a bundle of products offered by various firms. Krippendorf characterizes these relationships as *"collective production"*. The chances of satisfying demand and of achieving profits for the participating firms depend on the degree to which various service providers succeed in combining essential product elements in an attractive way. Krippendorf argues that a destination's original and unique, attractive characteristics should represent a normative basis for derivating its tourist products (cf. Geigant, 1963; Mill and Morrison, 1985; Jensen, 1992).

Many of the product elements in tourist destinations, and frequently the most attractive ones, are "public properties" like natural beauty, local traditions, and unique cultural attributes. Most of a destination's *original* characteristics or product elements are public properties. They have many similarities with *social goods* (Musgrave and Musgrave, 1980), which are basically "free" goods which may be consumed by everyone. *"The same benefits are available to all and without mutual interference"* (Musgrave and Musgrave, 1980: 56). The "image" of a destination may also be regarded as a social or a collective good (Nesheim, 1993; Olson, 1965), particularly for a destination's local suppliers of tourism services. All activities and performances which may influence a destination's image in a positive or a negative way will in some way affect the value of the collective product and/or single product elements offered by tourism service providers.

The Destination Northern Norway as an Example

Northern Norway is an example of a **rural, remote tourism destination**.[1] It has a few highlight-attractions (like North Cape, the Lofoten Islands, and The Coastal Express), and there are long distances between the different attractions and between population centers. Northern Norway is a "round-trip" product that includes visits to many destinations. In contrast, large tourism resorts and tourism to big cities (Rome, London and Paris) offer large concentrations of general and specific appeal to tourists. In this regard, northern Norway also contrasts with Alpine skiing-resorts and with mountain areas in southern Norway. Tourism to northern Norway so far has primarily been limited to the peak summer season. Surveys of individual tourists visiting northern Norway (Viken and Sletvold, 1988; Jensen, 1991; Jacobsen, 1992) indicate that natural beauty (including fjords/ocean), unpolluted environment, midnight sun, and the perception of freedom and solitude are the most attractive product elements of the destination. In addition, the indigenous culture of fishermen and of the Lapps may also be regarded as important contributions to the destination product.

Local suppliers of tourism services in northern Norway are mostly small firms and there is limited cooperation between firms. Among suppliers of accommodation, however, most larger hotels belong to horizontal chains or joint marketing arrangements. The major tasks of *Top of Europe Norway A/S*, the marketing organization of the destination's tourism industry, are the general promotion of the destination and the connecting of local tourist firms and tour operators. The destination's tourism potential, however, is yet to be exploited fully because of the limited coordination of tourism activities among individual firms and communities, as well as a lack of initiatives and a uniform level of competence on the local level. Though not yet empirically verified by research, there are indications that tour operators possess considerable power relative to the local tourist firms based on the tour operators' superior market information and market access (e.g. Rönningen and Nöstdahl, 1993).

DISCUSSION

In this sections we elaborate on some of the particularities of the resource base (or more generally of the "assets base") of local tourist firms under industry structural conditions described in the previous sections. We will suggest some advantages of developing dense local networks as means of obtaining control over and access to local tourism resources, as a way of increasing the learning capacity of small tourism firms and thus as an organizational form that can facilitate the development of competence by those firms.

The Competence Base of Tourist Destinations

We suggest that, from supply-side perspective, tourist destinations may be compared with industrial districts (Piore and Sabel, 1984). Regional competences, regional networks, and local governments organization can play an important role in developing and sustaining the resource base of local firms in such districts. However, from the demand-side perspective, the destination can also be perceived as a differentiated regional product, and its product elements considered as components of a resource base of tourist destinations. From the competence-based view, products are the *result* of the use of resources (Prahalad and Hamel, 1990), and the distinctive traits of a product result from specific competences in the use of resources (Bogner and Thomas, in this volume). Thus we consider product elements to be parts of a resource base, and distinctive product traits (that result when those elements are used effectively) to be a result of firm competences.

In assessing the competence-base of a tourist destination, it will be useful to make a distinction between a firm's or a region's *production-specific assets* and *product-specific assets* in the context of the tourism industry.

Production-Specific Assets

Tourism knowledge and skills are intangible firm-specific and destination-specific assets. Traditions and skills in organizing and promoting the distinctive elements of the tourism products within a region may provide the basis for competences of local firm and local firm constellations. These are "production-specific" assets and capabilities. They may form a sustainable competitive position by making possible the continuous production of an evolving range of differentiated products.

Product-Specific Assets

Within a tourist destination, local culture, history, and/or natural beauty may have multiple functions. They are *per se* substantial parts of a single destination product, and they may be consumed directly by tourists visiting that destination. At the same time, they may be parts of a "collective destination product", as well as elements used in "collective production" (Krippendorf, 1980). Therefore they may also be inputs to the production of organized tours (inclusive tours) to a region. If they are product elements for which consumption is free and not significantly restricted, they may function as public goods that enhance a variety of other products for other local industries (e.g. conventions, "theme parks").

Thus a destination's product elements may serve as resources in production processes for a number of products:

- The developing of specific inclusive tours in which one destination is mixed with several other product elements and other resources.
- The aggregated destination product (a regional product comprised of several related destinations).
- The development of managed, commercialized tourist attractions, like theme parks, which in turn may be inputs for further inclusive tour products.
- The destination image and its distinct profile used by other industries.

Such destination specific-assets are usually firm-addressable assets for firms. For local firms or networks of firms, destination-specific assets may have more strategic value than for other firms when destination-specific assets can be more closely coordinated or otherwise more effectively deployed by local firms. In such cases, location-specific, firm-addressable assets may be functionally equivalent to firm-specific assets and may become an integrated part of the firm's competence to the extent that they are integrated into and coordinated with other firm-specific assets and capabilities (Grant, 1991).

The Need for Regional Networks and Coordination of Local Resources

There is an important difference between simple aggregations of resources and collectives of well coordinated, effectively deployed resources within a destination. Production-specific and product-specific assets which are not coordinated on a destination level will exist as individual resources and will not function as parts of a destination competence. In such cases, external actors like foreign tour operators may basically "serve" themselves from an "à la carte" menu of single destination resources. A lack of coordination among local tourist firms may thus contribute to a weak negotiation position for local firms relative to tour operators, both collectively and individually. If accommodation is a necessary element of an inclusive tour, local hotels may (collectively or individually) establish a tie between utilization of their accommodation capacity and the consumption of certain local attractions or arrangements. They may therefore indirectly control access to local tourism products and may even gain control over the development and use of the attractions. By *interconnectedness* (Dierickx and Cool, 1989) between various local resources, the possibilities of exploiting their potentials will be enhanced, and teams of resources may be developed.

As pointed out earlier, resource control and resource dependency (Pfeffer and Salancik, 1978) represent basic elements of the network approach of Johanson and Mattsson (1987), and Håkansson and Johanson (1992). Figure 8.1 describes a simple relationship between local networks within a destination (composed of local actors, local resources and activities of local actors within the destination), external networks (of tour operators, etc.) and public-good tourist attractions (as a special type of local resource).

Coherence of a local network will result in increased local control (Brown and Butler, *op cit*; Johannisson and Gustavsson, 1984) over the local resource base. Many product-specific assets may be public goods and remain accessible to external actors like tour operators. Nevertheless, effective coordination processes within a local network lead to increased indirect control over such assets on a destination level giving local firms an advantage over external actors. One way of achieving control, for example, is to coordinate the utilization of capacities, like accommodation facilities, which then may become a "scarce" resource in the destination from the perspective of external actors.

The coordination of local product-specific and production-specific assets may support learning among local actors both directly and indirectly. It may effect a process of assembling and coordinating existing local skills and lead to more "intelligent" production of a more distinctive or acceptable product.

Moreover, dense local networks may create a basis for more effective "opportunity management" (Johannisson, 1991), with an enhanced capability for directly detecting and exploiting opportunities in end-user markets

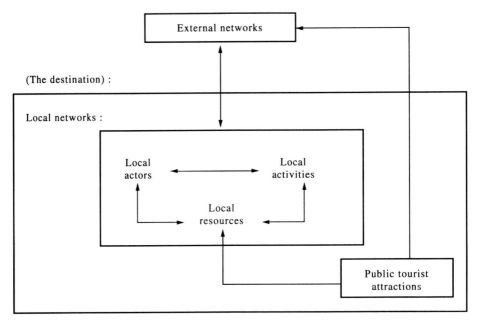

Fig. 8.1. Relationships between local networks and public attractions in the destination and external networks (adapted from Håkansson and Johanson, 1992).

(*i.e.*, independent of tour operators). Local networks may also support "qualitative growth" (*ibid*) by enhancing the learning capacity of local tourist firms. All of these effects may contribute to increased development of competences and sustainable competitive advantages by small local producers.

Uniqueness as a Value-Adding Source

Many local firms within a destination may be considered as suppliers of *support* services for tourists wanting to experience specific attractions of a destination. Facility services like accommodation and restaurants are examples of support services (Wahab *et al.*, *op cit*). These service elements may be duplicated by rivals in other destinations to the extent that they offer standardized product elements. However, by virtue of their location proximate to a destination's unique attractions, many tourists may readily associate product elements of these firms with these distinctive characteristics of a destination. Location therefore represents an important firm-addressable asset which local service providers like hotels and restaurants can use in creating competences to offer products with distinctive product traits.

The type and direction of interactions between unique product elements (*i.e.*, distinctive product traits) and standard elements (*i.e.*, threshold traits) within the destination are illustrated in Fig. 8.2. Indigenous, unique elements may have a substantial value-adding effect on a hotel or a restaurant, allowing it to create a bundle of product traits that result in a distinctive

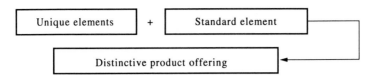

Fig. 8.2. The Influence of the unique product elements (assets) within the destination on standard product elements.

product offering (cf. Krippendorf, *op cit*). Unique product elements may therefore contribute to the development of well differentiated products (Porter, 1985).

By contrast, tourist products with little or no basis in indigenous characteristics may have a weak resource base and little basis for achieving sustainable competitive positions for the destination.[2]

Finally, it is important to note that many local tourist firms, like hotels, are heavily involved in other travel markets—e.g. business travel accommodations. In such cases, the competence base of these firms has to be analyzed relative to more than one main market and may result in various "parallel" strategies of competence-building and leveraging. Acquiring the use of flexible assets (Sanchez, 1995) which can serve multiple market needs will then become a central concern of competence building.

CONCLUSIONS

This paper has argued that from a competence-based perspective, dense local networks may contribute to increased control over/or access to and coordination of local assets and capabilities, as well as to enhanced learning capacity among local producers in fragmented industries. These effects can directly support the development of competence, as well as the production of more effective differentiated products.

Using the local tourism industry as an example, we may articulate some of the main points from the previous discussion and their generalizibility to other industries:

1. Local tourist firms are bound to their destination by their physical location. A main objective for these firms therefore should be to maximize the opportunities of their location. Although the assets of a location are mostly firm-addressable assets, a superior ability of a firm or network of firms to coordinate and deploy firm-addressable assets may convert such assets into the strategic equivalent of *firm-specific* assets. More generally, firms or networks of firms that can develop superior skills in accessing localized infrastructures (like university research programs, pools of trained technicians, specialized manufacturing capabilities, etc.) may be able to achieve the benefits of firm-specific assets with paying the full costs of ownership (Sanchez, 1993).

2. The assets of utmost strategic importance to (remote) destinations are specific attractive characteristics of the destination as perceived by the market (cultural, natural, character of the people, etc.). As long as such characteristics are scarce and desired by the market, they have the potential to generate tourism business. The attractive characteristics of a tourist destination are examples of distinctive product traits, the provision of which is a key objective of competence-based competition.

3. The uniqueness of tourism assets prevents imitation and replication by competing destinations. Many of the unique assets of a destination flow from a destination's natural or cultural properties and have been accumulated over a very long time. Unique assets—in tourism as in other industries—create possibilities for effective product differentiation, but require effective coordination and deployment to realize their full market value.

4. A great part of the uniqueness of a destination may be its public or collective goods (Musgrave and Musgrave, 1980; Olson, 1965) that are accessible for use by anybody. Public goods are therefore available to competitors and can only become a basis for competence when some firms are more effective in utilizing available public goods than other firms. In tourism as in other industries, firms may be able to make strategic use of public goods by developing dense regional networks or strategic alliances. These networks should have, *inter alia,* a specific strategy for more effectively utilizing public good assets than external actors. Such collective actions to capture significant benefits from public goods will be particularly important for small, local firms.

5. Development of regional networks composed of linked local networks may further strengthen the benefits achieved by local networks—e.g. creating enhanced opportunities for learning and market development.

6. Distinctive product specific assets must usually be combined with more standard resources and capabilities to create distinctive product offerings.

7. Locally networked assets and capabilities may create a greatly improved negotiation position for smaller firms relative to large firms in a vertical industry structure.

From a supply-side perspective, tourist destinations have much in common with industrial districts in that each can serve as a resource base that can support the creation of distinctive competences by local firms. Thus it will be important for local tourist (and other) firms to analyse their firm-addressable resource base, particularly those resources which are unique, to identify resources useful for the development of their own competences. The competence-based approach to analyzing competition helps to identify some particular strategic actions which can be taken by local tourist firms in competing in an increasingly global tourism industry.

NOTES

1. It has an area of 114.000 km^2 and the population has approximately 450,000 people, mostly living in towns and small communities along the coastline. The main international tourism attraction in Northern Norway is North Cape with 220,000 visitors during summer 1993, of which 92% were foreigners. (Top of Europa Norway A/S 1992).
2. On this criteria an attraction like "Eurodisney" would be judged a weak resource base as it is basically not rooted in the cultural area (Paris/France/Europe) where it is located.

REFERENCES

Amit, R. and Schoemaker, P. J. H. "Strategic Assets and Organizational Rent". *Strategic Management Journal*, Vol. 14, pp. 33–46, 1993.

Bonaccorsi, A. "What Do We Know about Exporting by Small Italian Manufacturing Firms". *Journal of International Marketing*, Vol. 1(3), pp. 49–75, 1993.

Borch, O. J. "The Process of Relational Contracting. Developing Trust-Based Strategic Alliances among Small Business Enterprises". Paper (draft) prepared for The 12th Annual International Conference of the Strategic Management Society in London, Moerkved, Norway, October 1992.

Borch, O. J. "Small Firms and the Governance of Inter-Organizational Exchange". Nordland College, Bodö, Norway. To appear in *Scandinavian Journal of Management,* 1993.

Bowersox, D. J. and McCarthy, E. J. "Strategic Development of Planned Vertical Marketing Systems". In Buckling, L. P., ed., *Vertical Marketing Systems.* Glenview, IL: Scott, Foresman and Company, 1970.

Brown, B. and Butler, J. E. "Networks and Entrepreneurial Development: The Shadow of Borders". *Entrepreneurship and Regional Development*, No. 5, pp. 101–116, 1993.

Clarkson, K. W. and Miller, R. L. *Industrial Organization. Theory, Evidence, and Public Policy*. MacGraw-Hill Inc., 1982.

Dierickx, I. and Cool, K. "Asset Stock Accumulation and Sustainibility of Competitive Advantage". *Management Science*, No. 12, December 1989.

Dandridge, T. C. "Children are not Little Grown-Ups. Small Business Needs its Own Organizational Theory". *Journal of Small Business Management*, No. 2, 1979.

French, J. R. P. and Raven, B. "The Basis for Social Power". In Cartwright, D., ed., *Studies in Social Power*. University of Michigan Press, 1959.

Friedmann, J. and Weaver, C. *Territory and Function. The Evolution of Regional Planning*. Norwich: Edward Arnold, 1979.

Geigant, F. *Die Standorte des Fremdenverkehrs. Eine sozialökonomische Studie über die Bedingungen und Formen der räumlichen Entfaltung des Fremdenverkehrs,* Universität München, 1962.

Goodall, B. and Bergsma, J. "Destinations—as Marketed in Tour Operators' Brochures". In Goodall, B. and Aschworth, G., eds, *Marketing Tourism Places*. London and New York: Routledge, 1990.

Grannovetter, M. S. "Business Groups". In Smelser, N. J. and Swedberg, R., eds, *The Handbook of Economic Sociology*. NJ: Princeton University Press, 1994.

Grant, R. B. "The Resource-Based Theory of Competitive Advantage: Implications for Strategy Formulation". *California Management Review*, No. 3, Spring 1991.

Hakanson, H. and Johanson, J. "A Model of Industrial Networks". In Axelsson, B. and Easton, G., eds, *Industrial Networks. A New View of Reality*. London: Routledge, 1992.

Heide, J. B. and John, G. "Do Norms Matter in Marketing Relationships?" *Journal of Marketing*, pp. 32–44, April 1992.

Holloway, J. C. *The Business of Tourism*. London: Pitman Publishing, 1989.

Jacobsen, J. K. "Ferieliv i Lofoten og Vesteraalen" (Report), Gjesteundersøkelse 1991. Nordland fylkeskommune, Bodö, Norway, 1992.

James, B. G. "Alliance: The New Strategic Focus", *Long Range Planning*, No. 3, 1985.

Jarillo, J. C. "On Strategic Networks". *Strategic Management Journal*, pp. 31–41, 1988.

Jensen, Ø. "Turister i Nordland: Muntlig Intervju-Undersøkelse av Turister Sommeren 1989". NF-rapport 04/91-70, Nordland Research Institute, Bodø, Norway, 1991.

Jensen, Ø. "Service and Service-Concepts Related to Tourist-Attractions". Two Discussion Papers, Bodø Graduate School of Business, Bodø, Norway, July 1992.

Johannisson, B. "Economies of Overview—Guiding the External Growth of Small Firms". *International Small Business Journal*, Vol. 9(1), 1991.

Johannisson, B. and Gustavsson, B. *Småföretagende på Småort—Nätverks-Strategier i Informationssamhället*, Växjö, Sweden: SFC/Högskolan, 1984.

Johannisson, B. "Lokalt Företak i ett Nätverksperspektiv". In Johannisson, B. and Spilling, O. R., eds, *Lokal Næringsutvikling*, Universitetsforlaget AS, Oslo, 1986.

Johanson, J. and Mattsson, L. G. "Interorganizational Relations in Industrial Systems: A Network Approach Compared with the Transaction-Cost Approach". *International Studies of Management and Organization*, No. 1, pp. 34–48, 1987.

Håkansson, H. and Johanson, J. "A Model of Industrial Networks". In Axelsson, B. and Easton, G., eds, *Industrial Networks: A New View of Reality*. London and New York: Routledge, 1992.

Kotler, P. *Marketing Management: Analysis, Planning and Control*. Englewood Cliffs, NJ: Prentice-Hall Inc., 1991.

Krippendorf, J. *Marketing im Fremdenverkehr*. Bern: Peter Lang A. G., 1980.

Macneil, I. R. *The New Social Contract: An Inquiry into Modern Contractual Relations*. New Haven and London: Yale University Press, 1980.

Middleton, V. T. *Marketing in Travel and Tourism*. Oxford: Butterworth Heinemann, Ltd., 1988.

Medlik, S. and Middleton, V. T. "The Product-Formulation in Tourism". *Marketing et Tourisme*, AIEST Publication No. 13, 1973.

Mill, R. C. and Morrison, A. *The Tourism System: An Introductionary Text*. Prentice-Hall, 1985.

Mintzberg, H. "Generic Strategies: Towards a Comprehensive Framework". In Mintzberg, H., ed., *Advances in Strategic Management*. Greenwich, CT: JAI Press, 1988.

Musgrave, P. B. and Musgrave, R. A. *Public Finance in Theory and Practice.* MacGraw-Hill, 1980.

Nesheim, T. "From Myths to Organizational Hybrid: Regional Organizations in Norwegian Travel and Tourism". Paper prepared for 11th EGOS Colloquim, Paris, 6–8 July 1993, Foundation for Research in Economics and Business Administration, Bergen, Norway.

Nilsen, R. *Med Hodet og Hendene. Fleksibel Spesialisering og Bedriftsstrategier i Nord-Toscana.* ISV, University of Tromsø, Norway, 1991.

Olson, M. *The Logic of Collective Action.* Cambridge, MA: Harvard University Press, 1965.

Pfeffer, J. and Salancik, G. R. *The External Control of Organizations: A Resource Dependence Perspective.* New York: Harper and Row Publishers, 1978.

Piore, M. J. and Sabel, C. F. *The Second Industrial Divide.* New York: Basic Books, 1984.

Porter, M. E. *Competitive Strategy.* Free Press, Division of Macmillan Publishing Co. Inc., 1980.

Porter, M. E. *Competitive Advantage: Creating and Sustaining Superior Performance.* New York: Free Press, 1985.

Porter, M. E. "The Competitive Advantage of Nations". *Harvard Business Review*, March–April, 1990.

Porter, M. E. "Towards A Dynamic Theory of Strategy". *Strategic Management Journal*, pp. 95–117, 1991.

Prahalad, C. K. and Hamel, G. "The Core Competence of the Corporation". *Harvard Business Review*, May–June 1990.

Rönningen, A. and Nöstdahl, A. *En Undersökelse av Relasjoner Mellom de Nord-Norske Reiselivsbedriftene og Turoperatørene Innenfor Internasjonale Turistmarkeder for Organiserte Reiser*, Bodö Graduate School of Business, Norway, 1993.

Sanchez, R. "Strategic Flexibility, Firm Organization, and the Nature of Managerial Work in Dynamic Product Markets: A strategic options Perspective". *Advances in Strategic Management.* JAI Press, Vol. 9, pp. 251–291, 1993.

Sanchez, R. "Strategic Flexibility in Product Competition". *Strategic Management Journal*, Vol. 16 (Summer Special Issue), pp. 135–159, 1995.

Stern, L. W. and El-Ansary. *Marketing Channels.* Englewood Cliffs, NJ: Prentice-Hall Inc., 1992.

Teece, D. J. "Competition, Cooperation, and Innovation. Organizational Arrangements for Regimes of Rapid Technological Progress". *Journal of Economic Behavior and Organization*, No. 18, pp. 1–25, 1992.

Viken, A. and Sletvold, O. *Bilturisme i Finnmark.* Finnmark College, Alta, Norway, 1988.

Wahab, S., Crampon, L. J. and Rothfield, L. M. *Tourism Marketing.* London: Tourism International Press, 1976.

Wernerfelt, B. "A Resource-Based View of the Firm". *Strategic Management Journal*, Vol. 5, pp. 171–180, 1984.

9

CHARACTERIZING ORGANIZATIONAL COMPETENCES: AN INDUSTRIAL NETWORKS APPROACH

Geoff Easton and Luis Araujo

INTRODUCTION

One of the most obvious features of recent work in the strategy field has been the attempt to understand what it is about firms, in a very specific sense, that drives economic performance. Thus strategy writers have been concerned with firms' value adding activities, resources, assets, capabilities and competencies and the relationships among them in order to understand the mechanisms within the firm that create wealth. However in doing so they have largely treated the firm as a bounded entity, only involving the environment when attempting to assess the effect of these entities on a firm's performance in product markets. However "no business is an island" (Hakansson and Snehota 1989). Firms are involved in a vast web of inter organizational relationships from which they draw, and to which they export, resources. It is therefore obvious that no view of how firms perform can be complete without taking into consideration the linkages it has with other organizations. This is not the place to develop a complete model of strategy formation as a network phenomena though we are in the process of doing precisely that. Our current objective is more modest. We seek to develop a characterization of resources enriching it by reference to a model of industrial networks and to show that this could provide the basis for one of the most basic competencies a firm could possess; an understanding of what its resource base is and how it might best be used.

THE INDUSTRIAL NETWORKS VIEW OF RESOURCES

The industrial networks approach to the study of industrial systems and interorganizational exchange relationships has had a long history. Its roots can be seen in the Swedish research into distribution channels and internationalization in the 1970s. A major development was the influential pan European study of buyer-seller dyads carried out by the I. M. P. group (Hakansson, 1982). During the 1980s there was a broadening of the focus to encompass networks at the level of industrial systems at the expense of dyadic relationships (Axelsson and Easton, 1992). For a recent review of the literature in this field see Easton (1992).

In this chapter, rather than provide a summary of the industrial networks approach in general, we have chosen to concentrate on two key aspects of the concept of resources within this paradigm. The first is the argument that relationships comprise resources that the firm must invest in so that they may continue to exist. The second is the relationship of resources to actors and activities in one particular model of industrial networks.

The definition of an industrial network is borrowed from social exchange theory and may be described as a set of two or more connected exchange relations (Hakansson, 1987). In social exchange theory, exchange is defined as consisting of a voluntary transaction involving the transfer of resources between two or more actors for mutual benefit. The key term 'resource' is defined as "...any valued activity, service or commodity" (Cook 1977: 64, emphasis added). In industrial network research such exchanges are largely confined to buyer–seller relationships. This definition of exchange, as pointed out previously (Easton and Araujo, 1992), places exchange of economic resources at the heart of industrial networks theory. Cook uses the term 'valued service, activity or commodity' which implies a metric of valuation, compatible with the usual definition of what constitutes an economic resource. In management accounting theory, the use of the term 'economic resource' is restricted to situations where future benefits in either cash or expected cash inflows accrue to the entity controlling the resource (Anthony and Reece, 1983).

The role of resources in industrial networks theory transcends this relatively narrow context. Industrial networks presuppose the establishment of exchange relationships. Such relationships are often found to be long standing and difficult to disrupt. Relationship specific investments in the form of mutual adaptations are made by each of the parties involved in the exchange. Some of these adaptations may take the form of specific, discrete investments in tangible assets (capable of being placed on a balance sheet) or acquisition of skills or knowledge. However most adaptations are taken to occur through routine, continuous processes resulting from the normal buyer–seller interaction processes (Johanson and Mattsson, 1987).

A crucial and related point made by Ford et al. (1986) is that resources are in themselves passive and fragmented. It is the company's exchange activities, rather than its production activities, that lead to an activation and integration of these resources. All the company's decisions in the allocation, control, and changes in the resource base occur due to current or anticipated interaction with others. It is these interactions which define the organization and confers on it an identity, by forcing it to deploy its resources.

The investment character of exchange relationships has been explored by Johanson and Mattsson (1985) and Mattsson (1987). In both cases, exchange relationships are treated as intangible assets (in our terms resources) that have accumulated as a result of the investment nature of the firm's activities. Johanson and Mattsson (1985) define investments as processes through which resources are committed in order to create, build or acquire assets which can be used in the future. Investments are characterized by the following dimensions:

(a) resource commitment: the end product of investment processes are seen as the building of assets resulting from the commitment and transformation of resources. The amount of resources and the process through which they are committed are crucial in determining the specificity–flexibility of assets and their future uses.

(b) asset aspects: assets can be described along a number of dimensions, namely tangible–intangible, flexible-specific and value. What defines the value of an asset is partly its assumed future uses and the extent to which future uses are dependent on the existence of other assets.

(c) time: investment processes are regarded as taking effect over a period of time and as being path-dependent—i.e. the sequence of steps involved in the process of resource commitment and accumulation matters.

(d) financial and monetary aspects: resource commitments and consequences of their use are often expressed in the metric language of money. Building and maintaining assets usually means negative cash-flows while the use of assets usually involves the generation of positive cash-flows.

(e) management aspects: investment processes require the management and control of resource commitments over a period of time.

Johanson and Mattsson (1985) use the terms 'marketing' and 'market' investments to refer to the long term and cumulative nature of the commitment of resources to the build-up of dyadic relationships and network positions respectively. These sets of intangible assets generate a position for the individual firm in the context of the network of other exchange relationships that define its strategic identity. Such a position parallels that of a role in social theory. Strategic change is defined in terms of major changes in the firm's network positions and strategy is defined as the set of principles governing a firm's conscious efforts to develop and direct its resources and its relationships to the environment. A firm's network position is thus looked at as a set of partially controlled, intangible assets that have arisen as a result of the investment nature of the firm's activities. These intangible assets generate revenue for the firm and, more importantly, serve to give access to other firms' internal resources (Easton, 1992).

A subsidiary point made by Johanson and Mattsson (1985) is that these intangible market assets are dependent not simply on the firm's investment decisions but also on activities and investments in complementary and competitive activities. In other words, the creation of intangible market assets are the consequence of the alignment and co-ordination of investments in complementary and co-specialized assets by the focal firm and its exchange partners. Thus the consequence of investment processes are also interdependent and timing of investment decisions is crucial.

These notions add to a picture of the individual firm embedded in a network of relationships, a social and historical entity whose location in space and time is crucial to the understanding of its acquisition and exploitation of resources. In analysing the firm's market and marketing activities as investments and the firm' position as an intangible asset, Johanson and Mattsson introduced a number of important concepts. First, they highlighted the crucial nature of exchange activities for the development of the firm's resources and capabilities.

Secondly, Johanson and Mattsson extended the meaning of the notions of investment and assets beyond their traditional signification in management accounting. In management accounting theory assets are defined as economic resources controlled by an entity whose cost at the time of the acquisition can be objectively measured (Anthony and Reece, 1983). In this context network positions can hardly be classified as assets since their creation is the product of interaction between different entities, the cost of purchase of a network position cannot be measured and, in any case, the ownership of the resulting asset is uncertain. This last point highlights the fact that whereas management accounting theory can deal with intangible assets whose ownership can be determined (e.g. patents, brand names), the treatment of intangible assets of dubious or uncertain ownership is beyond its frame of reference. Network positions depend, by definition, on the extent to which actors are able to use them by enrolling the support of other actors who recognize and value that network position.

As mentioned previously, the most comprehensive treatment of resources in the network approach is given by the actors–resources–activities model (Hakansson and Johanson, 1992) henceforth denoted as the ARA model. The most striking feature of the ARA model is the circular and mutual definition of its three building blocks. Actors perform activities and/or control resources while resources are means used by actors when they perform activities. An activity is said to take place when one or several actors develop, exchange or create resources by utilizing other resources. Activities can be categorized as either transformation or transfer. Transformation activities involve the change of resource in one or more dimensions and transfer activities involve the transfer of control over a resource between any two actors.

Activities thus always imply the transformation or transfer of resources. All resources are controlled by actors, either by single actors or jointly by a number of actors. Resources are heterogeneous. They have attributes in an unlimited number of dimensions. This means that the possibilities for the use of a specific resource can never be fully specified. Resources can be characterized, first, by the actors controlling the resource. A second characteristic is the utilization of the resource in activities. How many dimensions of the resource are used and how standardized is the utilization in each dimension? A third characteristic is the versatility of resources.

The three strands of the model—actors, resources and activities—form connected structures that again can be defined as networks. These three networks, in turn, form an intricate and interwoven pattern, again best described as a network. Instead of being simply building blocks of a network model, actors, resources and activities can also be regarded as products of shorter or longer networks, based on weaker or stronger associations. The network metaphor thus assumes a dual character: it is both constitutive and an end-product of actors, resources and activities. In other words, actors, resources and activities form and describe the medium of the networks they describe (Callon, 1991).

The ARA model provides a powerful and deceptively simple framework for the study of industrial systems as networks. By introducing the notion of resources as inextricably linked with the activities of actors in socio-technical systems, the ARA model anchors the industrial networks paradigm in the territories traditionally claimed by economics. But also by recognizing that actors can only be defined in interaction, in terms of their relationships, the ARA model moves the industrial networks paradigm closer to the concerns of sociological theory.

Previous network models have tended to have a structural (actor) or process (activities) bias and largely to ignore resources. Indeed the addition of resources is important as comparison with a related but very different model indicates. Porter (1985) in his value chain analysis concentrates on the equivalent of activities and includes actors by means of the concepts of value systems and relationships. The objective of this type of analysis is to disaggregate the firm into a number of strategically relevant activities with a view to identify areas contributing to potential competitive advantage. However he largely ignores resources as well as interactions between resources and activities, and as a result it is difficult to handle resource based competitive advantage.

The major limitation of the ARA model as it currently stands is the lack of a clear articulation of what types of actors and resources exist and how different configurations of ARAs give rise to different network structures and processes. In Hakansson and Johanson's (1992) model, actors differ mainly in terms of levels of aggregation: they can be individuals, groups of individuals, formal or informal organizations and supra-organizational actors. Resources can be both tangible and intangible and their character can only ascertained by their use, since they have virtually an infinite number of dimensions and actors may always find novel ways of using them. What the crucial dimensions are, if any, has not been discussed.

To summarize, Industrial Networks theory is concerned with explaining phenomena pertaining to the nature and evolution of industrial systems. It is positive and holistic in character. It recognizes the role of firms as one category of actor in an industrial system described as a network of actors, resources and activities. It does not purport to have a theory of the firm, nor does its theoretical framework reserve a special place for the treatment of the firm as one class of actor. The firm is only a subject of interest in its context, in the web of relationships it creates and maintains. The boundaries of firms are regarded as porous and fluid, continually reflecting the changes and adaptations imposed by the range of exchange relationships the firm is engaged in. The identity of the firm is not defined by the range of resources it has accumulated or the type of administrative framework it has chosen to co-ordinate activities and allocate resources. This identity is socially constructed and is a product of the firm's interactions with other actors (Hakansson and Snehota, 1989). As in most sociological theories, identity is a relational concept; identity cannot be dissociated from the relationship between actors in the common space they have built themselves (Callon, 1991).

THE CHARACTERIZATION OF RESOURCES

Multidimensionality of Resources

In this section we intend to further clarify and articulate the concept of resources. A concept takes its meaning from its context in a particular theory. We therefore propose to characterize the concept of resources with reference to the industrial networks model described in the previous section. In doing so we hope to focus more sharply and at the same time provide a richer picture. In the following discussion, we present a framework that attempts to dimensionalize resources as well as articulate the relationship of resources to both actors and activities.

The concept of a resource is clearly multidimensional. The difficulties in providing a precise definition are, in part, a result of the generality and complexity that the concept connotes. One, but only one, way of improving our understanding is to begin to identify what those dimensions might be. Obviously there are an infinity of such dimensions so that the issue of importance is raised. How do we decide which are the dimensions which will help us better understand the phenomena that study? Three criteria suggest themselves. The first is whether the dimension is consistent with and/or adds to existing theory, in this case industrial network theory. The second is whether the dimension offers insights into the phenomena under study. The extent to which the dimensions described meet these criteria is described at the relevant points in each of the four sections set out below. The third criterion is the extent to which it leads to managerial implications. This outcome is discussed in the final section of the chapter. First however we begin by reviewing previous efforts to dimensionalize resources.

Existing Schema

Amit and Schoemaker suggest that: " ... resources consist inter alia of know-how that can be traded (e.g. patents and licenses), financial or physical assets (e.g. property, plant and equipment), human capital, etc." (1992: 35). Barney (1991) provides a more helpful categorization of resources divided into three groups: physical capital resources, human capital resources and organizational capital resources. Under the first category Barney includes the technology used in firm and embodied in physical objects, plant and equipment, geographic location and access to raw materials. Human capital resources include the knowledge embodied in the firm's management team and other employees. Lastly, organizational capital resources include the administrative mechanisms that govern the firm's activities as well as the informal relations amongst groups within a firm and those in its environment. Grant (1991) includes items of capital equipment, human skills, patents, brand names and so on. Hakansson (1989) categorized resources under several headings: input, marketing, capital, personnel and techno-logy to which a sixth—relationship—was added. Axelsson (1992) mentions five areas—raw material, manpower, technological, marketing and financial resources. Similar taxonomies are used in classic works such as Ansoff (1965) or Hofer and Schendel (1978) who suggest that the firm's capabilities stem from five resource areas: financial, physical, human, organizational and technological. What is interesting from these categorizations is their breadth. Clearly there are no inhibitions among these authors about recognizing as resources whole categories which are difficult, if not impossible, to measure or value.

In two works at least, attempts have been made to use dimensions which reflect more profound ways of describing resources. Johanson and Mattson (1985) suggest that assets can be described in terms of the dimensions, tangible–intangible, flexible–specific and value. Grant (1991), cites four characteristics of resources and capabilities likely to be important determinants of sustainability of competitive advantage: durability, transparency, transferability and replicability. The emphasis of this latter approach is, paradoxically, to identify and articulate the very sources of idiosyncrasy of firms' resources and capabilities that are largely tacit, causally ambiguous or difficult to articulate.

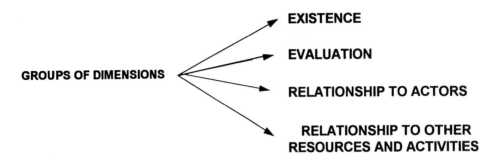

Fig. 9.1. Groups of dimension of resources.

DIMENSIONALIZING RESOURCES: A NEW SCHEMA

We will begin where previous authors have left off and present a list of 14 such dimensions within which all of the dimensions they propose are included, possibly after some minor transformation, together with some new ones. They are presented in four groups labelled; existence, valuation, relationships to actors and relationships to other resources and activities. The first two groups draw largely on the meanings attaching to resources in traditional strategy theory. The second two groups stem from the concerns of industrial network researchers. Figure 9.1 portrays the four groups used to dimensionalize resources.

The U.K. Temperature Control Industry—A Case Study

In order to test, in some sense, the face credibility of the dimensions described in the next section their use will be exemplified in a particular context. The UK temperature control industry is relatively small by the standards of many other manufacturing industries but has some feature which make it particularly interesting to study. The temperature control industry, though not described in this way by its participants, is one sector of a very much larger industry which provides means for the measurement and control of temperature in industrial processes. At one end of the scale this may involve thermometers; at the other, complex computer controlled process control systems. The industry in question is defined by the product it makes. Temperature controllers in this category are of a standard size for fitting into control panels, offer at least temperature indication but may also provide alarms, control, time profiling and communication and comprise input and output signal conversion devices as well as a microprocessor based logic processing. Such devices are priced anywhere from £100 to £1000. These instruments are fitted to a wide range of industrial plant from simple ovens to complex chemical process plant.

During the time that the research was carried out the industry contained around 15 competitors with a long tail of "garage" operations indicating that barriers to entry, at least at one level, were not high. Most of the firms were medium sized and either independent or the relatively independent subsidiaries/divisions of multinational corporations. Three specialist firms dominated the market in term of market share but there were also a number of small niche players as well as process control oriented multinationals which manufactured temperature controllers as part of a very broad product range.

The industry had developed from one based on electro-mechanical temperature control instruments. Some firms survived the transition; others did not. Thus the industry was neither old nor new but had many of the features of a maturing industry. Competitors were largely aware of one another but comprised perceptual strategic groups (Easton et al., 1992) The industry was geographically concentrated in two parts of the UK partly as a result of spin-offs as groups of individuals left established firms to set up on their own account.

The market, which was growing slowly, comprised three major segments. Original equipment manufacturers (OEMs) in sectors such as injection moulding machines and pottery kilns who took relatively large numbers of temperature controllers of more or less standardized form. They were mainly concerned with reliability and price. Large end users comprised a second segment. Such firms were buying to fit the instruments to new or existing plant and since the relative cost was low were more concerned with performance and the problem solving abilities of the sales engineers and technical after-sales services. Small end users were handled by distributors who were, in general, unable to provide the all round expertise of the manufacturers but could handle simple low cost standard applications for their price sensitive customers.

The manufacturing technology was a simple assembly operation. All of the components including the casing were bought in and hand assembled. While manufacturers had catalogues of specific products the ranges were both broad and deep and major customers could have a measure of tailor making. New product development was continuous but incremental. It was concentrated mainly on the algorithms in the software which could offer more options for the same money. It was widely believed in the industry that novel product features and problem solving abilities were the key to success in this market.

The Groups of Dimensions of Resources

Existence

The first group of dimensions, labelled existence, reflect the existential

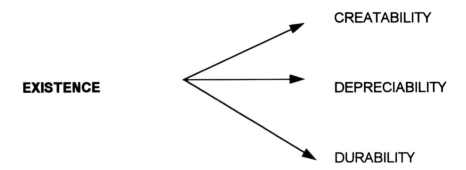

Fig. 9.2. The existence dimension.

characteristics of resources; how they come into being, change over time and are replaced. Figure 9.2 depicts the dimensions in this group.

The first dimension we have given the name of creatability. (It is only fair at this point to apologise for the labels we have attached to these dimensions. Turning verbs into nouns which capture the meaning we require has not been an easy task and the results are linguistically inelegant). It is meant to capture the ease or difficulty that a firm may experience in creating a new resource which they wish to employ. Firms cannot create "basic" resources such as land or minerals or employee's basic competences. They can only create "complex" resources by combining the existing resources under their control, which they can acquire control of or to which they have or can gain access. Part of the difficulty of creating a new resource may lie in gaining control of basic resources outside of the firm's current control. This relates to issues of relationships to actors dealt with in the next section. But part of the difficulty lies in the way in which the resources can be combined. It is related to the notions of versatility and complementarity of resources discussed later but differs in that it is a property of the emergent rather than existing resources.

In the temperature control industry it is widely perceived that competence in creating new products is a crucial success factor. This competence relies on the technological resources available to the firms involved. At least one firm turned itself round by buying in experienced staff from its competitors and from firms in adjacent industries and building a successful R&D team. However another firm tried a similar strategy and failed because the team simply did not gel for a number of technical, political and environmental reasons. One of sources of envy of the market leader has been their ability to sustain a powerful R&D team through good times and bad.

Depreciability measures the extent to which the stock of a resource changes over time if left to do so. Thus physical equipment, technical artefacts and instruments have a limited life-span and their ability to provide future benefits to the entity owning or controlling them is dependent on the stage they have reached in their projected life-cycle. Likewise, human skills decay and depreciate if not exercised and used. Firms invest continually in training partly so that employees can acquire new skills but also to refresh existing ones. Financial resources need to be continually replenished throughout the input–throughput–output cycle of the business. Other types of resources also have a limited life span and require regular maintenance and repair. Patents, licences and contracts are drawn for limited periods, need to be protected and updated and other intangible resources such as relationships with suppliers, customers or financial institutions are subject to decay and need rejuvenating. Indeed the very idea of an exchange relationship has associated with it an important time dimension, and interaction episodes can be seen as the 'replenishment' encounters that sustain and renew the relationship. The concept of a resource is thus linked with the idea of a stock-flow model. A resource is a stock that can be drawn upon, but that usually requires topping up by maintenance and repair (Dierickx and Cool, 1989).

We would suggest that a significant part of an organization's activities consists of such maintenance activities—in ensuring that the stock of resources it controls or has access to, is continually replenished and kept at levels that allow the organization to function. In this sense the relationships between resources and one kind of organizational activity is made obvious. Most of these maintenance activities only require well-working routines and automatic, non-reflective action—'action generators' in Starbuck's (1983) felicitous expression. These automatic behaviour programmes require no information-bearing stimuli and are simply activated through job assignments and descriptions, manuals and standard operating procedures, clocks and calendars.

In some cases, the maintenance and repair activities can be determined and programmed, and offer few problems in terms of what is required to maintain the stock of that resource at appropriate levels. In others, the relationship between stock and flows is rather uncertain and causally ambiguous. To maintain a stock such as a favourable image or reputation at high levels cannot rely on a stable framework of variables that are under the control of one actor or can be easily manipulated. These characteristics of some resources have led authors such as Itami (1987) to proclaim that these are precisely the kinds of resources which are crucial in firms' attempts to differentiate their offerings and at exploiting rents associated with those positions.

It should also be noted that resources can appreciate too, the stock increasing over time. For example the age of a workforce might be regarded as a surrogate for experience and provide reassurance to a customer. Land may increase in value. Depreciation is recognized in management accounting theory and included in balance sheets. However the stock of resource as described here is measured in terms of its natural units not in terms of the value to be placed upon it although the two are obviously related.

In the temperature control industry another important success factor is the reputation of the firm. The reputation appears to be largely a function of the age of the product line and the rate of new product introduction. Since, for at least one segment of the market, purchases are made infrequently customers are often unaware of the current state of affairs and base their initial approaches to potential suppliers on past reputation. This practice has two effects. It means that there is a lag in the reputation stocks of individual firms such that some firms live on past glories and others find it difficult to reverse a decline in their reputation. This in turn appears to provide incentives to firms to maintain their reputations by producing more new products and additional features than the market can effectively absorb.

A related characteristic of resources is their durability. Some resources can exist indefinitely if maintained (brand images). Others are subject to processes of depreciation which means that the stock eventually dwindles to nothing (e.g. some raw materials). Some have an obvious life span (e.g. an employee). This leads to notions of replacement cycles. These are likely to be more discontinuous than maintenance cycles though perhaps more predictable than creation cycles.

One of the most important resources in the temperature control industry is a firm's product line and the resources that support its existence. However, because of continuous incremental innovation, it is perhaps the least durable. Considerable energy is devoted to its maintenance and that of the resources, like R&D personnel, that support it. In addition, because of the history of spin-offs and inter firm migration, any of a firm's people dependent resources can quickly depreciate if personnel policies are not sensitive to perceptions of reward structures and morale. The manufacturing related resources, in terms of both the people employed and the knowledge of how to run a small batch system, however appear to be durable and low maintenance.

Introduction of these existential dimensions into the industrial network model allows us to articulate a relationship between resources and activities. Creation, maintenance and replacement activities constitute extensions to the typology used by Hakansson and Johanson (1992) to classify activities as either being transformation or transfer activities. They add a new process dimensions to those already described.

Evaluation

The second group of dimensions is concerned with issues of evaluation. Resources are generally held to possess a value. However there are at least 4 dimensions which may be used to describe the evaluation of any particular resource. Figure 9.3 depicts the dimensions grouped under evaluation.

The first concerns the actual value assigned to any particular resource; its valuation. Why do firms wish to value their resources and how do they do it? Money is the metric of a market economy. Firms wish to know what the

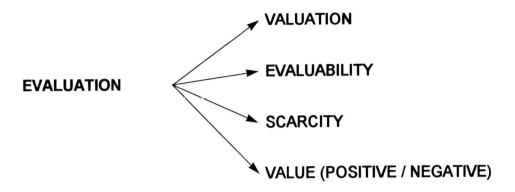

Fig. 9.3. The evaluation dimension.

totality of resources under their control are worth in order to measure how well they have been managing them or in order to sell the firm. Such valuations are, apparently, not difficult to make. Firms may be valued at book value; what the firm has paid for the resources it has paid a market price for. Alternatively it may be valued in terms of the expected future stream of earnings based upon past performance. In both cases, if the firm has traded shares, then a market valuation based upon both of these valuations, with some adjustment for sentiment, can be obtained.

As will be evident from some of the previous comments, what are perceived to be the key resources in the temperature control industry are precisely those that are most difficult to put a value on. An equally important fact is that there have been relatively few take-overs or mergers in the temperature control industry. This is partly due to the ownership patterns; private ownership at individual, family or corporate level in the case of wholly owned subsidiaries or divisions. Thus firm valuations are largely based upon acquired asset values, of which accumulated profit forms a major part, rather than market assessment.

Valuations made in this traditional way are not without flaws but even if one assumes that they are acceptable, there remains a substantial problem. For the same reasons that firms wish to value all of their resources they will also wish to know what any particular combination of resources is worth in order to make judgements about the management of parts of the firm. How firms do this leads on to a second dimension; evaluability. How easy is it for a firm to put a value upon its factory, stock, personnel or corporate image? There is one relatively straightforward route which parallels that used to value the firm; the market. Thus resources are often valued, for the purposes of the balance sheet, in terms of the money that was paid for them or the money that someone has or might offer for them. As in management accounting theory, we prefer to use the term 'asset' to describe a resource whose ownership, control and market valuation can be determined. Thus assets are simply a subset of economic resources whose valuation has some claims to be measurable.

It is clear however that even this approach to valuation is limited. The valuation is either historic and may have changed or is hypothetical and may never be realized. Further it relies on the existence of a relatively free market. These requirements, even if flawed, make it difficult, if not impossible, to place a value upon many types of the most important kinds of resources that firms control. One has only to point to the controversy over the valuation of brands as evidence in support of this statement. Many are simply not evaluable.

Even those that are evaluable, by virtue of some form of market evaluation, may be "wrongly" valued. The total value of a firm is assumed to be equal to the sum of the parts. In terms of resources this is not always, indeed may never be, the case. One implication of our definition of 'resource' is that the term only acquires meaning, and hence value, in a specific context in particular in relationship to other resources. To describe the content of a resource is inevitably to describe its context. A skill to operate and repair steam engines, for example, can hardly be qualified as a resource in most First World economies. Yet, in Third World countries operating outdated railway systems, or in science and technology museums it may constitute a vital resource. Put in another way, it is difficult to see what contribution any one resource makes to the value of the totality of resources which comprise a firm. How can one judge which part of the jigsaw puzzle is the most or least valued?

Yet firms have to make judgements for the reasons already outlined. How is it done? How can managers distinguish the valuable from the less valuable? They clearly have some model, however primitive, of the way in which the firm increases its value over time. In this model they ascribe greater value to those resources which they consider to be most essential to that value creation process. It may be that part of this evaluation is based upon the impact that the loss of a key resource (e.g. customer, salesperson) would have on the value creation process. Such judgements are bound to be highly subjective but are no less important because of that.

It was clear from our research in the temperature control industry that certain resources were seen as universally valuable in terms of their contribution to successful operation of the firms involved and these have already been discussed previously. However it is also clear that there were differences of opinion about what other resources are valuable. The top management of the market leader believes that their all-graduate engineer sales force is an important resource in that it provides end users with pre and post sale problem solving. No other firm in the industry has such a resource. Another leading competitor has chosen to develop strong relationships with the better distributors, training them to do the problem solving but concentrating on medium to small customers. None of the easily evaluable resources such as plant and machinery were regarded as particularly valuable.

The subjective judgement of resource value made in firms will be influenced, in part, by the relative scarcity or abundance of the resource in question. Scarce resources are usually competed for fiercely in economic systems both at the level of market exchanges and at the intra-organizational level. At the level of market exchanges the value of scarce resources is translated into high prices and incentives for exploitation of strong bargaining positions. In traditional strategic management approaches (Porter, 1980, 1985) suppliers and customers are regarded as competitors for scarce resources and market exchanges characterized by adversarial, arms-length forms of contracting. Inside organizations, scarcity of resources (say financial resources for capital investment projects) engenders structures designed to promote internal competition and to instil a degree of market discipline into internal transactions (Eccles and White, 1981).

When resources are in plentiful supply and easily accessible they lose their obvious character of providing benefits to the entities owning or controlling them. Thus energy management and conservation skills only became recognized as an important resource when the era of plentiful supply and cheap energy prices ended. The recent concern with training and continuing education can be partly explained by the realization that human capital is an important resource in organizations subject to decay and depreciation—with the consequence of elevating what was known as the 'personnel' function to the more prestigiously labelled 'human resource' management function.

In the temperature control industry most participants would identify technological resources, particular people and knowledge, as the scarcest resource. In particular the change from hardware to software driven solutions has meant that firms have had to go outside the industry to obtain the systems engineers and programmers that are necessary to create new product features. While such resources are not necessarily scarce in any absolute sense they are if you do not know where to find them or know precisely what skills you require.

It has been assumed so far that all resources contribute to the overall value of the firm. Some do not. They detract from the value; they are liabilities (poor brand image, ineffective management). The dimension may be called value negativity/positivity. It may be that other resources are used to overcome the impact of liabilities and hence there is an opportunity cost incurred.

The key liability which participants in the temperature control industry are concerned with is reputation. It is the asymmetry in the customer evaluation process which appeared to be most worrying. The perception was that a firm might perform well on all fronts for years with a particular customer and yet when a single mistake is made their reputation with that customer is ruined. A more idiosyncratic liability was identified in the person of a senior technical manager who moved from firm to firm in the industry creating havoc wherever he went. The managers in a firm he had just left firmly believed that he would profoundly affect the performance of the firm he went to.

The industrial network model avoids valuation issues. It models the processes by which resources create value, albeit it in a somewhat general way. However what it could incorporate is the notion that perceived resource values drive managerial decisions about how resources and activities are combined. While it is argued that heterogeneity of resources can lead to an infinite amount of choice with respect to particular resource configurations, in practice it is important to understand why particular configurations occur. Value connotations must form a part of the complex process which is involved.

Relationships to Actors

The third group of dimensions is called relationships to actors. In this case the actors may be either internal and external to the individual firm. Figure 9.4 depicts the dimensions subsumed under this group.

The first dimension is that of controllability. It measures the extent to which a resource can be controlled by an actor. Control implies the ability to deny a resource to other actors. Some resources are relatively easy to control (stocks of physical materials); others are more difficult (information). Control may involve ownership as with a patent; in other cases it may mean something less as in a contract or intellectual property rights. Other resources, such as images associated with brand names, reputations for quality, or for retaliation to competitive moves can only be built and maintained over time rather than being controlled. With human resources the issue of ownership does not arise and is a case where the concept of focal actor becomes important. For the firm, individual or groups of employees can be treated as resources. Conversely an individual employee as an actor can use, and may have control over, resources at the firm level (corporate image). Again the process of controlling this stock is fraught with ambiguities and uncertainties, resulting partly from poor understanding of cause-effect relationships in a dynamic environment and partly as a result of the time-lags involved in the investment process.

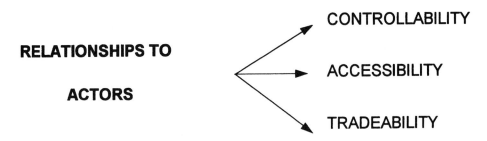

Fig. 9.4. The relationship to actors dimension.

In the temperature control industry we can cite two examples, one internal and one external, which illustrates the issue of controllability. It has already been pointed out that product lines are broad in the industry. One way that the marketing and sales people tend to further broaden the product line is by agreeing to manufacture tailor made "specials". There are any number of plausible reasons which may be used to justify such an action. However, even in small batch production, specials are expensive and disruptive. Thus there are always conflicts between the marketing and production people about the decision to do a special. The resource in this case is the product line and all that it represents, particularly its breadth. Considerable energy is required to control it, since decisions are often finely balanced. One external resource is the relationship a firm may have with a customer. The leading firms in the industry tend to have a few close relationships with customers which are not always the largest or most profitable. However they use these customers as sounding boards to test out new product concepts and prototypes. They have relatively little control over these customers who, in any case, regard themselves as experts doing their potential suppliers a favour, but they offer a useful resource.

Accessibility is an associated dimension. It is related to control in that, in general, the more accessible a resource is the less easy is it to control. Such control may refer to both internal and external actors. Internally, a resource which is inaccessible to one group of actors may limit the firm's performance (technical know-how, finance). Externally, firms wishing to enter into exchange relationships may find it difficult to access the resources they require and which are controlled by their potential partner and, of course, vice versa. Generalizing from extreme cases, the less accessible resources are and the easier it is to control and own them, the more valuable resources become and the more incentives firms have to rely on arms-length, market type contracts. Conversely, the more difficult it is to access, own and control resources the more firms have to rely on exchange relationships, specialization of resources and activities, and permeability of boundaries.

Information provides a good example of the issue of accessibility in the temperature control industry. The general product and process technologies used in the industry are widely known and available. They are described in technical journals in articles authored by leading technologists employed by competing firms as a form of promotion. However the specific technological solutions which define the performance of a particular instrument are closely guarded secrets, as are the prices actually charged as opposed to list prices and the features of any new products which may be about to be launched. Indeed there are unwritten rules of communication that apply to communication among competitors in the industry which prescribe what may or may not be discussed. Also a step change in the technology has changed the accessibility of a key resource. When instruments were configured in hardware it was possible to reverse engineer a rival's product to see how it worked. When instruments became configured in software this became virtually impossible to do. Thus a key resource became inaccessible and changed the balance of competition in the industry to favour the innovators at the expense of the followers.

A third dimension which impinges on the relationships between actors is tradability. This may be defined as the ease with which a resource can be exchanged between actors. Again there is a relationship with control; actors cannot exchange a resource they do not have control over. Traditionally this provides a major distinction between resources, based on an activities view of the firm. Firms exchange resources by both buying (raw materials and components), selling (products and services) and transforming them by means of other resources (machinery and labour) which, in general, are not normally consciously exchanged. However the distinction is not watertight. Information may be exchanged as part of an exchange relationship. Firms may allow their brand names to be franchised. They may even sell surplus capacity to other firms. "Hollow" corporations rely on the tradability of resources in order to exist.

It was rather surprising to discover in the temperature control industry that competitors traded "traditional" resources among themselves. At least one firm bought instruments from a competitor and sold them under their own trade mark. It was even more common for competitors to trade ancillary products, like sensors and thyristor stacks, with one another. In this way the boundaries between firms became more blurred. The more tradable resources that are available within an industry the more likely it is that firms will experiment with the exchange boundaries of their firms in an attempt to discover what resources they can and must own/control and what they merely require access to.

The industrial network model incorporates notions of access and control but not necessarily tradability. Indeed one of the central issues in this paradigm is the sharing of control over what is regarded as a key resource; exchange relationships. Control over this resource increases a firm's ability to access the resources of its partner. The balance of transformation to exchange activities must be, at least partly, a function of the accessibility of the required resources and the willingness of the owner/controller of those resources to exchange them.

Relationship to Other Resources and Activities

The final group of dimensions we have labelled relationships to other resources and activities. They represent some basic characteristics of resources which affect the way in which they may be combined with other resources or activities. A useful metaphor for these processes is that of chemistry and chemical reactions. Atoms and molecules react with each other and the characteristics of the reactants determine whether reaction is possible, what the processes involved may be and the nature of the combined product which results. Similar properties may be identified in resources and although the metaphor is not perfect it is useful in suggesting the characteristics upon which to concentrate in order to understand the dynamics of resource combination. Figure 9.5 portrays the dimensions grouped under this label.

The first dimension in this set is that of integrity. It measures the extent to which resources are simple or compound; that is already comprising a mix of resources or else representing some fundamental unit of resource which cannot be subdivided. The chemistry metaphor provides the distinction between an atom and a molecule as a direct analogy. The notion of integrity has important implications for other dimensions. In particular, if there is a basic resource unit which cannot be divided then it can be owned, controlled or accessed but not created by a firm. Similarly basic resource units may be easier to understand and less scarce than complex ones. The importance of the concept is, however, dependent on the practical issues that firms face in separating and recombining resources. If resources cannot be separated into component parts then they cannot be recombined and the firm may be constrained in significant ways.

The most obvious example of the integrity issue in the temperature control industry occurs where there are important teams of people involved. Is it sensible for a firm to move even non-key employees from a R&D team which is performing well or will this change the "chemistry" of their relationships? Another example concerns reputation. It is well established that there often exists a halo effect which results in firms being judged well or badly along all evaluative dimensions. This occurs as a result of peoples' inability or unwillingness to make complex judgements. Thus attempts to treat aspects of a firm's reputation separately may be doomed to failure.

A dimension widely acknowledged to be important in understanding resources is that of versatility. Resources may be versatile or specific in nature. In this context versatility refers to the ways in which a resource may be combined with other resources and/or activities. Using the chemical metaphor, some atoms or molecules are more reactive than others; they

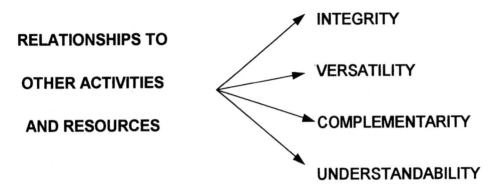

Fig. 9.5. The relationship to other activities and resources dimension.

have more active sites by means of which they can combine. A flexible manufacturing centre will be rather versatile; a service technician trained to repair only one kind of machine may be considered rather specific. Hakansson and Johanson (1992) argue that, in principle, resources can be used and configured in an infinite number of ways. In practice this versatility is unequally distributed among resources and, in any case, limited by the knowledge base of organizations and individuals, an issue which will be discussed later. Thus knowledge can be considered as a boot-strapping type of resource—as in Fiol (1991)—without which the versatile character of a resource or set of resources might never be recognized. The processes involved in the management and development of this knowledge base is thus a key problem in understanding the dynamics of industrial networks.

Versatility has been the subject of much discussion within the framework of transaction cost economics. Williamson (1991) identifies six sources of asset specificity: (1) site specificity; (2) physical asset specificity; (3) human asset specificity arising out of learning-by-doing; (4) brand name capital; (5) dedicated assets (e.g. customers); (6) temporal specificity. In industrial networks theory, the notion of resource versatility is more prominent and regarded as a feature of exchange activities. Specificity is not regarded as a fixed property of resources but a function of their use, namely in the context of exchange activities.

Two extreme scenarios for the purpose of illustration can be described. At one extreme we can imagine organizations engaged in interactions with a homogenous set of customers with a homogeneous set of needs, using a relatively inflexible set of resources. On the other extreme, we can picture, an organization engaged in project marketing or systems selling, handling a heterogeneous set of customer demands and discontinuous demand schedules. These demand characteristics require very versatile resources that can be subject to speedy depreciation. Activities are generally directing towards problem-solving but the ability to acquire, maintain and diffuse a stock of knowledge and experience is crucial if the need to start from tabula rasa for every new project is to be avoided.

In the first case most of the firm's highly specific resources are likely to be embodied in physical assets and in standard operating procedures and routines. Learning is accomplished at the intra-firm level and results from incremental, experience type effects. It would be, in conventional terms, very efficient though not effective in an environment with any degree of change. In the second example the firm's versatile resources are embodied in both human capital and in relationships—within teams of individuals at the intra and interfirm level. These resources can dissipate very quickly as individuals are moved between assignments, teams of individuals are disbanded and reassembled and relationships remain dormant for long periods of time. The firm's boundaries are constantly being extended and contracted as a result of interactions and its asset base is virtually negligible in relation to the resource base. The firm is relatively inefficient since versatile resources cost more to create and maintain than inflexible resources but it is likely to be more effective in adapting to long term change.

The small batch manufacturing systems used in the temperature control industry represent combinations of rather versatile resources. The workforce does not need very highly specialized skills and the capital equipment is low value and general purpose. In addition the instruments are configured in software which can be down loaded from a large suite of existing computer programmes. Thus within the scope of general temperature control product lines the manufacturing system may be said to be versatile.

The third dimension in this set is that of complementarity. Some resources are easier to combine with other resources, and with activities, than others. Chemical reactions can only take place among molecules where bonding is made possible by the compatibility of their relative physical structures. DNA provides a good example of how specific a fit must be for reaction to take place albeit between molecules of extreme complexity. In terms of firms, versatility may, of course, come into it. But there is a more subtle point to be made. Resources may be competitive as well as complementary even within the same firm. For example it may be difficult, and as a result economically disastrous, to combine a flexible manufacturing centre with a JIT delivery system. Complementarity is a measure of the processes of combination. It is concerned with the ease with which combinations with a specific resource may, in general, be carried out. To operationalize such a notion requires a better model than we currently have of such processes. Yet it is clearly an important dimension since it strongly shapes the constraints and opportunities for resource and activity combinations within a firm and thereby its potential scope and performance.

In the temperature control industry managers of the market leader would argue that the existence of close customer relationships with OEMs is a resource which is complemented by their all graduate engineer sales force. The sales personnel provide the customers with a service which matches or surpasses their own level of experience and expertise. Conversely the sales engineers are competent enough to be able to spot new customer requirements and translate them into product requirements that the R&D teams can work to. Another example of complementarity occurs in the case of firms which treat the temperature control industry as a sideline to their main interests in process control. In this case the resources devoted to the temperature control industry are complemented by some of the resources in the main division (e.g. multinational service operations) but not others (a product line designed for process control applications and not stand alone temperature control systems).

The final dimension in this set is understandability. It is a measure of how easy it is to comprehend the nature of a resource or even to recognize a resource at all. In terms of our metaphor the question is "how much do we know and understand about the properties of this chemical?" Some resources are easily recognized as such and are well understood. Money in the bank or physical resources come into this category. They have a simple metric and, as assets, also have a value. Other resources do not share these properties. They cannot be measured quantitatively and cannot easily be valued. As mentioned previously, individual and organizational competences fall into this category. Exchange relationships and managerial skills are other examples of this kind of resource. A common way of making a parallel distinction is to use the dimension of tangibility. However this simply refers to whether the resource is palpable or concrete; literally capable of being touched. The notion of understanding has wider connotations.

If a resource can readily be understood then it is more likely that the ways in which it can be combined with other resources will be understood and hence exploited successfully. However understanding is a necessary but not sufficient condition. The result of combining even quite simple resources may be quite complex. For example packaging a product in a new way can create all sorts of unforeseen difficulties even if the characteristics of both the product and the new pack are clearly understood.

It has already been emphasized that in the temperature control industry success is perceived to depend upon a flow of new and (marginally) improved products. The industry leaders would claim that they know how to combine technological resources with design and manufacturing to achieve this. The market leader would further claim that it understands how to combine the technological resources with its graduate sales force and customer relationship investments to ensure that the flow of innovations is successful not only in technical but also in market terms.

In the industrial network model understanding of resources or indeed activities is not considered to be a major issue. Versatility of resources is ignored at the expense of heterogeneity and complementarity of resources is not regarded as a quality that can distributed differentially.

CONCLUSIONS AND IMPLICATIONS

In this paper we have attempted to articulate the concept of economic resource. In doing so we have made suggestions as to how the industrial networks model might be developed to take into account the greater level of particularity we have described. It is hardly surprising that the directions suggested point to a degree of convergence between the industrial networks model and the strategic assessment models currently finding favour. However we do not see this as being inevitable or even desirable. Integration of different paradigms is not an intellectual but a social process and one that occurs rarely for all sorts of understandable reasons. Our concern has been merely to offer a prod in a somewhat different direction to each and leave the proponents to decide whether to react or not.

We have suggested that the industrial networks model should acknowledge the dynamics of resource creation, acquisition, maintenance and replacement since resources form one of the central bases for understanding firm behaviour. It should also broaden its view that resources are idiosyncratic to one where their capacity to be combined with other resources and activities offers a further source of heterogeneity which will affect that behaviour. The value of resources should help to drive the model and so the way in which value is attached to parts of a firm is of crucial import if intrafirm managerial behaviour is to be a key explanatory variable. Further articulation of the actors, resources and activities model is required if only to confirm that such articulation adds little to the power of the model while increasing its complexity in an unacceptable way. The inclusion of other forms of activities which relate to resource creation, maintenance and replacement comes into this category. Actors are concerned with control, valuation and combination of resources. Actors do not behave deterministically; they have human motivations and network behaviour is not a result of technical and material constraints and opportunities. Finally the link between strategic management and industrial networks deserves more study. The normative side of industrial networks is under-developed, for entirely understandable reasons, but perhaps the time has to come to bite the bullet and the links to the resource based model of the firm suggests ways in which this might be done.

What are the implications of this schema for managers? Four can be readily identified. First of all it offers a view of strategy which incorporates both the firm and its environment. In blurring the distinction between resources inside and outside the firm it helps managers to find the crucial balance point and a way of reconciling those who are internally and those who are eternally oriented by virtue of their positions. Secondly it provides a model of the firm which, unlike those derived from traditional economics, can be articulated, hierarchically, to levels of detail which meets managers needs for face validity in tackling the complexity that they regard as central to their tasks. Thirdly it gets them to look at resources in new ways, for example eschewing old distinctions between say capital and labour, and in doing so provides means by which they can think of new uses for resources and new combinations. Finally, it draws attention not only to the importance of resources per se but to the processes by which they are created, maintained, renewed and organized and links them to the tasks that they have to achieve for the firm to survive and perform.

REFERENCES

Amit, R. and Schoemaker, P. J. H, "Strategic Assets and Organisational Rent". *Strategic Management Journal*, Vol. 14, pp. 33–46, 1993.
Ansoff, H. I. *Corporate Strategy*. McGraw-Hill, 1965.
Anthony, R. N. and Reece, J. S. *Accounting: Text and Cases*, 7th edn, Irwin, 1983.

Axelsson, B. "Network Research: Future Issues". In Axelsson, B. and Easton, G., eds, *Industrial Networks: A New View of Reality*. Routledge, 1992.

Axelsson, B. and Easton, G., eds, *Industrial Networks: A New View of Reality*. Routledge, 1992.

Barney, J. "Firm Resources and Sustained Competitive Advantage". *Journal of Management*, Vol. 17(1), pp. 91–120, 1991.

Callon, M. "Techno-Economic Networks and Irreversibility". In Law, J., ed., *A Sociology of Monsters: Essays on Power, Technology and Domination*. Routledge, 1991.

Cook, K. S. "Exchange and Power in Interorganisational Networks". *The Sociological Quarterly*, Vol. 18, pp. 30–42, Winter 1977.

Dierickx, I. and Cool, K. "Asset Stock Accumulation and Sustainability of Competitive Advantage". *Management Science*, Vol. 35(12), pp. 1504–1513, 1989.

Easton, G. "Industrial Networks: A Review". In Axelsson, B. and Easton, G., eds., *Industrial Networks: A New View of Reality*. Routledge, 1992.

Easton, G. and Araujo, L. "Non-Economic Exchange in Industrial Networks". In Axelsson, B. and Easton, G., eds., *Industrial Networks: A New View of Reality*. Routledge, 1992.

Eccles, R. G. and White, H. C. "Price and Authority in Inter-Profit Centres Transactions". *American Journal of Sociology*, Vol. 94 (Supplement), pp. S17–S51, 1988.

Fiol, C. M. "Managing Culture as a Competitive Resource: An Identity Based View of Sustainable Competitive Advantage". *Journal of Management*, Vol. 17(1), pp. 191–211, 1991.

Ford, D., Johnason, J. and Hakansson, H. "How Do Companies Interact?". *Industrial Marketing and Purchasing*, Vol. 1(1), pp. 25–41, 1986.

Grant, R. M. "The Resource-Based Theory of Competitive Advantage: Implications for Strategy Formulation". *California Management Review*, Vol. 33(3), pp. 114–135, 1991.

Hakansson, H., ed., *International Marketing and Purchasing of Industrial Goods*. John Wiley, 1982.

Hakansson, H., ed., *Industrial Technological Development: A Network Approach*. Croom-Helm, 1987.

Hakansson, H. *Corporate Technological Behaviour: Co-operation and Networks*. Routledge, 1989.

Hakansson, H. and Johanson, J. "A Model of Industrial Networks". In Axelsson, B. and Easton, G., eds, *Industrial Networks: A New View of Reality*. Routledge, 1992.

Hakansson, H. and Snehota, I. "No Business is an Island: The Network Concept of Business Strategy". *Scandinavian Journal of Management*, Vol. 4(3), pp. 187–200, 1989.

Hofer, C. W. and Schendel, D. *Strategy Formulation: Analytical Concepts*. West, 1978.

Itami, H. *Mobilizing Invisible Assets*. Harvard University Press, 1987.

Johanson, J. and Mattsson, L.-G. "Marketing Investments and Market Investments in Industrial Networks". *International Journal of Research in Marketing*, Vol. 3(2), pp. 185–195, 1985.

Johanson, J. and Mattsson, L.-G. "Interorganisational Relations in Industrial Systems: A Network Approach Compared with a Transactions Cost Approach". *International Studies of Management and Organisation*, Vol. 17(1), pp. 34–48, 1987.

Mattsson, L. G. "Management of Strategic Change in a 'Markets-as-Networks' Perspective". In Pettigrew, A., ed., *The Management of Strategic Change*. Basil Blackwell, 1987.

Porter, M. E. *Competitive Strategy: Techniques for Analyzing Industries and Competitors*. Free Press, 1980.

Porter, M. E. *Competitive Advantage: Creating and Sustaining Superior Performance*. Free Press, 1985.

Starbuck, W. H. "Organizations as Action Generators", *American Sociological Review*, Vol. 48, pp. 91–102, February 1983.

Williamson, O. E. "Comparative Economic Organization: The Analysis of Discrete Structural Alternatives". *Administrative Science Quarterly*, Vol. 3, pp. 269–296, 1991.

10

SPINNING-OFF CAPABILITIES: COMPETENCE DEVELOPMENT IN KNOWLEDGE-INTENSIVE SERVICES

Tom Elfring and Geert Baven

INTRODUCTION

The aim of this chapter is to investigate the competence development of two service functions in the car industry in the United States, Europe and Japan focusing on the rationale behind make, cooperate or buy decisions. In particular, this study is an attempt at advancing understanding on development of competences in emerging markets for knowledge-intensive services. The central theme is how knowledge-intensive service functions are organized in a complex manufacturing environment, concentrating on the relation between internal and external resources and capabilities.

We have focused on the service functions because an increasing part of the organization of production is determined by the contribution of knowledge-intensive services (Elfring, 1993). When new markets develop as a reaction to the introduction of innovative service technologies, service functions gain relevance and consequently the issue of their outsourcing becomes more prevalent (Quinn, 1992). We shall investigate the forces which initiate the make, buy or cooperate decision, the role of competence building in service technologies, and we shall also consider how competence development can be enhanced by spinning-off service capabilities.

The car industry has been chosen for this study because it is considered to be on the leading edge in outsourcing a growing range of business functions. Competitive pressure, pollution control, globalization and continued technological change have all played a part in spurring the industry to become more oriented towards relational production strategies (Womack *et al.*, 1990).

The literature on internal development or external purchasing of knowledge-intensive services is limited and rather diverse. However, an increasing body of literature has been developed on the make or buy issue with respect to components production in the manufacturing sector. More relevant to our problem definition was the dynamic capabilities paradigm (Teece, Pisano and Shuen, 1990). The reasons for that paradigm being better suited to incorporate the particular characteristics of knowledge-intensive services are threefold: the unit of analysis is based on capabilities, learning is an important concept and dynamics in a historical context is central to its reasoning. The logic behind spinning-off knowledge-intensive service functies will be examined in terms of learning and capabilities.

With respect to the methodological approach in this investigation, we believed that given the current stage of development of knowledge-intensive services, it was crucial to collect observations from actual situations in order to enhance our insights on the issues at stake. The 'direct research' method as described by Mintzberg (1979) influenced our research approach. The observations have been collected in two research stages. First, a general overview of the importance of knowledge-intensive services in the organization of production, followed by in-depth interviews using open-ended questions with experts and relevant managers. This strategy was chosen to check the group of factors influencing make or buy decisions cited in the literature. Secondly, the services chosen for special focus are software and engineering. Both are knowledge-intensive services and they are of significant importance to the core competencies required for development, manufacturing, marketing and distribution in the car industry. Comprehensive case-studies were made to gain insights into the underlying mechanisms affecting those decisions and in order to develop concepts for analysis. These cases are referred to as A, B and C for reasons of confidentiality.

In section 2 the traditional factors affecting the make or buy decisions are presented and it is shown that for our purposes other factors need to be included. In section 3 a stages model of the development of service functions is discussed and the dynamic capabilities paradigm is used to introduce a more dynamic element into the analysis. In section 4 the concepts of leveraging, learning and capabilities are examined in order to understand the development of knowledge-intensive service functions.

FACTORS AFFECTING MAKE OR BUY DECISIONS

The literature dealing with make or buy decisions has grown substantially in the last fifteen years. A number of theories have been developed to explain the behaviour of firms choosing between the internal provision or the external supply of commodities and services (Harrigan, 1985; Helper, 1987; Nishiguchi, 1989; Porter, 1980; Quinn, 1992; Williamson, 1985). They have produced a range of variables which are most likely to affect the make or buy decision. The variables can be roughly divided into three groups of factors affecting management decisions. The three groups of factors are: strategic factors, environmental factors and operational factors. Important categories within these strategic factors are: core business issues, asset specificity and entry/exit barriers. Environmental factors like government regulations, degree of competition on supplier markets and pace of technological developments also play a role. The last group of factors influencing make or buy decisions is the one related to operational issues such as production costs and economies of scale.

Are these factors able to explain the make or buy decisions involving knowledge-intensive services in the car industry? Most of these functions were previously developed in-house such as: systems-engineering and software development and are now increasingly open to sourcing from outside parties. These are functions much closer to the core business of the car industry than the production of some simple components. In the make or buy literature these two functions have been studied more than any others. However, the expertise required to manage the external provision of knowledge-intensive service functions, which is labelled as the development of *interface skills* (Quinn *et al.* 1990), is quite different from the sourcing of components. It stresses 'coordinative, strategic and conceptual skills—and the capacity to manage contract relationships', as Quinn (1990: 83) termed it.

External Coordination and Learning

The notion that sourcing decisions concerning knowledge-intensive services functions required a different approach than the sourcing decisions of simple components was mentioned repeatedly during the case-interviews. Concepts such as external coordination and learning should be included if the emergence and expansion of knowledge-intensive services is to be understood (see also Ciborra, 1991). In addition, knowledge-intensive services require a different approach because of their particular characteristics, such as their interactive and knowledge-creating nature (O'Farrell and Moffat, 1991). On a conceptual level, these characteristics corroborate the arguments for the inclusion of external coordination and learning as key concepts in our approach.

The first of the two elements needing more emphasis is the external coordination. Traditional thinking tends to stress management as the coordination of functions performed internally. Increasingly, more tightly-knit interactions between customers and suppliers of services require a better understanding of interorganizational complementarities and coordination. Therefore we should like to add a new element to the make versus buy issue—the intermediate element of cooperation. Cooperation implies a more outward-looking perspective and is an example of external coordination. The management of external suppliers of knowledge-intensive services is gaining in importance (Baker and Faulkner, 1991). The few studies on outsourcing of knowledge-intensive services basically agree on the fact that in most cases these services are not provided exclusively in-house nor are they entirely contracted out. Usually, these are in-house capabilities which, to a certain extent, are supplemented with external resources.

The second of the two elements needing more emphasis concerns learning. The concept of learning is considered to be very important in understanding the strategies of firms dealing with the make, buy or cooperate issue of knowledge-intensive services. As well as an internal component, learning in this field almost always involves an important external component. It is these services in particular where demanding clients can act as a trigger for accumulating knowledge and exploring new product-market opportunities. The stimulating effect of 'demanding clients' (Moulaert, Martinelli and Djellal, 1990) and 'lead users' (Foxall, 1989; Von Hippel, 1986; Voss, 1985) has been examined in depth in the literature. In fact, our research corroborates the previous evidence that knowledge-intensive services have been learning from demanding clients and lead users. This learning is considered to be crucial to the enhancement of existing capabilities in the creation of competitive advantage.

Incorporation of the external coordination and learning dimensions make it imperative to find a more dynamic approach. Most of the theories underlying the traditional factors determining the make or buy outcome, are not suited to the incorporation of these dynamic elements. We have chosen the dynamic capabilities paradigm as the approach in this study largely because it is dynamic and includes concepts as learning and the development of capabilities.

THE STAGES MODEL AND THE DYNAMIC CAPABILITIES PARADIGM

Howells (1988) demonstrated that the development of software services often starts with internal development because initially there was no market for these services. This internal development may eventually lead to open-market relations and to the formation of a separate entity where the parent-company has either major- or minor-equity ownership. The case of software services provision for large European companies illustrates the stages. Howells demonstrated that a path can be seen along which these corporations have built internal units. In the end, as the current composition of leading European software suppliers shows, a number of them have emerged from an initial demand within large corporations. Playing a notable role are the French state-owned corporations such as CGE, Elf-Aquitane and the Government department for Atomic Energy (CEA), which spawned leading-edge software firms such as GSI and Groupe CiSi. Similarly, Groupe SG2 developed out of Banque Société Générale (Howells, 1988).

In the following section Howell's stages model is used as a starting point. We reduced the number of stage to four. In addition we will try to detect the mechanisms responsible for the shifts along the distinguished stages, because Howells did not explain the movement from one stage to the next. Besides these conceptual contributions, we will check whether our empirical material fits the four stage model. First, a large number of examples from trade publications and other sources were used to see whether they corresponded to one of the four stages and a selection of them were used to illustrate and describe the four stages. Secondly, three examples were investigated in more detail. On the basis of company documents, trade publications and interviews we were able to make three comprehensive case studies. These case studies cover all four stages in a longer time frame. The case studies have been helpful in expanding the concepts of learning and capabilities with respect to the general issue of development of service functions within the stages model.

The stages model consists in our view of four stages. The first stage resembles the internal development of an in-house demand for knowledge-intensive services. In the second stage the internal department also starts providing services to third parties. Stage three is characterized by the shedding of the in-house unit. And stage four can be seen as the move of the service supplier to offer a package of a number of related services and thereby offering one-stop-shopping to its clients.

Stage One

The internal development of knowledge-intensive services in large companies is the key characteristic of stage one. An often quoted reason for internal development is the non-existence of particular know-how externally and/or very intransparent and uncertain market conditions. For that reason, in the late sixties, Ford had to rely on the internal development of dealer software. It established a dealer computer services department, which provided computer systems to and communicated with a large number of the company's Ford and Lincoln-Mercury dealers. Instead of a gradual withdrawal, Ford entirely outsourced the service-department to an independent firm. It thereby resembles a move into stage three. The dealer computer services department was sold off to Universal Computer Systems Inc. in Houston. Ford commented that: 'UCS can provide better service for our dealers than we can at this point'. 'UCS is a small player in the dealership computer business with about 4% of the market' (Jackson, 1991).

A second example also relates to the Ford Motor Company. They formed an alliance with Hewlett Packard to collaborate on Computer Integrated

Manufacturing (CIM) and IT projects called the CIM Alliance team. Representatives of Hewlett Packard said that the alliance eventually hopes to sell products to other companies in the automotive industry (Computerworld, 1990). Thus in the near future they envisage a move into stage two.

Stage Two

In this stage we can perceive a more autonomous unit selling services to 'outsiders'. Revenue from captive services supply decreases, while service-provision through open market relations increases. When, at the same time, other parties start to offer their services to outsiders, a market develops which might preempt the purchase of services from captive units. One example relates to the Volkswagen group and its strategies towards services development, particularly engineering and software services. The VW data-processing unit—Gedas project management—set up in 1984 and majority-owned by VW, plans to expand outside the VW group. Current business with VW accounts for 70%, but with the take-over of Duer and Partner, a German software firm, the unit aims at market leadership for CAD software in the German-speaking market. Gedas employs 430 people and turnover in 1990 was DM 33 million. Services resulting from internal development efforts are now offered to third parties.

Another example of a firm which has moved into stage two is Porsche. In the eighties, the Porsche strategy was to build up the division that works on car engineering and design by offering these services to the major car producers (Wall Street Journal Europe, 1992). In this stage the service function is exposed to market discipline and may become a profit center.

Stage Three

The shedding of in-house units is characteristic for stage three. Knowledge-intensive services are generally provided to the users through arm's-length contracts during this stage. Interface skills to coordinate relational work practices become of importance. *Hawtal Whiting*, an engineering service supplier to the car industry, illustrates the typical positioning in the third stage. This company was launched by a group of senior design engineers who left Ford of Britain in 1970. Hawtal Whiting has now grown to some 800 employees. Their first big contract was with Volvo for the 760 model. Another major contract was with General Motors that rented 20 Hawtal Whiting designers to work for its Body Division in Detroit (Phelan, 1988). In the beginning 1990s Hawtal Whiting has won a number of large contracts, often by forming alliances with suppliers, with the main car manufacturers.

Another example of a stage three structure is the creation of a joint venture which has a highly independent stance in the marketplace. Gedas, previously an in-house supplier of Volkswagen, joined Control Data Corporation (CDC) to create companies in both Europe and the United States to provide software services to manufacturing industries. The alliance rests on both parties' specific expertise in respectively software development and batch manufacturing applications. Services based on these joint capabilities are offered to third-parties in the aircraft-, machine tool- and automotive industries by their joint venture named Icem Systems. CDC provides the management and development, while VW is providing the controllers and the marketing managers (Handelsblatt, 1990).

Stage Four

The fourth stage can be characterized by the capability of offering an integrated package of services to the customer. Another feature of this stage is the increasing geographical coverage by suppliers who are subject to demand-pull forces from their customers who, in many cases, have global outlays of production. At this stage, a cross-roads has been reached where both customer and supplier stand to benefit from service provision to third parties. A representative example is Masco, an independent supplier of engineering services. Masco has reacted to the requirement of supplier's capability with a twofold strategy. The first consisted of acquisition of firms which were able to deepen Masco's functional capability in design, from automotive components to entire vehicles (Marler, 1989: 10). This last aspect encompasses the necessity of confidentiality and trust in these relationships. The threat of losing the business is probably enough to deter any company from violating confidentiality issues and Masco has reduced the risk by isolating concept car projects for each individual client.

Secondly, to meet the demands of industry, Masco has developed the strategy of becoming a full-service supplier. Masco has positioned itself to be involved in the early stages of design, engineering and fabrication of concept vehicles. Creative Inc. is one of the engineering companies which is part of Masco. Currently employing 1,500 people, Creative's business has doubled twice over in the 1980s. The group's available services include computer-aided engineering (CAE), prototype body-engineering and construction, computerized marketing and one-off show vehicles. The firm works for the aerospace industry as well as car producers and has alliances with Comau Productivity Systems Inc. in Italy (Lowell, 1990). Masco has overseas manufacturing operations in England and Germany. It also has internalized design capabilities through their UK-based Canewdon Engineering Consultants Group. The engineering firm has facilities for styling, clay modelling, body design, and engineering of power train, suspension, steering, chassis, and vehicle electronics. Customers include Volvo, Ford (U.S. and Europe), Jaguar, Nissan and Austin Rover.

Coventry-based automotive design and engineering company *FF Developments* and Modern Engineering in Warren Michigan are also examples of stage four (see Elfring and Baven, 1993). They both show that in a full service context more responsibility is shifted to the service supplier. It often implies that coordination for the customer is reduced, but not their control over the project as a whole. Coordination for the project is shifted to the service supplier. It is important to note that coordination and control are separable.

Other Empirical Evidence On Stages

In the above section a number of the illustrative examples (mini-cases) of the four stages is given (see also Table 10.1).

The purpose was to see whether the four stages could be supported by empirical evidence from engineering and software services in and to the car industry. In addition, on the basis of the examples it was possible to distinguish and elaborate on some of the central features of each of the four stages. In the following section the three comprehensive case-studies are presented to substantiate the empirical basis of the stages model and elaborate on the contribution of concepts derived from the dynamic capabilities paradigm, i.e. learning and capabilities.

Table 10.1 presents also the three comprehensive case-studies A, B and C and their position in the stages model. The focus of the investigation was on the present position in the stages model. The present position concerns 1992, however information concerning 'some' years in the past (about 1989) and the planning for 1995 was gathered as well.

Table 10.1. Empirical Evidence on Stages model.

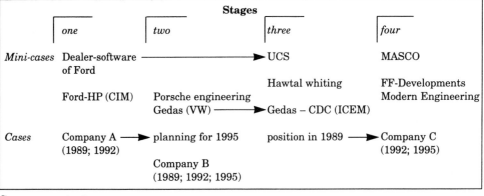

	Stages			
	one	*two*	*three*	*four*
Mini-cases	Dealer-software of Ford ——————————→		UCS	MASCO
			Hawtal whiting	FF-Developments
	Ford-HP (CIM)	Porsche engineering		Modern Engineering
		Gedas (VW) ——————→	Gedas – CDC (ICEM)	
Cases	Company A ——→ (1989; 1992)	planning for 1995	position in 1989 ——→	Company C (1992; 1995)
		Company B (1989; 1992; 1995)		

Sources: see text.

Company A	concerns engineering department of small-scale car producer.
Company B	concerns engineering department of small-scale car producer.
Company C	concerns large IT services firm.

Comprehensive Case Studies

Company A can quite clearly be placed in stage one; it is an engineering department of a relatively small car manufacturer and its engineering and design work is exclusively for internal use. Company B is comparable to case A with regard to the size and type of activity, however, it also delivers its knowledge-intensive services to outside clients. These clients are among the world's leading car producers. The third case, company C, is a large firm selling information technology services. Recently it has become a full-service supplier, in the sense that it offers a range of IT services dedicated to making their clients use their IT systems in the best possible way. During the interviews it became clear that the IT services supplier in the last few years had moved from offering one business to four related businesses. The shift from a focused service supplier to one offering a full-service concept marks the transition from stage three to stage four.

For all three cases dynamic elements were explicitly included. Although we did not follow the respective case-study companies for a longer time period, the policies over the last few years and the planning for the coming years was discussed in the interviews. In addition, documents concerning the case-study firms covered a period dating back to the end of the eighties and included statements about future goals regarding strategic planning as well. For example, company A states in a number of documents that they intend to sell services to outside parties based on their expertise. Presently, they are in a process of strategy formulation concerning this move to stage two. In this rather fragmented market of engineering and design services for the car industry they have to define quite clearly: first, what are their core capabilities; second, whether they can carve out a market segment or niche on the basis of their core capabilities and third, do the benefits in terms of, for example revenue and learning from demanding clients, exceed the potential disadvantages such as losing control over proprietary information in the provider–client relationship and consequently the risk of imitation.

Contrary to the companies A and C, company B has already for some time pursued a strategy in line with stage two and will continue to use that strategy in the near future. It is interesting to see how the routines to learn from clients and benchmarking if they are still delivering 'state of the art' engineering and design services are embedded in the strategies of the firm. For example, it is standard procedure that assignments for clients are handled by teams which consist of engineers from both the client's firm and company B as provider. These teams act very much as problem solvers to reach their goal, in that process each party has the opportunity of learning the special know-how of their partner. Company B has, on the one hand, a policy of openness to their client/partners, but at the same time a dedicated intention to learn. According to a study by Hamel (1991) the intent is one of the three factors which determine the successful learning from partners. The other two factors are receptivity and transparency. In the case of company B these last two factors are, to a certain extent, valid. The evidence is less clear-cut for this factor than for the intend factor. As a result in Table 10.2 we classified company B as successful in learning from clients, mostly demanding clients, and characterized that with a double plus. Compared to company A, with no positive learning from clients, and company C with a single plus, company B was the most professional and very organized with regard to the use of clients as resources for the internal development of services. They had already worked for quite a number of years for very demanding clients in an extremely competitive setting. While company C has been growing rapidly in the booming market of IT services, and had only recently found competition becoming rather severe. Just last year they set a reorganisation in motion which reflects their intention to exploit their position in the most competitive and advanced markets in Europe and the USA more fully.

Company C is in a much better position to ensure leverage of the client relationships than the companies A and B. Largely because it is offering a full-service concept to its clients and not a single-focus service. Company C is also trying to exploit that position by cross-marketing and cross-referencing. This implies that existing clients of one of their services receive information about potentially related services also offered by company C. The organizational complexity increases considerably when a company adopts the status of a full-service supplier. To run a smooth operation and exploit all business opportunities related to this stage four position requires the upgrading of internal organizational capabilities. Company C has been investing in IT solutions to upgrade organizational memory. The issues of leveraging, learning and organizational capabilities will be discussed in more detail in the following paragraph, because they are the key concepts to increasing the dynamics in the stages model.

Where do we go from here? After presenting this empirical evidence related to the stages model, a number of questions emerge which are addressed in the next paragraph.

Table 10.2 **Learning and Capability Development in Three Case-Studies.**

Firm	Present stage	External exposure	Learning from clients	Leverage of client relationship	Development of internal organizational capabilities
A	one	Some alliances	-	-	?
B	two	Some demanding clients	++	-	?
C	four	Alliances and demanding clients	+	++	++

- First, why is there a tendency to move along the stages?
- Secondly, how can we explain the occurrence of reverse movements in the stages trajectory?

CAPABILITIES AND DYNAMICS IN SERVICE FUNCTION DEVELOPMENT

The bulk of the empirical evidence shows a clear evolution in the development of service functions. The observed process can be generalized as a gradual move from stage one to stage two and successively to stage three and four. In a number of cases there was a direct shift from the organizational configuration in stage one, to one of those in stage three, thus it is possible to skip a stage. Furthermore, the process of evolution may stall at a certain stage and most certainly a substantial number of knowledge-intensive service firms will not make the move to stage four.

In the next section we will discuss the two factors, leverage and learning opportunities which have contributed to the movement along the trajectory of stages. These two factors have provided an incentive for the successive shifts of stages. However, the organizational capabilities must be developed sufficiently to reap the benefits from the expansion in opportunities (Chandler, 1992). The latter issue will be examined in the section on organizational capabilities. We will start with a distinction between functional and application capabilities.

Functional and Application Capabilities

At this point it is important to make a distinction between functional capabilities and industrial knowledge. The former relate to the software competencies of a software firm and the engineering competencies of an engineering firm. These functional capabilities have to be applied in a particular firm and in a particular industrial context. Generally, this involves some adjustments being made to the functional capabilities in order to fit customer-specific requirements. We want to label the ability of a service supplier to tailor their service capabilities to the specific needs of a client as its application capabilities. The customization can be done faster and better when the service supplier has prior knowledge about the industry from which the customer stems. As a result, clients increasingly require a degree of knowledge from service suppliers about the industry concerned. There is, however, a problem associated with the requirement of knowledge of the industry which often arises in the contract negotiations. The requirement of knowledge of the industry implies that the service provider has had clients from that industry and learning from those clients has contributed to their application capabilities. This process of enhancing service application capabilities will improve the competitiveness of the firm and it is inconsistent if a client benefits from that process but at the same time wants to discontinue that process in the case of the contract under review. It will endanger a crucial learning routine of the service supplier, namely to augment its application capabilities and thereby improve its competitive position as a disseminator. Company C, from our case-study sample, has resolved that conflict of interest by developing a policy that they only sign a contract if they have the possibilities to use the 'generic' knowledge acquired during the contract for other purposes as well. Thus the upgraded functional capabilities can be applied to tackle problems encountered in projects for competitors.

Increasing Leverage and Learning Opportunities

In our case-interviews, the possibilities of leveraging and learning were repeatedly mentioned as two of the main factors justifying the shift to the next stage. Also in the strategic management literature the concept of leveraging is gaining importance (De Fillippi, 1992; Lele, 1992). It refers to the means by which a firm exploits its distinctive competences in order to enhance its competitive advantage over rivals. To understand how the leveraging and learning opportunities increase in the dynamic process of the successive stages, we have to use the previously introduced concepts of functional and application capabilities (see Fig. 10.1) as described in the previous paragraph.

In stage one, an internal department is responsible for the development of knowledge-intensive services to be used by the parent company. Thus the functional capability can be 'sold to', 'tested by', or 'upgraded by' only one player, i.e. the parent company. Thus the leveraging of the functional capability is limited to one company and also the learning opportunities are constrained by exposure to one user.

Opening up possibilities for that department to sell services to third parties creates opportunities for leveraging the functional capabilities. This is particularly true of knowledge-related services. One of the characteristics of knowledge is that it does not disappear when sold, it can be sold again (Teece 1980). Instead of combining the functional capabilities (I) with one type of application (A), in stage two, the combinations IB and IC might have market value as well. They represent different applications of the same functional capability. These new users also create new learning opportunities, in particular when the outside clients are very demanding or act as lead users. They will not only enhance the application capabilities but strengthen the functional capabilities as well.

The shift to stage three, the shedding of the in-house unit, implies a rising level of independence for the unit. Often that shift has resulted in, first, a widening of scope in looking for potential clients, also outside the industry of the former owner. And secondly we have witnessed increasing focus, and consequently a rise, in the resources for the development of its functional capabilities. Leveraging and learning opportunities will be multiplied by

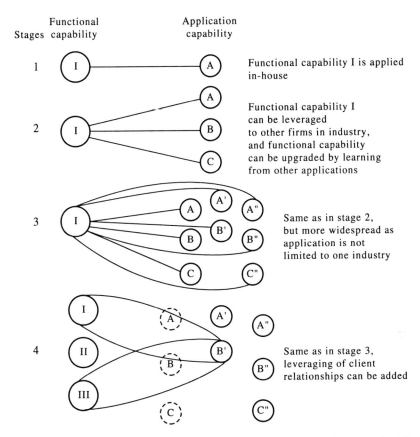

Fig. 10.1   Leverage and Learning Opportunities in the Stages Model.

marketing to clients in other industries (A', B' and A", B"); and selling a larger variety of combinations of functional and application capabilities (IA, IA', IA", IB, IB', IB"). Another reason for shedding the in-house unit is to assure clients of the independence of the venture and willingness to supply the best expertise.

The move to stage four implies the addition of functional capabilities. Leveraging can occur when the knowledge-intensive firm can accomplish the cross-marketing of its functional capabilities. When it sells a combination of its functional capability I and application capability B' and it is able to add to that existing relationship services based on its functional capability III, one can speak of cross-marketing and leveraging of the relationship with an existing client. We have encountered numerous examples. In the case of our European IT services firm, it often starts out initially with the idea of selling software services to a client. When, in the next phase, the implementation of the software is at stake, often the organizational advisory group of the IT services firm will take care of the implementation. Thus a second functional capability is added to the first one in serving one client. From the point of view of the client, this development is often referred to as one-stop-shopping (Nayyar, 1990). The competitiveness of the additional service provision is based on a combination of functional and application capabilities. In this case the latter are already largely available, because most relevant information about the user can be found in the internal department selling software services. The leveraging of this element of the application capability rests on the assumption that the client agrees with the information transfer within the supplier organization and on the organizational capabilities of the supplier.

Organizational Capabilities

In the previous section we have shown that the increasing leverage and learning opportunities have contributed to the successive movements along the stages. However, the firm does not in all cases have the means to exploit these opportunities. In our research we encountered a case of an IT department in a major food company, which had moved from stage one to stage two. Instead of only working for internal users, they deliberately chose to work with third parties as well. The positive impact on learning opportunities was however invalidated by the negative effects of human resource problems. IT staff working for third parties, experienced an increase in their status and related privileges. The resulting dual personnel structure had serious drawbacks on staff's morale and efficiency. Subsequently, the company decided to stop working for third parties and retrench to the configuration of stage one. The organizational capabilities of that firm were not sufficient to deal with the human resource problems associated with working for third parties.

One aspect of organizational capabilities concerns the creation of optimum conditions for pooling application expertise generated from completed projects. It becomes important in stage three and is even more crucial as a skill for full service suppliers in stage four. Three elements provide opportunities for upgrading organizational memory. The solutions implemented are aided by IT-based tools such as electronic bulletin boards and extensive electronic mail facilities (including voice mail). In addition, it appeared that these formal aspects of routines are complemented by the reliance on informal networks of professionals who cooperated in previous project-teams. Development of project routines has helped to structure project management. Organizing for cross-marketing opportunities is based on knowledge of the industry represented in relational databases developed by the supplier. Full service suppliers committed to cross marketing therefore face a large-scale investment in IT solutions which can be called upon by units involved in full-service supply to a specific client. It releases the client from the time and resource-consuming requirement of submitting application-specific data every time one of the units needs information.

CONCLUSION

The particular characteristics of knowledge-intensive services such as their interactive and knowledge-creating nature renders most of the traditional approaches to the outsourcing issue incomplete. Most of the strategic, environmental and operational factors as used in the make or buy decision concerning components are of importance in the outsourcing of knowledge-intensive services as well, however, other factors need to be included to understand the emerging markets for knowledge-intensive services. The empirical evidence supports this view and indicates that external coordination and learning need more emphasis.

The dynamic capabilities paradigm can fulfil the requirements for the research approach in this study. This paradigm includes important concepts such as learning and capabilities. It provides a framework to examine the dynamics underlying the development of knowledge-intensive services in a complex manufacturing environment and their relation to internal and external resources and capabilities. The ability to learn from demanding clients and lead users for software and engineering services appeared to be crucial to the enhancement of functional and application capabilities. A successful combination of the two can lead to competitive advantage.

The bulk of the empirical evidence shows a clear evolution in the development of service functions. The observed process can be generalized as a gradual move from in-house development to a more autonomous status in which clients also play a role. The service functions are then exposed to market discipline and may become a profit centre. This often leads to the shedding of the in-house unit and the final stage is the move of the service supplier to offer a package of a number of related services. The mini-cases and comprehensive case-studies confirmed that the stages model derived from Howells (1988) could be applied to the engineering and IT services and to the car industry. This stages model was used as a starting point, it was expanded to explain the movement from one stage to another. The concepts of leveraging and learning were introduced. Leverage and learning opportunities have contributed to the dynamics in the movement along the stages. These two factors have provided an incentive to the successive shift of stages. However, the organizational capabilities must be developed sufficiently to reap the benefits from the expansion in opportunities.

Thus we can conclude that competence-building cannot take place solely within the boundaries of the firm. Some firms have learned that their competences in knowledge-intensive service functions can be enhanced by spinning-off those functions. It promotes competence-building through learning from other firms and better brenchmarking and may achieve important economics of scale and scope by leveraging their capabilities.

REFERENCES

Baker, W. E. and Faulkner, R. R. "Strategies for Managing Suppliers of Professional Services". *California Management Review*, Vol. 33, pp. 33–45, 1991.

Brooke, L. "Outside Design Hangs On". *Automotive Industries*, pp. 59–61, February 1992.

Carrabine, L. "CAD/CAM Creates Car Complexion". *Computer Aided Engineering*, October 1990.

Chandler, A. D. "Organizational Capabilities and the Economic History of the Industrial Enterprise". *Journal of Economic Perspectives*, Vol. 6(3), pp. 79–100, 1992.

Ciborra, C. "Alliances as Learning Experiments: Cooperation, Competition and Change in High-Tech Industries". In Mytelka, L. K., ed., *Strategic Partnership; State, Firms and International Competition*. London: Pinter Publishers, 1991.

Clark, K. B., Chew, B. W. and Fujimoto, T. "Product Development in the World Auto Industry". *Brookings Papers on Economic Activity*, No. 3, pp. 729–781, Washington: The Brookings Institution, 1987.

Computerworld, 1990.

DeFillippi, R. J. "Resource Leverage, Relational Governance and Customer Commitment in Product Development". Paper for the 12th SMS-Conference, London, October 1992.

Elfring, T. "Structure and Growth of Business Services in Europe". In Jong, H. W. de, ed., *The Structure of European Industry*. Dordrecht: Kluwer Academic Publishers, 1993.

Elfring, T. and Baven, G. "Development of Knowledge-Intensive Service Functions: Challenges in the Make, Buy or Cooperate Decision". Management Report, No. 134, Rotterdam School of Management, 1993.

Foxall, G. R. "User-Initiated Product Innovations". *Industrial Marketing Management*, Vol. 18, pp. 95–104, 1989.

Griffiths, J. "Nissan in Venture with US Group". *Financial Times*, March 2 1989.

Gruhler, W. "Dienstleistungbestimmter Strukturwandel in Deutschen Industrie-unternehmen". Köln: DIV, 1990.

Hamel, G. "Competition for Competence and Interpartner Learning within International Strategic Alliances". *Strategic Management Journal*, Vol. 12, pp. 83–103, 1991.

Handelsblatt, November 15, 1990.

Harrigan, K. R. "Vertical Integration and Corporate Strategy". *Academy of Management Journal*, Vol. 28, pp. 397–425, 1985.

Harrigan, K. R. *Strategic Flexibility*. New York: Lexington Books, 1985.

Helper, S. "Supplier Relations and Technical Change: Theory and Application to the U.S. Automobile Industry". Unpublished PhD Dissertation, Harvard University, Boston, 1987.

Herzenberg, S. "Towards a Cooperative Commonwealth? Labor and Restructuring in the U.S. and Canadian Auto Industries". Unpublished PhD Dissertation, Massachusetts Institute of Technology, Department of Economics, Boston, 1990.

Howells, J. *Economic, Technological and Locational Trends in European Services*. Aldershot: Avebury, 1988.

Jackson, K. "Houston Firm Buying Ford Computer Group". *Automotive News*, December 9, 1991.

Lele, M. *Creating Strategic Leverage*. New York: John Wiley, 1992.

Lowell, J. "Hands Off Engineer Keeps his Hands in the Pot". *Ward's Auto World*, March 1990.

MacCharles, D. C. *Knowledge Production in Manufacturing: Its Impact on Business Services*, Vancouver: The Fraser Institute, 1990.

Marler, D. "The Post-Japanese Model of Automotive Component Supply: Selected North American Case Studies". *International Motor Vehicle Program*. MIT, May 1989.

Mintzberg, H. "An Emerging Strategy of 'Direct' Research". *Administrative Science Quarterly*, Vol. 24, pp. 582–589, 1979.

Moulaert, F., Martinelli, F. and Djellal, F. "The Role of Information Technology Consultancy in the Transfer of Information Technology to Production and Service Organizations". NOTA, working document W10, The Hague, 1990.

Nayyar, P. R. "Information Asymmetries: A Source of Competitive Advantage for Diversified Service Firms". *Strategic Management Journal*, Vol. 11, pp. 513–519, 1990.

Nishiguchi, T. "Strategic Dualism: An Alternative in Western Industrial Societies". Unpublished Doctoral Dissertation, University of Oxford, 1989.

O'Farrell, P. N. and Moffat, L. A. R. "An Interaction Model of Business Service Production and Consumption". *British Journal of Management*, Vol. 2, pp. 205–221, 1991.

Phelan, M. "Rent an Engineer Business Booms in Europe Too". *Ward's Auto World*, March 1988.

Porter, M. *Competitive Strategy*. New York: Free Press, 1980.

Prahalad, C. K. and Hamel, G. "The Core Competence of the Corporation". *Harvard Business Review*, Vol. 68(3), pp. 79–91, 1990.

Quinn, J. B., Doorley, T. and Paquette, P. "Rethinking Strategic Focus". *Sloan Management Review*, Winter 1990.

Quinn, J. B. *Intelligent Enterprise: A Knowledge and Service-Based Paradigm for Industry*. New York: Free Press, 1992.

Teece, D. J. "Economies of Scope and the Scope of the Enterprise". *Journal of Economic Behaviour and Organization*, pp. 223–247, 1980.

Teece, D. J., Pisano, G. and Shuen, A. "Firm Capabilities, Resources, and the Concept of Strategic Management". CCC Working Paper No. 90–8, University of California, Berkeley, 1990.

von Hippel, E. "Lead Users: A Source of Novel Product Concepts". *Management Science*, Vol. 32, pp. 791–805, 1986.

Voss, C. A. "The Role of Users in the Development of Applications Software", *Journal of Production Innovation Management*, Vol. 2, pp. 113–121, 1985.

"Troubled Porsche May Tell its Chairman to Step Down". *Wall Street Journal Europe*, February 20 1992.

Williamson, O. E. *The Economic Institutions of Capitalism*. New York: Free Press, 1985.

Womack, J., Jones, D. T. and Roos, D. *The Machine that Changed the World*. New York: Rawson Associates, 1990.

PART FOUR

LEVERAGING EXISTING COMPETENCES

The three chapters in Part Four investigate the efforts of firms to achieve more effective competence leveraging. Rather than emphasizing the importance of having scarce strategic resources, these chapters focus on the efforts of firms to improve their abilities to effectively coordinate and deploy their available resources.

Chapter 11 by Volberda explores the challenge of coordinating assets and capabilities in a highly dynamic market environment. Drawing on his studies of Philips Semiconductor division, Volberda explores the tension between the need to establish routines for deploying existing assets and capabilities, on the one hand, and the need to develop new (potentially disruptive) processes that embody new capabilities required to meet new market opportunities or demands, on the other. He proposes that firms can resolve this paradox by creating organizational flexibility, and he discusses the kinds of resources and managerial capabilities that appear to provide some degree of organizational flexibility in the context of Philips' semiconductor operations.

In Chapter 12, Winterscheid and McNabb investigate the evolution of AT&T's organizational configurations for developing telecommunications products as AT&T grew from a national to a global company. They describe three stages in AT&T's evolution marked by different organizational approaches to striking the best balance between serving specific customer needs in different national markets and achieving efficiencies in leveraging AT&T's technologies as widely as possible. They suggest that a firm's ability to evolve organizationally is constrained both by delays in managerial recognition of the need for new organizational structures and by the difficulties of building new coordinating mechanisms appropriate to each new organizational structure.

In Chapter 13, Sanchez discusses the use of computer-assisted design and development (CADD) programs and modular product design as "quick-connect" coordination technologies that may help a firm leverage its competence more effectively and broadly. He proposes that the standardized interfaces between shared CADD systems and between components in a modular product design can "embed coordination" of component development activities, allowing component developers to work autonomously and concurrently. Effective use of the quick-connect technologies to embed coordination is allowing some firms to leverage their competences more broadly by drawing on and coordinating an expanded network of firm-addressable resources.

11

FLEXIBLE CONFIGURATION STRATEGIES WITHIN PHILIPS SEMICONDUCTORS: A STRATEGIC PROCESS OF ENTREPRENEURIAL REVITALIZATION

Henk W. Volberda

INTRODUCTION

In the recent dynamic capability perspective of strategic management, organizational flexibility is considered as a strategic asset in situations in which anticipation is impossible and strategic surprise likely (Teece *et al.*, 1992). In the resource-based perspective to strategy formation the firm is seen as a bundle of tangible and intangible resources and managerial capabilities that must be identified, selected, developed and deployed to generate superior performance (Amit and Schoemaker, 1993). These superior capabilities and firm-specific resources may lead to a core competence. Nonetheless, Leonard-Barton (1992) rightly remarks that in highly competitive environments a core competence can become a core rigidity; firms develop core rigidities together with highly specialized resources to enhance profits at the price of reduced flexibility. An organization needs specific capabilities to develop competences, but at the same time remaining open for expanded search. Teece *et al.* (1992) therefore have suggested more recently that the relative superiority and imitability of managerial capabilities and organizational resources cannot be taken for granted and that, from a normative perspective, the firm must always remain in a dynamic capability building mode. Successfully competing in dynamic product markets requires resources, capabilities, and strategies that are intrinsically different from those likely to lead to competitive success in more stable markets (cf. Sanchez, 1993). These paradoxical requirements imply that there are balances to be struck if capabilities and resources are to remain vital.

This chapter proposes a new dynamic approach to understanding and investigating the managerial capabilities and organizational resources that are likely to enable a firm to achieve higher levels of flexibility. By considering flexibility as a strategic paradox, this paper distinguishes four strategies to configure the managerial capabilities and organizational resources of the firm for effective responses to strategic change, namely the rigid, the planned, the flexible and the chaotic mode. Each mode reflects a particular configuration strategy of dealing with change and preservation at a certain point of time. Furthermore, from this typology different path dependencies are derived for confronting the paradox over time; a firm's previous investments and managerial capabilities constrain its future behavior. Subsequently, the model is applied in an Assembly Department of Philips Semiconductors. The findings of this longitudinal case-study suggest that the risk of a "planned" configuration strategy is the transformation into a "rigid" organization as a result of "strategic drift." As a consequence of highly routine capabilities the firm may be "locked" into a specific set of irreversible, fixed assets inhibiting its ability to respond to environmental change or competitive threats. The inertia is due to, for intance, sunk costs in certain technologies (technological system), entrenched social structures (structural system), and also to organizational members becoming attached to certain cognitive styles, behavioral dispositions, and decision heuristics (cultural system). A trajectory of entrepreneurial revitalization can help firms in fundamentally unpredictable environments to more easily exploit unknown opportunities in technologies and product markets. The development of more dynamic managerial capabilities together with less tight technical, structural and cultural systems (resources) can endow the firm with flexibility.

ROUTINE PROLIFERATION VERSUS CAPABILITY DEVELOPMENT

How do strategists reconcile the conflicting forces for change and stability? How do they promote order and control, while having to respond, renew, and learn? Notwithstanding these provocative questions, most of the literature in strategic management is still rooted in stability, not change (cf. Mintzberg, 1990). Indeed, firms must develop certain unique and difficult to alienate routines as a part of their core competence. These *repositories of routines* endow the firm with a focus to search, yet at the same time suppress their attention span and their capacity to absorb new information. Nelson and Winter (1982) purpose that the routinization of activity in an organization, that is, investigating in tacit knowledge, constitutes the most important form of storage for the organization's specific operational knowledge. The developed routines spell out behavior that is appropriate and search for new ideas that are reasonable and consistent with prior learning. Teece (1984: 106) however has argued that a *limited repertoire of available routines severely constrains a firm's strategic choice.* This suppression of choice is probably a condition for the smoothness and effectiveness that routines and skilled behavior confer. Nevertheless, there are attendant risks that the things done well may be the wrong things, or that unnoticed abnormalities may render the performance ineffective or irrelevant. Similarly, Utterback and Abernathy's (1975) model posits that a firm which does pursue the evolution of its processes and products to the extreme may find that it has achieved the benefits of high productivity only at the cost of decreased flexibility and innovative capacity. It must face competition from innovative products that are produced by other flexible firms. When environmental changes become increasingly undefined, fast moving, and numerous, it is risky to rely upon routine proliferation. Routines restrict the development of new knowledge and continued competence by imposing old understandings. Therefore, some researchers in strategic management considered organizational flexibility as a strategic option (cf. Aaker and Mascarenhas, 1984; Eppink, 1979; Quinn, 1985).

In this chapter we will further elaborate the flexibility concept and explicitly develop various configuration strategies to deal with capability development and routine proliferation. By considering some recent theoretical developments in strategic management from the linear towards the learning and dynamic capability model, we will show that flexibility is inherently paradoxical and requires a constructive friction between change and preservation. In this regard, an organization needs explicit strategic intentions in order to develop competences (Prahalad and Hamel, 1990), but at the same time remaining open for expanded search (Leonard-Barton, 1992). A clearer formulation of the strategic paradox of flexibility can be derived based on some insights drawn from systems theory of control. In this approach flexibility is treated as a two-dimensional concept. First, flexibility is perceived to be a managerial task. In this connection, the concern is with the managerial capabilities of the management that endow the firm with flexibility. Second, flexibility is perceived as an organization design task. The concern here is with the 'controllability' of the organizational resources under different conditions: is it possible to activate flexible managerial capabilities within the technological, structural and cultural system.

This two-dimensional conception of flexibility can be portrayed in a conceptual model or variance model. From this model some specific hypotheses are derived which state under which environmental characteristics certain flexible managerial capabilities and organizational resources are likely to lead to organizational competences. In addition, on the basis of the dimensions of the variance model, a typology of configuration strategies is developed, namely the rigid, the planned, the flexible, and the chaotic mode. Each mode reflects a particular way of dealing with the flexibility paradox of change versus preservation at a certain point of time. Furthermore, from this typology different path dependencies can be derived for handling the paradox over time. These path dependencies serve as hypotheses with respect to the process of strategic change.

By connecting the variance model and the organizational typology, the Flexibility Audit and Redesign (FAR) method is developed. Subsequently, the method is applied within the Assembly Department Glass-Bead Diodes of Philips Semiconductors. This selected longitudinal case-study serves as a test or 'hold out' sample of the underlying variance and process hypotheses of the FAR method.

FLEXIBILITY FROM THREE STRATEGIC PERSPECTIVES: THE LINEAR, THE LEARNING, AND THE DYNAMIC CAPABILITY MODEL

Historically, an organization's strategy has been thought of as an integrated plan. The most frequently cited definitions of organization strategy are provided by Andrews (1971: 28) and Chandler (1962: 13), and emphasize concepts such as goals, resource allocations, and especially plans. These concepts form the essential elements of the *linear model* of strategic management (Chaffee, 1985), corresponding to what others have called the 'planning' (Mintzberg, 1973), 'rational' (Peters and Waterman, 1982), 'rational comprehensive' or 'synoptic' (Fredrickson, 1983) approach.

This linear model still pervades the literature on the process of strategic management. It characterizes the strategic process as a highly rational, proactive process that involves activities such as establishing goals, monitoring the environment, assessing internal capabilities, searching for and evaluating alternative actions, and developing an integrated plan to achieve the goals (Hofer and Schendel, 1978; Lorange and Vancil, 1977). Emphasis is on planning "What to do," rather than on planning "What the organization might be capable of doing in the future."

Surprisingly enough, it was Ansoff (1978), one of the founders of the linear model, who suggested that the nature of environmental change was changing and giving rise to strategic surprises, making strategic anticipation and strategic planning of the sort that proceeds in an outside-in, market-to-product development manner no longer useful. The basic effect of uncertainty is that it limits the ability of the organization to preplan or make decisions about activities in advance of their execution (Galbraith, 1973: 4). Because of this effect, organizations must search for flexibility (Thompson, 1967: 148). The more uncertain the situation, the more an organization will need flexibility as a complement to planning (Eppink, 1978: 14–15, 59–61). Therefore, Ansoff (1978) asserted that in these situations the use of traditional action strategies ("in which direction do we change the firm's position in the environment") would be increasingly supplemented and sometimes replaced by preparedness or flexible configuration strategies ("How do we configure the resources of the firm for effective responses to unanticipated surprises"). Rather than adhering single-mindedly to a predetermined set of goals and course of action, it is better to be capable of adapting to a variety of possible events, exigencies or unpredictable states of nature.

In line with this *learning model* of strategic management, Mintzberg and Waters (1985) argue that the focus is not placed on deliberate planning and control, but on developing an organizational capacity for strategic thinking and learning, which means being open and responsive. As a result, strategies emerge which are not guided by explicit *a priori* intentions. Patterns or consistencies are realized despite, or in the absence of, intentions. Nevertheless, the *emergence of these ex-post* strategies does not have to mean that management is out of control, only—in some cases at least—that it is open, flexible and responsive, in other words, willing to learn. Such behavior is especially important when an environment is too unstable or complex to comprehend, or too imposing to defy. Openness to such emergent strategy enables management to act before everything is fully understood— to respond to an evolving reality rather than having to focus on a stable fantasy. As an example, Mintzberg and Waters (1985) describe that a distinctive competence cannot always be assessed on paper *a priori*; often, perhaps usually, it has to be discovered empirically, by taking actions that test where strengths and weaknesses really lie.

Until recently, this learning model of strategic management is reinforced by the *dynamic capability model*. In this perspective, flexibility refers to management's ability to develop those capabilities that will be effective in different future positions. It is aimed at identifying and evolving those core capabilities that are important in multiple segments under alternate scenarios (Schoemaker, 1992). The objective of the firm's strategy therefore becomes the acquisition of the set of resources and capabilities which endow the firm with its optimal set of strategic options (Sanchez, 1993).

These developments within strategic management from the linear towards the learning and more recently the dynamic capability model contributed substantially to the concept of organizational flexibility. Organizational flexibility from a strategic perspective means creating a flexible configuration of managerial capabilities and organizational resources for facilitating emergent strategies. It results in a process of the management of 'unintended order' (Mintzberg and Waters, 1985) or 'controlled chaos' (Quinn, 1985), in which capability development as well as routine proliferation is possible. That is, the organization is capable of responding to surprises and initiate novel actions (core capability renewal), but also able to continuously improve its capabilities (core capability upgrading).

FLEXIBILITY AS A CONFIGURATION OF MANAGERIAL CAPABILITIES AND ORGANIZATIONAL RESOURCES

A clearer formulation of the strategic paradox of flexibility can be derived based on some insights drawn from systems theory of control (De Leeuw and Volberda, 1992). In this approach flexibility is treated as a two-dimensional concept (see Fig. 11.1). First, flexibility is perceived to be a managerial task. In this connection, the concern is with the managerial capabilities that endow the firm with flexibility, e.g. manufacturing flexibility to expand the number of products the firm can profitably offer to the market or innovation flexibility to reduce the response time for bringing new products to the market. Second, flexibility is perceived as an organizational task. The concern here is with the 'controllability' or changeability of the organization resources under different conditions: is it possible to activate these managerial capabilities within the technological, structural, and cultural system. For instance, manufacturing flexibility requires a technological system with multi-purpose machinery, universal equipment, and an extensive operational production repertoire. In the same way, innovation flexibility requires a structural system which consist of multi-functional teams, few hierarchical levels, and few process regulations. These two dimensions result in the following definition (Volberda, 1990, 1992; Volberda and Cheah, 1993):

Flexibility is the degree to which an organization possesses a variety of actual and potential managerial capabilities, and the rapidity by which these can be activated, in order to increase the control capacity of management and improve the controllability of organizational resources.

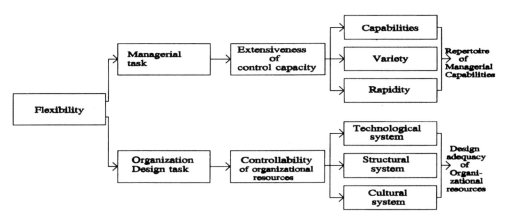

Fig. 11.1. Organizational flexibility and the associated management and organization tasks.

The Management Task: Developing Dynamic Capabilities

As a management task, flexibility is concerned with the creation or promotion of managerial capabilities, especially in situations of unexpected disturbance. It must be noted that these managerial capabilities cannot be equated only with the activities of the manager. While in most situations managers do indeed dominate this process, in principle every organizational member participates to some extent in the managerial process of capability development. The managerial system of an organization therefore is a partsystem the relation of which to the system as a whole varies greatly with the type of organization. That is, the managerial system might be a subsystem that is identical to the managerial subsystem. In this case of extrinsic management, management is exerted by some authoritarian manager(s). On the other hand, the managerial system might as well be an aspectsystem, for instance, when groups have self-control. In this case, there is not a separate managerial subsystem, but the control consists of a specific bundle of relations between the members of the group. In contrast with extrinsic management, the latter intrinsic mode of control refers to more democratic and more participative forms of decision-making in organizations. Core components of this managerial task are:

(a) *the existence of actual and potential managerial capabilities*—not only the actual arsenal of capabilities is important, but also the collection of potential flexibility-increasing capabilities. The possible emergence of opportunities or threats require management to have some potential capabilities to rely upon as an insurance against risk (see Scott, 1965);

(b) *the variety of managerial capabilities*—Ashby (1964) demonstrated that the required variety of a firm's managerial capabilities must, at a minimum, be equal to the variety of disturbances in the environ ment. The variety of managerial capabilities can be in terms of either the quantity, that is the number of capabilities, or the quality of the capabilities (such as one-off versus durable flexibility-increasing capabilities). For instance, the training of multi-skilled personnel results in a more durable mode of flexibility, while the contracting out of certain peripheral activities or 'hire and fire' employment practices tend to result in a one-off improvement in flexibility; and

(c) *the rapidity by which management can activate its capabilities*—management may possess the right capabilities, but this does not necessarily mean that the management can activate these capabilities in time. Flexibility is not a static condition, but it is a dynamic process. Time is a very essential factor of organizational flexibility.

These dynamic capabilities which endow the firm with flexibility are manifested in the *'flexibility-mix.'* This refers to the repertoire of flexibility increasing capabilities that management possesses, and the rapidity by which

	Internal Flexibility (I)	External Flexibility (E)
Operational (R) Flexibility	internal routine control (IR)	external routine control (ER)
Structural (A) Flexibility	internal adaptive control (IA)	external adaptive control (EA)
Strategic (G) Flexibility	internal goal control (IG)	external goal control (EG)

Fig. 11.2. Types of flexibility.

management can activate these capabilities. The flexibility-mix consists of three types of flexibility (see Fig. 11.2): operational flexibility, structural flexibility, and strategic flexibility (Ansoff and Brandenburg, 1971; Volberda, 1990). For each of these types a distinction can be made between internal and external flexibility. Internal flexibility is defined as management's capability to quickly adapt to the demands in the environment, while external flexibility refers to the capability of management to influence the environment, so that the firm becomes less vulnerable to changes in the environment.

Operational flexibility or routine maneuvering capacity consists of routine capabilities that are based upon existing structures or goals of the organization. This most frequently occurring type of flexibility relates to the volume of activities rather than the kinds of activities undertaken within the organization. These routines are primarily directed at the operational activities and are reactive in nature. The time horizon involved is short term. Even though the variety in the environment may be high, the sort of combinations is reasonably predictable so that management, on the basis of experience and extrapolation, is able to develop certain routines to reduce this uncertainty. An example of internal operational flexibility is the variation of production volume in the organization. Examples of external operational flexibility are the contracting out of certain peripheral activities or obtaining resources from more than one supplier.

Structural flexibility or adaptive maneuvering capacity refers to managerial capabilities to adapt the organization structure, and its decision and communication processes, to suit changing conditions, as well as the rapidity by which this can be accomplished (Krijnen, 1979). Examples of internal structural flexibility are the application of horizontal or vertical job enlargement, the creation of small production-units or work cells within a production line, or the transformation from a functional grouping to a market oriented grouping, with personnel and equipment that is interchangeable. Examples of external structural flexibility are forms of 'JIT-purchasing,' 'co-makership,' 'co-design,' or even 'joint-ventures' and other co-alignments.

Strategic flexibility or non-routine steering capacity refers to managerial capabilities related to the goals of the organization or the environment (Aaker and Mascarenhas, 1984). This radical type of flexibility is much more qualitative and goes together with changes in the kind of organizational activities, such as the creation of new product market combinations (external strategic flexibility) or the application of a new technology (internal strategic flexibility). Strategic flexibility is, by definition, unstructured and non-routine; the scarce information is very 'soft' and fuzzy. Totally new values and norms are required and past experience is more of a disadvantage rather than an advantage (Newman *et al.*, 1972). The creation of new activities in new situations has great importance.

Besides these three different types of flexibility, we can distinguish the *metaflexibility* of management, that is, the supporting monitoring or learning system. Metaflexibility involves the processing of information to facilitate the continual adjustment of the composition of management's flexibility-mix in line with changes in the environment. This requires the creation, integration and application of managerial capabilities in a flexible way.

The Organization Design Task: Creating Adequate Organizational Resources

The ability to initiate these managerial capabilities is dependent upon the design adequacy of the organizational resources, namely the organization's technological system, structural system, and cultural system. These determine the volume and composition (operational, structural, strategic) of the flexibility-mix, and its limitations. The creation of specific organizational resources constitutes the organization design task. This second dimension of flexibility, namely the 'controllability' of the system, is an organizational task which involves designing the appropriate technological, structural, and cultural systems necessary to effectively realize certain types of flexibility. These tangible resources (such as the mode of production, physical layout and transformation means of the technical system and basic organizational form and planning and control systems of the structural system) and intangible resources (such as the process regulations of the structural system and the identity, leadership style, and unwritten rules of the cultural system) are indispensable elements for the realization of flexibility (see Van Ham, Pauwe and Williams, 1987). While the tangible resources normally depreciate, the intangible resources involved in activating capabilities can cumulate over time.

In sum, this two-dimensional conception of flexibility creates a paradox: management must possess some dynamic capabilities which enhance its potential flexibility to avoid becoming rigid, but the firm must also be anchored in some way by distinctive resources in order to avoid chaos. There has to be a constructive tension (Kanter, 1983) between dynamic managerial capabilities which must be easily changed and the distinctive organizational resources which are necessary to preserve. This anchoring can be a result of the identity, leadership, unwritten rules and external orientation stemming from the cultural system, the basic organizational form, planning and control systems and process regulations of the structural system, or the mode of production, physical layout, means of production and operational production repertoire of the technological system.

In this connection, the *technological system* refers to the hardware (means of transformation, like machinery and equipment) and the software (knowledge) by which and the configuration in which the organization transfers materials and/or information. The characteristics of the technological system can range from routine to non-routine corresponding to the opportunities for routine capabilities.

By the *structural system* is meant not only the actual distribution of responsibilities and authority among the organization's personnel, but also the planning and control systems and the processes of decision-making, coordination and execution. The former is related to the construction of the organization in functions and units (organizational form or 'Aufbau' [Kieser and Kubicek, 1978]). The latter is related to the organizational regulations of processes ('Ablauf'). The structural system of the organization can range from mechanistic to organic (Burns and Stalker, 1961) corresponding to the opportunities for adaptive capabilities.

The *cultural system* can be defined as the shared interpretations about the kind and usefulness of work and cooperation. It is the idea system of the organization, which is contained in the minds of the organization members (Hofstede, 1980). As a consequence, the cultural system cannot be observed directly, but can only be felt. The cultural system may constrain the managerial capabilities by specifying broad, tacitly understood rules for appropriate action under unspecified contingencies. It can range from conservative to innovative depending upon the slack within the existing norms and value systems for strategic capabilities.

THE VARIANCE MODEL: BASIC ASSUMPTIONS AND HYPOTHESES

Up to this point, we have considered the managerial and organization design challenge of flexibility. On the one hand, we have argued that the management challenge of flexibility is concerned with the creation of a sufficient flexibility mix. On the other hand, we have claimed that the organization design challenge of flexibility is concerned with designing appropriate technological, structural, and cultural systems to generate the potential for flexibility within the organization necessary to realize the flexibility mix. If the potential for flexibility within the organizational resources is much smaller or much larger than the required flexibility mix, it will be necessary to redesign these organizational resources.

Nonetheless, we have not explicitly dealt with the factors that determine the sufficiency of the flexibility mix and thereby the adequacy of the organizational resources. When can management confine itself to operational flexibility together with tight organizational resources or when does it have to develop structural or even strategic flexibility together with looser organizational resources? We assume that the sufficiency of the flexibility mix and the adequacy of the organizational resources depend on the turbulence in the environment. That is, the more dynamic, complex, and unpredictable the environment, the more difficult it is to handle the managerial and organization design challenge.

This two-dimensional conception of flexibility together with the turbulence characteristics of the organizational environment can be portrayed in a conceptual model or variance model (see Fig. 11.3). This model explains which organizational resources and turbulence characteristics generate variations in the composition of the flexibility mix. In this connection, the flexibility mix represents the actual flexibility of management. Furthermore, the architecture of organizational resources indicates the potential for flexibility available within the organization, while the environmental turbulence characteristics determine the required volume and composition of the flexibility mix. The basic assumptions of our conceptual model are that

(i)   *the volume and composition of management's flexibility mix must be in line with the degree of environmental turbulence (**sufficiency of the flexibility mix**);*

(ii) *in order to activate a sufficient flexibility mix, the design of the organizational resources must facilitate enough potential for flexibility (**design adequacy of the organizational resources**);*

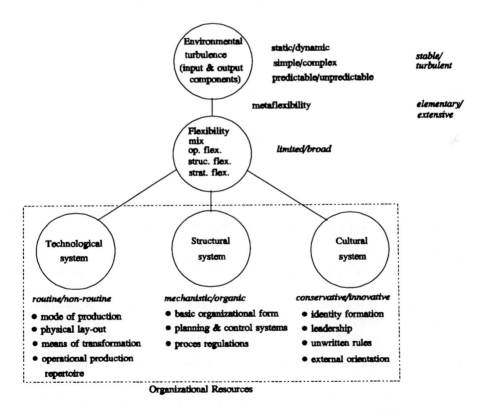

Fig. 11.3. A conceptual model of organizational flexibility.

(iii) the sufficiency of the flexibility mix (i) and the design adequacy of the organizational resources (ii) are continuously threatened by shifts in the degree of environmental turbulence and autonomous changes in the organizational resources.

These assumptions are based on our definition of flexibility. In this two-dimensional conception of flexibility, flexibility corresponds with large or at least sufficient dynamic capabilities of management (i) and high controllability of the organizational resources (ii). Consequently, the first assumption reflects the managerial challenge of flexibility, the second assumption reflects the design challenge of flexibility, while the third assumption indicates the difficulty of both these challenges by putting them in a dynamic context.

From these basic assumptions of the model, three central hypotheses can be derived which combine the degree of environmental turbulence, the flexibility mix, and the organizational resources.

H.1 organizations functioning in a static, simple, and predictable environment (stable) employ a limited flexibility mix and possess a routine technological system, a mechanistic structural system, and a conservative cultural system. In addition, the sensor and information processing capacity as a part of management's metaflexibility is very elementary.

This first hypothesis is very straightforward. In a stable environment, management does not have to activate a flexibility mix, nor do the organizational resources have to generate potential for flexibility. As a consequence, the sensor and information processing capacity is restricted to the primary functions of the organization.

H.2 organizations functioning in a dynamic and/or complex, but largely predictable environment (moderately turbulent) employ a more comprehensive flexibility mix, dominated by operational flexibility, and possess a more non-routine technological system, a relatively mechanistic structural system, and a conservative cultural system. In addition, management's sensor and information-processing capacity is very extensive and directed towards routine proliferation.

According to our second hypothesis, in a dynamic and complex, but largely predictable environment, management must activate many sophisticated routines to deal with these complex changes. This requires a potential for operational flexibility originating from a non-routine technological system. In addition, management needs an extensive information-processing capacity to anticipate complex changes and to facilitate routine development.

H.3 organizations functioning in a fundamentally unpredictable environment, which may also be dynamic and complex (turbulent), employ a very broad flexibility mix, dominated by structural and strategic flexibility, and possess a totally non-routine technological system, an organic structural system, and an innovative cultural system. Moreover, the sensor and information processing capacity as a part of management's metaflexibility is very rudimentary and directed towards enhancing the receptiveness to new environments through routine reduction.

The third hypothesis suggests that in unpredictable environments management must activate strategic flexibility together with structural flexibility originating from innovative cultural systems and organic structural systems. In such highly turbulent environments, management has no specific experience nor data, and therefore pure anticipation in the form of routine proliferation is impossible. The latter may even reduce its receptiveness to change. Instead of increasing its information-processing capacity, management should reduce the need for information processing and enhance its structural and strategic flexibility to cope with unexpected changes.

A TYPOLOGY OF CONFIGURATION STRATEGIES

On the basis of the two central dimensions of the variance model—the composition of the flexibility mix (preponderance of operational, structural, or strategic flexibility) and the controllability or design adequacy of the organizational resources (low or high changeability of organizational resources)—we can roughly distinguish four ideal types: the *rigid*, the *planned*, the *flexible*, and the *chaotic* configuration (see Fig. 11.4). In this typology, each ideal type is a result of a deliberate or emergent *configuration strategy* of management regarding the composition of the flexibility mix and the design of the organizational resources. In the '*rigid configuration*,' management possesses a very

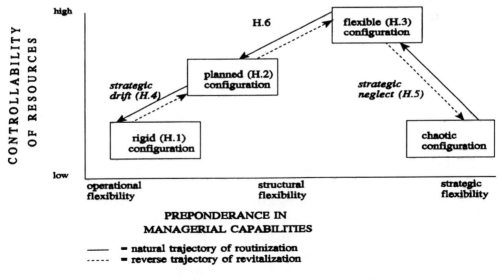

Fig. 11.4. A typology of configuration strategies.

small flexibility mix and the changeability of the organizational resources is low. The flexibility mix, as far as it exists, is dominated by simple routines. In addition, the choice and variation possibilities are limited; improvisation is a taboo in this organization. The mature technology (routine technological system), the functionalized and centralized structure with many hierarchical layers (mechanistic structural system) together with a monotonous and narrow-minded culture (conservative cultural system) do not allow any potential for flexibility and result in a fragile and vulnerable organization. The 'rigid configuration' reflects our first hypothesis (H.1).

In the 'planned configuration' management also has a narrow flexibility mix, but the variety of routines is less limited than in the 'rigid organization.' In addition, the controllability of the planned form is much higher. The flexibility mix mainly consists of specific rules and detailed procedures, which are very sophisticated and complex. This proliferation of routines requires a very extensive information-processing capacity. As a result of the surplus of operational flexibility, for every possible change the organization has developed a certain routine. Hence the mix is much more sophisticated than that of the rigid configuration.

The rigidity of the organizational resources is not a result of the technological system or the basic organizational form of the structural system, but more an outcome of strong process regulations of the structural system, like standardization, formalization and specialization, and very detailed planning and control systems (intangible resources). Also, the shared cultural beliefs and assumptions give very little leeway for deviant interpretations of the environment. Dissonance with this idea system is potentially threatening to the organization's integrity. As long as there are no unexpected changes, the controllability of organizational resources is high. However, if changes occur which are not calculated in the planning repertoire and are threatening to the shared idea system, the result is a situation referred to as 'strategic drift'; a situation in which consciously managed incremental changes do not necessarily succeed in keeping pace with environmental changes (Johnson, 1988: 88). As a consequence of this strategic drift, the incremental changes only result in further attempts to perfect the process regulations of the structural system and basic beliefs and assumptions of the cultural system, which are the very sources of inertia. Accordingly, slowness of response is characteristic of the 'planned configuration.' This configuration strategy corresponds with our second hypothesis (H.2).

In the 'chaotic configuration' management possesses a very extensive flexibility mix dominated by strategic flexibility, but the required organizational resources are totally uncontrollable. In such a firm, the possibilities of variation are unlimited; there are not firm-specific resources. There are innumerable initiatives for change, but it is impossible to implement them. A distinct technology, administrative structures, and some basic 'shared values' stemming from a cultural system are missing. Consequently, the environment can directly force the organization into a certain direction, that is, the organization is controlled by the environment. The lack of admini-strative stability is caused by 'strategic neglect.' According to Burgelman (1983: 234–237), 'strategic neglect' refers to the more or less deliberate tendency not to pay attention to the administrative structure of the organization. As a result, emerging administrative problems deteriorate from petty and trivial to severe and disruptive. In his study of new internal corporate ventures (ICV), Burgelman concluded that this administrative instability is exacerbated by the fact that there is no strong strategic orientation, while there is still a lot of opportunistic behavior on the part of some participants of the venture. The range of possible procedures is so large that it is very hard to make a choice. As a consequence of this lack of decisiveness, the decision-making capacity of the management is strongly reduced (Eppink, 1978: 41; Scott, 1965). Decisions are delayed, while the situation requires an immediate decision.

In the 'flexible configuration,' finally, management possesses a large and rich flexibility mix dominated by strategic and structural flexibility, while in addition the controllability of the organizational resources is reasonably high. Disturbances are fought against effectively with alert adaptations without management losing its distinctive capabilities. The resistance to signals of threat to the existing idea system is low, and results, in fact, in the adapting of the actual (innovative) idea system. Furthermore, the associated stimuli for change can easily be implemented with some supple adaptations within the existing non-routine technological system and organic structural system (Ansoff and Brandenburg, 1971). On the other hand, the organization is able to resist the threat of incorporation in its immediate environment, and the consequent loss of its distinctive competence. It develops some dominance over its environment to preserve its identity. The paradox between change and preservation is well manag-ed here. The flexible configuration complies with our third hypothesis (H.3).

Trajectories of Transformation

Each of the modes of our typology reflects a particular *configuration strategy* (deliberate or emergent) of dealing with the change–preservation paradox at a certain point in time. In the rigid, and to a lesser degree, in the planned mode, there is a lack of structural and strategic flexibility caused by a preference of preservation to change. In the flexible and especially the chaotic mode dominance of structural and strategic flexibility indicates a preference for change. From this organizational typology, therefore, different *strategic trajectories of transformation* can be obtained for dealing with the change–preservation paradox over time.

We hypothesize that

H.4 the risk of the 'planned mode' is the transformation into the 'rigid organization' as a result of 'strategic drift.'

The surplus of operational flexibility, consisting of sophisticated routines, creates inertia in the form of a very mechanistic structural system and a very narrowly focused cultural system. The growing resistance to 'deviant' interpretations of the environment reflects a tendency toward 'overbalance' of the planned mode.

H.5 the risk of the 'flexible mode' is turning into a 'chaotic organization' as a result of 'strategic neglect.'

The surplus of structural and strategic flexibility leads to unfocused actions with disconstructive results. The lack of firm-specific assets, administrative structures, a sense of direction, shared beliefs, and institutional leadership is characteristic of a tendency towards 'underbalance' of the flexible mode.

H.6 In order to survive, an organization has to shift from the 'planned' towards the 'flexible' mode and vice versa in line with changes in the level of environmental turbulence.

It is important to understand that the planned and the flexible mode are different stages in a cyclical process. Mintzberg (1978), too, shows how organizations go through periods of strategy adjustment characterized by continuity, flux or incremental change, but also require more global changes. In addition, Greiner (1972) charts periods of evolution and revolution in corporate development. Moreover, the tenor of this hypothesis is in line with the 'classic' of Burns and Stalker (1961), who concluded as early as then that the organic form was temporary because the necessary internal dynamics could not be sustained. Their speculations of an oscillating organizational mode are supported by many other scholars (e.g. Duncan, 1976; Weick, 1982).

The above process hypotheses can each be conceived in terms of path dependencies in which the extreme positions are undesirable states characterized by an inappropriate composition of the flexibility mix and an inadequate design of organizational resources. Figure 11.4 distinguishes two path dependencies, the natural trajectory of routinization from a chaotic state to a rigid organization and the reverse trajectory of revitalization from a rigid organization to a chaotic state.

The natural trajectory of routinization suggests that starting firms or new ventures operate chaotically. In this earliest stage of development, these organizations have a preponderance of strategic flexibility in their flexibility mix, which helps them to be more sensitive to the possibilities for creating 'new combinations.' For such an organization, however, to 'get off the ground,' the firm must be sufficiently well organized to be lifted from a chaotic state of random, disconnected and uncoordinated impulses. This requires a capacity for achieving some degree of *strategic focus*. Furthermore, the organization has to develop the necessary technological as well as the structural and cultural systems which would enable it to increase its controllability. If the organization is successful in these efforts to manage chaos, it begins to establish itself as a 'flexible configuration' of resources and capabilities. Its very success produces the consolidating forces which transform the environment within which it operates. As its dominant environment becomes more and more predictable, the flexible configuration faces a crisis. Since experience is gained by management of the flexible form, environmental turbulence will be correspondingly reduced. At this point, it has to become more efficient in its operations in order to be able to extract greater benefit from the changes that it introduced previously. The organization needs to be transformed in a manner which best permits it to exploit the existing knowledge and opportunities. To do this, it has to introduce a greater number and variety of operational procedures or routines and reduce its structural and strategic flexibility. As a consequence, the organizational culture becomes more conservative in nature and matched to those opportunities which management has chosen to exploit. At the same time, the organizational structure has to be adapted in a congruent fashion. This transition from a flexible towards a planned form can be portrayed as a process of *maturation*. Thus, the 'planned' organization is able to alertly exploit existing knowledge and opportunities because it has the appropriate (conservative) culture, (mechanistic) structure (in terms of many process regulation and detailed planning and control systems), and a large number and variety of operational routines which have been adapted to match the needs of the situation. However, in the process of adapting and refining the organizational conditions in order to become increasingly focused and specialized, the 'planned' organization runs the risk of losing its strategic and structural flexibility, as it concentrates increasingly upon the accumulation of a large number and variety of operational procedures and routines. Moreover, the increased rationalization of the work flow and the replacement of general-purpose machines and skilled workers by dedicated, highly 'specific' equipment promotes a routine technological system. Together with an excessively mechanistic structural system and unduly conservative cultural system, this adversely affects the controllability of resources. In these circumstances, the firm becomes progressively rigid. In this process toward *stagnation* (Miller and Friesen, 1980: 283–284), the routinization and systematization of organizational resources bring bureaucratic momentum, traditions, and resistance to change. As a result, the rigid form is characterized by a reduced emphasis on product-market innovation, risk taking, and proactiveness.

For many organizations, indeed, the transition from chaotic state towards a 'rigid' organization may be regarded as a 'natural trajectory.' However, a transition in the reverse direction may, in our typology, also be perceived as a trajectory, though it may not be as easy to achieve or seem as 'natural' as the former process. As these organizations are confronted by a situation of low and diminishing returns from, for instance, established product lines, and intense competition from numerous rivals in the same field, these rigid organizations must seek to exploit opportunities flowing from more unstable environments, or attempt to generate major innovations. In connection with the latter, they face the task of promoting a shift back towards the flexibility mix and the organizational resources of the planned configuration. Such a transition of *professional revitalization* involves the comprehensive and often dramatic movement away from traditions, conservatism, and rigidity and toward adaptiveness, vigilance, and diversification (Miller and Friesen, 1980: 281). Perhaps most important for this transition is a concerted effort to track the external environment, to discover the new market forces in order to be able to adapt to them. It requires that the limited basic scanning procedures are expanded to a more formalized set of information gathering and processing programs. The resulting increased capacity for processing information facilitates the development of a variety of sophisticated routines with a view to becoming more adaptive and sensitive to market forces. As a consequence, product lines become broader and more diverse and change more frequently. The organization becomes more aggressive and innovative in dealing with competitors and more imaginative in meeting the needs of customers. On the other hand, this non-routinization of technology increases the administrative complexity of the task of running the firm (Miller and Friesen, 1980: 282). It is not surprising, then, that we find highly developed intelligence systems and more structural process regulations (formalization, standardization, specialization). Ad hoc committees become standing committees, and performance appraisals become routine and systematized. In addition, the activities usually call for a higher level of expertise than was available within the rigid form, and so the level of professionalization increases.

Where this professional revitalization proves inadequate, the 'planned' organization has to transform itself further into a more flexible form. These efforts should aim to create greater structural and strategic flexibility, and reduce the number of operational routines. Strategic flexibility encourages the exploitation of new opportunities or new ideas, while structural flexibility facilitates the restructuring of the organization in line with these new opportunities or ideas. With respect to the organizational resources, this change in the composition in the flexibility mix can only be realized if the organization moves towards an even more flexible or multi-purpose technology, develops a more organic structure, and adopts a more heterogeneous, open and externally oriented culture. The above process of *entrepreneurial revitalization* is promoted by changes such as new leadership composed of visionary entrepreneurs, reduction of process regulations (specialization, standardization, formalization, centralization), loose basic organizational forms (grouping by target market, flat structure, and broad management tasks), a more open external orientation, and a high tolerance for ambiguity. Thus, the transition from the 'planned' to the 'flexible' configuration would significantly transform the existing culture and structure, while it violates the established operational routines in the organization. However, if the organization is successful in achieving a major transformation, it faces the opposite danger of 'overshooting' its target and becoming 'chaotic.' This possibility arises from the danger of strategic neglect, that is, the failure to retain the necessary strategic focus and the resources which will enable it to organize itself sufficiently to create and/or to implement radical innovations. Kanter (1988: 195) also points out that, ironically, creating change requires stability. Organizational structures and cultures have to allow continuity and preserve the organization in the midst of change. In particular, Kanter proposes to encourage strong social ties within flexible units (socialization) and to facilitate strong beliefs in fundamental values.

THE FAR METHOD IN PRACTICE

So far, we have developed a theoretical basis for the paradox of flexibility, a conceptual model for describing flexible configurations, and a typology of configuration strategies. From this, we postulated hypotheses about the configuration of dynamic capabilities and organizational resources (H.1, H.2, H.3) and strategic trajectories of change for dealing with the flexibility paradox over time (H.4, H.5, H.6). By subsequently integrating the conceptual model and our typology of configuration strategies, we developed an enriched process model of flexibility improvement (see Figure 11.5). In combination with the observation and analysis instruments, this process model formed the basis of a method for diagnosing organizational flexibility and guiding the transition process.

   This so-called Flexibility Audit and Redesign (FAR) method provides the practitioner with instructions for systematically describing, analyzing, and assessing the organization's actual flexibility versus the desired flexibility in terms of the dimensions of our conceptual model. Moreover, the method supports the consultant in deriving recommendations for redesigning the organization in order to reduce the gap between required and actual flexibility. In the various phases of the process of flexibility improvement, the FAR method poses the following questions:

Orientation: What is the point of departure of the organizational unit? (strategic group, stakeholders analysis, adequacy of flexibility label, boundary decisions, history)

Analysis:
- What are the inputs, throughputs, and outputs of the organizational unit and which external elements or constituents are important for attaining these inputs and disposing of the outputs? (specification of primary process)
- How flexible does the organizational unit have to be? (desired state depending on the degree of environmental turbulence)
- How flexible is the organization at the moment? (current state depending on the actual flexibility mix and flexibility potential within the organizational resources)

Assessment: Is there a gap between the required flexibility mix and the actual flexibility mix? (discrepancy analysis)
- If so, what are the relevant flexibility aspects, types of flexibility, and lacking information activities?

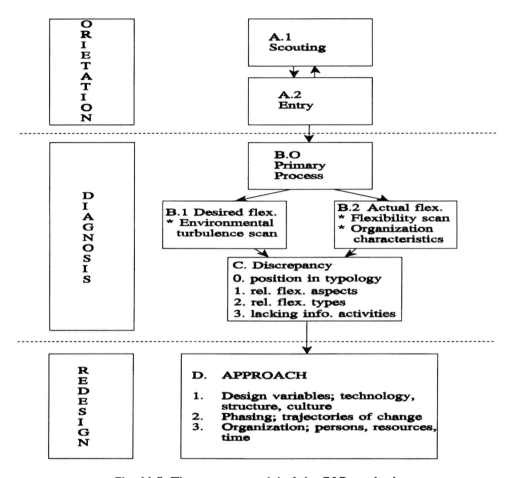

Fig. 11.5. The process model of the FAR method.

Redesign: How should a more flexible organization be redesigned?
- What are possible design variables for varying the flexibility potential of the organization? (technological, structural, and/or cultural design variables)
- What steps have to be taken? (strategic trajectories of change)
- What persons and resources should be involved and at what time?

The Multi-Case Longitudinal Study

When we want to justify the above method on empirical grounds, the underlying hypotheses of the method must be tested. Therefore, we started with a multi-case longitudinal study in which we undertook flexibility efforts within real organizations by using the FAR method. In this way we were able to study only a very small number of cases. In an attempt to provide more validly generalizable knowledge, however, the multi-case longitudinal study was designed in such a way that three cases differed on the construct dimensions of the conceptual model of flexibility. In particular, we selected three extreme cases to fill our theoretical typology and provide examples of polar types (Eisenhardt, 1989; Yin, 1989). Such *theoretical sampling* of cases on the basis of a tentative conceptual model and typology is a particularly effective means of testing the empirical claims of the FAR method. The selected cases serve as a tests or 'hold out' samples, but they also serve to extend or negate the underlying hypothesis of the empirical claims.

In this chapter we will limit ourselves to the longitudinal case within Philips Semiconductors. For a more detailed treatment of the other longitudinal case-studies within the Dutch Postbank and the Dutch Gas Corporation, we refer to Volberda (1992).

Within Philips Semiconductors there was a clear need for flexibility due to a shift in the level of environmental turbulence. As a part of an Integral Organization Renewal (IOR) program, the assembly department Glass-Bead Diodes was a pilot case of a Redesign Production Systems (RPS) project, in which the total plant tried, among other things, to increase the production flexibility. Instead of rigid central planning, production units were now themselves responsible for reacting to variations in demand. The assembly unit used to operate in a dynamic, complex, but largely predictable environment. Now they had to cope with a fluctuating work load, an increase in the volume of specialties, changes in quality requirements of key customers, and a varying composition of the product mix.

On the basis of the architecture of the organizational conditions and environmental characteristics, we generated predictions concerning the composition of the flexibility mix. Subsequently, by conducting a pre-measurement of the level of environmental turbulence, the flexibility potential within the organizational resources, and the composition of the flexibility mix, we were able to test the *'variance' prediction*. Furthermore, the pre-measurement allowed us to generate a prediction concerning an effective strategic trajectory of change for flexibility improvement. By conducting a post-measurement, these *'process' predictions* could be tested, too. Thus, if these predictions were replicated, our hypotheses were accepted. If not, we had to revise our hypotheses and the related empirical claims of the FAR method.

ENTREPRENEURIAL REVITALIZATION OF ASSEMBLY DEPARTMENT GLASS-BEAD DIODES

In this section we will describe the longitudinal case-study of Philips Semi-conductors according to a standardized format. We will successively provide a brief introduction, a preliminary description of the unit's problem in the entry phase which formed the basis for subsequent phases of the FAR method, the results of the analysis, an assessment of the actual flexibility, the redesign of the unit in order to vary its flexibility potential, and the results of a post-measurement conducted one year later.

Introduction

In 1987 the new plant manager of *Philips Semiconductors Stadskanaal,* a large plant of the Dutch multinational *Philips,* started an Integral Organization Renewal (IOR) program directed at improvement of the work, organization, and labor relations. In the past, strong pressures from competitors (far east and Eastern Europe) had forced the multinational *Philips* to close down one of the plant's production departments and to dismiss 400 employees. Still, the low competitiveness of the plant's major products together with the depressing atmosphere throughout the whole plant required a more radical change. In order to improve the plant's competitiveness in terms of market share, the management team of *Philips Semiconductors Stadskanaal* organized an integral change program with four basic objectives.

1. improving control and accelerating innovation of manufacturing processes within the plant in order to quickly anticipate new market developments
2. redesigning production systems of the product lines in order to satisfy customer demands more easily
3. making arrangements with regular suppliers of the plant in such a way that they do what they promise
4. training employees of the plant in such a way that they can meet new market challenges

As a part of this integral renewal program, the Redesign Production Systems (RPS) project was initiated within the four major product lines of the plant (see Fig. 11.6), namely Tube Bases (TB), Medium Power Rectifiers and Stacks (MPRS), Small Signals Diodes (SSD), and Power Transistors (PT).

In line with this strategic reorientation and new philosophy, each product line had to redesign its product organization and equipment. In the product line Medium Power Rectifiers and Stacks (MPRS), which is a part of the product group 'Diodes and Transistors' of the business unit 'Discrete Semiconductors,' this RPS project resulted in the formulation of four design criteria.

- increase of quality of working life within the product line
- increase of production flexibility in terms of output volume and assortment
- increase of process control in terms of lead times, delivery reliability, product quality and cost price
- increase of innovativeness of the product line in terms of new products and new production processes

The product line MPRS consisted of one diffusion department and three assembly departments, namely the Implosion Diode (ID) assembly, the Stack (S) assembly, and the Glass-Bead (GB) assembly (see Fig. 11.7). In

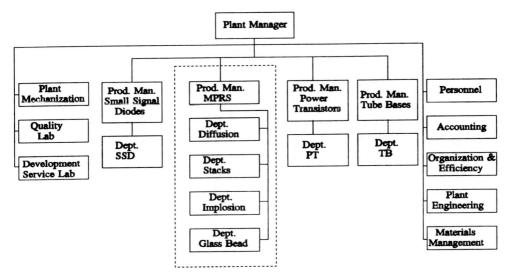

Fig. 11.6. The organigram of Philips Semiconductors Stadskanaal.

these assembly departments, leads were mounted to the diffused crystals with studs and pellets. Subsequently, these compositions were enveloped by means of the glass-bead or implosion technology. The function of the envelope is to passivate the crystal, while the leads are necessary to fix the diodes to print boards. The main application of these diodes is in power supplies of consumer as well as professional equipment. Another important application is in the line output systems of TV-sets. In addition, other market segments include the car industry (alternator regulators, motor management systems, ignition systems, etc.), and the telecommunication area (polarity-guard diodes, transient suppressors).

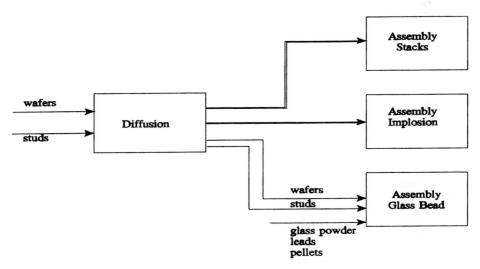

Fig. 11.7. The production process within the productline MPRS.

Before the implementation of the RPS project, fluctuations in demand required the product line MPRS to rely on high buffer stocks between the various steps in production and assembly. In this traditional, stable, and high-volume manufacturing approach, errors in the planning forecast of the Central Planning Department (CPD) within the headquarters of the multinational resulted in large inventories and high cost prices (see Fig. 11.8a). Moreover, these high volumes for various product types within a single line caused long waiting and lead times, many defects in the production process, very high part per million (ppm) rejects scores (sometimes as high as 50%), and a limited quality of working life. Furthermore, most performance measures were directed at the input of the production departments (e.g. the number of batches, the technical capacity utilization) and not at the quantity and quality of the output of the production departments.

With the introduction of the RPS project within the product line MPRS, production departments were now themselves responsible for reacting to variations in demand (see Fig. 11.8b). That is, they had to offer a variety of diode types in smaller quantities within ever shorter delivery times. On the one hand, they had to cope with a more fluctuating workload, an increase in the number of specialties, higher quality requirements of key customers, and a varying product range. On the other hand, they had to take care of low stock levels and high efficiency rates in production.

Customers expected them to satisfy their specific needs and at the same time to maintain a reasonable price-quality relation. To deal with this dilemma, the product line MPRS had to strongly increase its logistic performance and its information-gathering capacity regarding customer needs. In 1989, within the pilot Assembly Department Glass-Bead (GB) the partial implementation

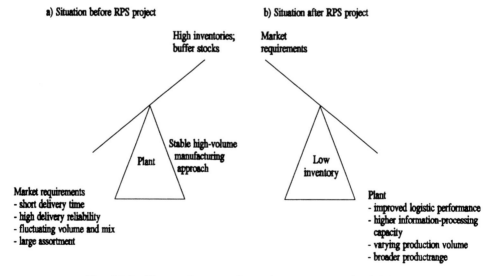

Fig. 11.8. Change in manufacturing strategy of MPRS.

of the RPS trajectory had resulted in a higher market share due to:

- drastic decreases of throughput times within the assembly;
- shorter lead times (order acceptation plus delivery) and an improvement of the delivery reliability;
- increase of the number of custom-made diodes or specialties. For instance, diodes with preformed leads for special applications;
- higher product quality.

The above professionalization of the assembly department had helped the department to more routinely react to new market forces. Consequently, the product range had become broader and more diverse.

Entry

In February 1989, we had a series of conversations with the manager Organization and Efficiency and the project manager Logistic Improvements of the plant. They were curious about the results of the RPS project and therefore asked us to audit one of the production departments within the product line MPRS in terms of flexibility improvement. We jointly decided to choose for Assembly Department GB, because this department had successfully undergone a revival and was the first pilot case of the RPS project. In 1980 the product manager of the product group Diodes and Transistors intended to gradually close down this assembly department. The industrial plan of MPRS showed glass-bead diodes being rapidly superseded by implosion diodes. However, the evolution of ID cost prices was not in line with expectations. In addition, the GB cost prices declined much faster while the demand of GB increased. Furthermore, the RPS project, which started in 1987, further improved the performance of Assembly Department GB. Still, not all the changes suggested by the RPS had been implemented. Also, there was a low commitment from production workers to participate in the project.

Following this first meeting, we had a second meeting with the Production Manager MPRS, the Assembly Manager, and the operational group (OG) of the Glass-Bead Department (see Fig. 11.9), in which we presented a systematic plan for conducting the FAR method. We decided that the flexibility audit had to measure the progress of the RPS project in terms of managerial flexibility-improving capabilities within the assembly department and eventually support the further implementation of the RPS trajectory.

On the basis of this preliminary orientation, we predicted that

Assembly Department Glass-Bead Diodes, which was now more professionally organized within the product line MPRS for a reasonably turbulent environment (dynamic, complex, but largely predictable), would employ an extensive flexibility mix, dominated by operational flexibility, and possess a

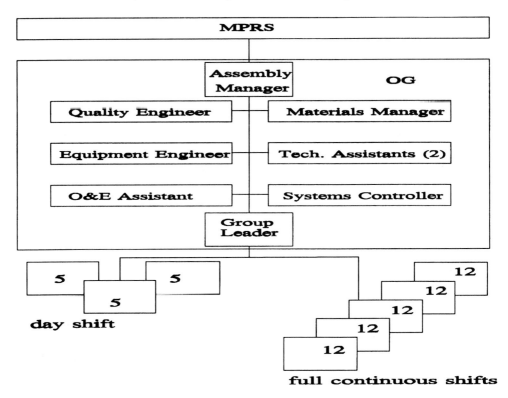

Fig. 11.9. The organigram of the assembly department GB.

more non-routine technological system, a mechanistic structural system, and a conservative cultural system. Also, as the non-routinization of its technological system had increased the administrative complexity of the task of running the Assembly Department Glass-Bead, we expected to find highly developed intelligence systems as a part of the metaflexibility and more structural process regulations.

Analysis

After this first orientation and our variance prediction, we conducted a pre-measurement within Assembly Dept. GB. From our data of the structured interviews with the Assembly Dept. Manager, the Group Leader of the shifts, the Production Manager MPRS, the Planner/Materials Manager, and the Marketing Manager of MPRS, we specified the primary process of Assembly Dept. GB and measured the level of environmental turbulence the department was confronted with. Furthermore, the flexibility scan filled in by the OG was converted by a computer program FARSYS into a flexibility profile and a metaflexibility score. Also, the answers of the OG regarding the types of flexibility indicated which types were applied most in Assembly Dept. GB that moment. Finally, structured interviews regarding Assembly Dept. GB's technological system, structural system, and cultural system enabled us to classify the flexibility potential within the Assembly Dept's organizational resources. Appendix I shows the profiles resulting from the data incorporated with FARSYS. Below, we will contrast and supplement these profiles with the data we obtained from document analysis, archival records, and direct observation.

The representation of the *primary process* shows that Assembly Dept. GB received subcomponents such as crystals from diffusion, leads, studs, pellets, and glass powder from suppliers, and basic materials such as chemicals and packing materials from the plant's stores. In addition, with the use of machines, equipment, information systems, financial budgets, a full continuous shift and a day shift, these subcomponents were assembled to glass-bead diodes. In the glass-bead assembly there were two product flows running on the same assembly line, namely envelopes for crystals with a 1.5 mm diameter and envelopes for a 2.0 mm diameter. In both standard envelope diodes (SED) there were several diode types, namely general purpose rectifiers and efficiency diodes (GP), fast rectifiers (F), ultra fast rectifiers (UF), Zener diodes (Z), and special selections (e.g. preformed leads). Subsequently, these diodes were transported to the main distribution store. From there, they were distributed by national sales organizations and various outlets to internal as well as external customers. The workload of the department consisted of commodities (70%) and of specialties (30%). The sales volume to external customers (e.g. IBM, Siemens, Bosch, Olivetti) was increasing, while the volume to internal customers decreasing. Moreover, many of the external customers were located in communist countries, which resulted in unclear forecasts and long-term prospects.

The *environmental turbulence profile* indicates that Assembly Dept. GB was confronted with dynamic, especially complex changes, and that some of these were highly unpredictable. The major developments in Assembly Dept. GB's environment which caused this turbulence profile are illustrated in Fig. 11.10. Assembly Dept. GB had to deal with dynamic changes in its outer technologies. The glass-bead diodes are glass passivated and assembled in the glass-bead. Plastic technology had been abandoned by the plant in the early 1980s. In the low-end market, where price is of utmost importance and quality clearly comes second, however, the high quality glass-bead diodes could not compete with the cheap plastic rectifiers of the competition. With their current 'state of the art,' Assembly Dept. GB could not penetrate this 'stay-out pricing' market. Furthermore, the 1.5 mm diameter glass-bead diodes could be replaced by an equivalent implosion diode of the Assembly Dept. Implosion Diodes. Finally, there was a tendency in the components world to absorb more and more discrete sockets into Integrated Circuits (ICs). The high power dissipation and high voltages of GB diodes conflicted with the demand towards lower power dissipation and miniaturization of ICs.

Besides these technological changes, Assembly Dept. GB was continuously confronted with new quality audits carried out in order to acquire certain

DYNAMISM	COMPLEXITY	UNPREDICTABILITY
— introduction of high quality plastic diodes, ID diodes, and rapid advance of ICs (*outer technologies*) — various quality audits of key customers and higher standards imposed by Quality Lab, MIS Dept. (*regulations*)	— increase of number of suppliers (*suppliers*) — varying composition of the workload resulting in high resetting times and many bottlenecks (*workload*) — increase of number of specialties and variety of customer requirements (*customers*) — non-transparent and related application markets together with price erosion (*PMCs*)	— rapidity of technological developments such as substitute diodes, new crystal types, faster higher voltage diodes, advances of ICs (*outer technologies*) — volume developments in GP, F, UF, and Z markets (*PMCs*)

Fig. 11.10. Developments within the environment of Assembly Dept. GB.

certificates as well as new regulations imposed by the Quality Lab and Manufacturing Instructions and Standardization Dept. (MIS).

In addition to dynamics in technology and regulations, the department was faced with an increasingly complex environment. Firstly, the number of suppliers was increasing. Secondly, the workload was becoming more heterogeneous while the relatedness between the assembled products was increasing. Within both standard envelopes there were more than 25 types and each type had several subtypes. Nonetheless, the maximum possible mix of 1.5 mm and 2.0 mm diameter envelopes was 60/40. Moreover, the composition of the product mix was changing from 1.5 mm to 2.0 mm diameter envelopes, which are more complex to produce. As a consequence, the assembling of more 2.0 mm diameter diodes required longer resetting times. Furthermore, the assembly of zeners required resetting times of as long as 4 hours. These changes in the product line caused large bottlenecks in the testing and marking of diodes. Thirdly, the complexity regarding customer requirements was increasing as a consequence of the enlargement of the number of specialties for key customers (preformed leads, special packing, etc.) together with higher quality requirements of these customers. Unfortunately, the quality requirements of these key customers differed strongly. Also, Assembly Dept. GB was not able to arrange stable annual contracts with external customers. Fourthly, the application areas for diodes were very non-transparent and strongly related. The range of their area of application is similar to that of salt. While there are of course some major application areas, such as consumer electronics, professional equipment, telecommunication, and automobiles, it was impossible for marketing to distinguish homogeneous market segments. Furthermore, there were very strong substitution effects between these market segments. For instance, in order to decrease the size of the costly supply transformer, there was a tendency to increase the operating frequencies of SMPSs. Consequently, GP diodes were replaced by UF rectifiers. In other words, the high growth rate in the UF market was accomplished by a decreased growth rate of the GP market.

While most of these complex and substantial changes were predictable, some of them were unclear or even fundamentally unpredictable. Many developments within outer technologies, such as the introduction of better and cheaper substitute diodes for GB diodes (plastic diodes, ID diodes), the release of higher-voltages versions, 2.25 mm diameter crystal diodes, and the advance of ICs in the application markets, were unclear. Furthermore, the developments within PMCs were to some extent unpredictable.

When we conducted our pre-measurement, the fact that the market demand turned out to be 6% higher than foreseen caused overload problems for the department. Specifically, the GP market was a very mature market in which the main Taiwanese competitor followed a 'stay-out-pricing' policy to discourage others to jump in. The sudden withdrawal of some smaller competitors, however, caused fluctuations in demand. In addition, the F market was also a maturing market, but the UF and Z markets were growth markets. The growth rates were 9 and 10% respectively. Because Assembly Dept. GB did not work with annual contracts, like their major competitors, they had to cope with fluctuating demands in these markets. For an illustration of the growth rates and market shares we refer to the Boston analysis in Fig. 11.11.

The *flexibility profile* illustrates that Assembly Dept. GB scored high on managerial capabilities regarding products (e.g. short lead time, large assortment, complementary product mix, many specialties) and information systems (e.g. decentralized information systems, modular construction, short response times, high accessibility, various application possibilities), but low on labor markets and outer technologies. The use of temporary workers within the department was restricted because of the high quality requirements in the assembly process. Similarly, flexibility-increasing capabilities directed at outer technologies were restricted, too. The glass-bead technology in general is a relatively mature technology; product innovations resulting from new semiconductor technologies had been undertaken within other assem-

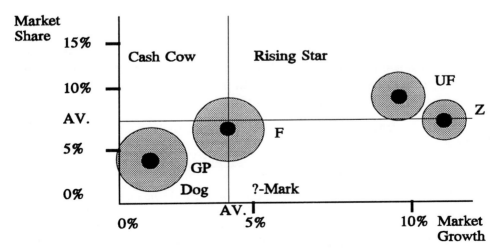

Fig. 11.11. Boston analysis PMCs Assembly Dept. GB.

bly departments (e.g. the application of implosion technology was started within the relatively young Implosion Diode Assembly Dept.).

Furthermore, the internal flexibility score was significantly higher than the external flexibility score, indicating that Assembly Dept. GB adapted to its environment more than it tried to shape that environment. In this connection, management responded that the department mainly adapted in the form of operational flexibility, more specifically short-term volume and mix flexibility. By changing the capacity utilization within the installed capacity and by changing the production capacity between various product types, short-term fluctuations could be offset. Nonetheless, due to the overload, the department operated with a maximum capacity utilization, which resulted in bottlenecks in the production line and high stress among the work force. Moreover, the information coefficient was 47.9, indicating that the metaflexibility was very extensive and directed towards routine proliferation. In order to routinely react to market developments the department used highly developed intelligence systems and highly systematized performance appraisals such as:

- automatic order scheduling with weekly resolution; the LOgistics Planning and Information Control (LOPIC) system resulted in a weekly order scheduling instead of a monthly order scheduling, thereby further decreasing the lead time of products and improving the delivery reliability;
- automatic replenishment of the main store and real selling stores;
- Statistical Process Control (SPC) throughout the product line in order to provide various measurement and control circuits;
- Shop Floor Control; an order progress system for determining which types are located in each stage of the assembly process, and in which quantities;
- Logistic Performance Indicators such as Confirmed Line Item Performance (CLIP), Confirmed Volume Performance (CVP), or Part Per Million rejects (PPM).

Consequently, for every possible change the management could develop a sophisticated routine.

Finally, the characteristics of the technological, structural, and cultural system represent the potential for flexibility within Assembly Dept. GB's resources. On the basis of the *technology characteristic* provided in Appendix I, we may conclude that there was some potential for operational flexibility within the technological system, but that

- the single assembly line hampered the production of various product types and fluctuating volumes;
- the many interdependencies in the assembly process made it very difficult to absorb disturbances;
- the limited repertoire of workers within a single assembly line caused a low quality of working life.

Furthermore, the *structure characteristic* illustrates that Assembly Dept. GB had a mechanistic structural system, that is, a functional structure with a dominant grouping according to process or operation, many hierarchical levels, but a low degree of functionalization of management tasks. The latter was one of the advancements of the RPS project; all staff workers from supporting staff departments together with the assembly manager and group leader were integrated in the multidisciplinary operational group of the Assembly Dept. GB (see Fig. 11.9). In addition, there were very elaborate planning and control systems within the department together with many tight process regulations. The structure characteristic reveals that the potential for structural flexibility within the structural system was seriously limited by the sophisticated planning and control systems and strong process regulations, or, in more detail,

- the far-reaching specialization (limited scope and depth) led to single-skilled personnel, few learning opportunities, and no self-regulation of work teams. Consequently, participation and delegation levels remained low;
- the many formal and informal liaison devices limited the autonomy of the interdisciplinary OG and further destroyed the development of self-contained Task Groups. The increased integration boosted the vulnerability to disturbances of the department and harmed its stability. Faced with strategic changes, liaison devices led to very long and overloaded horizontal communication lines which inhibited quick reactions to unanticipated market developments.

Finally, the *culture characteristic* indicates that the department had a relatively conservative cultural system emanating from:

- a narrow and homogeneous identity; it was based on a limited assortment of values, beliefs, and cultural practices;
- a management attitude directed towards routine proliferation; for every possible change they tried to develop a sophisticated routine;
- many unwritten rules shaped by the discipline dominance among the organization members; the department was predominantly made up of employees with a technical education (Technical College, Technical School). Consequently, problems were often framed in technical terms, while the more social problems were ignored. Furthermore, supplementary unwritten rules were only transmitted on a limited scale by socialization processes;
- the low tolerance for renewal and innovation.

Consequently, the potential for strategic flexibility was not satisfactory.

Assessment

In the above pre-measurement, we found that Assembly Dept. GB, which was intended to function in a complex and dynamic environment, employed merely operational flexibility and possessed a mechanistic structural system and conservative cultural system. Also, we found highly developed intelligence systems as a part of the metaflexibility and many structural process regulations meant to facilitate the development of routines. However, due to the partial implementation of the RPS project, the technological system was not as non-routine as we had predicted. Consequently, the management still had problems activating operational flexibility. Thus, our variance prediction is only partly replicated. The department did not totally correspond with t he planned mode, but was positioned somewhere between the rigid and planned mode in our typology of configuration strategies (see Fig. 11.12). Furthermore, the environmental turbulence profile shows that the environment of Assembly Dept. GB was no longer only complex and dynamic, but also unpredictable, especially regarding the developments in outer technologies and PMCs. According to our typology, this shift in environmental turbulence towards unpredictability requires a much broader flexibility mix, dominated also by structural and strategic flexibility originating from a more organic structural and innovative cultural system. In this connection, pure anticipation in terms of routine proliferation is insufficient. A strong commitment to a likely future may even reduce the assembly department's receptiveness to change. Instead of further increasing its information-processing capacity, management should reduce the need for information processing. This transition from a merely planned configuration to a more flexible configuration is referred to as a process of *entrepreneurial revitalization* (see Fig. 11.12).

The planned configuration is seriously handicapped when confronted with fundamentally unpredictable environments. A process of entrepreneurial revitalization could help Assembly Dept. GB to more easily exploit unknown opportunities in technologies and PMCs. In addition, management still needed operational flexibility for short-term fluctuations in demand. Therefore, we predicted that

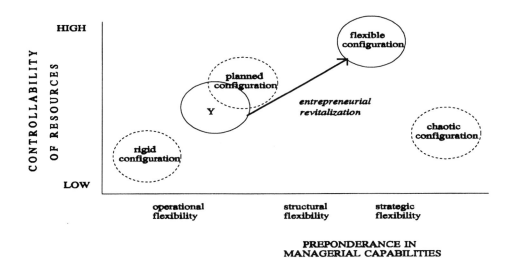

Fig. 11.12. Entrepreneurial revitalization of Assembly Dept. GB.

Assembly Dept. GB, which in addition to a complex and dynamic environment was confronted with increasing unpredictability, would have to employ a broader flexibility mix, dominated by operational and strategic flexibility originating from a non-routine technological system and innovative cultural system. Moreover, management's sensor and information-processing capacity would have to be very rudimentary for strategic flexibility and directed towards enhancing the receptiveness to new environments.

In the management conference, in which we presented the results of the analysis, the OG judged that *operational flexibility in the form of load flexibility* and *strategic flexibility in the form of capacity flexibility* were most important. On the one hand, Assembly Dept. GB had to adapt the production volume concerning crystal families and crystal types on the short term to the demand within the limits of a given production capacity. On the other hand, they had to be able to adapt the production capacity on the long term to changes in the demand pattern.

Subsequently, on the basis of a comparison of the environmental turbulence profile with the flexibility profile, management selected the production system, personnel, outer technologies, and external customers as the important aspects for improving operational and strategic flexibility. Regarding the *production system*, consisting of machines, equipment, and devices to process and assemble subcomponents into diodes, most managerial capabilities were directed at reducing the throughput time. Nonetheless, the most urgent problem regarding production system flexibility was the lack of a fluctuating production capacity for various product types. As a consequence of the maximum capacity utilization, there was very little leeway in the assembly process. In the actual situation, however, the demand was higher than the existing capacity within the department so that fluctuations in demand had no consequences; the assembly could produce at top capacity. If the production capacity expansion were to be realized as a part of the RPS project, however, fluctuations in demand would have far-reaching consequences for production (see Fig. 11.13). Because there were few capabilities directed towards improving the applicability of existing machines and equipment and the rapidity by which they could be adjusted, this would be very problematic. Furthermore, there was less attention for the combination of operations in a flexible work station or the reduction of variations in operation times between machines.

Furthermore, the load and capacity flexibility also required a more variable work force as a part of flexibility of *personnel*. At the time of our pre-measurement, the flexibility regarding personnel mainly consisted of improvement of the workers' skills, continuous quality review by the employees involved (intrinsic quality control), and shift work. The first two are examples of durable flexibility-increasing managerial capabilities, while the shift work only results in a one-off improvement of flexibility. That is, the use of day shifts (consisting of 3 shifts) and a full continuous shift

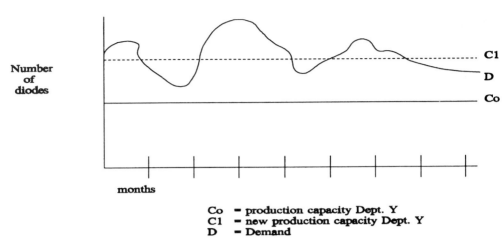

Co — production capacity Dept. Y
C1 — new production capacity Dept. Y
D   — Demand

Fig. 11.13. Demand and production capacity of Assembly Dept. GB.

(consisting of 5 shifts) resulted in a poor volume flexibility due to the high production volume. At the very most, the OG could shrink the work force at the cost of large efficiency losses. A more managerial capability to vary the utilization of the work force is the use of crash teams, or the enlargement of the skill repertoire of employees. This task or functional flexibility in the form of multi-skilled personnel was extremely low within Assembly Dept. GB. Job rotation within the full continuous shift could decrease the vulnerability of the assembly of certain product types.

Besides choosing a more variable production capacity and a multi-skilled work force, management decided to increase its external flexibility regarding *external customers*. At that time, they only made arrangements regarding new products (co-design) or certain specialties. By also making arrangements with regular clients regarding the number and kind of products in terms of annual contracts they could affect the sales patterns. Finally, in order to react to unclear developments in *outer technologies*, the assembly department intended not only to more easily incorporate technological developments in the assembly process, but also to develop new diodes in the glass-bead technology (crystal redesign to anticipate changed market demands, 2.25 mm diameter crystal series glass-bead diodes, leadless glass-bead diodes, diodes with higher voltages).

Management's choice of relevant flexibility capabilities was largely supported by our decision matrix, which presents the most relevant flexibility gaps for Assembly Dept. GB (see Appendix I). The matrix indeed shows high flexibility deficits for technology, production system, personnel, and external clients. However, there are also large flexibility deficits for the external aspects such as components (raw materials), suppliers, and labor markets. The first two could only be marginally influenced by Assembly Dept. GB; in order to receive scale effects these tasks were performed by the Purchasing Dept. Nonetheless, multi-sourcing of suppliers could certainly reduce the vulnerability of the production process and improve the quality of incoming subcomponents. Moreover, the OG intentionally chose not to increase its labor market flexibility. Because of the extreme quality instructions imposed by key customers and the required on-the-job training, temporary workers could only be used to a small degree in the day shift.

Redesign

Management's ability to realize a process of entrepreneurial revitalization as specified in the assessment is demarcated by the flexibility potential available within the organizational resources. That is, the initiation of operational and strategic flexibility by means of the specified flexibility aspects depends on the design adequacy of the department's organizational resources. According to our process prediction, operational flexibility requires a further non-routinization of the assembly department's technological system (H.2). Furthermore, a more innovative cultural system together with a more organic structural system facilitates strategic and structural flexibility (H.3). On the basis of a closer scrutiny of the technology, structure, and culture characteristics, the OG was asked to select those design variables which severely restricted the potential for flexibility or which allowed them to better control the flexibility potential. In addition, only those design variables were considered which management could change. This exercise added supplementary design variables to the RPS project.

Regarding the department's technological system, as a part of the RPS project management intended to subdivide the single assembly line into two parallel mini-lines, one for the simple 1.5 mm diameter crystal glass-bead diodes and one for the more complex 1.5 and 2.0 mm diameter crystal diodes. In addition, batch sizes had to be decreased. This shift towards a group lay-out and a small batch mode of production would result in two homogeneous work flows with less dependencies. However, if these product flows were to operate as autonomous and flexible mini-lines, the skills repertoire of employees and the applicability of machines had to be increased. If not, the possibilities for operational flexibility would be seriously restricted.

Regarding the department's structural system, the OG intended, in line with the RPS project, to group activities according to product flows instead of according to operations (see Fig. 11.14). Indeed, this basic form with one OG and two Task Groups (TGs) would allow a larger potential for flexibility because there would be fewer coordination problems, resetting problems, and so on. The RPS project, however, largely ignored the elaborative planning and control systems and strong process regulations.

Finally, the RPS project totally neglected Assembly Dept. GB's cultural system. Nonetheless, the culture characteristic revealed that the potential for strategic flexibility was severely restricted by the department's conservative culture. Therefore, the OG decided to enlarge the scope of the department's identity by broadening the mission and goals and paying more

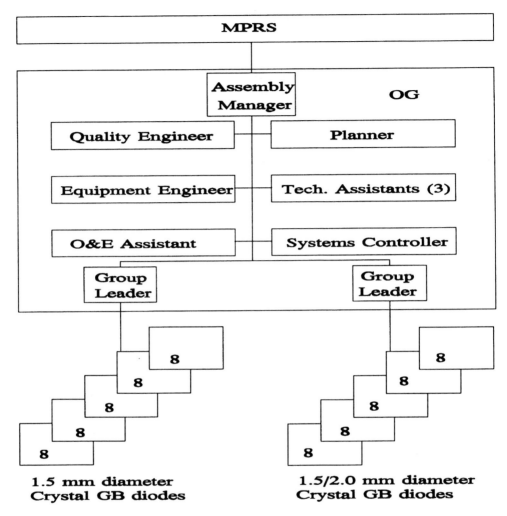

Fig. 11.14. The new basic organizational form according to the RPS project.

attention to various cultural practices such as celebrations, shared symbols, etc. Moreover, in order to facilitate a more open external orientation, they tried to increase the communication with the TGs in such a way that they would become more involved in new market developments or new product types. Furthermore, more information about new developments, redesign projects, and so on could also increase the workers' tolerance for new ideas. This again could remove the strict isolation between the OG and TGs. Finally, in order to guarantee an adequate flexibility potential within the department's culture, some preservation was necessary. Management decided that by stronger socialization processes (career policy, rotation programs, regular assessments), supporting rules could be more thoroughly explained and maintained within the department.

To conclude, in the RPS project management applied an exclusive engineering approach which focused on the architecture of the tangible technological resources. The application of the FAR method supported the selection of these design variables. However, the FAR method also generated design variables of the more firm-specific intangible resources in order to develop certain critical managerial capabilities to reach that state and deal with it over time (see Fig. 11.15). These design variables can be clustered in three categories. The first cluster improves the potential for task or functional flexibility; it facilitates a higher self-regulation, which is required for autonomous, flexible task groups. The second cluster improves the potential for strategic flexibility regarding new market developments or technological developments. The third cluster is necessary to maintain an adequate potential within Assembly Dept. GB.

Post-Measurement

The new flexibility profile of Assembly Dept. GB, which gives an idea of the flexibility mix one year later, shows that the external flexibility had strongly increased, while the internal flexibility had decreased. This implies that the department had become less vulnerable to changes in its environment, but that its internal adaptability had further diminished. Consonant with our specified flexibility aspects, we can observe that management's external flexibility capabilities regarding customers and outer technologies increased. Management had succeeded in arranging more stable contracts and could more easily implement process improvements in the Glass-Bead technology. Also its external flexibility capabilities regarding suppliers and workload had to some extent increased. The Purchasing Dept. had arranged second suppliers for certain subcomponents (second-sourcing). Also, the volume of the workload could be influenced better, due to the closer links of the planner of Assembly Dept. GB with the Central Planning Department. Regarding the internal flexibility capabilities, the expensive flexibility originating from inventories had decreased significantly; specifically, the buffer stocks between

	RPS Project	FAR Project
ENGINEERING APPROACH	(1) • mode of production (small batch) • physical layout (group layout) • grouping (product flow)	idem
DEVELOPMENT APPROACH		(1) • operational production repertoire • interchangeability • reduction liaison devices
		(2) • scope of identity • openness of external orientation • tolerance for ambiguity
		(3) • socialization

Fig. 11.15. Design variables of the FAR project to complete the RPS project.

the various steps in the assembly process had diminished. However, the flexibility score regarding our specified internal flexibility aspects, namely the production system and personnel, had not increased. At the moment of our post-measurement, the replacement of the old solder and alloy ovens by modern computerized ovens was causing many running start problems for flexibility improvement of the production system. Regarding the personnel, 75% of the day shift was transferred to the full continuous shift. These shifts now consisted of 16 employees. While the department had not introduced crash teams for rush orders, the workers within the full continuous shift were better skilled and more self-regulating. More workers were able to handle the tinning machine, and workers of the jig filling group also performed other operations in the assembly line. Due to this increase of functional labor flexibility, the department could suffice with a lower numerical labor flexibility. Therefore, no increase was observed in the total flexibility score regarding personnel.

Thanks to the above changes in the management's flexibility profile, the operational flexibility in terms of load flexibility and the strategic flexibility in terms of capacity flexibility were much higher. The radical enlargement of its production capacity had helped the department to more easily exploit new volume developments in the F, UF, and Z markets. When we conducted our post-measurement, the production capacity was even higher than demand. While for some product types the department could fill its safety stocks, for the other product types load flexibility was very important. Because production capacity and personnel could more easily be switched to produce other product types, management could more quickly react to short-term fluctuations.

Furthermore, the management's information-processing capacity was less extensive; the information score had decreased from 47.9 to 34. Regarding the specified information activities, the information gathering was more rudimentary. Assembly Dept. GB was now producing according to the ISO-9000 norm, while the Ford Q-1 norm was the leading standard for its diodes. Moreover, the application areas for GP diodes were still unclear. Also, the volume developments in the long term and the substitution effects were hard to assess. Finally, the numerous informal and formal liaison devices had been reduced to 5 regular meetings.

Regarding the organizational resources, the department's technological, structural and cultural system provided a larger potential for flexibility. The smaller batch sizes, the larger skill repertoire, the extra production capacity and improved switchability of machines and equipment, and the incorporation of tinning and certain operations of the Diffusion Dept. within the assembly line facilitated a larger potential for operational flexibility. For instance, the resetting times for the production of zeners had decreased with one and a half hours as a consequence of the introduction of computerized ovens. Nonetheless, the department was still operating with a single assembly line, which was now segmented into three parts. For each part one technical assistant was responsible.

The department's structure was an intermediate form of the old and the desired structure. The OG had been enlarged with a planner and a technical assistant in such a way that all staff departments were fully integrated in an interdisciplinary group. However, because the equipment was not organized in mini-lines, there were no self-contained task groups. The OG was still striving to create two task groups but not in its layout of equipment. Although there were still no autonomous task groups, the larger shifts were more self-regulating than before. As a consequence of increased on-the-job training and the training in process control, the interchangeability within the shifts increased. For every worker a skills matrix had been developed, linking skills to operations. The increased self-regulation of the shifts facilitated the delegation of more routine tasks to the shifts. Also, the information rounds regarding the redesign of the department and the development of task groups had resulted in higher participation levels. For each shift, the OG had chosen two contact persons who functioned as intermediaries in the redesign of the department.

Finally, the department's cultural system had become more innovative. By stimulating various cultural practices such as the celebration of the twelve-and-a-half-year existence of the department, attention for the silver jubilees of production workers, the organization of an 'open house' of the assembly for the workers' relatives and other social events, the development of a unique logo for the department, and the start of special mailings for informing the shift workers, the OG had succeeded in broadening the scope of the department's identity. Furthermore, by ongoing information rounds regarding the development of the IOR program and the RPS project, special IOR training for the assembly department's workers, and participation in the decision-making regarding the implementation of the RPS project, the openness and the tolerance for ambiguity increased within Assembly Dept. GB. Besides these communication channels, the product line MPRS had started with a news bulletin, directed by an editorial staff, informing the employees about the goals of the change program. Moreover, by developing a human resources planning, a re-evaluation of the functional levels, an explicit career policy, and regular assessments of production workers, the appropriate rules could be transmitted.

In sum, Assembly Dept. GB was transformed from a hybrid of a rigid/planned configuration into a hybrid of a planned/flexible configuration. Still, management had not yet succeeded in creating two mini-lines with two autonomous task groups. Consequently, the remaining interdependencies in the assembly process restricted especially the strategic flexibility of the assembly department.

SUMMARY AND CONCLUSIONS

In this chapter, we have developed a definition for the paradox of flexibility, a conceptual model for describing flexible configurations, and a typology of configuration strategies. This allowed us to postulate variance-hypotheses about flexible configurations of managerial capabilities and organizational resources and process-hypotheses of strategic change for dealing with the flexibility paradox over time.

Furthermore, by integrating the conceptual model with our typology, we developed an enriched process model of flexibility improvement. In combination with the observation and analysis instruments, the process model formed the basis of the Flexibility Audit and Redesign (FAR) method for diagnosing organizational flexibility and guiding strategic transition processes.

In our longitudinal case-study within Philips Sermiconductors, we showed that most of the hypotheses of the FAR method were confirmed. Of course, we have to realize that on the basis of extreme cases, it is often difficult to test the hypotheses with much complexity, and their empirical grounding is likely to be insufficient (cf. Eisenhardt, 1989: 545). Still, with the theoretical foundation of these hypotheses and this empirical study, our hypotheses are at least logically and empirically plausible.

The pre-measurement within the Assembly Department GB summarized in Fig. 11.16 makes clear that our variance prediction is replicated for a reason which supports our second hypothesis (theoretical replication). Assembly Dept. GB, which was intended to function in a dynamic and complex environment, indeed employed merely operational flexibility and possessed a mechanistic structural system and a conservative cultural system. Also, in line with our prediction we found highly developed intelligence systems as a part of the metaflexibility and many structural process regulations, issued to facilitate the development of routines. Nonetheless, due to the partial implementation of the Redesign Production Systems (RPS) project, the technological system was not as non-routine as we had expected. Consequently, Assembly Dept. GB was still experiencing problems activating operational flexibility. Our case therefore did not totally correspond with the planned configuration (H.2), but was positioned somewhere between the rigid and planned configuration in our typology of strategic configurations (hybrid rigid/planned configuration).

Besides the replication of our variance prediction, the empirical results of the post-measurement largely conform our process prediction. Deviations from our process prediction were caused by the fact that not all changes in the design variables could be implemented within one year. The partial implementation of the design variables on the basis of our process prediction resulted in a hybrid of a planned/flexible form with a higher external flexibility, and less extensive information scanning, but a lower internal flexibility (entrepreneurial revitalization). Assembly Dept. GB, which was confronted with increasing unpredictability, was able to activate operational load flexibility and some strategic capacity flexibility originating from an increasing non-routine technological system, a moderately organic structural system (organic form with strong process regulations), and a more innovative cultural system. The internal flexibility score, however, was temporarily curtailed because the replacement of the old solder and alloy ovens by modern computerized ovens caused many running start problems,

		CASE PHILIPS	
Environmental shift	dynamism	+	++
	complexity	+	++
	unpredictability	–	+/–
Trajectory		Entrepreneurial revitalization	
Measurement		pre	post
Flexibility types	operational	+/–	+
	structural	–	–
	strategic	–	+/–
F scores	F internal	46.7	35.2
	F external	31.6	38.5
	F total	39.2	36.9
Metaflex.	I score	47.9	34.0
Flexibility potential	technological system	+/–	+
	structural system	–	+/–
	cultural system	–	+
Configuration strategy		rigid/planned	planned/flexible

- = low
+/– = moderate
+ = high
++ = extremely high

Fig. 11.16. Empirical results of the Philips Semiconductors case.

while the expensive internal flexibility originating from large inventories significantly decreased. Moreover, in order to cope with unexpected changes, pure routine proliferation was impossible. In line with our process prediction, therefore, management reduced its need for information processing. Not surprisingly, Fig. 11.16 shows that the metaflexibility score diminished further as a consequence of this more rudimentary information scanning. Finally, because the department had not yet succeeded in creating two mini-lines with two autonomous task groups, the remaining interdependencies still hampered the activation of strategic flexibility.

To conclude, the concrete output of the FAR research project is a method with a strongly theoretical, conceptual, process-oriented, and instrumental basis. From an *analytical* point of view, the study contributed *'universal knowledge'* to the scientific discipline of strategic management in terms of theoretically and empirically plausible hypotheses. That is, the study generated validly generalizable knowledge stating under which environmental characteristics certain configurations of dynamic managerial capabilities and organizational resources are likely to be found, and also which strategic trajectories of transformation for improving flexibility are appropriate.

From a *clinical* point of view, the study contributed *'existential knowledge'* to the practice of management as a profession. That is, the study provided situationally dependent knowledge as to how to change the dynamic managerial capabilities in terms of types of flexibility, flexibility aspects, and information activities, and how to redesign the organizational resources in given contexts so as to achieve and maintain improved flexibility as measured by the FAR method.

REFERENCES

Aaker, D. A. and Mascarenhas, B. "The Need for Strategic Flexibility". *The Journal of Business Strategy*, Vol. 5(2), pp. 74–82, Fall 1984.

Amit, R. and Schoemaker, P. J. H. "Strategic Assets and Organizational Rent". *Strategic Management Journal*, Vol. 14(1), pp. 33–46, 1993.

Andrews, K. R. *The Concept of Corporate Strategy*. Homewood, IL: Dow Jones-Irwin, 1971.

Ansoff, H. I. "The Changing Shape of the Strategic Problem". In Schendel, D. E. and Hofer, C. W., eds., *Strategic Management: A New View of Business Policy and Planning*. Boston and Toronto: Little, Brown and Company, pp. 30–44, 1978.

Ansoff, H. I. and Brandenburg, R. "A Language for Organizational Design: Parts I and II". *Management Science*, pp. 350–393, August 1971.

Ashby, W. R. *An Introduction to Cybernetics*. London: Methuen, 1964.

Burgelman, R. A. "A Process Model of Internal Corporate Venturing in the Diversified Major Firm". *Administrative Science Quarterly*, Vol. 28, pp. 223–244, June 1983.

Burns, T. and Stalker, G. M. *The Management of Innovation*. London: Tavistock, 1961.

Chaffee, E. E. "Three Modes of Strategy". *Academy of Management Review*, Vol. 10(1), pp. 89–98, 1985.

Chandler, A. D. Jr. *Strategy and Structure*. Cambridge, MA: MIT Press, 1962.

De Leeuw, T. and Volberda, H. W. "On the Concept of Flexibility". In Trappl, R., ed., *Cybernetics and Systems Research '92*. Singapore: World Scientific, Vol. 2, pp. 1079–1086, 1992.

Duncan, R. B. "The Ambidextrous Organization: Designing Dual Structures for Innovation". In Kilmann, R. H., Pondy, L. R. and Slevin, D. P., eds., *The Management of Organization Design*. New York: Elsevier North-Holland, Vol. 1, pp. 167–188, 1976.

Eisenhardt, K. M. "Building Theories from Case Study Research". *Academy of Management Review*, Vol. 14(4), pp. 532–550, 1989.

Eppink, D. J. "Managing the Unforeseen: A Study of Flexibility". Dissertation, Ermelo: Administratief Centrum, 1978.

Fredrickson, J. W. "Strategic Process Research: Questions and Recommendations". *Academy of Management Review*, Vol. 8(4), pp. 565–575, 1983.

Galbraith, J. R. *Designing Complex Organizations*. Reading, MA: Addison Wesley, 1973.

Greiner, L. E. "Evolution and Revolution as Organizations Grow". *Harvard Business Review*, pp. 37–46, July–August, 1972.

Hofer, C. W. and Schendel, D. *Strategy Formulation: Analytical Concepts*. St. Paul, MN: West Publishing, 1978.

Hofstede, G. "Motivation, Leadership and Organization: Do American Theories Apply Abroad?". *Organizational Dynamics*, pp. 42–63, Summer 1980.

Johnson, G. "Rethinking Incrementalism". *Strategic Management Journal*, Vol. 9, pp. 75–91, September 1988.

Kanter, R. M. *The Change Masters*. New York: Simon and Schuster, 1983.

Kanter, R. M. "When a Thousand Flowers Bloom: Structural, Collective, and Social Conditions for Innovation in Organization". In Staw, B. M. and Cummings, L. L., eds., *Research in Organizational Behavior*. Greenwich, CT: JAI Press, Vol. 10, pp. 169–211, 1988.

Kieser, A. and Kubicek, H. *Organisationstheorien I und II*. Stuttgart: Kohlhammer, 1978.

Krijnen, H. G. "The Flexible Firm". *Long Range Planning*, Vol. 12, pp. 63–75, April 1979.

Leonard-Barton, D. "Core Capabilities and Core Rigidities: A Paradox in Managing New Product Development". *Strategic Management Journal*, Vol. 13, Summer Special Issue, pp. 111–125, 1992.

Lorange, P. and Vancil, R. A. *Strategic Planning Systems*. Englewood Cliffs, NJ: Prentice-Hall, 1977.

Miller, D. and Friesen, P. "Archetypes of Organizational Transition," *Administrative Science Quarterly*, Vol. 25(2), pp. 268–300, 1980.

Mintzberg, H. "Strategy-Making in Three Modes". *California Management Review*, Vol. 16(2), pp. 44–53, Winter 1973.

Mintzberg, H. "Patterns in Strategy Formation". *Management Science*, Vol. 24, pp. 934–948, 1978.

Mintzberg, H. "Strategy Formation: Schools of Thought". In Frederickson, J. W., ed., *Perspectives on Strategic Management*. New York: Harper, pp. 105–235, 1990.

Mintzberg, H. and Waters, J. A. "Of Strategies, Deliberate and Emergent". *Strategic Management Journal*, Vol. 6, pp. 257–272, 1985.

Nelson, R. R. and Winter, S. G. *An Evolutionary Theory of Economic Change*. Cambridge: Harvard University Press, 1982.

Newman, W. H., Summer, W. H. and Warren, E. K., *The Process of Management: Concepts, Behavior and Practice*. Englewood Cliffs, NJ: Prentice-Hall, 1972.

Peters, T. J. and Waterman, R. H. Jr. *In Search of Excellence*. New York: Warner Books, 1982.

Prahalad, C. K. and Hamel, G. "The Core Competence of the Corporation". *Harvard Business Review*, Vol. 68(3), pp. 79–91, 1990.

Quinn, J. B. "Managing Innovation: Controlled Chaos". *Harvard Business Review*, Vol. 63(3), pp. 78–84, 1985.

Sanchez, R. "Strategic Flexibility, Firm Organization, and Managerial Work in Dynamic Markets". In *Advances in Strategic Management*. JAI Press, Vol. 9, pp. 251–291, 1993.

Schoemaker, P. J. H. "How to Link Strategic Vision to Core Capabilities". *Sloan Management Review*, pp. 67-81, Fall 1992.

Scott, B. W. *Long-Range Planning in American Industry*. New York: American Management Association, 1965.

Teece, D. J. "Economic Analysis and Strategic Management". *California Management Review*, pp. 87–110, Spring 1984.

Teece, D. J., Pisano, G. and Shuen, A. "Dynamic Capabilities and Strategic Management". Working Paper, University of California, Berkeley, August 1992.

Thompson, J. D. *Organizations in Action*. New York: McGraw-Hill Book Company, 1967.

Utterback, J. M. and Abernathy, W. J. "A Dynamic Model of Process and Product Innovation". *Omega*, The Int. Jl of Mgmt Sci., Vol. 3(6), pp. 639–656, 1975.

Van Ham, J. C., Pauwe, J. and Williams, A. R. T. "Flexibiliteit en Stabiliteit vanuit Individu en Organisatie". In Buitendam, A., ed., *Arbeidsmarkt, Arbeidsorganisatie, Arbeidsverhoudingen, Sociaal Beleid*. Deventer: Kluwer, Chapter 6, pp. 74–90, 1987.

Volberda, H. W. "Een Flexibele Organisatie als Voorwaarde voor Innovatie" (A Flexible Organization as Condition for Innovation). *M&O Tijdschrift voor Organisatiekunde en Sociaal Beleid*, Vol. 44(3), pp. 215–242, May–June, 1990.

Volberda, H. W. "Organizational Flexibility: Change and Preservation". Research Paper 10th EGOS Colloquium, "Societal Change Between Market and Organization", Vienna, July 15–17 1991.

Volberda, H. W. *"Organizational Flexibility: Change and Preservation—A Flexibility Audit and Redesign Method"*. Dissertation thesis. Groningen: Wolters-Noordhoff, 1992.

Volberda, H. W. and Cheah, H-B. "A New Perspective on Entrepreneurship: A Dialectic Process of Transformation within the Entrepreneurial Mode, Type of Flexibility and Organizational Form". In Klandt, H., ed., *Research in Entrepreneurship*. Aldershot: Avebury, pp. 261–285, 1993.

Weick, K. E. "Management of Organizational Change Among Loosely Coupled Elements". In Goodman, P. S. and Associates, eds., *Change in Organizations: New Perspectives in Theory, Research, and Practice*. San Francisco: Jossey-Bass, pp. 375-408, 1982.

Yin, R. K. *Case Study Research: Design and Methods*. Applied Social Research Methods Series. Newbury Park: Sage Publications, Vol. 5(Revised Edition), 1989.

APPENDIX I

DIAGNOSTIC RESULTS OF THE LONGITUDINAL CASE-STUDY

The data collected within Philips Semiconductors by means of the standardized questionnaires (environmental turbulence scan, technology, structure, and culture checklist) and quick survey (flexibility scan) were analyzed with the FARSYS computerprogram and generated the profiles presented in this appendix: a turbulence profile, a flexibility profile, and the organizational characterists of the pre-measurement, a decision-matrix, and a new flexibility profile of the post-meaurement. For a more elaborate discussion of the measurement procedures we refer to Volberda (1992).

Pre-Measurement

Environmental Turbulence

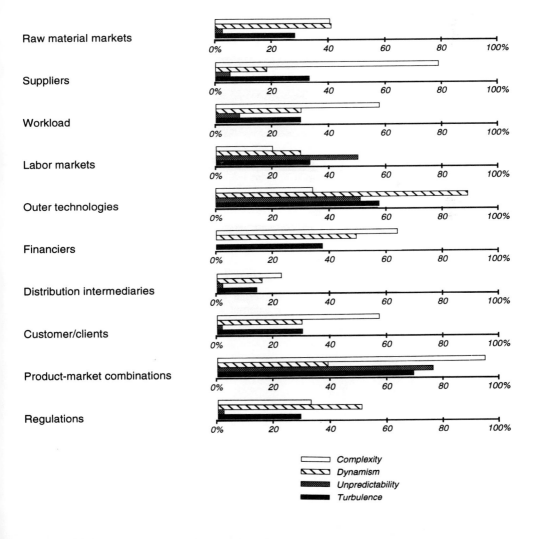

Raw material markets

Suppliers

Workload

Labor markets

Outer technologies

Financiers

Distribution intermediaries

Customer/clients

Product-market combinations

Regulations

Complexity
Dynamism
Unpredictability
Turbulence

Flexibility Profile

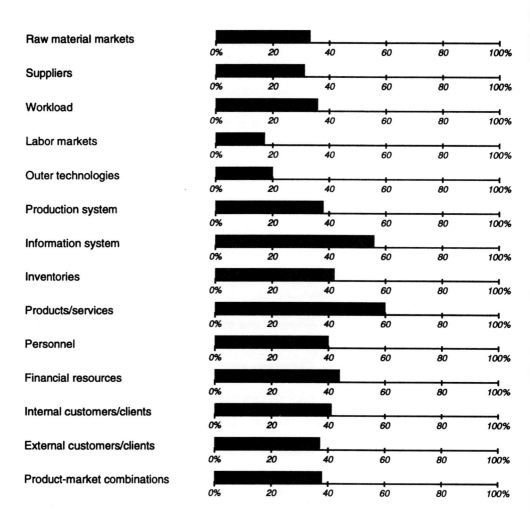

I = 47.9
F internal = 46.7
F external = 31.6

Technology Characteristic

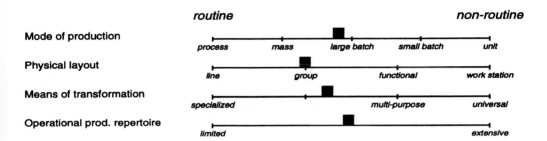

Structure Characteristic

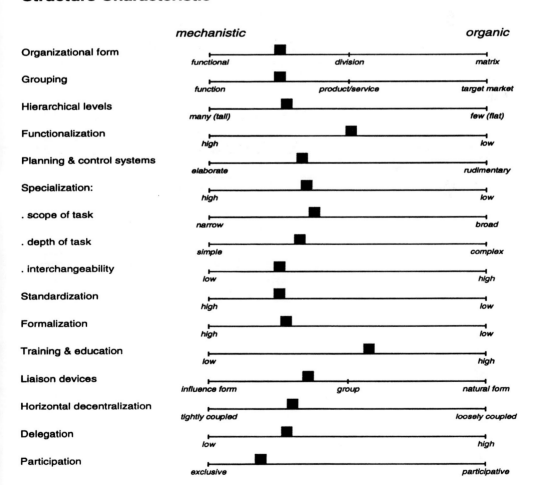

Culture Characteristic

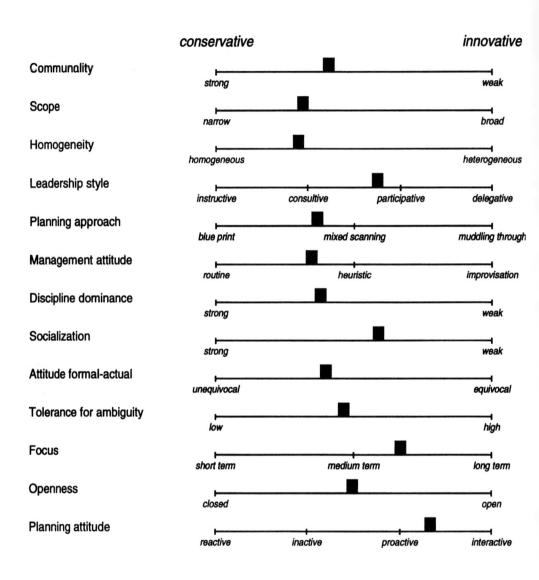

ASSESSMENT

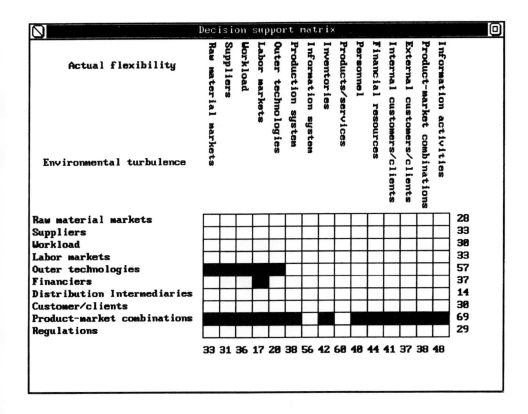

Post-measurement

Flexibility Profile

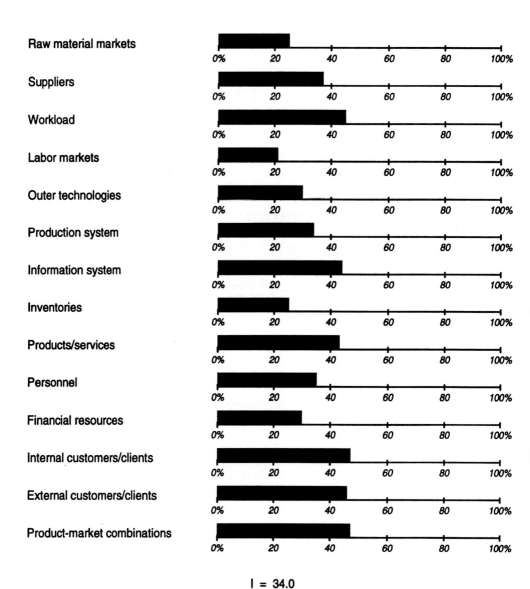

Raw material markets

Suppliers

Workload

Labor markets

Outer technologies

Production system

Information system

Inventories

Products/services

Personnel

Financial resources

Internal customers/clients

External customers/clients

Product-market combinations

I = 34.0
F internal = 35.2
F external = 38.5

12

FROM NATIONAL TO GLOBAL PRODUCT DEVELOPMENT COMPETENCE IN THE TELECOMMUNICATIONS INDUSTRY: STRUCTURE AND PROCESS IN LEVERAGING CORE CAPABILITIES

Beverly C. Winterscheid and Sandra McNabb

INTRODUCTION

Rapid technological change and global competition is radically changing the face of competition across the globe. The impact of rapid technological change coupled with radical market changes is no where more evident than in the European telecommunications industry. Today it is impossible to define members of this industry group in the same way as ten years previous. Former competitors are new collaborators seeking to integrate technological strengths, market access, and national infrastructures. Foreign entrants such as AT&T, MCI or Nippon Telephone and Telegraph now attempt to compete in European national markets previously excluded to outsiders. The differing speed of privatization and industry deregulation across European countries have made it difficult for companies, such as these foreign entrants, to pursue global strategies to take advantage of economies of scope and scale. In short, firms competing in this industry, whether European national champions or global players, are evolving new behaviors trying to create new competences that they hopefully can sustain.

This paper examines the development of global competence in the product development function of firms in the telecommunications industry, and proposes a three-stage normative model of organizational evolution that can effectively link dispersed technological capabilities with diverse customer needs. We begin by describing the current competitive dynamics in the European telecommunications industry. Using the first-hand experience of AT&T Network Systems Europe, we outline the required product development competencies that, in our view, are essential for success in the European telecommunications industry.

We argue that product development competence requires a dynamic matching process between customer needs and firms' technological strengths. Further, as telecommunications companies leave their positions as national champions and move to contest international markets, the nature of the matching process between technology and customer need is changing, requiring new individual and organizational capabilities. We demonstrate this argument using an evolutionary model derived from the international experience of AT&T.

AT&T AND COMPETITIVE DYNAMICS IN THE EUROPEAN TELECOMMUNICATIONS INDUSTRY

AT&T Network Systems is a global manufacturer and marketer of network telecommunications products, which include the hardware and software information service providers need to build and operate their communication networks. It is organized into five business groups: switching systems, transmission equipment, operations systems that develops and markets network management systems, network cable and network wireless systems. Major customers for these five divisions include European PTTs, cable television providers and wireless service providers.

AT&T is the world's networking revenue leader, providing communications services and products, as well as network equipment and computer systems. Its customers are businesses, consumers, telecommunications service providers and government agencies. From its historic position of strength in the United States, AT&T began competing in international markets in the late 1800's when it acquired International Telephone and Telegraph.

Today, however, the competitive challenges for AT&T in Europe are dramatically different than in the U.S. AT&T is a new entrant in the European networking business, rather than the national champion. It routinely has small market shares in European countries, in contrast to national champions such as Alcatel of France and Siemens of Germany. Further, many of AT&T's competitors are subsidized by their governments. AT&T must deal with multiple cultures and business practices, as well as differing technological standards within these countries. In short, the rules of competition (if indeed, there are any at this stage in the European telecommunications industry) are vastly different than those in the U.S., and AT&T must adjust its practices to extend its national success globally.

There are three key aspects of the European telecommunications industry that will affect companies that do business with PTTs, national public telephone companies. First of all, PTTs are governmental or quasi-governmental organizations. Secondly, the PTTs' markets will be protected until 1998 due to an extension granted by the European community. Finally, industry experts anticipate that PTTs will choose between two and three vendors for each type of network equipment: switches, fiber, cable, and so on. Each of these facts has significant implications for the competencies required to successfully compete in this industry. We now deal with each in turn, and discuss the shifts in competence required by a company such as AT& T.

PTTs are Governmental or Quasi-Governmental Organizations

Despite the increased trend towards privatization in Europe, telephone and other types of communications companies remain closely tied to national governments, typically due to national governments' reluctance to give up control on a profitable monopoly, and to maintain some control on a strategic industry. Due to the size of contracts in this industry, which typically range from 10 to 500 million dollars, companies who win these contracts must show benefit to the local economy. Thus, local value-added is critical. This value-added takes the form of local-content, local hiring, and local expertise requirements. Increasingly, countries are demanding a substantive local contribution in technology, in hopes of upgrading technological skills in the country and creating spin-off industries. Therefore, technology transfer agreements are usually part of the contract. Technology transfer agreements are new to AT&T, requiring new competence in identifying what technologies are proprietary, and which can be given away so as not to create new competitors in a decade's time.

Further, new knowledge transfer and collaboration skills are required to develop and sell high quality products with "employees" from different nations and cultures. Finally, new political skills are required to win the contract. Protected, national champion competitors can frequently point to impending job loss in the national economy if their firm loses the contract to the foreign outsider. AT&T, as the new upstart, typically does not have the local employment levels prior to the contract to make as compelling an argument as the national champion. Thus, AT&T must leverage its technological strengths to achieve meaningful local content in technology and human resource terms in order to win the contract.

PTTs Will Choose Two or Three Vendors for Each Product

The implication here is that AT&T will never achieve the market dominance experienced in the U.S., which places a high priority on choosing which technology/product offerings to go with in each country. AT&T's historic strengths in technology must be maintained at the same time that international marketing skills are learned and refined. Thus, the marketing and R&D relationship in the company must be managed well, with information that is timely and relevant to each function. This requires the placement of international marketing individuals in targeted countries that U.S. AT&T technologists trust to provide an accurate "read" on environmental demand and product offerings. The task is challenging enough to a traditional tech-push company if the competitive domain is a single nation; the task can be daunting spread over multiple countries and cultures.

Since the PTTs will always choose multiple vendors, the additional technology/marketing task of attempting to figure out *in advance* which products will sell in that market emerges. New competence in simultaneously predicting technological development, market demand, and competitor's moves across multiple countries is required.

PTTs' Markets are Protected Until 1998

PTTs have negotiated a short, protected window of opportunity in a volatile market to upgrade their quality, productivity, and technical competence. PTTs also realize that if they do not do this, they may very likely disappear as an independent entity come 1998. Thus, PTTs are motivated to upgrade their networks to world-class standards in short order, and realize that they must partner with a dominant telecommunications player to do this. They also realize that their partner of today may be their competitor in 1998. Thus, PTTs do not want to be locked into a single vendor, and want to stimulate competition among their chosen vendors. Companies such as AT&T realize that they will have to share small, national markets for a period of time, thus placing more emphasis on technologies and products offering synergy across multiple nations.

To summarize, the industry specific competencies emerging in the European telecommunications industry include the capacity to distinguish which technologies can become part of technology transfer agreements and which should remain proprietary; the organizational ability to transfer technologies and new product design and manufacturer to different national partners, and produce and deliver to world-class standards; and finally, to develop a strategic vision of which technologies and product offerings should exist in each country to take advantage of firm-wide economies of scale and scope, as well as the emergent political and economic situations. In all cases, competence in technology development is essential. It is this topic to which we now turn.

PRODUCT DEVELOPMENT COMPETENCE: A DEFINITION AND KEY COMPONENTS

While each firm requires certain specific competencs in product development in order to be successful within its industry, we believe that a generic definition is of value to establish certain baseline competence, regardless of industry:

> Competence in product development is derived from a *dynamic and recursive match* between *technical capabilities* and *market knowledge* where individual and organizational processes mediate the flow of information between these two.

This definition builds upon existing literature (Allen, 1977; Cooper, 1979, 1983 Dougherty, 1992; Zirger and Maidique, 1990) regarding the integration or tension between technical capabilities (i.e. R&D, engineering, product design) and market knowledge (i.e. customers, competitors, and the regulatory environment). We suggest that it is not enough for a firm to have expertise in these two areas; product development competence is dependent upon a dynamic and recursive matching process between technology and market knowledge. This matching process is accomplished by individuals involved in product development activities, as well as through standard operating procedures within the firm. The focus of our paper is to elucidate the dynamics surrounding this matching process, as a firm-specific competence.

Assumed within the definition are the following key components of competence within product development. Each of these components will be expanded in the remainder of the paper:

1. **technical capabilities**, typically originating from the R&D and engineering functions, and which encompass individual intelligence, and expertise to innovate and design products;
2. **customer knowledge**, typically originating within the sales and marketing function or other individuals wit outside customer contact. This component includes translating customer needs into existing or new technical capabilites within the firm;
3. **customer relationships**, which can reside anywhere in the organization with customer contact. The main point is that relationships are required to create an information flow between customers and the firm. Typical information is customer needs, technical requirement with R&D people, product prototype performance in real-time customer situations, and strategic information on customer/competitive priorities;
4. **product technology platforms**, which include software/hardware environments and associated tools, Product technology platforms enable the firm to efficiently customize products by assembling standardized components in unique combinations to meet specific customer need.

Finally, we argue that dynamic matching, and therefore competence, occurs when individual cognitive processes and organizational processes such as routines and standard operating procedures, electronic information processing capability, and cultural assumptions mediate the flow of information regarding technology and the external environment. Aoki (1990) makes the distinction that organizational coordination is the essence of a firm's distinctive competence. We make the distinction between individual and organizational processes to clearly separate individual learning and expertise from organizational learning and competence captured in firm-level systems and procedures. We proceed by examing the three organizational arrangements that AT&T has used to deploy its product development capability over time in Europe, in order to raise these structural and process issues.

THE THREE STAGES OF PRODUCT DEVELOPMENT IN AT&T

AT&T has moved through the following three stages in their shift from national to global product development which will be described below: the single customer approach; the multiple customer, multiple nation approach; and most recently, the competence center approach. The following sections will first present a factual description of each stage, followed by the authors' analysis of the functional and process competencies required to successfully implement each stage. Finally, the strengths and limitations of each stage are presented.

The data for this study were made available through personal, managerial experience within AT&T of one co-author, and the action research and analysis by the other author over a two year period. Primary research methodology was the constant comparison method (Glaser and Strauss, 1967). While the real-time experience of AT&T involved an incremental and, at times, circuitous journey, the three stages are clearly distinguishable, and have been used as reference points in discussions with AT&T managers regarding the global deployment of product development activities within the firm.

STAGE ONE: THE SINGLE CUSTOMER APPROACH

AT&T Network Systems first began their international operations with one overseas customer. The expectation was that product development activities were to be handled as was done in the U.S. market—in the U.S. labs. Since early business was anticipated to be existing products adapted for foreign use, new product development was anticipated to be a minor activity, except for product adaptation activities for the foreign market.

In order to support this market entry strategy, it was necessary to establish local development activities to please the government which could grant or withhold market access, as is currently the case today in Eastern

Stage One: Single Customer Approach

Remote developments from a central R&D Lab to serve a specific customer

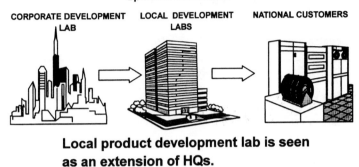

CORPORATE DEVELOPMENT LAB   LOCAL DEVELOPMENT LABS   NATIONAL CUSTOMERS

Local product development lab is seen as an extension of HQs.

Fig. 12.1. Stage One: Single customer approach.

Europe and Russia. The product development structure, depicted in Fig. 12.1, involved remote developments from a central R&D lab in the States to serve the specific national customer, and insure a close match between customer need and AT&T technology. Specific national adjustments to the product were interpreted by local engineers and marketers, and transmitted to the corporate lab for design and technical integration into the existing product. The organizational assumption was that the local product development lab would serve as an extension of the corporate lab.

Functional Capabilities

Required capability for the technology function at the corporate lab was that competence was created and dispersed from a central lab. The marketing function at HQ required the flexibility to respond to customer need as interpreted by the local lab. Flexibility refers to a technological capability and cultural openness to interpret and respond to the requests of the often foreign, engineer.

At the local lab site, marketing competence included the assessment of customization details; in other words, translating the customer requirements into technically doable tasks at the corporate level. Technological competence involved the ability to build from central lab specs and customize particular details as required.

Process Capabilities

According to our definition, capabilities in technology and customer functions are matched dynamically by individual and organizational processes.

Table 12.1. Stage One—The single customer approach required capabilities.

| | FUNCTIONAL | |
	Technology	Customer/Environmental
Corporate	Competence created and dispersed from central lab	Flexibility to respond to customer need as interpreted by local lab
Local	Ability to build from central lab specs	Assessment of customization details to central lab

| | PROCESSES | |
	Individual	Organizational
Corporate	"Creators"	Centralized systems that support top-down information flow
Local	"Interpreters" and "Implementers"	Local labs mirror HQ processes and systems

At the corporate level in Stage One, individuals in the central lab are the "creators" and "innovators", while at the local level individuals are the "interpreters" of local customization need and corporate technology and "implementers" of the top-down designs.

At the corporate level, organizational processes must be dominated by centralized systems that support top-down information flows as a basis of its competence. The organizational processes at the local lab mirror those found at the central lab because tasks are the same at both locations. The local lab reuses project management tools and decision-making processes made centrally. The tasks are perceived by both the corporate and local labs to be the same, but they are done in different places. The processes at both locations facilitate technical and customer information flow between locations, and project management, in general. Table 12.1 displays the functional and process competencies of Stage One.

To summarize, the strength of a Stage One product development structure is the total focus on the customer. Product development efforts create a seamless integration between customer needs and product traits, because all organizational efforts are geared towards the single customer's satisfaction. Further, it is a relatively easy and inexpensive way to meet local content and technology transfer requirements imposed by the national customer. As long as there is only one foreign customer, there are no apparent weaknesses to this arrangement.

STAGE TWO: THE MULTIPLE CUSTOMER/MULTIPLE COUNTRY APPROACH

Stage Two arises when the international strategy has been successful, and the company has national customers in many different nations. When the second customer in a different country was obtained, the organizational problem of how to manage repeated product customization activities emerged. If the second country was close to the first one, it was possible to run product development activities out of the first foreign lab for a period of time. However, the economic and political forces which led AT&T to establish its first international product development outpost are equally strong determinants of the second customer's contract.

Thus, Stage Two, depicted in Fig. 12.2, involves product development labs positioned close to the customer in multiple nations. As an example, product development labs for AT&T Network Systems are located in Belgium to serve Belgacom, Spain to serve Telefonica, and Holland to serve PTT-Telecom. The organizational assumption is the same, however ... each lab is a remote site charged only with performing local product customization. An important distinction in this stage is that the customization activities in each country begin to differ from each other based upon the needs and demands of the local customer. Thus, the competences within each national lab begin to diverge to match their markets, and products begin to differ, as well.

Functional Capabilities

At the local product development labs, the capabilities required in Stage One are still the same; technical capabilities rest on the ability to build from central lab specs to meet local customer requirements. At this stage, due to increased time and experience with each national customer, national

Stage Two: The Multiple Customer/Multiple Nation Approach

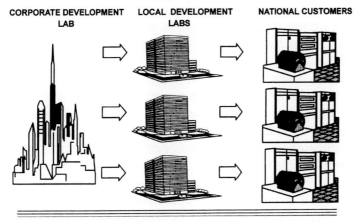

Fig. 12.2. Stage Two: The multiple customer/multiple nation approach.

product families emerge as the product offerings in each country are expanded to serve the national market. Customer capabilities at the local labs also remain the same as Stage One: the assessment and communication of local customization details to the corporate lab.

However, Stage Two provokes the recognition that new capabilities are required at the corporate lab. Corporate technology and customer functions now serve multiple product development labs, and multiple national customers. Complexity has increased dramatically, not only in sheer numbers, but in subtle product differences as well. While the technology task is still the same, i.e., product design dispersed to the remote local sites, the possibility of product platforms emerge because the functions and features of the products in each national market are similar, but organizational recognition of this fact is typically obscured. Why? Traditionally, corporate-level product development engineers have been organized to serve separate national product development labs. In this corporate structure, the recognition of the similarity in product features between Country A and B go unrecognized. The task of each group of corporate product development engineers is to serve the needs of their local lab counterparts. Thus, a potential opportunity to establish a competitive advantage through product platform design is missed due to corporate structure.

Process Capabilities

The corporate-level task to accomplish the dynamic matching between technology and customer functions also becomes more complex. In AT&T's experience, corporate individuals were not assigned to separate countries; they had to cover the technical demands of multiple local labs. Since AT&T did not add additional individuals to handle separate countries, corporate individuals have more local counterparts to deal with, and wider technical challenges. Eventually, product commonalities are perceived across multiple nations, as corporate product developers recognize similar solutions across nations and/or product groups in solving "unique" problems at the national level. Organizational-level processes at the corporate level remain the same as Stage One: centralized systems to facilitate predominantly top-down information flows.

At the local, national labs complexity increases for individuals, but the complexity is different from the challenge of multiple clients in different nations experienced at the corporate level. Staffing levels at the local labs are kept to a minimum, due to the inherent assumption that the local labs are merely remote sites which do not do fully-fledged product development. The reality in a Stage Two structure is that there typically is not enough revenue from each customer to support robust product development for every product that you want to sell. A local lab is a cost of market entry, and it is acknowledged that development costs can not be recouped on the sale of initial products. However, development costs can be recouped on the second and third products, if headcount is kept to a minimum. Therefore, product development teams are reused, asking people to cover a greater variety of technologies. These distinctions are depicted in Table 12.2.

To summarize, a Stage Two product development organization still meets customer needs through a close match between technology and customer need. It still gets products out on time, if communication and project management processes between the local and corporate labs function well. In fact, Alcatel and Ericsson run very effective Stage Two product development organizations. If an organization could stay at a Stage Two organization, it would because customer needs are being met in an effective fashion from the customer's standpoint.

Ultimately however, Stage Two organizations become overly expensive and inefficient because multiple labs in multiple nations are doing similar development tasks. No economies of scale or scope from a product standpoint can be obtained with this structure. Further, a Stage Two organization drains the skills of all of its employees, regardless of corporate or national location. The organization will eventually search for a new product development structure, when costs escalate due to market success in multiple foreign locations.

Table 12.2. Stage Two—The multiple customer/multiple nation approach required capabilities.

| | FUNCTIONAL | |
	Technology	Customer/Environmental
Corporate	Recognition of product platform possibilities	Flexibility to respond to multiple needs as interpreted by multiple local sites
Local	Ability to build from central lab specs	Assessment of customization details to central lab

| | PROCESSES | |
	Individual	Organizational
Corporate	HQ has more local counterparts	Centralized systems that support top-down information flow
	Redundancies eventually perceived across multiple sites	Additional complexity due to multiple sites
Local	Capabilities become shallow Competes for HQ attention	Local labs mirror HQ processes and systems

STAGE THREE: THE COMPETENCE CENTER APPROACH

A competence-based product development structure is radically different from Stages One and Two, because it involves a complete reassessment and restructuring of organizational capabilities. Why are companies such as AT&T willing to undergo such drastic change? As described earlier, product cost structures have gradually moved out of line as more engineering redundancies across national labs have emerged.

Consider for example, that the same product is designed in three different labs, but this product can be offered with minor variations in multiple markets. The product introduction in each national market is bound by the timing of the local lab. There is no reuse of software code; further, an individual lab will not have the organizational processes to allow them to reuse code because each product developed is significantly different. Finally, a local lab will not even see that coordination is possible.

Add to this scenario the competition at the corporate level between the different national lab priorities, and the increased difficulty experienced by any one local engineer to gain the ear of their corporate counterpart due to the sheer number of local developers attempting to get corporate attention. Finally add to this scene national customers who demand increasingly global roles in technological and product development in order to grant product contracts. At Stage Three, it is simply not enough to offer local content for the local market to win the contract; increasingly, companies must offer local content for global markets.

As depicted in Fig. 12.3, local product development labs are disbanded in Stage Three, and regional competence centers that specialize in particular product or service components which match regional assets are distributed throughout the globe. Locational decisions for competence centers are still driven by technology transfer and local content priorities, as in the prior two Stages. Product or service components are shipped in electronic or physical form depending upon the component to a product integration center, where components are assembled in customized combinations for particular markets. Finally, products are shipped to national customers.

The primary assumption for this stage is that the HQ possesses the expertise to identify and allocate capabilities and product development activities throughout the organization. As new research (Hamel and Heene, 1994) in the resource-based view of the firm indicates, this assumption may be ill-founded due to sheer lack of experience in activities of this sort. The second assumption in Stage Three is that information technology within the company supports real-time information flow. The intent of the competence center structure is to create a virtual organization and reduce geographic, national and functional barriers through the use of firm-wide information technology.

While the tight match between national customer need and technology

Stage Three: Competence Center Approach

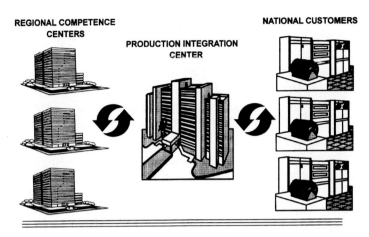

REGIONAL COMPETENCE
CENTERS

PRODUCTION INTEGRATION
CENTER

NATIONAL CUSTOMERS

Fig. 12.3. Stage Three: Competence center approach.

experienced in Stages One and Two is missing in the competence center approach, the company is attempting to meet the larger national/customer needs of bootstrapping the national economy, increasing the technical competence of the national population by the larger, regional distribution of product or service components made by the local population. In addition to product revenue, companies may receive additional compensation in the form of tax credits in Stage Three.

In many respects, competition in this still largely regulated, European market is a curious mixture of political and business factors. In a regulated market, a firm must make the decisions described above, in order to compete. But taking these actions does not lead to a competence center approach. Gaining market access is a Stage One problem. Getting costs out of the product using a core competence structure and product platforms is the problem faced in Stage Three.

Functional Capabilities

In the Stage Three diagrams, the corporate level is synonymous with regional product integration centers because of the similar coordinative role that each organization plays. In the technology function, product platforms and supporting technical expertise (Sanchez, 1991) are essential capabilities at the corporate/integration center level. Correspondingly at the competence center level, product platform components and supporting technical expertise is required. In order for a Stage Three organization to function well, an equalization of competence and power between the corporate and local levels is desirable. A change in roles for both the corporate-level and local-level individuals must occur. Local-level individuals might now participate in the *original* designs of product components or project management systems, rather than simply being on the receiving end of the designs. Equally, corporate-level or integration center individuals might find themselves on an implementation or assembly team executing, rather than designing a product component. The point here is that both product design and implementation competence is widely dispersed through the organization. Every location provides distinctive and creative technical contributions in contrast to the top-down, colonial approach of Stages One and Two.

A major weakness of Stage Three is the apparent lack of match between the customer functions and the organization. For example, Stage Three optimizes regional technology and product design competences by grouping core expertise together. An internal technology focus predominates, at the expense of the previously tight match between national sales and marketing with the national product development labs. This lack of customer focus is equally shared at both the corporate/integration center and regional competence center levels.

Process Capabilities

In addition to the structural upheaval discussed above, new skills are required for individuals. Individuals must shift from working primarily with a face-to-face team of product developers to a virtual team of individuals worldwide. Regardless of location, individuals face team issues of electronic counterparts geographically dispersed with subtle, perhaps personal differences in approach that previously were resolved face-to-face. Additionally, well-known cross-cultural differences (Hofstede, 1991) in communication, work style, and work approach are experienced.

As mentioned earlier, the competence center structure more broadly distributes power and competence within the organization. Original product design and corresponding customization expertise is now distributed throughout the global product development structure, potentially requiring changes in interpersonal as well as technical skills.

Organizational processes must be reconsidered, as well. Systems are required to assess individuals' capabilities throughout the organization and flexibly deploy these capabilities to meet specific, and changing, product design tasks. This is easier said than done due to the dynamic nature of human capability which is difficult, if not impossible, to capture in a systematized form. A competence center structure provokes a reconceptualization of human capabilities available to the firm. The metaphor of the individual as a platform of capabilities, and individual expertise as modular components of skills fits well here. Changes in organizational systems to support the platform concept are equally required. While organizational systems must still be centralized as in Stages One and Two, systems to support flexible allocations such as human skill data bases, product feature data bases, or accounting formats that charge headcount expense to project instead of departmental location must be established or enhanced.

Table 12.3 outlines the major distinctions of the competence center product development structure. To summarize, the competence center approach is a response to the perceived and real weaknesses of increased product cost, late or inappropriate product introductions, and the organizational redundancies of Stage Two, the multiple customer/multiple nation approach. The competence center approach seeks to bundle product development expertise into pockets of technological critical mass spread throughout the world matched to regional assets and future product opportunities. It necessitates a reexamination of the product in terms of platform and modular components, a reexamination of human capability in terms of deployable skills, and finally, a reexamination of the firm's systems and processes in order to support the other two.

The nature of the match between customer need and available technology shifts in Stage Three. While the match was explicit, close and visible through national product offering and product development lab expertise in Stages One and Two, the match expands to encompass political, social, and economic factors of the region, at the expense of the product match. A potential weakness of this approach is that attention in the product development lab shifts away from product to component expertise. Product

Table 12.3. Stage Three—The competence center approach required capabilities.

	FUNCTIONAL	
	Technology	**Customer/Environmental**
Corporate	Product platform and supporting technical expertise	Allocates components to meet customer needs
Local	Product platform components and technical expertise	Loss of customer focus shifts to product integration centers

	PROCESSES	
	Individual	**Organizational**
All Locations	Product designers and assemblers	Assessment and deployment of "bundles" of capabilities
	Global team issues: electronic and cultural	Centralization, but shift in systems to support flexible allocations
		Human capabilities are reconstrued as platforms and modular
		Information technology as main organizational link
		Global team issues: electronic and cultural

emphasis was relocated to the regional product integration centers potentially far away from the national customers, which was the strength of the other two stages.

THE NECESSITY OF INCREMENTALISM IN THE COMPETENCE CENTER APPROACH

The AT&T example also provides an example of a company who has linked a resource-based strategy with global expansion. It is important to note that the competence center approach was not undertaken as an independent strategic activity simply for its own merits. Rather, it was prompted by the strategic necessity to provide local content and technology transfer to each national customer. The first remote international product development lab was established due to requests/demands by the customer in order to win the contract. The company could justify the expense of the lab by the new revenue. Revenues increased as the products contained in the first contract grew to a family of related products to serve the national market, further justifying the remote lab decision. Since the Stage One model worked so well for the first international customer, it was continued with the second and third international customers, moving the company to a Stage Two model.

The decision to shift to Stage Two was not explicit, it was the natural result of a customer-driven approach to product development. This distinction is important because issues of organizational capability and competence were not recognized by the organization and thus, unconsidered and lost (Winterscheid, 1994). Capability and competence were technology and product driven, a position taken by many other competitors in the European telecommunications industry, such as Alcatel and Siemens. The battle for distinctive competence between these competitors was fought only on the technology and product battlefields.

Because AT&T Network Systems was in the small, scrappy, upstart position in Europe, two discoveries occurred. AT&T realized that they had to compete differently than in the States. This awareness led to an early examination, or fresh look, at product development systems and processes. Secondly, because AT&T was not a European national champion, their financial resources were not underwritten by a target market's government, and their resources were spread throughout the world. AT&T had less financial slack than some of their European competitors which surfaced the inefficiencies of the Stage Two structure earlier. It was simply not cost effective to continue a global strategy with a Stage Two product development structure. This realization only came after late product introductions, mismatches between product features and markets, and most importantly, the awareness of product platform possibilities made possible by a multi-nation, multi-customer approach. The combination of the fresh look and minimal financial slack enabled AT&T to recognize the potential advantages of the competence center approach.

FROM NATIONAL TO GLOBAL PRODUCT DEVELOPMENT COMPETENCE: DISCOVERIES FROM THE FIELD

AT&T Network Systems experience in Europe suggests a number of empirically-based insights concerning the relationship between structure and managerial process as a source of distinctive competence in product development activities. Of course, these conclusions are firm specific. New research is required to identify whether this evolutionary model of global product development competence holds for other firms and industries. Regardless, firms which have an administrative heritage (Bartlett and Ghoshal, 1989) of historic market success are faced with the same challenges that AT&T has faced—how to evolve new organizational responses to changing market conditions without compromising the technological and market strengths which brought market leadership in the first place.

The experience of AT&T is an appropriate exemplar for these insights due to the:

- historic technical competence of AT&T driven in part by research at Bell Labs.
- American telephone industry legislation which not only deregulated phone service, but decoupled AT&T facilitating internationalization and heightened product development.

These two developments forced AT&T to reconsider technology-market linkages and become more customer responsive, and forced them to implement a series of structural changes and a focused internationalization strategy beginning in the early 1980's. The structural changes enabled the company to experiment with a variety of relationships between Bell Labs, product developers at the business units, and customers.

The following insights can be offered from this research.

1. Each evolutionary stage of movement from national to global product development competence, from Stage One: the single customer, to the multiple customer–multiple nation, to the competence center approach requires its own organization structure and coordinating capabilities. Each structural variation of the product development function assumes specific individual and organizational competencies and creates certain demands on the individual and the organization. This research has outlined the required relationships between the technology and customer functions at both the corporate and local levels.

In Stage One, the technology relationship is primarily top-down: product design expertise is tightly controlled at the corporate level with the local level providing customization details.

Stage Two arises from success in the international arena in which the primary product development challenge eventually becomes how to handle multiple customization details, and growing product families of related technologies. Multiple product development labs in multiple countries with little innovation in coordinative processes at the corporate level ultimately lead to poor performance; late product introductions and high engineering costs. Structural arrangements are the same as in Stage One, only there are more product development centers spread throughout the globe. Coordinating capabilities at the corporate level increase in complexity with the proliferation of multiple labs.

Stage Three, the competence center approach, offers a potential solution to the problems presented in Stage Two by looking inward to optimize internal efficiencies in product development structure. The structural challenge for the firm is to determine which competencies to build competence centers around, and where to locate these competencies. AT&T answered this problem by identifying leading regional products and pairing competence centers with the necessary technological expertise for those products. The required coordinating capabilities for this structure represented substantial innovations for AT&T at the corporate level in breaking apart existing country structure arrangements, refocussing human resources towards competence objectives, electronic virtual product development teams, and the planning and control mechanisms to support all of this.

2. Each evolution in organization structure, from the single customer, to the multiple customer-multiple nation, to the competence center approach was motivated by the need to strike a new balance between maintaining match and achieving efficiencies in leveraging technologies as widely as possible. The Stage One structure solves a relatively simple problem and offers an equally simple solution. A firm will change existing centrallized product development arrangements **only when** a market opportunity is better fulfilled by relocating product development activities to the local market. The motivation to restructure is driven by maintaining a better match between technological resources and customer need by locating close to the customer.

The Stage Two evolution is still motivated by maintaining the match between technology and customer. However, the potential to leverage technologies as widely as possible becomes more clear as redundancies are perceived across the product families that emerge from the separate product labs. When the balance tips towards the technology/customer match to the expense of efficiencies in product cost and customer deliveries, Stage Three evolves.

A competence center organization shifts the firm squarely towards the efficiency solution. The firm loses its primary focus on maintaining the technology/customer match and seeks, instead to leverage technologies as widely as possible through product platforms. However, as the firm gazes inward to reallocate resources and organizational processes to support a competence center approach, market attention is secondary. This is a serious shift, as market competence was the source of competitive advantage in Stages One and Two.

3. This paper has demonstrated that the movement between stages is constrained by delays in managerial recognition and delays in the process of building new coordinative capabilities in firm-wide systems. Building new coordinative capabilities in the firm that are necessary to sustain the evolution described in this paper require individual and organizational processes that:

- facilitate the flow and interpretation of information between individuals around the firm; and
- focus attention on customer, design and product goals, and monitor achievement towards these goals.

The above capabilities are dependent upon the structural arrangement of the firm (Chandler, 1962; Bartlett and Ghoshal, 1989; Kim and Mauborgne, 1991), and tend to develop in a path dependent manner. That is, the longer a particular structural arrangement is in place, the stronger a particular capability is aligned with an organizational location.

4. Finally, it is possible that the competence center approach can work now precisely because telecommunications technology has developed to the point where a large "inventory" of standardized components has been developed, and as a result, virtually all the variations in products needed for a particular national market can now be obtained by combining various components that now are frequently used in common across many national markets. Such a development would greatly mitigate the need for any strong technical capabilities in customizing products in each national market. In other words, technological evolution is bound to be a key determinant of what strategies and organizational structures are likely to work best at different points in time.

However, we argue that a company will not willingly embrace the competence center approach, even if technological evolution permits standardized components, without experiencing the dysfunction of more traditional organizational arrangements, as demonstrated by the AT&T example. The competence center approach requires a radical reconstruction of firm-wide functional, human and organizational capabilities as described in this paper. This reconstruction is expensive, and potentially disruptive to the execution of on-going business within the firm.

Finally, the competence center approach is not a greenfield option, either. The market entry strategy of Stage One must always come first—there is little motivation to move operations to a foreign market without the promise of revenue. Our point is that firms will **evolve** to a competence center approach, only after discovering that other, more preferable organizational arrangements (i.e. Stage Two) no longer work. This realization, coupled with product platforms and component modularity enable the technological coordination that allows organizational decentralization into competence centers.

REFERENCES

Aoki, M. "Rents and the Theory of the Firm". In Aoki, M. *et al.*, eds., *The Firm as a Nexus of Treaties*. London: Sage, 1990.

Allen, T. *Managing the Flow of Technology*. Cambridge, MA: MIT Press, 1977.

Bartlett, C. and Ghoshal, S. *Managing Across Borders: The Transnational Solution*. Boston: HBR Press, 1989.

Chandler, A. *Strategy and Structure: Chapters in the History of the American Enterprise*. Cambridge, MA: MIT Press, 1962.

Cooper, R. "The Dimensions of Industrial New Product Success and Failure". *Journal of Marketing*, Vol. 43, pp. 93–103, 1979.

Cooper, R. "A Process Model for Industrial New Product Development". *IEEE Transactions on Engineering Management*, Vol. 30, pp. 2–11, 1983.

Dougherty, D. "A Practice-Centered Model of Organizational Renewal through Product Innovation". *Strategic Management Journal*, Vol. 13, pp. 77–92, 1992.

Glaser, B. and Strauss, A. *The Discovery of Grounded Theory*. Chicago: Aldine Press, 1967.

Hamel, G. and Heene, A., eds., *Competence-Based Competition*. New York: Wiley, 1994.

Hofstede, G. *Culture's Consequences: International Differences in Work-Related Values*. Beverly Hills, CA: Sage, 1991.

Kim, W. and Mauborgne, R. A. "Implementing Global Strategies: The Role of Procedural Justice". *Strategic Management Journal*, Vol. 12, pp. 125–143, 1991.

Sanchez, R. *Strategic Flexibility, Real Options, and Product-based Strategy*. Doctoral dissertation, Cambridge, MA: Massachusetts Institute of Technology, 1991.

Winterscheid, B. C. "Building Strategy from Within: The Insiders' View of Core Competence". In Hamel, G. and Heene, A., eds., *Competence-Based Competition*. New York: Wiley, 1994.

Zirger, B. and Maidique, M. "A Model of New Product Development: An Empirical Test". *Management Science*, Vol. 36, pp. 867–883, 1990.

13

"QUICK-CONNECT" TECHNOLOGIES FOR PRODUCT CREATION: IMPLICATIONS FOR COMPETENCE-BASED COMPETITION

Ron Sanchez

INTRODUCTION

The resource-based view of the firm has emphasized the importance of a firm's stock of strategically useful and difficult-to-imitate resources and capabilities in achieving competitive advantage (Wernerfelt 1984; Dierickx and Cool 1989; Barney 1991; Grant 1991; Amit and Schoemaker 1993; Peteraf 1993). The theory of competence-based competition adds to the resource-base view by emphasizing the importance of a firm's relative effectiveness in *coordinating* resources in determining a firm's ability to achieve competitive advantage with a given endowment of resources (Sanchez, Heene, and Thomas 1996, in this volume). In addition, the competence perspective explicitly recognizes that many useful, difficult-to-imitate resources lie outside the firm but may be accessible by a firm under certain conditions. This chapter investigates the ways in which recently developed *coordination technologies* enable new modes of coordinating both firm-specific and firm-addressable resources in creating, producing, distributing, and marketing products. Building new competences based on the new coordination technologies enables new kinds of product strategies, makes possible new forms of organizations for creating new products, and results in transformed competitive environments.

This chapter first discusses *systemic interdependencies* among competences in product creation, product strategies, organization designs for carrying out product strategies, and the competitive environments of product markets. Two recent changes in coordination technologies make possible new kinds of product creation competences and, as a result, are inducing rapid changes in product strategies, the organization of processes for creating new products, and competitive environments in product markets. A number of new interrelated *computer technologies* have created unprecedented means for firms to *quick-connect* in an electronically mediated product creation environment. Major developments in computer-assisted design and development (CADD), computer-integrated manufacturing (CIM), and electronic data integration (EDI) are assessed for their contribution to creating quick-connectivity among firms. The emerging *design technology* of modular product design also enhances quick-connectivity among firms by creating modular product architectures that allow concurrent, autonomous development of components for new products.

The combined use of CADD/CIM/EDI systems and modular product design by a product developing firm can *embed coordination* of the various component development and other activities required to fully develop a new product, eliminating the need for much, if not all, overt managerial coordination of development activities. Embedding coordination through effective use of the new quick-connect technologies makes possible new *modular forms of organization* for linking firm-specific and firm-addressable resources in product creation processes. Several examples suggest how some firms are using the quick-connect technologies of CADD/ CIM/EDI and modular product design to achieve embedded coordination and evolve new product creation environments.

The implications of the new quick-connect technologies for competence-based competition are substantial in markets where product development is—or has the potential to be—a driver of competition. *Building competence* in using the quick-connect technologies to coordinate a network of firm-addressable development resources can greatly increase the ability of a firm to *leverage its competences* more effectively and broadly. Achieving this new potential for leveraging competences, however, requires *managerial recognition* of a *new strategic logic* for competing through new product strategies and new approaches to organizing product development. Emerging possibilities for reconceptualizing product creation processes include using new quick-connect technologies to establish a kind of *electronic kanban system* in which changing customer preferences are monitored at point-of-purchase to create a real-time demand pull that drives product design and development processes.

SYSTEMIC INTERDEPENDENCIES OF TECHNOLOGIES, COMPETENCES, PRODUCT STRATEGIES, ORGANIZATION DESIGNS, AND COMPETITIVE ENVIRONMENTS

A basic premise of the competence-based perspective on competition (Sanchez, Heene, and Thomas 1996) is that competence arises from an ability of a firm to sustain "the *coordinated deployment* of assets and capabilities" [emphasis added]. In essence, the competence which a firm can derive from its own endowment of assets and capabilities and from the firm-addressable resources of other organizations will depend fundamentally on the firm's ability to coordinate those assets and capabilities in creating, producing, and marketing products.

The resources a firm can use and its coordination capabilities in using those resources determine the product strategies which a firm can effectively pursue. To coordinate resources effectively in carrying out a product strategy, a firm must adopt an organization design suited to the processes required to realize its intended strategy. It may be most effective for a firm to adopt a divisional structure based on products, for example, if its product strategy is based on achieving superior product performance in "global" products, or a regional division structure if its strategy is to tailor products to specific preferences or requirements of regional markets (see, for example, Winterscheid and McNabb 1996, in this volume). Firms' individual choices of organization forms and associated product strategies collectively determine the nature of the competitive environment in a product market. Competitive conditions in product markets, in turn, determine what kinds of new technologies may be most strategically useful and what kinds of competences may be especially important for a firm to have now and in the future.

These relationships suggest that technologies, competences, product strategies, organization designs, and competitive environments are interdependent and form a positive feedback system like that shown in Fig. 13.1. In a positive feedback system, a change in one element of the system tends to induce a like change (*i.e.,* "in the same direction") in one or more other system elements, which induces further change in other system elements, and so on, in a spiral of increasing change affecting all system elements. In this case, changes in technologies—which may be developed by firms in a given product market or which may originate in another product market—may lead to changes in available technological resources or in the technological means to coordinate resources that in turn make possible new product strategies. The desire of a firm's managers to carry out a newly feasible product strategy may encourage them to adopt or innovate a new organization design. If one or more firms manage to carry out a new product strategy more effectively through a new organization design, the superior competence of those firms may lead to significant changes in competitive conditions in that product market. New competitive conditions brought about by firms with new competences based on new technologies may stimulate other firms to acquire or develop new technological capabilities, to imagine new product strategies, to explore new organizational forms for building new technology-based competences, and so on, in spiraling cycles of change.

Discussions of technological change commonly recognize two forms of

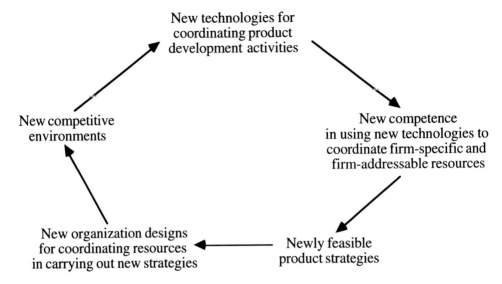

Fig. 13.1. Systemic interdependencies of technologies, competences, strategies, organization designs, and competitive environments.

technological change (which are often closely interrelated): changes in *product technology* that make possible new kinds of products (*i.e.*, products with new functionalities), and changes in *process technology* that make possible new ways of making products. Recent changes in information technology, for example, have led to new kinds of products like laptop computers and to new kinds of production processes like flexible manufacturing systems. New information technology, however, is also making possible significant changes in the ways firms *coordinate* product development, production, distribution, and marketing activities. The sweeping nature of these changes suggest the need to recognize a third form of technological change—change in *coordinating technology*—that may have an even more profound impact on firm competences, product strategies, organization designs, and competitive environments than more commonly recognized changes in product or process technologies.

The following sections discuss ongoing changes in two coordinating technologies that are precipitating fundamental changes in the competences firms must have in order to compete effectively in a growing number of product markets. Rapid development of these technologies is enabling some firms to achieve unprecedented *quick-connectivity* with other firms, defined as follows:

Quick-connectivity:
The use of *standardized interfaces* between interrelated processes to quickly establish communication and achieve coordination among organizations carrying out those processes.

Computer systems that provide standardized interfaces between processes for designing, manufacturing, distributing, and marketing products have enabled some firms to establish quick-connect *electronic interfaces* with networks of other firms. Building new competences based on using these computer-based quick-connect technologies is enabling some firms to leverage their own technological, marketing, and other capabilities more broadly by coordinating effectively with more diverse, often global networks of firm-addressable resources, creating and offering more new products to more markets than ever before.

In addition, a growing number of firms appear to be adopting a modular product design methodology in which standardizing interfaces between components creates *modular product architectures* that serve as *information structures* for coordinating component development and production activities. Modular product architectures based on fully specified and standardized component interfaces enable component developers to work independently and concurrently in developing components for a new product, leading to greatly increased speed of product development.

Firms that have developed new competences in creating products by making effective use of these new computer-based and design-based *quick-connect technologies* are able to pursue new kinds of product strategies and adopt newly flexible "modular" forms of organization that are transforming the nature of product competition. In building these new competences, these firms are redefining the competences required to remain competitive in a growing number of product markets (Sanchez 1995).

COMPUTER-BASED QUICK-CONNECT TECHNOLOGIES

Computer-based technologies in support of product design, development, manufacturing, distribution, and marketing have been evolving rapidly in the last three decades. The ability of computer systems to increase the speed of information processing within organizations has been recognized for some time. This section discusses other impacts of these new computer technologies that make possible new kinds of interorganizational competences in product creation and marketing that are transforming the nature of product-based competition in many product markets.

Computer-Assisted Design and Development (CADD)

Since the introduction of basic computer-assisted drafting (CAD) systems in the 1970s, computer systems for designing and developing products have progressed with surprising alacrity through five generations of design capabilities. These generations and their increasing product design capabilities are:

- Generation 1: Two-dimensional electronic drafting capabilities (line drawings)

- Generation 2: Three-dimensional "wire figures" defining edges of objects, with ability to capture the spatial configuration of only simple geometric shapes
- Generation 3: Three-dimensional surfaces are defined, but with limited ability to assure continuity of all the defined surfaces in a solid shape
- Generation 4: True three-dimensional solids in which both precise definition and continuity of all surfaces is assured. An extensive menu of flat and curved surface-generating algorithms assures designers the ability to create and analyze surfaces of virtually any complexity. Common engineering analyses of parts and product designs can be performed, allowing designers to refine design concepts and evaluate alternative designs "in real time"
- Generation 5: Protocols for managing distributed design and manufacturing processes are introduced. Designs created on computer systems generate "3-D files" that can be used to perform various simulations and to drive automated manufacturing and assembly processes.

Use of fourth and fifth generation computer–assisted design and development (CADD) software programs is growing rapidly in a number of industries in the United States, Europe, and Japan (Åstebro, 1992a, b). The ability of these systems to perform complex design modeling and engineering analyses has also been increasing rapidly. As a result, current CADD systems offer radical reductions in the costs and time required to design new products (Cardaci 1992). Total development time can often be reduced by half or more by using CADD (Parker 1993), and in some product development projects, the reductions in costs to create a new design may exceed two orders of magnitude (1/100th or less) relative to design and engineering by humans in a paper documentation environment (Hughes 1992).

Of even greater importance to competence-based competition, however, is the way fifth generation CADD systems can be used to define *standardized communication interfaces and procedural protocols* that enable a product-developing firm to *connect with and coordinate* other firms having similar CADD systems in an electronically mediated product development network (Malone, Yates and Benjamin 1987). Shared CADD systems provide protocols for defining the task to be performed by each participant, monitoring each participant's progress in meeting project milestones, assuring the compatibility of the designs of components and parts developed by each participant with those of other participants, and creating archives that document participants' technical analyses and design decisions.

The standardized communication interfaces and procedural protocols of a shared CADD system provide a means to link and coordinate firms with various capabilities in industrial design, component development, manufacturing, and other capabilities in creating new products, as suggested in Fig. 13.2. Especially when used with modular product design (discussed below), CADD's standardized communication interfaces and procedural protocols enable diverse and geographically dispersed firms to be linked in a quickly assembled "resource chain" (Sanchez 1995) that can carry out a multitude of interrelated development tasks concurrently and autonomously. Using the quick-connect electronic interfaces of a shared CADD system may largely relieve the firm coordinating a product creation project from direct involvement in the development processes carried out by each participating firm, allowing each participating firm to be regarded as a "black box" within a resource chain assembled from a network of firm-addressable product development resources.

The rapid growth of fifth-generation CADD systems with quick-connect capabilities has been accompanied by the development of a number of related computer technologies for accelerating and improving product development (Ulrich 1990), including technologies for simulation, virtual reality, rapid prototyping, virtual assembly, and rapid tooling.

Simulation

Product designs created on CADD systems can be used as the basis for a variety of engineering analyses and computer simulations that investigate the technical suitability of designs for parts, components, or products for their intended use (Whitney 1988; Port 1989; Skerrett 1992; Winter 1994). Using CADD-generated 3D files, the manufacturability of parts and

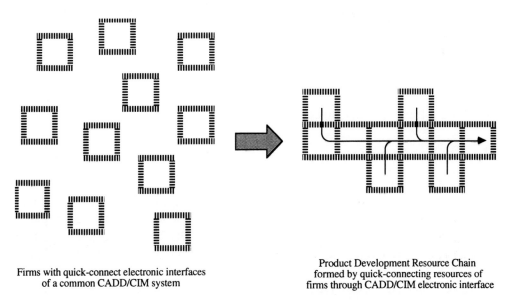

Firms with quick-connect electronic interfaces
of a common CADD/CIM system

Product Development Resource Chain
formed by quick-connecting resources of
firms through CADD/CIM electronic interface

Fig. 13.2. Formation of product development resource chains from quick-connect electronic interfaces of shared CADD/CIM systems.

components can be simulated (Yeich 1992). Designs of production systems can also be dynamically simulated to evaluate flows of parts and work-in-process before deciding on the final configuration of production equipment (Hill 1994; Schulz 1994; Swain 1993). Black and Decker Co., for example, simulates the performance capabilities of production systems under a range of future scenarios before deciding on the configuration of equipment for a new plant (Cosco 1994). The increasing sophistication of software for simulating products and production systems is suggesting new possibilities for evaluating potential applications of new product and process technologies *electronically* before committing to production of physical products or systems. Researchers at Xerox, for example, are developing ways to simulate impacts of a new technology on various processes and users "...in a way which evokes its power and possibility. Put another way, we are trying to prototype a use before we prototype a system" (Thackara 1994). The capability to simulate uses and assess the performance of potential new products, production systems, and technologies enables a firm to make better choices and to achieve quicker, more predictable adoption.

Virtual Reality

Many CADD systems provide photo-realistic images of proposed new product designs, complete with a choice of lighting effects and backgrounds (Dutton 1993). Recently developed virtual reality devices for visually representing new product designs permit designers to see and interact with a new product design which exists only as a CADD 3-D file, allowing designers to check and improve the ergonomic and esthetic aspects of a new product design (Sheridan and Zeltzer 1993). In many cases, these virtual reality devices can greatly reduce or eliminate the need for physical tests or physical mock-ups of a product design. Some firms now use virtual reality devices to gather detailed reactions to proposed new product designs from suppliers and targeted customers (Bylinsky 1991; *Economist* 1993; *IEEE Spectrum* 1993; Sawyer 1994a) in an increasingly interactive process for improving new product designs.

Rapid Prototyping

New technologies have also been developed for rapid prototyping of new parts, components, and even entire products. Many kinds of parts in a new product design can be now be fabricated in a few minutes by rapid prototyping machines controlled directly by the CADD design file for that part (Ashley 1991; Schrage 1993; Stevens 1993; Wall, Ulrich, and Flowers 1992). In a few hours or less, advanced rapid prototyping systems may even produce working prototypes of mechanical assemblies in which "gears engage, shafts turn, ball and socket joints swivel, even bearing and race assemblies spin freely" (Kobe 1992: 55). In addition to improving design processes and reducing the time required to engineer assembled products (Cook 1991; Winfield 1991), prototyped parts, components, and products are becoming widely used to elicit suggestions from customers and suppliers about proposed new product designs (Comerford 1993; Sawyer 1994b). The rapidly developing ability to quickly produce physical prototypes from CADD 3-D files is encouraging a growing "culture of prototyping" (Schrage 1993) that enables expanded involvement of suppliers and users in creating new products.

Virtual Assembly

A recent extension of CADD is the ability to simulate the part-by-part assembly of a new product. In developing its 777 aircraft, for example, Boeing developed a CADD-based virtual assembly system that allowed it to "assemble" electronically the 3 million individual parts of the 777 aircraft before actually producing any physical parts (Woolsey 1994). Electronic assembly enabled Boeing to check for the proper fit of all the parts designed by its global network of component suppliers before asking its suppliers to commit to the substantial costs of tooling for producing physical parts.

Rapid Tooling

CADD design files can be used to control a growing number of flexible manufacturing systems (FMS) for machining individual metal parts or for making molds for injected plastic or cast metal parts. The rapid tooling capability of linked CADD and flexible manufacturing systems allows production of many kinds of products to begin within a few days—or in some cases, within a few *moments*—after completing product design, simulation, and virtual assembly.

Computer-Integrated Manufacturing (CIM)

Increasingly, 3-D files created by CADD systems can link to and drive computer–integrated manufacturing (CIM) systems. The creation of integrated CADD/CIM systems is extending the reach of computer-based quick-connect technology in coordinating widely dispersed component manufacturing and assembly processes (Sawyer 1994b; Schulz 1994; Sykes 1994). The quick-connectivity of integrated CADD/CIM systems is allowing some firms to form and coordinate global networks of development and production resources. By quick-connecting with the most appropriate suppliers of components and services, some firms are quickly establishing and coordinating a large number of resource chains for creating and producing products. IKEA, for example, uses its computer system to effectively coordinate a global network of 1800 suppliers of modular furniture components in 50 countries (Normann and Ramirez 1993) to provide a broad and changing array of furniture products to its growing international chain of stores.

Electronic Data Integration (EDI)

Electronic data integration (EDI) creates standardized formats for electronically gathering, transmitting, and processing many kinds of data related to products. By adopting universal product codes (UPC) and using EDI to quick-connect with retailers, for example, a firm can gather "real time" sales data about its products through retailers' bar-code scanners or other point-of-purchase (POP) devices. Data about current sales of product models can be transmitted "upstream" in standardized form to computer-based inventory and ordering systems and to suppliers' production systems to assure the most advantageous scheduling of deliveries of parts, components, and assembled products throughout a supply chain (Davis 1994, 1995; Parker 1994; *Manufacturing Systems* 1994). The standardization of exchanges of data typified by EDI is essential to the eventual linking of CADD, CIM, inventory, and POP systems into integrated product development, production, distribution, and marketing systems (T. Schulz 1992; K. Schulz 1994).

The product creation and delivery environment made possible by EDI creates, in effect, the possibility for a new *electronic kanban system* in which real-time sales data gathered through POP devices create a "demand pull" that drives upstream distribution, production, and even product development activities. This newly feasible approach to coordinating product creation and delivery processes radically transforms the potential ability of a firm to use computer-based quick-connect technologies to discover and respond quickly to current and new product opportunities.

DESIGN-BASED QUICK-CONNECT TECHNOLOGIES

Product design is the process in which the overall functionality desired in a product is decomposed into functions that will be performed by individual components, which are in turn decomposed into individual functional parts. Interactions between components occur through the *interfaces* between components, such as the interfaces for attaching components to each other, for transferring power between components, for sending and receiving control signals, etc. (Sanchez 1994). A complete set of component interface specifications that fully specifies the functional input and output relationships between all components in a product design defines a *product architecture* (Abernathy and Clark 1985; Clark 1985; Henderson and Clark 1990; Morris and Ferguson 1993).

Traditional engineering design consists of a methodology for obtaining the highest feasible level of product performance subject to some cost constraint, or the lowest possible cost for a product subject to some minimum performance constraint (Marples 1961; Alexander 1964; Clark 1985). This design methodology results in product architectures that are typically composed of highly integrated component designs (Ulrich and Seering 1990). In product architectures based on integrated components, interfaces between components reflect the individual characteristics of each component and thus tend to be both complex and idiosyncratic for each new product.

Recently, *modular product design* has emerged as an alternative design methodology. Rather than seeking a design optimized to some cost or performance constraint, the objective of modular product design is creation of a modular product architecture that can serve as the basis for a number of product variations with different performance and cost characteristics. This key flexibility of a modular product architecture is derived from component interfaces that *are not allowed to change* during a product development project (*i.e.,* they are *standardized*) and that are specified to permit a range of variations in any given component (Stevens, Myers, and Constantine 1974; Parnas, Clements, and Weiss 1987; Sanchez 1991, 1994; Ghazanfar, McGee, and Thomas 1992; Sanchez and Mahoney 1994).

The variations in components that can be accommodated by a modular product architecture allow a potentially large number of product model variations to be leveraged relatively quickly and inexpensively from a modular product design by "mixing and matching" different combinations of modular components to create different product variations (Sanderson and Uzumeri 1990; Sanchez 1994; Baldwin and Clark 1994), as suggested in Fig. 13.3. The ability of modular design to generate many product variations has led to its growing use in industries as diverse as automobiles, computer hardware, software, photocopiers, consumer electronics, household appliances, test instruments, and power tools (Sanderson and Uzumeri 1990; Sanchez 1991; Ghazanfar, McGee, and Thomas 1992; Sanchez and Mahoney 1994). The growing use of modular product design has been accompanied by the rise of new product strategies based on offering a large number of product variations to targeted markets. Some firms that have learned to use modular design to quickly create low-cost product variations are creating "learning models" to investigate customer preferences in "real time" (Sanchez and Sudharshan 1992). Thus, modular product design can make possible an important new form of *strategic flexibility* (Sanchez 1993, 1995) to discover and respond to changing market preferences by rapidly and inexpensively leveraging product variations derived from different combinations of modular components.

Modular product design has had an even more profound impact, however, on the organization of product development processes. The standardized component interfaces in modular product designs create a complete *information structure* (Sanchez and Mahoney 1994) that defines the *output* desired from each component development effort. By clearly

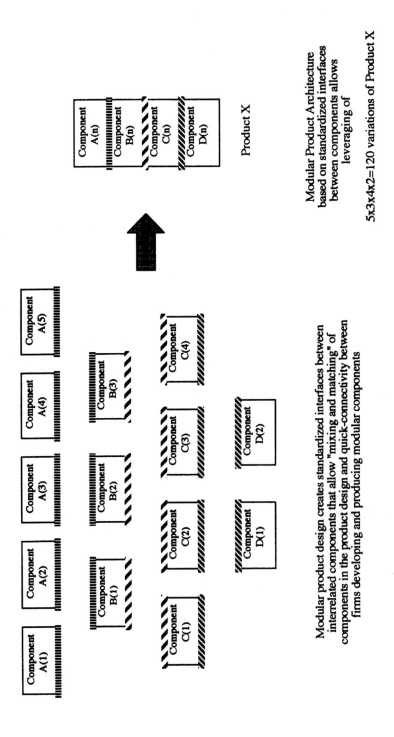

Fig. 13.3. Modular product design allows leveraging of product variations and quick-connectivity among firms providing components.

defining the desired outputs of component development efforts, a modular product architecture enables a product developing firm to quick-connect with any number of component developers that are capable of understanding and meeting the specifications for component interfaces in a given modular component. Thus, the standardized component interfaces of a modular product design constitute a design technology[1] that can enable a firm to quick-connect with and coordinate the activities of a network of component developers and suppliers (Kogut and Kulatilaka 1994; Normann and Ramirez 1993). Boeing's ability to coordinate a global network of component suppliers in developing the 777 was derived jointly from the modular product architecture of the 777 and from Boeing's global CADD system linking Boeing designers and suppliers (O'Lone 1992; Woolsey 1994).

NEW COMPETENCES BASED ON QUICK-CONNECT TECHNOLOGIES

When integrated CADD/CIM/EDI systems and modular product architectures begin to appear in an industry, a new *product creation environment* becomes possible in which firms that can build competences based on effective use of modular product architectures and CADD/CIM/EDI systems may gain substantial competitive benefits. In particular, firms that develop superior capabilities in using these new quick-connect technologies to *embed coordination* of a network of firm-addressable resources may be able to initiate significant changes in their product strategies, organization designs, and competitive environments.

Effective joint use of modular product architectures and the standardized protocols of CADD systems allows the processes for developing a new product to be partitioned into tasks (von Hippel 1990) that can be performed *autonomously and concurrently* by a dispersed network of product designers and component developers. Thus, a product developing firm that is skillful in using modular design and CADD systems to partition and define component development tasks may not need to directly manage component developers' processes in order to assure the result of various development processes will be a product that works as planned. In essence, the means to achieve effective coordination of the overall product development process is "embedded" in the standardized interfaces of the modular product architecture and CADD system (Sanchez 1995). When a firm can embed coordination of development processes through skillful use of the quick-connect technologies, it may achieve effective coordination without the need for continuous exercise of managerial authority (Sanchez and Mahoney 1994). Thus, embedding coordination through the quick-connect technologies may reduce the cost and difficulty of coordinating development resources and thereby increase the scope and geographic extent of the firm-addressable resources a firm can access.

Indeed, in a growing number of dynamic product markets, the ability to use modular product architectures and CADD systems to quick-connect with and embed coordination of specialist component development firms anywhere in the world is rapidly becoming a *necessary* competence. In the early 1990s, for example, Ford designed its Mondeo world car on a global CADD system linking Ford designers in the USA and Europe, Mazda designers in Japan, and key modular component developers in many locations around the world (Lowell 1993). BMW and other car makers are creating comparable global CADD systems (Brooke 1994). Similarly, major U.S. software development firms now routinely develop new applications programs through networks that link the system design work of systems analysts in the USA with programmers in India who write the detailed code for program modules (Gargan 1993). The diffusion of modular design and CADD-based product creation environments that can quick-connect firms anywhere in the world is greatly diminishing the need for, and relative benefits to be derived from, physical co-location of participants in a product development process.

Daft and Lewin (1993) have suggested the evolution of a new form of "modular organization" that uses "interconnected coordinated self-organizing processes" to support continuous learning and flexible responses to a changing environment. The ability to embed coordination of concurrent, autonomous product creation processes through modular product design and CADD/CIM systems may make possible the modular form of organization Daft and Lewin describe (Sanchez and Mahoney 1994). Product development firms in a network coordinated by a modular product architecture and a shared CAD/CIM system are interconnected, co-ordinated, and (largely) self-organizing. Learning in developing and producing individual modular components can take place independently of other component development processes. And quick-connect development networks can rapidly link together the resources and capabilities of its organizations to form product development "resource chains" to respond flexibly to new market and technology opportunities (Sanchez 1994, 1995).

Building competence based on use of quick-connect technologies to connect with and coordinate an expanded set of firm-addressable resources may increase the ability of a firm to *leverage* its other competences more broadly. By quick-connecting its competences with the resources of other firms serving product markets the firm does not currently serve, the firm may be able to leverage its competences by indirectly "diversifying" its competences into new product markets. Alternatively, when a firm can quick-connect with firms that have technologies or product development and manufacturing resources the firm can use in its current product markets, it may be able to "intensify" the use of its own competences in its existing markets by combining with other firms' competences to offer an expanded range of products.

EXAMPLES OF QUICK-CONNECT TECHNOLOGIES IN COMPETENCE-BASED COMPETITION

There is evidence that strategic managers in a growing number of firms are beginning to develop competences in using modular product design and CADD/CIM/EDI systems to coordinate networks of firm-addressable resources and thereby to increase the ability of a firm to leverage its own competences more effectively and broadly. This section briefly describes how some firms are using quick-connect technologies in this manner in competence-based competition.

RubberMaid Corporation

RubberMaid Corporation is the leading producer of injection-molded plastic products for home, office, and industry in the USA. RubberMaid has adopted an aggressive product strategy based on sustaining a high rate of new product introductions in its various product markets. The foundation of this strategy is RubberMaid's intensive use of an integrated CADD/CIM system that quick-connects RubberMaid's own product designers with a network of industrial design firms, rapid prototyping services, and contract mold makers. Use of a common CADD/CIM system at RubberMaid has created a "seamless" product creation environment among participating firms that has radically reduced the time required for creating new products. The firm's goal for 1994 was to reduce to six weeks the time to fully develop a new product concept into a product ready for production and distribution. When RubberMaid achieves a six-week development cycle time, the firm expects to be capable of introducing, on average, one new product *per day*— a level of intensity of new product creation unmatched in its industry. RubberMaid's competence in using its CADD system to quick-connect with and coordinate a network of product development resources gives the firm remarkable speed and flexibility in leveraging its own and others' competences into a greatly expanded set of new product opportunities.

Sony

New product concepts innovated by Sony are developed as modular product architectures that allow a number of variations in modular components (*e.g.,* casings, batteries, electronic components, headphones) to be mixed and matched to produce large numbers of product variations. The standardized interfaces between modular components, used in conjunction with a CADD system that links Sony's product development staff with Sony's network of component suppliers, allows Sony's network of product development organizations to work concurrently and largely autonomously in develop-ing new component and product variations (Sanderson 1992). Sony uses its ability to develop large numbers of product variations to engage in "real-time market research" (Sanchez and Sudharshan 1992) to discover the preferences of different market segments for functionalities, features, performance, and price levels in its new product innovations.

AT&T

To coordinate a global manufacturing and marketing network for its products, AT&T has developed a Global Information Systems Architecture (GISA) that defines standard data formats and transfer interfaces that are eventually to be used by AT&T operations worldwide. Standardizing the description and form of information generated by one AT&T operation facilitates ready access to and correct interpretation of that information by any other AT&T operation. An order received by an AT&T operation in Europe, for example, can be correctly understood and provided by an AT&T unit elsewhere in Europe, the USA, or the Pacific Rim. The GISA system, moreover, intends to provide an architecture for capturing and disseminating many forms of organizational learning. Improvements made in production processes at one AT&T plant, for example, can be defined, cataloged, and diffused in standard formats readily accessed and comprehended by other production units in AT&T, thereby providing a means to more effectively leverage local learning throughout the AT&T system worldwide (Sykes 1994).

Boeing/Sikorsky

Boeing, which pushed the envelope of CADD/CIM capabilities in the virtual assembly of the 777 aircraft, jointly developed the RAH-66 helicopter with Sikorsky Aircraft in the "paperless" product creation environment of a CADD/CIM system linking the two firms. The product architecture of the RAH-66 was defined to consist of a number of major component modules that could be developed concurrently by teams of engineers from Boeing, Sikorsky, and key component suppliers. Coordination among the design decisions made by various component development teams is accomplished through the protocols of the CADD/CIM system that control the designs of interrelated components to assure compatibility. Managers of the RAH-66 project maintain that the new helicopter is so complex that it could not have been developed without this critical coordination capability of the CADD/CIM system shared by Boeing and Sikorsky (Hughes 1992). Modular product architecture and a shared CADD/CIM system allow both Boeing and Sikorsky to leverage their own competences more effectively by quick-connecting to each other's specialized capabilities.

Sun Microsystems

To compete against makers of proprietary engineering workstations, Sun Microsystems uses an "open system" modular product architecture. Sun's product architectures are based on modular components (*e.g.,* hard disk drives, monitors, modems) that conform to industry standards for each component, allowing Sun's customers to "substitute" a wide variety of available components in any Sun workstation to configure a system that best suits each customer's needs (Garud and Kumaraswamy 1993). To assist its customers in selecting the most appropriate peripheral devices and software, Sun has established an electronic information network that allows its customers to quick-connect directly with its component suppliers to obtain the latest performance specifications and prices (*Information Week* 1993). By using modular product architecture and an electronic information network that enable customers to make their own selections of components for customized Sun workstations, Sun leverages its distinctive capabilities in designing high performance microprocessors and systems software into an industry-leading competence in providing "customer customized" engineering workstations.

CONCLUSIONS: IMPLICATIONS FOR COMPETENCE-BASED COMPETITION

Advances in the *coordination technologies* of modular product design and CADD/CIM systems are creating new possibilities for competence leveraging through new product strategies based on new approaches to organizing processes for creating new products. Building competence based on the use of quick-connect coordination technologies frees firms from having to rely primarily on firm-specific resources in creating new products. Firms may build new competences based on using quick-connect technologies to coordinate a network of firm-addressable development resources. When used most effectively, the new coordinating technologies may be the basis for a new product creation environment in which a "modular organization" of product development firms can work concurrently and autonomously. This new product creation environment is enabling some firms to access a greater diversity of resources and to deploy them more quickly. Thus, the quick-connect technologies make possible a new competence that is enabling some firms to sustain higher rates and expanded scope of new product creation.

   Research on product development has recently emphasized managerial and "team work" approaches to improving firm performance in product development (*e.g.,* Takeuchi and Nonaka 1986; Clark and Fujimoto 1991; Clark and Wheelwright 1993). This discussion, however, suggests that recent developments in modular product design and CADD/CIM systems enable a fundamental reconceptualization of how processes for creating new products might be organized and managed. The ability of modular product architectures and CADD/CIM systems to embed coordination of product development processes raises the possibility of a new *strategic logic* (Sanchez, Heene, and Thomas 1996, in this volume) for creating products.

This new strategic logic seeks to expand the number and scope of product creation processes a firm can initiate and coordinate, while at the same time greatly reducing the level of direct managerial involvement required to coordinate those processes. Thus, although much current research in product development suggests that intensive management is essential to good product development performance, when the potential of quick-connect technologies to embed coordination of networks of firm-addressable resources is fully understood, new concepts of coordination and organization structures that span the boundaries of many firms become possible.

Increasingly, product markets that reward variety and change in products are being served by firms capable of providing a growing level of variety and change in products, leading to emergence of an increasingly dynamic competitive environment. Such transformations of the competitive environment appear to be triggered by *managerial recognition* of the potential of modular product design and CADD/CIM/EDI to support new kinds of product development processes, organization structures, and product strategies. Managers in some firms are now seeking competitive advantage by using the new coordinating technologies to access and coordinate expanded sets of firm-addressable product development resources and by experimenting with new organizational forms that try to exploit those capabilities more effectively. The activities of these firms suggest that the ability to derive greatest competitive advantage from the new quick-connect technologies depends on the abilities of managers to imagine new ways of managing the *dynamic, systemic interdependencies* of technologies, strategies, and organizations. To succeed in using the new coordination technologies to create new competence-based competitive advantage, managers must be able to lead a firm to adopt systemic changes in product strategies and organizational structures (Moad 1994).

The emerging electronically mediated product creation environment is not yet "seamless." The quick-connectivity of current CADD/CIM/EDI systems across all product development processes is currently limited by incomplete standardization of interfaces between CADD and CIM systems in many industries (Murphy 1990; Strehlo 1994). Until developers of CADD/CIM systems can provide a seamless "off-the-shelf" product creation environment with fully standardized interfaces between CADD and CIM systems, the capability to create interfaces linking non-standardized computer systems may be an important means to achieve superior competence in product creation. As one manager commented on Raytheon's efforts to create interfaces among available but nonstandardized systems, "How are we different from another company in the same business? If we can perfect some of those interfaces better or faster or more efficiently, then I think we give our people a competitive advantage—and that's why we have our own [standardized interface] development projects" (Hughes 1992: 47).

As the interfaces between commercial CADD and CIM systems become more standardized, off-the-shelf CADD/CIM systems will offer the seamless product creation environments currently available only to the relatively few firms capable of creating their own system interfaces. Achieving superior competence in this new product creation environment will then require a superior ability of managers to solve the organizational challenges of redefining product strategies, work processes, and organization structures capable of realizing the strategic potential of seamlessly linked CADD/CIM systems (Adler 1989; *Automotive Industries* 1994; Bryant 1991; Liker and Fleischer 1989; Majchrzak and Salzman 1989). As off-the-shelf seamless CADD/CIM systems become available in more industries, managing processes for quick-connecting firm-specific resources to a global network of firm-addressable resources within a CADD/CIM-mediated product creation environment is increasingly becoming a coordinating capability essential to maintaining competence in the competitive environments of the near future (Bartmess and Cerny 1993; Haeckel and Nolan 1993; Malone and Rockart 1991).

Similarly, as modular product design principles become more widely understood, creating modular product architectures that offer both large numbers of product variations through the flexibility to "mix and match" modular components (Kotha 1995; Sanchez 1994, 1995) and high levels of perceived product integrity (Clark and Fujimoto 1990) will become a key engineering design competence. Developing this competence will require new capabilities in gathering and interpreting current market data which can be readily integrated into processes for defining and designing new products (Rasmus 1993). Achieving close integration of market information into modular design processes will require establishing quick-connect electronic linkages throughout a product creation chain, from real-time market information gathered through electronic point-of-purchase devices to design processes that respond quickly to changing market preferences by providing appropriate modular product variations. Achieving competitive advantage in dynamic product markets may therefore require establishing electronic data interchange (EDI) systems linked not just to distribution and production processes, but also to processes for defining and designing new products in CADD/CIM environments.

Recent years have witnessed widespread re-engineering of production processes around "demand pull" concepts, typically based on using physical kanban cards to drive production systems by signaling downstream demand for more parts (delivered just-in-time). In the near future, product creation processes may undergo an analogous, but more profound, transformation. An integrated CADD/CIM/EDI system may provide a form of *electronic kanban system* in which real-time market preferences for product variations will provide the "demand pull" that drives modular product creation processes seeking to create and deliver new product variations just-in-time to evolving consumer preferences. In the electronically mediated product creation environments of the near future, competence in creating new products may increasingly require competence in quick-connecting with *markets,* as well as with networks of development and production resources.

NOTE

1. CADD systems increasingly offer protocols that not only prevent or limit, but also *coordinate* changes in interfaces between components. To the extent that these interface protocols can mediate changes in component interfaces during development to assure that the ability to carry out autonomous, concurrent development processes for interrelated components is not disrupted, the need to standardize component interfaces during development to achieve coordination of concurrent development processes is reduced. In the limit, perfectly flexible design and manufacturing systems would allow unlimited variations in interfaces between components provided by concurrent, autonomous component development and production processes. Conversely, standardization of the interfaces that determine outputs of component development and production processes can achieve (otherwise unobtainable) *organizational flexibilities* that increase with decreases in the actual flexibilities of given component development and production processes.

REFERENCES

Abernathy, W. J. and Clark, K. B. "Innovation: Mapping the Winds of Creative Destruction". *Research Policy,* Vol. 14, pp. 3–22, 1985.

Adler, P. S. "CAD/CAM: Managerial Challenges and Research Issues". *IEEE Transactions on Engineering Management,* Vol. 36, pp. 202–215, 1989.

Alexander, C. *Notes on the Synthesis of Form.* Cambridge, MA: Harvard University Press, 1989.

Amit, R. and Schoemaker, P. "Strategic Assets and Organizational Rent". *Strategic Management Journal,* Vol. 14(1), pp. 33–46, 1993.

Ashley, S. "Rapid Prototyping Systems" (Special Report). *Mechanical Engineering,* pp. 34–43, April 1991.

Åstebro, T. "Computer Aided Design". In Ayres, R. U., Haywood, W., Merchant, M. E., Ranta, J. and Warnecke, H.-J., eds, *Computer Integrated Manufacturing, Volume II: Models, Case Studies, and Forecasts of Diffusion.* New York: Chapman and Hall, pp. 83–95, 1992a.

Åstebro, T. "The International Diffusion of Computer Aided Design". In Ayres, R. U., Haywood, W. and Tchijov, I., eds, *Computer Integrated Manufacturing, Volume III: The Past, the Present, and the Future.* New York: Chapman and Hall, pp. 171–196, 1992b.

"No DDL? No TQE". *Automotive Industries,* p. 15, February 1994.

Baldwin, C. Y. and Clark, K. B. "Modularity-in-Design: An analysis Based on the Theory of Real Options". Working Paper, Harvard Business School, 1994.

Barney, J. "Firm Resources and Sustained Competitive Advantage". *Journal of Management,* Vol. 17, pp. 99–120, 1991.

Bartmess, A. and Cerny, K. "Building Competitive Advantage Through a Global

Network of Capabilities". *California Management Review*, pp. 78–103, Winter 1993.

Brooke, L. "Carolina Motor Works". *Automotive Industries*, pp. 44–46, January 1994.

Bryant, A. "The Art of Car Styling Adapts to Computers". New York *Times*, p. C5, December 4 1991.

Bylinsky, G. "The Marvels of Virtual Reality". *Fortune*, pp. 138–142, June 3 1991.

Cardaci, K. "CAID: A Tool for the Flexible Organization". *Design Management Journal*, Vol. 3(2), pp. 72–75, 1992.

Clark, K. B. "The Interaction of Design Hierarchies and Market Concepts in Technological Evolution". *Research Policy*, Vol. 14, pp. 235–251, 1985.

Clark, K. B. and Fujimoto, T. "The Power of Product Integrity". *Harvard Business Review*, Vol. 68(6), pp. 107–118, November–December, 1990.

Clark, K. B. and Fujimoto, T. *Product Development Performance: Strategy, Organization, and Management in the World Auto Industry.* Boston: Harvard University Press, 1991.

Clark, K. B. and Wheelwright, S. C. *Managing New Product and Process Development.* New York: Free Press, 1993.

Comerford, R. "The Flexible Factory: Case Studies". *IEEE Spectrum*, pp. 28–42, September 1993.

Cook, B. "Rapid Prototyping: Designing a New Industrial Revolution". *Industry Week*, pp. 46-48, June 3 1991.

Cosco, J. "Black and Deckering Black and Decker". *Journal of Business Strategy*, Vol. 15, pp. 59–61, 1994.

Daft, R. L., and Lewin, A. Y. "Where are the Theories of the 'New' Organization Forms? An Editorial Essay". *Organization Science*, Vol. 4(4), pp. i–iv, 1993.

Davis, D. "PDM Caps the Enterprise Strategy". *Manufacturing Systems*, pp. 38–56, May 1994.

Davis, D. "Stock of Warehouse Systems on the Rise". *Manufacturing Systems*, pp. 28–34, May 1995.

Dierickx, I. and Cool, K. "Asset Stock Accumulation and Sustainability of Competitive Advantage". *Management Science*, Vol. 35, pp. 1504–1511, 1989.

Dutton, B. "Engineering the Aesthetic". *Manufacturing Systems*, pp. 20–22, March 1993.

"Virtual Reality gets Real". *Economist*, pp. 61–62, February 20 1993.

Gargan, E. A. "India Among the Leaders in Software for Computers". New York *Times*, pp. 1–A4, December 29 1993.

Garud, R. and Kumaraswamy, A. "Changing Competitive Dynamics in Network Industries: An Exploration of Sun Microsystems' Open Systems Strategy". *Strategic Management Journal*, Vol. 14, pp. 351–369, 1993.

Ghazanfar, A., McGee, J. and Thomas, H. "The Impact of Technological Change on Industry Structure and Corporate Strategy: The Case of the Reprographics Industry in the United Kingdom". In Pettigrew, A. M., ed., *The Management of Strategic Change*. London: Basil Blackwell, pp. 166–191, 1992.

Grant, R. M. "The Resource-Based Theory of Competitive Advantage: Implications for Strategy Formulation". *California Management Review*, pp. 114–135, Spring 1991.

Haeckel, S. H. and Nolan, R. L. "Managing by Wire". *Harvard Business Review*, pp. 122–132, September–October 1993.

Henderson, R. and Clark, K. B. "Architectural Innovation: The Reconfiguration of Existing Product Technologies and the Failure of Established Firms". *Administrative Science Quarterly*, Vol. 35, pp. 9–30, 1990.

Hill, S. "Simulation Software Builds Models to Solve Genuine Problems". *Manufacturing Systems*, pp. 59–61, September 1994.

Hughes, D. "Sikorsky Exploits Workstations in Rah-66 Cad/Cam Design Work". *Aviation Week and Space Technology*, pp. 52–54, June 22 1992.

"Virtual Reality is for Real". *IEEE Spectrum* (Special Report), pp. 22–39, October 1993.

"A New Way to Follow the Sun". *Information Week*, p. 58, June 14 1993.

Kobe, G. "Cubital's Unknown Soldier". *Automotive Industries*, pp. 54–55, August 1992.

Kogut, B. and Kulatilaka, N. "Operating Flexibility, Global Manufacturing, and the Option Value of a Multinational Network". *Management Science*, Vol. 40(1), pp. 123–139, 1994.

Kotha, S. "Mass Customization: Implementing the Emerging Paradigm for Competitive Advantage". *Strategic Management Journal*, Vol. 16, Summer Special Issue, 1995.

Liker, J. K. and Fleischer, M. "Implementing Computer-Aided Design: The Transition of Non-Users". *IEEE Transactions on Engineering Management*, Vol. 36(3), pp. 180–190, 1989.

Lowell, J. "Global Design". *Ward's Auto World*, pp. 41–44, November 1993.

Majchrzak, A. and Salzman, H. "Introduction to the Special Issue: Organizational Dimensions of Computer-Aided Design". *IEEE Transactions on Engineering Management*, Vol. 36(3), pp. 174–179, 1989.

Malone, T. W. and Rockart, J. F. "Computers, Networks, and the Corporation". *Scientific American*, Vol. 265, pp. 128–136, 1991.

Malone, T. W., Yates, J. and Benjamin, R. "Electronic Markets and Electronic Hierarchies". *Communications of the ACM*, Vol. 30, pp. 484–497, 1987.

"Special Supplement on Supply-Chain Strategies". *Manufacturing Systems*, November 1994.

Marples, D. L. "The Decisions of Engineering Design". *IEEE Transactions on Engineering Management*, Vol. 2, pp. 55–71, 1961.

Moad, J. "Welcome to the Virtual IS Organization". *Datamation*, pp. 32–35, February 1 1994.

Morris, C. R. and Ferguson, C. H. "How Architecture Wins Technology Wars". *Harvard Business Review*, pp. 86–96, March–April 1993.

Murphy, E. E. "Reconciling Conflicting Design-Automation Standards". *IEEE Spectrum*, p. 44, March 1990.

Normann, R. and Ramirez, R. "From Value Chain to Value Constellation: Designing Interactive Strategy". *Harvard Business Review*, pp. 65–77, July–August 1993.

O'Lone, R. G. "Final Assembly of 777 Nears". *Aviation Week and Space Technology*, pp. 48–50, October 12 1992.

Parker, K. "Solids-Based Design Cuts Development Time in Half". *Manufacturing Systems*, pp. 48–50, November 1993.

Parnas, D. L., Clements, P. C. and Weiss, D. M. "The Modular Structure of Complex

Systems". *IEEE Transactions on Software Engineering,* SE-11, pp. 259–266, 1985.

Peteraf, M. A. "The Cornerstones of Competitive Advantage: A Resource-Based View". *Strategic Management Journal,* Vol. 14, pp. 179–191, 1993.

Port, O. "The Best Engineered Part is no Part at all". *Business Week,* p. 150, May 8 1989.

Rasmus, D. "Learning the Waltz of Synthesis". *Manufacturing Systems,* pp. 17–29, June 1993.

Sanchez, R. "Strategic Flexibility, Real Options, and Product-Based Strategy". Ph.D. Dissertation, Massachusetts Institute of Technology, Cambridge, MA 02139, 1991.

Sanchez, R. "Strategic Flexibility, Firm Organization, and Managerial Work in Dynamic Markets: A Strategic Options Perspective". In Shrivastava, P., Huff, A. and Dutton, J., eds, *Advances in Strategic Management.* Greenwich, CT: JAI Press, Vol. 9, pp. 251–291, 1993.

Sanchez, R. "Towards a Science of Strategic Product Design: System Design, Component Modularity, and Product Leveraging Strategies". *Proceedings of the Second International Product Development Management Conference on New Approaches to Development and Engineering,* Gothenburg, Sweden, Brussels: EIASM, pp. 564–578, May 30–31 1994.

Sanchez, R. "Strategic Flexibility in Product Competition". *Strategic Management Journal,* Vol. 16, Summer Special Issue, pp. 135–159, 1995.

Sanchez, R., Heene, A. and Thomas, H. "Towards the Theory and Practice of Competence-Based Competition". In Sanchez, R. Heene, A. and Thomas, H., eds, *Dynamic of Competence-Based Competition: Theory and Practice in the New Strategic Management,* London: Elsevier, 1996.

Sanchez, R. and Mahoney, J. T. "The Modularity Principle in Product and Organization Design". Working Paper No. 94-0157, Department of Business Administration, University of Illinois, Champaign, IL 61820, 1994.

Sanchez, R. and Sudharshan, D. "Real-Time Market Research: Learning-By-Doing in the Development of New Products". In *Proceedings of the International Product Development Management Conference on New Approaches to Development and Engineering,* Brussels, Belgium, pp. 515–529, 1992. Reprinted in *Marketing Intelligence and Planning,* Vol. 11, pp. 29–38, August 1993.

Sanderson, S. W. "Design for Manufacturing in an Environment of Continuous Change". In Susman, G. I., ed., *Integrating Design and Manufacturing for Competitive Advantage.* New York: Oxford University Press, pp. 82–99, 1992.

Sanderson, S. W. and Uzumeri, V. "Strategies for New Product Development and Renewal: Design-Based Incrementalism". Working Paper, Center for Science and Technology Policy, Rensselaer Polytechnic Institute, Troy, New York 12180, 1990.

Sawyer, C. A. "CAD Zooks". *Automotive Industries,* pp. 34–38, January 1994a.

Sawyer, C. A. "Up and Running". *Automotive Industries,* pp. 34–38, 1994b.

Schrage, M. "The Culture(s) of Prototyping". *Design Management Journal,* Vol. 4, pp. 55–65, 1993.

Schulz, K. "The Evolving 'Information Hub' ". *Manufacturing Systems,* pp. 16–21, 1994.

Schulz, T. "Object-Oriented Methodology, Technology, and Data Base". *Data Base Management*, pp. 24–33, November 1992.

Sheridan, T. B. and Zeltzer, D. "Virtual Reality Check". *Technology Review*, pp. 20–28, October 1993.

Skerrett, P. J. "The Teraflops Race". *Popular Science*, pp. 50–90, March 1992.

Stevens, T. "Rapid Prototyping Moves to Desktop". *Industry Week*, pp.38–44, February 1 1993.

Stevens, W. P., Myers, G. J. and Constantine, L. L. "Structured Design". *IBM System*, Vol. 2, pp. 115–139, 1974.

Strehlo, K. "A Standard for Workflow". *Datamation*, p. 7, January 7 1994.

Swain, J. J. "Flexible Tools for Modeling". *OR/MS Today*, pp. 62–65, December 1993.

Sykes, C. "AT&T Adopts a Global Manufacturing Architecture". *Manufacturing Systems*, pp. 34–39, January 1994.

Takeuchi, H. and Nonaka, I. "The New New Product Development Game". *Harvard Business Review*, pp. 137–146, January–February 1986.

Thackara, J. "Leap to an Interactive Future". *Financial Times*, p. 9, June 13 1994.

Ulrich, Karl T. "Computer-Supported Product Design". *Design Management Journal*, Vol. 1, pp. 62-67, 1990.

Ulrich, K. T. and Seering, W. P. "Function Sharing in Mechanical Design". *Design Studies*, Vol. 11, pp. 223–234, 1990.

von Hippel, E. "Task Partitioning: An Innovation Process Variable". *Research Policy*, pp.407–418, 1990.

Wall, M. B., Ulrich, K. T. and Flowers, W. C. "Evaluating Prototyping Technologies for Product Design". *Research in Engineering Design*, Vol. 3, pp. 163–177, 1992.

Wernerfelt, B. "A Resource-Based View of the Firm". *Strategic Management Journal*, Vol. 5, pp. 171–180, 1984.

Whitney, D. E. "Manufacturing by Design". *Harvard Business Review*, pp. 83–91, 1988.

Winfield, B. "Stereolithography: Laser Sculpture Speeds Product Development and Shortens Lead Times". *Automobile*, pp. 45–49, August 1991.

Winter, D. "Special Effects". *Ward's Auto World*, pp. 31–35, November 1994.

Winterscheid, B. C. and McNabb, S. J. "From National to Global Product Development Competence in the Telecommunications Industry: The Role of Structure and Process in Leveraging Core Capabilities". In Sanchez, R. Heene, A. and Thomas, H., eds, *Dynamic of Competence-Based Competition: Theory and Practice in the New Strategic Management*, London: Elsevier, 1996.

Woolsey, J. P. "777". *Air Transport World*, pp. 22–31, 1994.

Yeich, C. R. "Manufacturing Simulation". *Automotive Industries*, p. 95, October 1992.

PART FIVE

COMPETENCE BUILDING AS THE DRIVER OF INDUSTRY DYNAMICS

Dynamic change in a competitive environment may result from both the competence building and competence leveraging activities of firms. The chapters in this section explore ways in which causal ambiguities and managerial cognitions impact the way firms try to build competence and thereby shape industry dynamics and evolution.

In Chapter 14, Wright investigates the impact of the imitability *vs* inimitability of competence on the evolution of the semiconductor industry through several generations of DRAM chips. Wright proposes that the degree of imitability of a new generation technological knowledge determines the specific trajectories of ensuing industry evolution. Wright suggests that identifying the tacit *vs* non-tacit and apprehensible *vs* not-apprehensible characteristics of knowledge provides a means of assessing the relative imitability of knowledge. A firm's ability to imitate new knowledge underlying an important new competence will be influential in determining whether that firm achieves intergenerational change or fails to advance in the industry.

In Chapter 15, Tallman and Atchison propose that industry evolution is shaped both by the uncertainty of managers about the imitability of some new knowledge and by their perceptions of the risks of deploying that new knowledge in a firm's current or potential product markets. The perceptions and attitudes of specific managers about technological uncertainty and business risk lead them to make investment decisions that result in firm-specific patterns of competence-building. An individual managers' perceptions and preferences, however, are likely to be shared to some extent by managers of other firms with similar backgrounds, leading to patterns of similar decision making about competence building by managers in an industry. Similar patterns of decision making over time lead to "strategic configurations" of firms with similar competences and competence-building trajectories.

In Chapter 16, Roehl investigates the path-dependency of managerial decisions about alternative approaches to competence building. Studying the approaches to internationalizing research and development activities of Japanese pharmaceutical firms, Roehl argues that pharmaceutical firms in Japan pursued one of five patterns of competence building and leveraging that appear to depend on the scope and depth of a firm's prior competences. Competence building and leveraging responses ranged from seeking international partners to more broadly leverage proven capabilities to repositioning within the Japanese market to focus a firm's competence leveraging on the Japanese market.

14

THE ROLE OF IMITABLE VS INIMITABLE COMPETENCES IN THE EVOLUTION OF THE SEMICONDUCTOR INDUSTRY

Russell W. Wright

INTRODUCTION

The fundamental theme pursued in this chapter is that the importance of firm resources over time is a function of the imitability of those resources. The imitability of resources in turn, is a function of two conceptually distinct attributes: tacitness and tangibility. For example, resources such as product design, product development, or manufacturing capability are tacit to the extent they have not been written down, codified or transferred into a machine. Resources such as brand image, technological skill, management skill, or corporate culture, are intangible resources to the extent that they are difficult to observe or apprehend. The exploitation of tangible resources in a firm often requires the use of intangible resources. Several firms may possess the tangible resources to develop a product and get it to market, but only one of these firms may possess the intangible resources to get to market fast and efficiently enough to make a profit. If these intangible resources are not subject to imitation, the firm may obtain a sustained competitive advantage from exploiting its physical technology more completely than other firms, though competing firms possess the same physical technology.

This paper can be read in two ways. It is, in the broadest sense, a contribution to understanding the role of resources in the process of technological innovation; more narrowly, it can also be read as an analysis of the evolution of one of the most important technologically innovative industries of our time. In this paper, I suggest a series of propositions regarding the role of resources in the process of innovation and I briefly describe the evolution of the U.S. semiconductor industry. Central to the framework is the idea that a firm is an integrated set of resources and that the task of top management is to invest in a portfolio of resources and related competences which yield high returns over a sustained period of time. The existing resource and competence configuration constrains the strategic direction of a firm. An innovation is the product of cumulative resources and the ability of the firm to carry out the innovation is constrained by the amount of relevant resources and competences it has developed and acquired. When a firm seeking innovation lacks the necessary resource configuration, the managers face a dilemma—where and how to get the necessary resources.

THE ROLE OF RESOURCES IN INNOVATION

From a resource-based view, a firm is an integrated set of resources (Penrose, 1959; Moss, 1981; Wernerfelt, 1984). In this perspective, the task of top management is to invest in a portfolio of resources which yields high returns sustained over a period of time. Top management's role is to seek out and invest in unique or difficult-to-copy resources (Rumelt, 1987). Hard-to-copy resources of the firm are potential sources of economic rent and the fundamental drivers of competitive advantage (Barney, 1986; Rumelt, 1984, 1987; Conner, 1991).

Resources can be described in terms of classes or categories. Penrose (1959) distinguishes between two classes of resources: physical and human. The physical resources of a firm are tangible assets such as plant and equipment, land and natural resources, raw materials, and semi-finished goods. The human resources of a firm are the managerial resources of the management team, skilled and unskilled labor including clerical, administrative, legal, and technical staff, etc.

Barney (1991) distinguishes among three classes of resources; physical capital resources, human capital resources, and organizational capital resources. Barney's physical capital and human capital resources are similar to Penrose's definition of resource types. Barney adds organizational capital resources which include the formal reporting structure, its formal and informal planning, controlling, and coordinating systems, as well as informal relations among groups within a firm and between a firm and those in its environment. Human capital and organizational capital resources tend to be knowledge-based. I will argue that it is these knowledge-based resources that are the primary productive resources of the firm. Indeed, knowledge-based resources are the primary enabling and constraining factors in the development of innovation and competitive advantage.

Schumpeter conceptualized the process of innovation as a new combination of resources and skills. Schumpeter described five different examples of innovation:

> (1) The introduction of a new good—that is, one with which consumers are not yet familiar—or of a new quality good. (2) The introduction of a new method of production that is, one not yet tested by experience in the branch of manufacture concerned, which need by no means be founded upon a discovery scientifically new, and can also exist in a new way of handling commodity commercially. (3) The opening of a new market, that is a market into which the particular branch of manufacture of the country in question has not previously entered, whether or not this market has existed before. (4) The conquest of a new source of supply of raw materials or half manufactured goods, again irrespective of whether this source already exists or whether it has first to be created. (5) The carrying out of new organization of any industry, like the creation of a monopoly position (for example through trustification) or the breaking up of a monopoly position (Schumpeter, 1934: 66).

Therefore, innovation can be conceptualized as a new combination or a recombination of conceptual and physical materials that were previously in existence (Barnett, 1953; Nelson and Winter, 1982).

Firms do not generate innovations in a haphazard or random fashion. The identification and assessment of potential research and development projects require an intimate knowledge about related technology. Such knowledge may be readily available if the knowledge and skills required for the project are "in the vicinity" of the firm's own skills (Cyert and March, 1963: 86, 121–122). A project may be less costly and less risky the closer and more related it is to the firm's existing knowledge base. Baysinger and Hoskisson (1989) find that firms pursuing related diversification stress technological knowledge development more than do unrelated diversifiers. Prahalad and Hamel's (1990) analysis of NEC and GTE demonstrates that some firms (e.g. NEC) strategically pursue new opportunities that exploit their existing technological competences. Pavitt (1984) argued that technical change at the firm level is cumulative and specific. Any acquisition of knowledge or skills external to the firm would have to be supported and integrated within the existing knowledge base. The existing resource configuration of the firm therefore simultaneously enables and constrains the direction of innovation and change of the firm. We can expect, therefore, that firms with accumulated knowledge in a preceding technological generation will be more likely to enter a new but related technological generation and will enter it earlier.

Therefore:

Proposition 1.1: The more a firm has accumulated related R&D resources, the more likely the firm will enter the emerging technology generation.

Proposition 1.2: The more a firm has accumulated related R&D resources, the earlier the firm will enter the emerging technology generation.

The Role of Resources

When routines assemble and coordinate engineering resources in integrated clusters spanning individuals and groups to enable distinctive activities to be performed, these activities constitute organizational capabilities (Teece, Pisano, and Shuen, 1992). The idea that organization or coordination of resources are a source of differences in firm performance is not new. Gavin (1988) found that quality performance was a function of organization routines such as information processing, linking customer experience with engineering design and coordinating factories and component suppliers. Clark and Fujimoto (1991) found a significant degree of variation in the ways in which firms coordinate their various product development activities and demonstrated performance differences due to the variation in coordination activities.

As the complexity of a technology increases, the amount and variety of resources required to design a new product increases (Methé, 1992). With the increased technological complexity, the list of customer required specifications grows longer. Areas covered by specifications also grow more numerous and diverse. Examples might include specifications not just of the finished product, but of the composition and grade of processing equipment, operating procedures, or a combination of these factors. Specifications gradually synthesize know-how about the ways in which a product design is translated from an initial design on a sheet of paper into an actual product. Specifications become the means by which engineers communicate with one another within a firm to divide the various tasks of making the product among them. This allows many engineers to work in parallel since each can proceed with assumptions on the work being performed by others. (See Sanchez 1996 in this volume for a discussion of this process.)

Generally, when a product initially comes out of its production process, it does not easily conform to the characteristics it is designed to have, even when the design specifications have all been met (Jaikumar and Bohn, 1988). In the semiconductor industry, such non-conformance is the rule rather than an exception. These non-conformances can usually be explained by the existence of variables that govern the characteristics of the product but remain unspecified in the design of the product. Product designs tend to be underspecified because the completeness of specifications is usually not a necessary condition for a product to be produced and it is virtually impossible for a design to comprise a comprehensive list of specifications. Once the product design is complete in every respect which can be anticipated in specifications, a large effort may still be required to make the actual product meet targeted customer needs.

It is already well accepted that firms enable certain activities to be organized more efficiently than markets and vice versa (Coase, 1937; Williamson, 1975, 1985). Some firms may also be better at coordinating product innovation activities than others. Since organizational or coordinating capabilities vary across firms (Teece, Pisano, Shuen, 1992), a firm's specific coordinating capabilities in product design and process engineering can directly influence its ability to develop new products and the speed at which it can develop those products.

Therefore:

Proposition 2.1: The more efficient a firm is at coordinating its product design resources, the more likely a firm will enter the emerging technology generation.

Proposition 2.2: The more efficient a firm is at coordinating its product design resources, the earlier a firm will enter the emerging technology generation.

Proposition 3.1: The more efficient a firm is at coordinating its process engineering resources, the more likely a firm will enter the emerging technology generation.

Proposition 3.2: The more efficient a firm is at coordinating its process engineering resources, the earlier a firm will enter the emerging technology generation.

RESOURCE ATTRIBUTES

I will use the attributes of knowledge-based resources as my main theoretical constructs in examining the changing importance of competences in the technological evolution of an industry. Resources work together in bundles to confer firm competences. Firm resources can be best differentiated with two conceptually distinct attributes: tacitness and tangibility.

Tacitness

Tacit is defined as (1) expressed or carried on without words or speech, (2) implied or indicated but not actually expressed (Webster's Dictionary, 1986). An asset or skill is considered tacit if it is difficult to articulate, specify, or explain.

The following diagram lays out two dimensions I will use to describe degrees of resource tacitness. A position near the left end of the continuum is an indicator that the resource is relatively tacit while a position near the right end of the continuum indicates that the resource is not very tacit.

not articulable ⬅——➡ articulable
 not articulated ⬅——➡ articulated

The first of the continua ranges from not articulable to articulable. A skill is tacit if it is "achieved by the observance of a set of rules that are not known as such to the person following them" (Polanyi, 1958: 49). Tacitness can imply that even the most skilled workers may not be able to 'codify' or explain the decision rules that underlie performance. In other words, the skill is not articulable. In contrast, fully articulable knowledge or skill can be transferred to another worker in oral or written form and the recipient would receive the same understanding.

The second of the continua characterizes the distinction between articulable knowledge that is articulated and articulable knowledge that is not. The ease of imitation of an asset or skill will depend upon the tacitness of the underlying knowledge (Nelson and Winter, 1982: 123). At one extreme, if the resource is tacit, acquiring the know-how underlying the knowledge is difficult. At the other extreme, imitation may be relatively easy through 'reverse engineering'. Then, the underlying knowledge of the product is deducible from the product itself, and there is little tacitness in the production process. The tacitness of a resource is directly related to the tangibility of that resource but as I will explain below, the words are not perfect synonyms.

Tangibility

Tangible is defined as (1) capable of being realized; readily apprehensible by the mind, (2) capable of being perceived or observed (Black's Law Dictionary, 1979). I will refer to intangible resources as assets or skills that (1) cannot be apprehended or understood, (2) cannot be perceived or observed. The following diagram lays out two dimensions I will use to describe degrees of resource tangibility. A position near the left end of the continuum is an indicator that the resource is relatively intangible while a position near the right end of the continuum indicates that the resource is relatively tangible. Apprehensibility refers to whether the mind can conceive of or understand

not apprehensible ◀——▶ apprehensible
                    not observable ◀——▶ observable
                         in use   in use

the underlying knowledge of the resource in question. Observability in use refers to the extent of disclosure of underlying knowledge that is necessitated by use of the knowledge (Winter, 1987). The central issue is the extent to which underlying knowledge can be transferred simply through observing the process or product. For example, in the semiconductor industry the design of a new integrated circuit is a secret that is hard to keep once the device is made available for purchase. Semiconductor manufacturers have attempted to reduce the observability of product design by encasing (potting) the IC devices in a non-removable resin casing that cannot be removed without destroying the device (Shapley, 1978). Manufacturing firms have sought to reduce the observability of process knowledge by segmenting the production process and only allowing a few key people to view the entire process from beginning to end.

The tangibility of a resource or competence refers to the degree of difficulty in apprehending or observing the underlying knowledge. The ability to apprehend or observe the underlying knowledge within a skill is based on two kinds of awareness: focal and subsidiary (Polanyi, 1958). Polanyi uses the following example to illustrate:

> When I am riding a bicycle or picking out my mackintosh, I do not know the particulars of my knowledge and therefore cannot tell what they are; when on the other hand I know the topography of a complex three dimensional aggregate, I know and could describe its particulars, but cannot describe their spatial relationship (Polanyi 1958: 90).

A focal awareness refers to an ability to focus on the whole, while subsidiary awareness allows one to see specific parts. In an organizational context, firms often segment the design or manufacturing process so that individual members of a firm cannot understand the whole picture, only their small part of the whole. This insures that no single employee can possess all the knowledge and skill of the firm. Employees act according to rules not known to all members. Skills may be observable, specifiable and explainable at the individual employee level (i.e., subsidiary awareness), but not on the organizational level (i.e., focal awareness). In such a case, the organization level skills would be considered intangible.

An intangible resource is often tacit, but a tacit skill or knowledge is not necessarily intangible. Skills often include tacit knowledge. Skills based on tacit knowledge may be teachable though not articulable. A competent supervisor or trainer can provide an observable model of tacit skill for the trainee to follow and imitate. It is the non-apprehensible, non-observable (i.e., non-teachable) skills that are intangible. For example, in many Japanese companies, the coordination of dozens of engineers in the development of a new semiconductor device is an organizational level skill that has developed over time and remains a relatively informal process. Even though project management software is used to monitor the critical process events, apprehending and observing the underlying knowledge of this organizational level skill by anyone external to the team is very problematic. The underlying knowledge of this type of organizational level skill tends to be intangible.

In summary, tacitness and intangibility are conceptually distinct and can be construed as two resource attributes. The following examples illustrate possible combinations of tacitness/non-tacitness and tangibility/intangibility of knowledge-based resources.

	Intangible	Tangible
Tacit	New Idea/Thought	Individual Skill
	Org. Level Skill	Non-codified task
Non-Tacit	Patent Submission	Common knowledge/
	Original Drawings	Technology
	Potted IC	Cited Patent
	Specifications	Computer Software

New ideas tend to begin as images not words. Written language, which we now regard as a way of representing speech, was originally an independent language, as it has remained to this day in China. Written language consisted originally as pictures, which gradually became conventionalized, eventually, to represent syllables, and finally letters Russell (1921) argues that written language began as a direct pictorial representation of what was to be expressed.

> The essence of language lies, not in the use of this or that special means of communication, but in the employment of fixed associations (however these may have originated) in order that something now sensible—a spoken word, a picture, a gesture, or what not—may call up the "idea" of something else (Russell, 1921: 191).

Therefore, new ideas, images or thoughts start out intangible and tacit, but do not necessarily remain as such. A new idea tends to be tacit and intangible until someone puts it into words, sketches it, or codifies it in some meaningful way. Once this is done, the knowledge has become non-tacit. It is the words, sketches, symbols, etc., that represent the idea and convey meaning. However, just because it has been written in words, sketched, or codified does not mean that the underlying knowledge is tangible to anyone other than the originator of the idea. The apprehensibility and observability in use of the underlying knowledge determine the accessibilty of the knowledge to anyone other than the originator of the idea. In essence, the tangibility of knowledge is relative and dynamic.

For example, a new idea in an engineer's head tends to be tacit and intangible until he/she puts it on paper or draws it. At that point it becomes non-tacit. However, this does not mean that anyone other than the originator apprehends the idea or understands how to use it. If the engineer wants to patent the idea, he/she must go one step further. Knowledge and ideas are not patentable. Indeed, it is that distinction between the idea and its application that defines the area of patentability. A potential patentee must be prepared to demonstrate that he/she has developed a new, useful, and nonobvious process or product. In the patent process, some of intangibility of the knowledge will be lost. However, demonstrating novelty, utility and nonobviousness does not require full disclosure of the underlying knowledge or applicability of the idea. Once the patent has been diffused through the industry the idea has become non-tacit and tangible.

A new idea can also move from being tacit and intangible to being tacit and tangible. The know-how for performing an individual skill or task may not be codified or put in words at first, but may still be apprehensible and observable in use. Automation tends to replace individual skills and tasks. Once the skill has been written into a robotics program, the knowledge has gone from being tacit and intangible to non-tacit and tangible.

THE TRANSFERABILITY OF RESOURCES

New firms or firms implementing new strategies often do not have all the needed resources and are forced either to internally develop needed resources or to acquire them from outside the firm. New ventures typically begin with a scarce number of strategy relevant resources (Lippman and Rumelt, 1982; Kimberly, 1981). Firms seeking to implement a particular strategy such as diversification may do so by buying resources or acquiring other firms. Firms pursuing a strategy of product innovation might seek research and development skills (research scientists) in the labor market. Barney (1986) argues that "whenever the implementation of a strategy requires the acquisition of resources, a strategic factor market develops." However, not all resources are equally transferable and equally marketable.

The transaction cost approach can be applied to analyzing the marketability of resources. The transaction cost approach typically attempts to identify a set of factors that explain the circumstances under which complex contracts involving contingent claims will be costly to write, execute, and enforce (Williamson, 1985). Uncertainty, complexity, transaction specific investment, and small numbers are some transactional factors which can lead to market failure. Williamson joins these market factors with a set of human factors such as bounded rationality and opportunism to explain market failure.

From my discussion of resource attributes above, intangible resources tend to be difficult to apprehend or observe. To commercialize an intangible resource a firm must articulate its tacit knowledge and be able to transfer that knowledge to the purchasing firm. Identifying an intangible resource and attaching value to it is likely to be highly problematic and may require significant transaction specific investments to be made before the resource value can be determined. The transaction cost model suggests that the selling or trading of intangible resources under these conditions is very unlikely. A resource that is intangible and tacit is relatively difficult to transfer (except in the form of hiring a human asset); ex ante, there may be no market value for it. Tacitness and intangibility tend to create transaction difficulties not just because the buyer does not fully recognize the value of the resource, but also because full disclosure of the know-how (which would make its value known to the prospective buyer) is not in the best interest of the seller. This is the paradox of information: "Its value for the purchaser is not known until he has the information, but then he has in effect acquired it without cost" (Arrow, 1971: 152).

Resource Attributes and Transferability

Resource attributes in combination with the transaction cost approach can be used to explain why some resources seem more marketable and transferable than others. Resource attributes and transaction costs might therefore usefully be applied to the analysis of exchanges between firms at different stages of technology development. Uncertainty and the need for transaction-specific investments create a variety of exchange problems in the transfer of technological innovations between firms. Because of uncertainty, contracts cannot anticipate all future states of the relationship and because the need for transaction-specific investments, parties to an exchange have an incentive to appropriate the difference between the value of that investment in the current transaction and its value in its next best use (Barney, 1990). As a result of the potential for opportunism, economic transactions characterized by high uncertainty/ complexity and high transaction-specific investment will be more efficiently governed through vertically integrated hierarchical relations than through market relations (Williamson, 1975).

Incumbents

During the early stages of the development of a technology, exchanges are characterized by uncertainty and complexity. This is especially the case for possible Schumpeterian innovations that are potentially far reaching in their impact on existing technologies and have highly uncertain future economic value. In these stages of technology development, the strategic factor market often 'fails' and transfers of resources among firms tend not to occur. Firms with any experience in an industry have usually acquired some relevant resources. Among these are product development skills, manufacturing skills, and distribution channels consisting of sales people and service representatives. Given that the strategic factor market fails in the early stages of technology development, incumbents with any experience relevant to the new technology would have an advantage over non-incumbents.

When technological innovation spans multiple generations, as with many of the semiconductor markets, a market gradually develops for many of the resources needed to compete. The more tangible, non-tacit resources diffuse through the industry and many of the skills of incumbent firms do not remain unique. To the extent that firms operating in other industries and markets can obtain similar resources and can transfer those resources efficiently to the industry and market in question, the relative advantage of the incumbents decline. As many of the resources required to commercialize a new product become common and transferable throughout an industry, non-incumbent firms with relevant skills can be expected (1) to enter emerging technologies and (2) to enter as quickly as incumbents.

Therefore:

Proposition 4.1: In the earlier generations of a market's technology development, incumbents will be more likely to enter and will enter earlier than non-incumbents.

Proposition 4.2: In the later generations of a market's technology development, non-incumbents will be as likely to enter and as likely to enter early
as incumbents.

Non-Tacit/Tangible Resources

In terms of this model, as an R&D resource evolves from tacit understanding in an engineer's head to a non-tacit description on a design
drawing or a patent submission it increases in transferability. At this point,
the patent may be non-tacit and still intangible. The knowledge or skill may
still be unteachable and possibly not observable in use. However, when a
company has an important technological advance it may attempt to patent
around it to obtain "defensive patents" on the periphery of the advance
(Albert *et al.* 1991). Important innovations are often represented by a cluster
of patents and not just a single patent. As the cluster of resources evolves
from tacit to non-tacit, they move from intangible to tangible and the
transferability of the competence increases. Once the R&D resources
become non-tacit and relatively tangible, a strategic factor market can
develop (Barney, 1986).

For example, with the advent of computer aided engineering (CAE),
design engineers can enter semiconductor design schematics directly into
the computer and then have the computer automatically draw the physical
representation of the design. Each single schematic represents only a small
part of a semiconductor design and structure. However, many engineers
began immediately to create design libraries of these structures (Davidow
and Malone, 1992). In such a process, as the number of schematics stored
in the design libraries increases the underlying knowledge of a firm's design
competency moves from a state of tacitness to nontacitness. The more
comprehensive the design library, the more apprehensible and observable
the underlying knowledge.

As R&D resources move from "people embodied" to being "machine
embodied," innovations become more diffusible, and strategic factor
markets form. Eventually, these resources become common among
industry participants, and they are no longer a source of advantage. Firms
lacking that knowledge or technology can now easily purchase or replicate
it. Prior accumulation of machine embodied resources is therefore no longer
easily translated into early market entry or product success.

Therefore:

Proposition 5.1: In the earlier generations of a market's technology
development, firms having accumulated related, non-tacit/tangible, R&D
resources will be more likely to enter and will enter earlier than other firms.

Proposition 5.2: In the later generations of a market's technology
development, firms not having accumulated related, non-tacit/tangible, R&D
resources will be as likely to enter and as likely to enter early as other firms.

Tacit/Intangible Resources

Nelson and Winter (1982) and Dosi (1984) observed that technologies evolve in patterns according to natural trajectories. These trajectories are shaped by technological paradigms or regimes. Nelson and Winter (1982) use the example of the Douglas DC-3 airplane. The DC-3 technology dominated the technological regime in terms of metal skin, low wing, piston engines, etc. for more than two decades. Dosi (1984: 193), in his study of the semi-conductor industry, observed that movement along a technological trajectory followed a trend toward increasing incorporation of technology into capital equipment and into complex institutions. This also can be described as a movement from "people embodied" technology toward "organization-embodied" technology.

In parallel with the evolution of product design, the production process also develops toward states of higher productivity through incremental changes. A cumulative effect is achieved that significantly alters the general nature of the process. As the product technology matures, production systems become more efficient, and price competition may become more intense. Firms seek to standardize their designs, processes etc., so that production efficiencies can be achieved. The production system becomes elaborate and tightly integrated through automation and process control (Utterback and Abernathy, 1975). As investment increases and the process becomes well integrated, coordination across multiple functions becomes increasingly routine. It is these coordinative routines that become an important source of advantage during later stages of technology development.

Firms can be characterized as consisting of more or less structured clusters of routines. Routines are thus the organizational counterpart to individual skills. Grant (1991) suggests that coordinative routines have some of the same attributes as individual skills.

> Just as the individual's skills are carried out semi-automatically, without conscious coordination, so organizational routines involve a large component of tacit knowledge, which implies limits on the extent to which the organization's capabilities can be articulated (Grant, 1991: 110).

As described earlier, organizations often attempt to codify their organizational routines with procedures, control programs, and project management softwares. However, as the complexity of the routine increases, the underlying knowledge becomes less apprehensible and less observable in use. Organizational level routines tend to remain somewhat tacit and intangible. Organizational routines also evolve over time and vary across firms (Teece, Pisano, Shen, 1992).

Nelson and Winter (1982) describe the process of technological evolution as proceeding in two stages. The first stage takes place within the firm and entails the search for better routines or ways of doing things. The second stage takes place at the industry level. Firms that have put superior routines in place drive out those firms that have not. For example, if a firm has routines that are able to take advantage of unforeseen outcomes, it may be able to proceed with a development project that another would not (Mitchell, 1988). In the early stages of technological evolution, firms are "searching" for appropriate routines. In the later stages of technological evolution, however, those firms with better routines begin to have an advantage over those lacking the necessary routines.

Therefore:

Proposition 6.1: In the later generations of a market's technology development, firms having accumulated related, tacit/intangible, product design resources will be more likely to enter and will enter earlier than other firms.

Proposition 6.2: In the earlier generations of a market's technology development, firms not having accumulated related, tacit/intangible, product design resources will be as likely to enter and as likely to enter early as other firms.

Proposition 7.1: In the later generations of a market's technology development, firms having accumulated related, tacit/tangible, process engineering resources will be more likely to enter and will enter earlier than other firms.

Proposition 7.2: In the earlier generations of a market's technology development, firms not having accumulated related, non-tacit/tangible, process engineering resources will be as likely to enter and as likely to enter early as other firms.

I have presented two sets of propositions in the preceding discussion. The first set (propositions 1.1–3.2) is concerned with the nature of the firm and the role of resources and coordination capabilities in the process of innovation. The second set (propositions 4.1–7.2) deals with the attributes of firm resources and how those attributes affect the role of resources and coordination capabilities in the process of innovation over the stages of technology development. In the remainder of the paper, I present a brief history of the semiconductor industry.

THE SEMICONDUCTOR STORY

The semiconductor industry is a fascinating example of technological evolution and an interesting case for this study for several reasons. It is an industry in which knowledge-based resources are the primary productive resources of the firm. It has been one of the fastest growing and most innovative industries over the last four decades. Firms within the industry have had to deal with constantly changing technologies, competitors, and customers, and the sources of competitive advantage have therefore changed rapidly. The semiconductor industry is an excellent example of an industry in which the Schumpeterian "perennial gale of creative destruction" (innovation) has played a major role.

In the early stages or generations of semiconductor technology development, several design and process technologies were available. The technology was uncertain and its future applicability unclear. A long series of linked innovations followed. There was a continuous stream of new electronic devices based on semiconductor materials. However, the technology evolution was discontinuous with several early significant innovations. During these early stages there was limited transfer of strategically relevant resources. Engineers were in short supply, much of the design and manufacturing equipment was made in-house, and the future potential of the technology was uncertain. The possession of the necessary knowledge and skills both enabled and constrained the firms in their choices of strategic action. In several cases, simply having the right equipment, a few patents, and a few knowledgeable semiconductor engineers made all the difference.

However, as standards and dominant designs emerged, the technology matured, and the possession of the right equipment, patents, and engineers was not enough to be competitive. As the level of uncertainty in the industry dropped off, a market for relevant knowledge and skill emerged. Firms began to transfer relevant resources and imitate each other's strategic actions. Much of the knowledge and skills that in the early stages were unique to a small number of firms became increasingly available to a large number of firms. Gradually, the possession of non-transferable knowledge and skills became the primary source of advantage in the increasingly competitive race to market. The following synopsis of the industry will provide a brief historical background and summarizes the role of the transferability of knowledge in shaping industry evolution at key stages of industry technology.

Early Origins

The birth of the semiconductor industry was in December of 1947 with the invention of the point-contact transistor at Bell Laboratories. But, the story does not begin there. Bell announced the transistor as a challenger to the vacuum tube, the simplicity of which would allow for mass-production economies. Vacuum tubes were originally very large, relatively expensive, and energy inefficient. These electron amplifiers were used in the early radio receivers. Gradually, advances in packaging placed multiple amplifying devices in one common glass bulb. The size of the glass tubes was eventually scaled down to 2 inches long and 3/4 inch in diameter. Vacuum tube technology continued to advance into the 1950s and for a time, attempted to compete directly with transistors. Attempts were made to put all the vacuum tubes needed for a standard radio into a large glass bulb, but the arrival of the germanium transistor gradually reduced interest in improving the vacuum tube further.

The transistor ushered in a new technological paradigm or regime replacing the old one based on electron tubes. It used semiconductor materials and was based on advances in solid-state physics. Science played an important role and scientists were the main protagonists of the invention because only scientists who had a knowledge of solid-state physics could understand the workings of the device.

The Transistor

When the point-contact transistor was announced, the world took little notice at first. The initial device was not very effective, its stability and reproducibility were poor, and it was extremely difficult to manufacture. The point-contact transistor announcement initiated a battle for suitable manufacturing technologies. In April of 1952, Bell laboratories held a symposium and publicly divulged what progress they had made towards the manufacture of transistors (Tilton, 1971). Through the mid-1950s, most of the innovations continued to emerge from Bell laboratories and other well established vacuum tube and electronic valve companies.

Gradually, the source of new ideas and innovations shifted from the larger, well-established firms to smaller start-up firms. Many of the most critical innovations eventually emerged from newer firms that had lured away key engineers from the larger, better established firms. Texas Instruments (TI) entered the electronics industry in 1949 and established its first research laboratory in 1953. TI produced the first silicon transistor one year later in 1954. Fairchild Semiconductor was started in 1957 and within three years developed the first batch production method for semiconductors using a different semiconductor design than TI. TI created the first semiconductors and Fairchild demonstrated how to mass-manufacture them.

The Integrated Circuit

TI's invention formed a complete circuit on a single piece of semiconducting material. The device combined several transistors, diodes, and capacitors, on a bar of germanium. Fairchild's mass-manufacturing technique was called the planar process and made it possible to connect the circuits using a batch process which allowed the large scale production of semiconductor devices. Because Fairchild was clearer than TI in specifying the mode of interconnection, Fairchild was allowed to share in the integrated circuit patent. The planar process became the standard means used by semiconductor manufacturers to produce integrated circuits.

With the introduction of the planar process, oxide masking, and other batch process technologies, technological change became increasingly cumulative. Manufacturing techniques continued to improve rapidly with major innovations in chemical vapor deposition, clean-room technology, lithography, and computer aided design. Technological innovations were increasingly based on already existing technologies. Contrary to earlier periods, product and process innovations emerged and evolved independently of each other. As semiconductor technology became more complex, organized R&D became more important and required larger amounts of investment. The coordination of R&D, manufacturing, marketing, and other functions also increased in importance.

During these years of the semiconductor industry, a new breed of competitor began to emerge in the US: the scientific entrepreneur. Venture capital made entry relatively easy and scientists with knowledge of semiconductor physics and technology were able to begin their own small manufacturing operations. The industry experienced an increasing pattern of scientific entrepreneurs leaving established firms to form new ventures and of experts being recruited away by competitors. In the 1960s and early 1970s more that 50 new firms entered the semiconductor industry. Many of these new companies went into business with the aim of producing a low-cost, high performance semiconductor memory that could replace the existing computer core memory.

In these early years of the semiconductor industry, much of the knowledge required to design, manufacture, and bring devices to market, was tacit and stored in the heads of a small number of scientists. The manufacture of semiconductor devices was an individual skill. The first IC was made by hand. Early IC manufacturers had to design and manufacture their own processing equipment in addition to the IC itself. Gradually, the attributes of the knowledge required to compete in the industry began to change. Designers began to put the architecture or layout of the ICs on paper. The number of patent submissions surrounding IC design and process technology shot up quickly. To the extent possible, knowledge was being written down, drawn, symbolically represented, or transferred into a machine. The critical knowledge began moving from a state of tacitness to non-tacitness.

Large-Scale Integration (LSI)

When Intel was founded in 1968, the largest silicon memory device available held only 256 bits of information. The ferrite core, invented by researchers at MIT, was the dominant memory device. Largely due to this device, computers were large and expensive, usually costing well over $10,000 each. During the next three years, Intel developed and introduced the three critical components of the personal computer—the working memory, the permanent memory, and the microprocessor. Even though other companies were pursuing similar technologies, and in many cases the same technologies, Intel's threefold announcement—the microprocessor (MPU), the working memory (DRAM), and the permanent information storage device (EPROM) established a "dominant design" across these three devices. In the November 15, 1971, issue of *Electronic News*, Intel submitted a half-page advertisement proclaiming "a new era of integrated electronics." This announcement ushered in the period of large-scale integration (LSI).

LSI refers to semiconductor devices with between 100 and 100,000 gates. The LSI period covers the years between 1971 and the early 1980s. Much of the process equipment used during this period was made internally by the semiconductor manufacturing firms. The effort to move to LSI manufacturing was hampered by wafer damage and other defects caused by the contact aligners and other process equipment available at the time. Indeed, most of the available process equipment represented, in one way or another, a barrier to the volume production of higher-level integrated circuits (Van Zant, 1990). Those manufacturing firms that developed and patented their own process innovations enjoyed an early lead. In addition, a thorough understanding of the device's complex end use was critical. The manufacturer had to have the design capability as well as the processing technology to make the device.

The possession of the appropriate process technology and talented knowledgeable engineers was a source of advantage in the early 1970s. Indeed, many of the critical innovations in the 70s emerged from the newer firms which attracted people of ability and concentrated on the development of production technology (Braun and MacDonald, 1978). Process equipment and talented engineers were in short supply. Early semiconductor participants enjoyed temporary monopolies in terms of resources. Various techniques and equipment were not equally understood or available to all competitors.

LSI production moved the semiconductor business from a laboratory-based, small batch manufacturing process to an equipment-based, automated, high-volume manufacturing process. Before LSI, most of the equipment was basic and manually controlled with process effectiveness being a function of the way the equipment was run by any given operator at any given moment. The state-of-the-art gradually shifted from manual to computer-controlled processes with on-board solid-state controllers and sequencers. The knowledge of how to control the process was gradually transferred into the equipment. The process knowledge became part of the machine.

The semiconductor firms began to get added help from specialty equipment vendors. Companies like Kodak, Waycoat, and Shirley Company gradually improved their photoresist products and materials. Monsanto and Dow Corning provided increasingly pure polished silicon wafers. The Perkin-Elmer Company eliminated some of the mask and aligner defect problems by developing the first projection aligner for the photomasking operation (Van Zant, 1990). Improved photolithographic equipment began appearing using several different technologies such as ion implantation and electron beams. Equipment vendors gradually became reliable sources of state-of-the-art equipment and often quickly spread any advances in process technology.

Many of the resources that gave early incumbents an advantage moved from people-embodied to machine-embodied and became easily transferred. With the advent of computer-aided engineering (CAE), design engineers could enter semiconductor design schematics directly into the computer and then have the computer automatically draw the physical representation of the design. Engineers almost immediately began creating design libraries of these structures (Davidow and Malone, 1992). The product design knowledge moved from being people-embodied to being machine-embodied. In addition, competitors routinely engaged in reverse engineering to obtain competitor's product designs. Product design innovations quickly diffused through imitation and the movement of engineers. Much of the product design knowledge that provided advantage in the early stages of the technology lost its value as competitors imitated or acquired it.

During the LSI years of the semiconductor industry, much of the knowledge required to design, manufacture, and bring devices to market was increasingly non-tacit and tangible. The knowledge required to compete became increasingly easy to transfer. Strategic factor markets developed for many of these critical resources. Much of the product design and manufacturing knowledge that had been a source of advantage had diffused widely throughout the industry. The non-tacit/tangible resources were diffusing at an increasing rate. The source of advantage for most firms began to shift from easily transferable resources to those resources that are difficult to transfer. The source of advantage gradually shifted from non-tacit/tangible resources to tacit/intangible resources. Organizational level skills such as coordination of product design and process engineering resources became an increasingly critical form of knowledge.

A New Era

As the industry approached the era of very-large-scale integrated circuits (VLSI), many of the industry's resources were purchasable and available to all participants. Indeed, the purchase of the right equipment became one of the key success factors of the industry. A high level of process capability became pervasive across all participants. For memory circuits to be successful, they had to be capable of being produced in large quantities at costs that were competitive with those manufactured with alternative methods and equipment. In addition, a new expectation developed in which the circuit had to be capable of performing its functions at very high levels of reliability throughout its intended lifetime. Yield and reliability became the basis of competition.

The periods of LSI and VLSI in the semiconductor industry seem to parallel Nelson and Winter's (1982) two stage model of technological evolution. The first stage proceeds within the firm with a search for better "routines" or ways of doing things. The second stage consists of a selection process at the industry level during which the evolved firms (those having better routines) force the other firms out. With the emergence of VLSI, most of the individual manufacturing processes had been automated. The focus of process change became the elimination of operators from the fabrication areas and the automation of material delivery and movement. The elimination of operators is desirable because human beings are one of the major sources of contamination in the process. In addition, subtle, incremental adjustments during the fabrication process to increase yield became absolutely critical to success in the industry. Better routines achieved through superior automation became an important source of advantage in the semiconductor industry.

The efficiency of the product development process is a function of two coordinative routines: product design and process engineering. By the early 1980s, so many product designs had been developed on CAE systems that semiconductor firms had developed vast libraries of circuit designs. The impact of these new design methodologies and equipment was significant. Design cycles for new chips dropped from years to months, even though newer products were often hundreds of times more complex. The constant race to meet and exceed current requirements caused Dynamic Random Access Memory (DRAM) design processing to become one of the most difficult design processes in the industry. The coordinative routines involved have had a significant impact on such performance variables as development cost, development lead times, development productivity, and quality of the design.

The evolution of the semiconductor industry also dramatizes the role of process engineering. The minimum feature size of DRAM devices has shrunk by about one-third every year since 1970. The number of bits stored has quadrupled every three years. The same sort of persistent progress has also been observed in other performance criteria such as access time and power consumption. Performance improvement like this is partially attributable to incremental improvements in design engineering, as well as to the introduction of new design ideas. But process engineering undoubtedly has played the central role in this continuous, and surprisingly regular, progress of the IC semiconductor technology.

By the end of the VLSI era, much of the design and process equipment required to manufacture ICs was available to all industry participants. The knowledge had become tangible and non-tacit. The tangible/non-tacit knowledge in the industry was diffusing at a phenomenal rate. Devices had become relatively standard so that one competitor's product could usually be replaced by another competitors product. As described above, the basis of competition had become yield and reliability. Tacit/intangible, organizational level skills had become the source of advantage in the industry.

Further, preventing the diffusion of resources had become a critical aspect of a firm's strategy.

CONCLUSION AND IMPLICATIONS

Two firms facing the same environment will often follow different technology strategies and innovation paths. Many conditions may constrain a firm in its decision to experiment, to acquire a new process or product, or to change organizational practices in general. A firm's decision to innovate may be constrained by a variety of factors in its environment, by search routines imposed by its own history, by its inertia resulting from organizational size, and by its existing portfolio of competences. The aim of this paper has been to understand the role of resources and their attributes in the process of innovation.

Innovative firms are those that constantly seek better capabilities and processes to overcome the perceived constraints and exploit opportunities. Since these activities entail risks, the role of management is to gauge the trade-offs between acceptable risk and the potential rewards to developing new capabilities. The optimal growth of the firm thus requires a balance between capitalization of existing resources and formation of new ones (Penrose, 1959; Rubin, 1973). However, substantive questions remain as to what new capabilities would be optimal to acquire.

It is tautological to argue that successful firms must already possess the necessary resources. What keeps the competence-based argument from being equally tautological is that firms exiting high-technology markets such as semiconductors in recent years possessed many of the same resources as those that continued to compete. What distinguishes exiting and entering firms with the same resources must therefore be their differing abilities to use resources and capabilities. In other words, their differing competences in key dimensions of competition.

As mentioned above, this paper argues that when technological innovation spans multiple generations, such as in DRAMs, firms that seek to enter the new technological generations enjoy a significant advantage in their entry efforts if they have accumulated relevant resources and capabilities. An interesting proposition of this paper, however, is that the relevance of resources appear to change over time. Thus proposed relationships change as the technology matures. This paper further argues that the attributes of the resources can be used to predict the ways in which the relationships change. The more tacit and tangible a resource, the longer its probable duration as a source of advantage. Resources that are not articulable, not observable in use, and not apprehensible and are elements of a system are the longerterm sources of advantage.

Much of the literature on market entry and entry timing view firms as primarily constrained by environmental conditions. Managers are seen as individually rational with a limited set of options from which to choose when pursuing their goals. Economic arguments have been used to explain entry timing decisions. Several of these studies have found that the first firms to introduce "major" production innovations frequently are newcomers to an industry, with "major" defined as either cost-reduction or quality-enhancement (Jewkes, Sawyers and Stillerman, 1958; Nelson, 1959; Abernathy and Utterback, 1978). Incumbents in one technology generation are usually described as having disincentives for early entry into the next generation. For example, cutting into sales of existing products creates a disincentive to introduce new products (Arrow, 1962; Reinganum,1983; Tushman and Anderson, 1986). Competitive pressures such as the number of current and potential competitors or their threats to core products are described as influencing entry decisions (Bain, 1956; Phillips, 1966; Barzel, 1968; Mitchell, 1988). Obviously, incumbents do introduce new products. Indeed, about half of the new semiconductor product introductions over the last fifty years have been introduced by incumbent companies (Dosi, 1981; Freeman, 1982). This has usually been explained, however, by whether the incumbent's incentives to enter early outweigh the incentives to enter late.

This paper has demonstrated that other constraints internal to the firm limit a decision maker's actions even beyond the limits posed by the environment, past experience, size or economic tradeoffs. Other firm-specific attributes such as capabilities and processes have not been adequately discussed in the literature and need to be added to the debate.

At any given time, a firm can only pursue a limited set of strategic directions. The existing resource configuration of the firm enables and constrains the direction of the firm. Innovative firms search for better resource configurations, new capabilities, and better coordinating processes. Whenever there is perceived inadequacy in its resource configuration, capabilities, or processes, managers face a decision of where and how to remedy the firm's inadequacies. Not all resources or capabilities are equally available. As this paper has suggested, availability of resources and capabilities is a function of their attributes and the stage of technological development.

This paper has research implications for the competence-based view of the firm and therefore for corporate strategy. This study highlights the tension that exists between the need to invest in assets and skills and the need to appropriate the value of those investments. Many resources may be good to own when pursuing technological innovation, but few will retain their value over long time periods. To understand the patterns of entry in evolving industries, we need to understand the roles resources, capabilities, and processes play in creating competences.

This paper also points to the need to possess a full set of relevant resources in order to succeed in the pursuit of innovation. This study highlights the interaction between firm competences, the transferability of competences and the number of firms possessing them. As the number of firms possessing a specific competence increases, the value of that competence diminishes as a source of advantage. As a result, some of the most valuable and critical competences a firm can possess are not transferable or marketable. Indeed, some of the most valuable competences a firm can possess are deeply embedded organizational skills or coordination routines.

The process of identifying and investing in requisite competences is particularly problematic. New firms or firms implementing new strategies are often forced to acquire resources from the environment. Firms pursuing a strategy of product innovation might seek research and development skills in the labor market for research scientists. However, if a specific firm can purchase a needed competence in such a market, chances are that all firms can. Possessing a portfolio of easily transferable competences therefore is not likely to lead to competitive success; we can rather expect that to be successful, every firm will need to develop more tacit, less tangible, and thus less transferable competences.

REFERENCES

Abernathy, W. J. and Utterback, J. M. "Patterns of Industrial Innovation". *Technology Review*, Vol. 80, pp. 97–107, 1978.

Albert, M. D. and Avery, D. "Direct Validation of Citation Counts as Indicators of Industrial Important Patents". *Research Policy*, Vol. 20, pp. 251–259, 1991.

Arrow, K. J. *Essays in the Theory of Risk-Bearing.* Chicago, IL: Markham, 1971.

Arrow, K. J. "Economic Welfare and the Allocation of Resources of Invention". In Nelson, R. R., ed., *The Rate and Direction of Inventive Activity—Economic and Social Factors*, Princeton: National Bureau of Economic Research, pp. 609–625, 1962.

Bain, J. *Barriers to New Competition.* Cambridge, MA: Harvard University Press, 1956.

Barnett, H. G. *Innovation: The Basis of Cultural Change.* New York: McGraw-Hill, 1953.

Barney, J. "Firm Resources and Sustained Competitive Advantage". *Journal of Management*, Vol. 17(1), pp. 99–120, 1991.

Barney, J. "The Debate between Traditional Management Theory and Organizational Economics: Substantive Differences or Intergroup Conflict?". *Academy of Management Review*, Vol. 15, pp. 382–393, 1990.

Barney, J. "Strategic Factor Markets: Expectations, Luck, and Business Strategy". *Management Science*, Vol. 86, pp. 1231–1242, 1986.

Barzel, Y. "Optimal Timing of Innovation". *Review of Economics and Statistics*, Vol. 50, pp. 348–355, 1968.

Baysinger, B. and Hoskisson, R. E. "Diversification Strategy and R&D Intensity in Multiproduct Firms". *Academy of Managment Journal*, Vol. 32, pp. 310–332, 1989.

Black, H. C. *Black's Law Dictionary.* St. Paul, MN: West Publishing Co, 1979.

Braun, E. and MacDonald, S. *Revolution in Miniature.* Cambridge: Cambridge University Press, 1978.

Clark, K. and Fujimoto, T. *Product Development Performance: Strategy, Organization and Management in the World Auto Industries*. Cambridge, MA: Harvard Business School Press, 1991.

Coase, R. H. "The Nature of the Firm". *Economica*, Vol. 4, pp. 386–405, 1937.

Conner, K. R. "Resource-Based Theory as a New Theory of the Firm: A Comparison to the Transaction Cost Perspective". Working Paper: Presented at the 1991 Academy of Management Meetings, Miami, FL, 1991.

Conner, K. R. "A Historical Comparison of Resource Based Theory and Five Schools of Thought Within Industrial Organization Economics: Do We Have a New Theory of the Firm?". *Journal of Management*, Vol. 17(1), pp. 121–154, 1991.

Cyert, R. M. and March, J. G. *A Behavioral Theory of the Firm*. Englewood Cliffs, NJ: Prentice-Hall, 1963.

Davidow, W. H. and Malone, M. S. *The Virtual Corporation*. New York: Harper-Collins Publishers Inc, 1992.

Dosi, G. *Technical Change and Industrial Transformation*. London: Macmillan, 1984.

Dosi, G. *Technical Change, Industrial Transformation and Public Policies: The Case of the Semiconductor Industry*. Sussex European Research Centre, University of Sussex, 1981.

Garvin, D. *Managing Quality*. New York: Free Press, 1988.

Grant, R. M. *Contemporary Strategy Analysis: Concepts, Techniques, Applications*. Cambridge, MA: Blackwell Publishers, 1991.

Jaikumar, R. and Bohn, R. E. "The Development of Intelligent Systems for Industrial Use". In Rosenbloom, R., ed., *Research on Technological Innovation, Management and Policy*. Greenwich, CT: JAI Press, Vol. 3, 1988

Jewkes, J., Sawers, D. and Stillerman, R. *The Sources of Innovation*. London: MacMillan, 1958.

Kimberly, J. R. "Managerial Innovation". In Nystrom, P. C. and Starbuck, W. H., eds, *Handbook in Organizational Design*. New York: Oxford University Press, pp. 84–104, 1981.

Lippman, M. B. and Rumelt, R. P. "Uncertain Imitability: An Analysis of Interfirm Differences in Efficiency under Competition". *Bell Jounal of Economics*, Vol. 13, pp. 418–438, 1982.

Methe, D. T. "The Influence of Technology and Demand Factors on Firm Size and Industrial Structure in the DRAM Market—1973-1988". *Research Policy*, Vol. 21, Vol 13–25, 1992.

Mish, F. C. *et al.*, eds, *Webster's Ninth New Collegiate Dictionary*. Springfield, MA: Merriam–Webster Inc, 1986.

Mitchell, W. G. "Dynamic Commercialization: An Organizational Economic Analysis of Innovation in the Medical Diagnostic Imaging Industry". Unpublished Ph.D. Dissertation, School of Business Administration, University of California, Berkeley, 1988.

Moss, S. *The Economic Theory of Business Strategy*. New York: Halsted Press, 1981.

Nelson, R. R. and Winter, S. G. *An Evolutionary Theory of Economic Change*. Cambridge, MA: Harvard University Press, 1982.

Nelson, R. R. "The Simple Economics of Basic Scientific Research". *Journal of Political Economy*, Vol. 67, pp. 297–306, 1959.

Penrose, E. *The Theory of Growth of the Firm*. Oxford: Blackwell, 1959.

Polanyi, M. *Personal Knowledge: Towards a Post-Critical Philosophy*. New York: Harper Torchbooks, 1958.

Prahalad, C. K. and Hamel, G. "The Core Competence of the Corporation". *Harvard Business Review*, Vol. 68(3), pp. 79–91, 1990.

Reinganum, J. F. "Uncertain Innovation and the Persistence of Monopoly". *American Economic Review*, Vol. 56, pp. 301–310, 1983.

Rubin, P. H. "The Expansion of Firms". *Journal of Political Economy,* pp. 936–949, 1973.

Rumelt, R. P. "Towards a Strategic Theory of the Firm". In Lamb, R., ed., *Competitive Strategic Management*. Englewood Cliffs, NJ: Prentice-Hall, pp. 556–570, 1984.

Rumelt, R. P. "Theory, Strategy, and Entrepreneurship". In Teece, D., ed., *The Competitive Challenge: Strategy and Organization for Industrial Innovation and Renewal*. Cambridge, MA: Ballinger, 1987.

Russell, B. *The Analysis of the Mind*. London: Routledge, 1921.

Schumpeter, J. A. *The Theory of Economic Developmen*. Cambridge, MA: Harvard University Press, 1934.

Shapley, D. "Technology Creep and the Arms Race: ICBM Problem a Sleeper". *Science*, Vol. 201, pp. 1102–1105, 1978.

Teece, D. J., Pisano, G. and Shuen, A. "Dynamic Capabilities and Strategic Management". Working Paper, University of California, Berkeley, 1992.

Tilton, J. *International Diffusion of Technology: The Case of Semiconductors*. Washington, D.C.: The Brookings Institution, 1971.

Tushman, M. L. and Anderson, P. "Technological Discontinuities and Organizational Environments". *Administrative Science Quarterly*, Vol. 31, pp. 439–465, 1986.

Utterback, J. and Abernathy, W. "A Dynamic Model of Process and Product Innovation". *Omega*, Vol. 33, pp. 639–656, 1975.

Van Zant, P. *Microchip Fabrication: A Practical Guide to Semiconductor Processing*. New York: McGraw-Hill Publishing Company, 1990.

Wernerfelt, B. "A Resource-Based View of the Firm". *Strategic Managment Journal*, Vol. 5, pp. 171–181, 1984.

Williamson, O. E. *Markets and Hierarchies*. New York: Free Press, 1975.

Williamson, O. E. *The Economic Institutions of Capitalism*. New York: Free Press, 1985.

Winter, S. G. "Knowledge and Competence as Strategic Assets". In Teece, D. J., ed., *The Competitive Challenge: Strategies for Industrial Innovation and Renewal*. Cambridge, MA: Ballinger Publishing Company, 1987.

15

COMPETENCE-BASED COMPETITION AND THE EVOLUTION OF STRATEGIC CONFIGURATIONS

Stephen Tallman and David L. Atchison

INTRODUCTION

Existing studies of strategic groups do not provide a cohesive set of theoretical explanations and empirical findings for the observation that firms in an industry appear to employ strategies which fall into a limited number of configurations. Barney and Hoskisson (1990) provide a typical commentary on the shortcomings of strategic grouping studies. They show that while group studies rely on two basic assertions—that groups exist and that groups affect firm performance—neither of these central issues has been conclusively demonstrated. This essay examines the formation, persistence, and performance effects of strategic groups or configurations from a rent-seeking, competence-based perspective on business strategy to replace these assertions with conceptual reasoning based on empirical evidence.

Both Barney and Hoskisson (1990) and Thomas and Venkatraman (1988) argue that no theoretical justification for strategic groups exists outside of Industrial Organization (IO) theory. Then both sets of authors show that empirical studies done to date do not support predictions derived from IO theory. When the heterogeneity of performance within industries was established empirically (Hunt, 1972; Porter, 1979; Newman, 1978), contrary to IO expectations, industry sub-structures, or groups, were proposed as a device which could reconcile the industry structure—firm conduct—group performance (SCP) model of IO with this new evidence

(Caves and Porter, 1977). McGee and Thomas (1986), working within the SCP construct of IO, speculate that groups provide the necessary link to explain how performance differences in an industry might be related to factors other than firm size. This modified version of industrial organization economics suggests that performance variation within industries consists of performance homogeneity within groups of firms and heterogeneous performance results across groups. Studies have provided mixed support at best for inter-group performance differences (Thomas and Venkatraman, 1988). For instance, Cool and Schendel (1987, 1988) and Feigenbaum and Thomas (1990) test for risk-adjusted performance differences among groups in different industries both cross-sectionally and over time, and find little evidence of such difference. Because the determinative relationship of industry structure to firm performance is at the heart of IO theory, these and other (e.g., Johnson and Thomas, 1987; Frazier and Howell, 1983) empirical findings have reduced the credibility of the IO concept of structurally determined homogeneous groups.

Barney and Hoskisson (1990) and Johnson (1993) show that empirical methodologies designed to discover groupings of observations will always describe groupings, yet provide no measure of the validity or reliability of such findings. Empirically based models of strategic groupings (Galbraith and Schendel, 1983; Miller and Friesen, 1984) distinguish clusters of strategic configurations through multivariate analysis, but offer little conceptual justification for why the groupings of firms which they have identified might have formed. Describing this literature, Thomas and Venkatraman note that "...very little work has been done to explore the question of the formation of [strategic] groups, and more importantly the key determinants for the structure of strategic groups" (1988: 551). They also suggest that "If adequate theoretical reasoning can not be brought to bear [regarding] equifinality..." (1988: 548) of performance results, then studies should refocus on the resources of individual firms and drop groups as a meaningful construct.

Three major research questions are addressed from a new perspective in this paper:

- Why and how do strategic groups form?
- Why do groups persist?
- What are the performance implications of strategic groups to firms in an industry?

To begin to answer these questions, this paper proposes a model of how innovation and imitation can result in the evolution of strategic configurations under competitive conditions. A typology of firm-level competences is developed and applied to firms engaged in competitive interactions to suggest that unique competences play a critical role in shaping strategic configurations of firms and in creating sustained performance differences among firms. Finally, a case study of the personal computer industry is used to demonstrate the ability of the proposed model to explain the evolution of competition in that industry.

THE EVOLUTION OF STRATEGIC CONFIGURATIONS

This section argues that *firms in competitive situations tend to cluster their strategies in a limited number of configurations formed by alternating innovation and imitation of key competences*. In this process, firms are characterized as pursuing a variety of strategies in an ongoing search for economic quasi-rents to their unique competences. This effort results in performance differences among firms both within a common configurations of competences and across such configurations.

Strategic groups are defined here as collections of businesses which have similar strategic configurations; that is,

- they occupy similar product/market positions
- they are organized in similar manners
- they pursue the same economic rents with similar (although not identical) sets of resources.

Miller (1986) and Miller and Friesen (1984) argue that firm strategies are closely tied to firm structure and control systems and can be grouped in "strategic configurations", based on consistent modes of deploying resources. We extend the configurational model by proposing that the innovation or imitation of strategies requiring certain skills and resources drive the evolution of industry structure into groupings of firms with similar configurations of market position and competences. To distinguish the sets of firms described here from the "strategic groups" derived from IO theory, we will use the term "strategic configurations" to refer to sets of firms with similar market strategies, organizational structures, and competences.

In order to examine the interaction of market position, firm strategy, and organizational competences in generating persistent configurations, we first explain just what is meant here by "competences". While the resource-based view of the firm typically focuses on the rent-generating capabilities of truly idiosyncratic firm-level resources, the model of strategic configurations presented here suggests the existence of firm-specific competences and two additional competence types.

The most general type of competence is the Industry Competence (**IC**). ICs are defined as ways of conducting economic activity that are common to firms in an industry, but that are not freely available to other firms. Within the industry, these competences are observable and imitable by competitors, and therefore provide no rents in a competitive market (although they may generate rents when industry membership is limited). These competences fill the role of entry barriers described in IO, in that potential entrants must acquire the competences in order to compete in the industry. Although the competences may be available in the market (through hiring experienced individuals, licensing patents, buying plants, or acquiring existing firms), they can be expected to be priced to absorb all excess profits, making new entry costly, with no expectation of rent generation. Entry is rational only if an entrant can acquire the needed ICs and believes itself to also have unique firm-specific competences which will be rent producers in the industry.

A more narrowly distributed type of competence is the Strategy-Specific Competence (**SSC**), common to firms with a particular configuration and necessary to pursue the strategy which defines the group (Mascarenhas and Aaker, 1989; Mehra, 1990). Strategic configurations are defined by the market strategies and the SSCs of the firms in the configurations. Strategy-specific competences are those skills and resources necessary to pursue the particular strategy that conforms to the industry niche targeted by the firms with that configuration. For instance, Mascarenhas and Aaker (1989) describe the specialized drill rigs and technical skills required by different groups of firms within the oil-drilling industry as specific to each group and distinctly different across groups. In the way that ICs act as industry entry barriers, SSCs act as mobility barriers across groups. Although firms in the industry may be able to identify and potentially imitate these competences, the marginal value of doing so does not justify the risk and opportunity costs entailed for most firms. In this way, SSCs provide what Ghemawat (1986) calls contestable advantage. If the rents to the SSCs in any configuration grow too far above the industry norm, mobility into the configuration will take place until additional competition eliminates the rents. Ghemawat does suggest, however, that investment in contestable advantage is of considerable importance to competitive advantage.

The resource-based view of competition proposes that sustainable, as opposed to contestable, competitive advantage for a firm is dependent on its possession of idiosyncratic, rent-yielding, non-imitable, and non-substitutable resources. True Firm-Specific Resources—FSRs—are said to develop internally as the firm grows and operates (Penrose, 1959; Dierickx and Cool, 1989) or are purchased at below their eventual true market value by the exceptionally insightful or lucky firm (Barney, 1986). Rumelt (1984) describes FSRs as isolating mechanisms which provide protection for competitive advantage among superior performers. The major aspect of competitive isolation is the causal ambiguity of success. Reed and DeFillippi (1990) describe tacitness, or organizational embeddedness, complexity, and specificity as the key sources of causal ambiguity.

In keeping with our terminology, and to differentiate the dynamic aspect of competences from the static conceptualization of resources, we characterize the unique capabilities of the firm as Firm-Specific Competences (**FSCs**). FSCs are ways of acting or routines (Nelson and Winter, 1982) developed internally or acquired through special insights (which are themselves FSCs) at below true market value. FSCs are characteristic of the firm, closely related to its unique history, and as such are ambiguous and inimitable. Acting as isolating mechanisms, FSCs provide sustained, rather than contestable, competitive advantage. Where the firm's SSCs are directly related to *what* strategy the firm pursues, FSCs are more properly seen as related to *how* the firm pursues its market strategies; that is, whether it innovates or imitates, its procedures for acquiring resources, and its methods of interacting with its competitors and customers. Penrose (1959) says that advantage comes from better use of resources rather than inherently superior resources. This is the role of FSCs.

Innovation and Imitation: The Formation of Configurations

Figure 15.1 suggests how the different competence types interact with strategic decisions to affect the evolution of distinct configurations of strategies within an industry. In this section, the dynamics of innovative and imitative cycles in an industry are examined to show that strategic decision making under uncertainty and investment in differentiated competences can result in "strategic groups" of firms with common configurations and how these impact competitive interaction and performance differences.

Innovation

Schumpeter's model of entrepreneurial rents (1934) provides a useful starting point for examining the development of strategic configurations based on competences. The entrepreneurial cycle begins with an industry stuck in a "circular flow" of undifferentiated activity in which no businesses are earning profits in excess of a fair market return. In this stage of industry development, all competences would be classified as ICs, as no firms are earning rents through either contestable or sustainable advantage. Thus, undifferentiated competence bases can do little to support

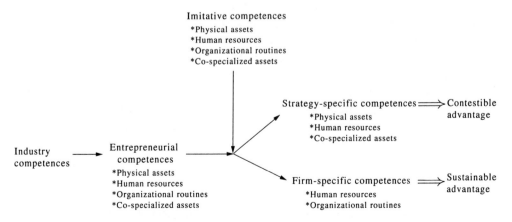

Fig. 15.1. Competence types and competitive advantage.

anything but undifferentiated strategies. At some point, though, new entrants or the managers of some existing businesses (entrepreneurs or innovators) will begin to try new strategies in search of improved performance. Whether through luck or exceptional market insight, some innovators will discover combinations of market demand and competences which generate supernormal performance.

The innovators may have combined external capabilities in a new way in an intentional effort to fill a perceived market opportunity (Schumpeter, 1934), or may have found a new way to apply capabilities already internal to the firm (Penrose, 1959). While Schumpeter focuses on the entrepreneur who brings together externally supplied resources and skills, modern resource-based theory suggests that product/market innovation often involves new applications of existing firm-specific, rent-yielding resources. In either case, industry renewal comes when *some* innovators find a unique match of potential firm- and strategy-specific competences with a market opportunity for a new product (or an industry need for a more efficient process and so forth) and begin to accumulate excess profits or entrepreneurial quasi-rents (Rumelt, 1987). The superior performance of such innovative businesses will provide the motivation for less entrepreneurial firms to undertake strategic change in imitation of success, and begin the process of strategic group formation.

Firm-level competences at this initial stage of innovation are described as "Entrepreneurial Competences" in Fig. 15.1. All the unique resources of the firm perhaps could be considered FSCs at this point. Competition surely will show some of these competences to provide only contestable advantage in the marketplace, but the degree of imitability of competences in the long run is not likely to be apparent in the first innovative stages of the industry. Therefore, both true FSCs and eventual SSCs are equally parts of the innovator's entrepreneurial competences. Figure 15.1 classifies rent-generating competences according to Barney's (1991) scheme of Physical, Human, and Organizational resource types as a means of maintaining a grounding in resource-based theory. That is, the firm may rely on unique hard assets, key people, or organizational routines to generate profits when competition is weak. Also, Fig. 15.1 identifies the existence of co-specialized assets (Teece, 1987). These are assets which do not provide advantage in themselves, but which permit the more effective exploitation of the FSCs. Possession of co-specialized assets often is important to the firm's ability to fully appropriate the rents due to its unique competences. Superior product design, for instance, usually cannot generate profits in the absence of complementary production facilities, distribution systems, and sales forces.

Imitation

Entrepreneurism is risky. Therefore, many managers avoid the uncertainty of strategic innovation (DiMaggio and Powell, 1983; Casson, 1982).

Institutional theory suggests that fear of uncertainty, combined with high returns to successful innovation, provides the mechanism which initiates strategic group formation. Innovators who are observed to succeed in the marketplace are assumed, whether through luck or skill, to have picked a product or process strategy which in some way fits an unfilled market need for a different or less costly product (Casson, 1982; Schumpeter, 1934). Schumpeter recognizes that the successful entrepreneur will be followed by imitators who attempt to appropriate some of the profits accruing to the entrepreneur before they are completely eroded. Imitation of market position strategies often is relatively simple, owing to the observable nature of market position decisions made by a firm.

Imitation of the internal competence strategy of the innovator, however, is constrained by the indefinite nature of core competencies (Rumelt, 1984) and by the slow diffusion of new assets into the imitator's pool of resources (Dierickx and Cool, 1989). Causal ambiguity, resulting from the organizational embeddedness and diffuse nature of organizational processes, makes determination of the competence basis for performance success problematic (Reed and deFillippi, 1990; Rumelt, 1984). So, while new products or lower prices may be apparent, the strategic reasoning that led to the changes, the technological capabilities which made them possible, and the skills of the people who executed the new strategy are likely to be much more difficult to define and copy. Imitators apply their own competencies to recognized market segments. Attempts at competence imitation, however, will demonstrate which of the innovator's competences result in sustainable advantage (FSCs) and which eventually are imitable (SSCs). When imitated, SSCs provide the necessary means for firms to enter into a new configuration while FSCs maintain the isolation of the first-mover and generate profits. In this way, both competence types contribute to the further development of stable configurations.

Competence Strategies and the Persistence of Strategic Configurations

Sustainable Advantage, Performance, and Competences

Ghemawat (1986) suggests that many innovations in product, process, and market are imitated easily, but that some innovators may retain their competitive advantage and superior performance levels for extended periods. Sustained advantage occurs for two reasons. First, a period of delay occurs as each potential competitor evaluates the potential rewards and risks of the new configuration. Second, resource-based models (Wernerfelt, 1984; Dierickx and Cool, 1989) maintain that a successful market position strategy must have an appropriate resource strategy associated with it to generate sustained above normal performance. While market strategies, as discussed above, are apparent to potential imitators, resource-based models focus on the difficulty of identifying and imitating critical resource positions (Barney, 1991; Dierickx and Cool, 1989; Reed and DeFillippi, 1990). Imitators are forced to operate during a period of adjustment while their resources—competences in our model—are not exactly matched to their market strategy, a condition likely to limit performance.

Early followers which imitate the SSCs of a successful strategy should appropriate some of the rents that accrue to contestable advantage. As indicated in Fig. 15.1, such competences are likely to be the more easily identified and copied or acquired physical and human resources or co-specialized assets. Indeed, in a situation in which an early follower possesses critical co-specialized assets (Teece, 1987), or has superior firm-specific routines or other competences, this superiority may overcome first-mover advantages and permit the close follower to supplant the innovator as the focal firm of the group. In any case, a small group of early entrants should establish the dominant configuration of market and competence strategies, accrue contestable rents, and become the entrenched core of the group. Continued imitation will eventually eliminate any excess profits from the once-unique market position or imitable SSCs. As the configurational cluster gets larger, only firms with truly idiosyncratic FSCs will continue to earn an economic profit. As noted in Fig. 15.1, these competences are most likely to be complex human capabilities and organizational processes that are tacit, deeply embedded, and essentially inimitable. These FSCs will provide intra-configurational differences in performance levels even as SSCs delineate differences in performance across strategic configurations.

Strategy-Specific Investment and Limits to Mobility

Resource-based strategy models (Wernerfelt, 1984) suggest that firms must invest in certain SSRs in order to support a product/market strategy at a minimum level. Reed and DeFillippi (1990) argue that increasing levels of competition will erode competitive advantage despite isolating mechanisms unless the firm continually reinvests in its resource base. Similarly, in this model both innovator and imitator businesses can be expected to invest in building additional competences to improve their competitiveness within the particular strategy. Firms make a variety of investments, but investment in competences to enhance efficiency or refine competitive advantage **for a given market position** can be considered strategy-specific investment. Strategy-Specific Investment (**SSI**) adds significant value in a particular strategic context, but has much lower value in a second-best use (i.e., in another strategic configuration). SSI is investment in acquiring or creating SSCs, the resources which permit or enhance competitiveness under a particular strategic configuration but which are shared by the firms within that configuration. As previously stated, these competences act in a manner similar to the IO concept of group- level mobility barriers by making entry more expensive and more uncertain of providing positive returns.

Firms may use SSI to refine their firm-specific competences as well, enhancing their isolating characteristics in one context at the cost of reducing their generalizability to an alternative configuration.

SSI is essential to sustaining advantage and performance (for the first mover) or overcoming isolating mechanisms (for the innovators) in the face of increasing competition under the competence-based model of competition. However, when firms invest in SSCs in order to improve their efficiency in a particular configuration, they increase commitment to their chosen strategic configuration and create their own limitations on inter-group mobility. Mobility barriers between configurations therefore need not be the result of consciously directed collaborative activity by group members. Rather, most limitations on mobility reduce to issues of capital requirements and uncertainty of returns to the new strategy (Rumelt, 1987). As firms invest ever more in strategy-specific competences, the cost to them of changing to an alternative strategic configuration becomes ever greater. Continuing in an efficient strategy may only generate average returns. However, switching to an alternative strategy will entail new SSI and will also result in opportunity costs due to inefficiencies in applying new resources in an unfamiliar strategy. In addition, direct competition with a new set of competitors while following an unfamiliar strategy raises the risks of strategic change. The same risk avoidance that limits the number of truly innovative strategies during the entrepreneurial stage also limits movement into new configurations.

SSI raises the capital requirements for adopting a configuration, as a new entrant must invest to develop the appropriate pool of strategy-specific competences and must develop its idiosyncratic capabilities if it is to attain superior performance (Mascarenhas and Aaker, 1989, make an analogous argument for investments in physical resources). SSI by firms with a particular configuration therefore acts to make new entry both more costly and more risky for entrants, and should act to deter late entrants. At the same time, SSI raises the opportunity cost of exit by creating a situation where investments in superior competences specific to the configuration have little value with a different strategy. Therefore, moving *out* of the group will also be deterred—a condition which makes potential movement to other groups even more difficult. However, reduced mobility does not necessarily imply that mobility barriers have been built intentionally, only that mobility somehow becomes constrained.

Thus, when businesses spend on SSI to improve their competitiveness within a strategic configuration in order to gain or to protect competitive advantage against their closest competitors, they are likely to reduce their strategic flexibility (Sanchez, 1993). Porter (1980) states that movement from one strategic configuration to another—e.g., Cost Leader to Product Differentiator—is difficult and very costly. The argument presented here suggests a similar outcome for the competence-based perspective.

CONFIGURATIONS AND PERFORMANCE IN CONTEXT: AN EXAMPLE

The perspective on the formation of strategic configurations developed here is intended to accommodate a variety of specific industry contexts. In this section, the model is applied in the context of a dynamic industry to demonstrate its robustness even under rapidly changing circumstances. The model presented here suggests that the development of strategic configurations in changing contexts leads to changing interactions among firms and in turn to different combinations of active strategic configurations in an industry at different times. These contextual changes may be associated with major environmental changes which open new possibilities for innovation, or with the cumulative effects of more incremental changes in a more or less uniform environment. This section looks at strategic configurations in the context of the life cycle development of the U.S. personal computer industry in the 1970s and 1980s to demonstrate the ability of the model to explain the evolution of strategies in a highly dynamic industry. To facilitate the discussion of the stages in that industry's development, Fig. 15.2 diagrams the evolution of strategic configurations in that industry through its innovation, entrepreneurial, growth, shakeout, and maturity stages.

The Innovation and Entrepreneurial Contexts

In the innovation and early entrepreneurial stages of a new product market, innovators focus on perceived market opportunities. The specific competences that will be rent generators cannot be positively identified until they have been applied successfully in the marketplace (Barney, 1991). During the early innovation phase of the lifecycle of a new technology, the highly uncertain response of the market to any innovation will result in a high rate of new strategy introduction and a relatively low rate of imitation. In a developing industry, firms will be small, cospecialized assets will be limited[1], organizational competences will be in early stages of development, and most firms will rely on the skills of individuals or small groups for key technological developments because organizational processes for coordinating diffuse capabilities will not be developed. In this early stage, competitive success does not typically depend on efficiency as much as on strategic flexibility. As a result, SSI will be limited. Strategic configurations will include small numbers of firms and will be transient, with limited commonality of market position, strategies, and competences as firms try alternative technologies and strategies, but make only low levels of commitment to specific resources and capabilities.

The personal computer (PC) industry provides a recent example of how industry structure might evolve as new technology becomes established and firms move into the new market. In the early innovation stage of this

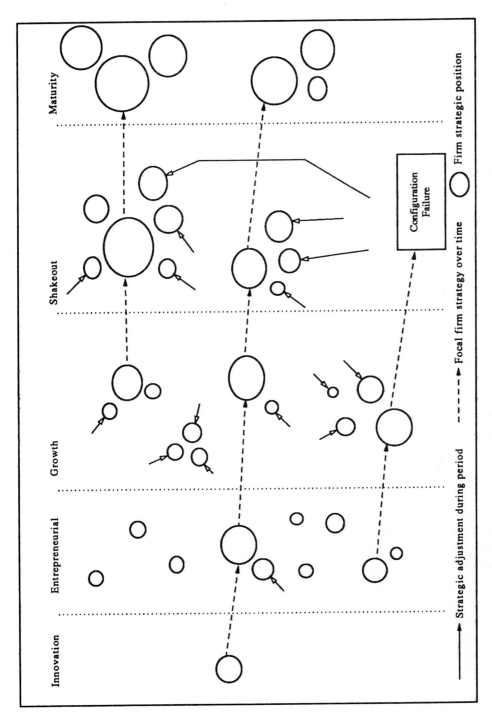

Fig. 15.2. The evolution of strategic configurations in an industry context.

industry, before the 1981 entry of IBM's version of the PC, the proliferation of incompatible standards fragmented the personal computer industry. The dawn of the "PC Age" dates from the first commercially available general purpose computer "kit" in 1975. The cover story of the January, 1975 issue of Popular Electronics detailed the design of the Altair 8800, a functional personal computer suitable for assembly by hobbyists. The Altair, made by MIPS, a company in Albuquerque, New Mexico, was based on a new generation of microprocessor manufactured by Intel, the 8008. Priced at $395.00 and consisting of little more than a collection of circuit boards and memory chips, the Altair 8800 was judged "an absolute, runaway, overnight, insane success," with sales greatly exceeding expectations (Freiberger and Swaine, 1984: 37). While the availability of kit computers such as the Altair was a breakthrough which enabled computer enthusiasts to pursue their interests, a practical personal computer for less technically adept users had yet to be realized. There was essentially no prewritten commercial software for the Altair, so the proud owners of newly assembled computers had to write programs in an arcane low level programming language to accomplish even simple calculations. The next significant development in the early history of the industry was the invention of a high level programming language with a more meaningful, intuitive structure that would enable users to more easily create programs on their computers. Two young computer entrepreneurs, Paul Allen and Bill Gates, offered MIPS a high level language called BASIC designed to run on the Altair, providing the first sale for a company destined to become a major influence in the microcomputing industry—Micro-Soft as it was then called (Freiberger and Swaine, 1984: 40; Manes and Andrews, 1993: 74).

While the Altair was the first commercially available personal computer, it was not long before imitators appeared on the scene. By early 1976, other manufacturers were dogging MIPS and coming up with alternative designs that had both hardware and software technologies which were incompatible with the Altair. Personal computers based on microprocessors made by Motorola and Zilog appeared. In addition to their differences in microprocessors, these new models had "busses" (a frame of "slots" for holding and electronically connecting computer components) that were incompatible with the Altair (Freiberger and Swaine, 1984: 49). In effect, each computer maker defined a standard applicable only to their specific machine that, as a consequence, precluded any potential synergies in software creation and impeded the further advancement of the industry.

Many of the early microcomputer makers, such as Sphere, Southwest Technical Products, Commodore, and even MIPS itself, would later find themselves out of business at least in part due to their early adoption of technologies that eventually proved to be inadequate in the face of increasing competition. Arthur (1988) has defined notions of technological "lock-in" and path dependent innovation that seem to explain the causes of the mortality of some of these early computer manufacturers. In the model presented here, these firms made investments in strategy- and technology-specific competences which provided some early competitive advantages, but which made successful adaptation to later technological changes difficult or impossible.

Rise of the First Industry Standards

The next important development in the personal computer industry centers around the creation of technical standards. In the absence of some standard hardware and operating system configuration, the personal computer industry continued to be fragmented into small, "proprietary" market segments, too small to support efficient manufacturing capacity or software development. Flamm (1988: 256) asserts that the economic importance of standards flows from the fact that "the cost or benefit of producing or using a [computer] depends on the number of other users." For example, when the cost of writing a software program can be spread over a large base of computer users who can run the program on their machines, the share of the program development costs which must be charged to each user decreases. The development of a standard operating system followed from what was perhaps the first professionally organized personal computer company, IMSAI Manufacturing, the creation of Bill Millard, a former IBM salesman. In contrast to other personal computer pioneers, Millard was not focused on the technological aspects of computing. Rather, the IMSAI organization was created to sell a hardware product, floppy disk drives. Floppy disk drives were a key component of the early personal computers. "What [IMSAI] needed was a way to sell floppy-disk drives. CP/M is what did it" (Freiberger and Swaine, 1984: 68). The CP/M operating system that helped IMSAI to sell floppy disk drives became one of the first successful standards in the personal computer industry. Running under CP/M, floppy disk drives provided such efficient, low cost information storage that virtually all computer manufacturers began to design their systems for standardized floppy disk operating systems. Moreover, CP/M had the advantage of incorporating a high level programming language, BASIC-E, with which users could write their own applications programs. A final contributory factor in the standardization of personal computers on the CP/M operating system was the availability of a more or less user-friendly wordprocessing program, WordStar, that ran on CP/M compatible machines (Manes and Andrews, 1993: 156). CP/M was thus the first true standard in the personal computer industry and demonstrated some of the advantages that would later be realized when operating systems converged to a few standardized types.

Development of Improved Functionality

Another important event in the early history of the PC industry was the introduction of the Apple II computer in 1977. Apple computers were unique in a number of critical ways. The company itself was professionally managed, with Mike Markkula providing business experience drawn from his previous employment with Fairchild Semiconductors and Intel. It also had two innovative young computer designers, Steve Jobs and Steve Wozniak. At least part of the early success of Apple was due to their innovative approach to improving floppy disk storage. Early disk storage techniques were derived from IBM's mainframe computer technology. This technology required complicated circuitry to synchronize the writing of data to the disk. Wozniak invented an alternative approach, eliminating the complex, expensive circuitry while enhancing reliability (Freiberger and Swaine, 1984: 226). Even more important, Apple provided connectivity for printers and modems, thereby offering novice users greater utility from their Apple II's than was available from other computers.

Another contributory factor to Apple's success was the invention of the first commercially available spreadsheet, VisiCalc, by Dan Bricklin in 1979. VisiCalc, written for the Apple operating system, was the first personal computer application software that allowed computer users to use the analytical power of the personal computer without having to write the application program themselves. Until Bricklin's pioneering effort, most applications were either written by computer owners for their own use, or were simple games and utilities (short programs to make computers easier to use). VisiCalc in the Apple environment and WordStar in the CP/M operating environment opened a whole new era of functionality that led to the development of the personal computer software industry. With its ease of use following from its fully assembled status, peripheral support, and availability of commercial application programs like VisiCalc, the Apple II was to become the first personal computer to gain wide acceptance in the marketplace. With that, the personal computer finally evolved from a technological curiosity to a useful tool. Operating systems such as Apple's proprietary system and CP/M appear to have acted as strategy-specific competences. They provided temporary competitive advantages, but were fairly transparent and market related. As such, they provided only contestable advantages which were eventually matched or superseded, rather than the sustained advantage which might be expected from organizational routines for strategic activities such as product development.

By 1980 Apple was the leading firm among a number of firms offering different combinations of hardware and operating systems. Customers were usually technologically sophisticated and were attracted to different personal computers for their unique combinations of technologies. Soon, however, the industry began to move into a phase of converging technology that led to more rapid growth. In 1981, IBM entered this market with the introduction of the IBM PC. While some strategic and technological convergence had occurred prior to the entry of IBM, the introduction of the

IBM PC was to be a watershed event that precipitated a prolonged period of rapid growth for the personal computer industry.

Growth and Shakeout

Most industries appear to move from a stage of tentative technological and strategic trials into a growth phase of consolidating technologies, rapid entry, market growth, and larger, more distinct strategic configurations of firms. The model developed here suggests that firms in specific configurations of market positions, competences, and strategies should achieve superior performance (probably in the form of increasing share) and should begin to attract serious imitators. Typically, technology converges rapidly on successful models, and differentiation becomes based on aspects of the business other than technology or market position. In this case, the number of groups compared to the number of competitors should drop. Performance differences should be greater within than between configurations, because SSI has not yet reached significant levels. Those configurations with the weakest performance will disappear, but firms with these configurations may migrate to other strategies rather than exit or fail. Again, the relatively low level of SSI makes strategic repositioning more feasible at this stage.

Eventually, a growth period will end in a shakeout as supply overshoots demand, the weaker firms fail, and the industry makes the transition into maturity. The shakeout will result not only in the further disappearance of non-viable configurations, but is also likely to witness outright firm failures within weak configurations and on the margins of surviving configurations (see Fig. 15.2). In the shakeout stage, failure results from the impact of a sudden drop in or slowing of demand on (1) inadequately funded new entrants and (2) firms trying to close large investment-intensive gaps between existing competences and those needed to pursue viable market strategies.

To continue the example of the personal computer industry, the watershed entry of IBM into the personal computer when it was poised for rapid growth did not completely surprise incumbent firms. Market-leading Apple had been preparing for increased competition by developing the Lisa and Macintosh computer lines (Freiberger and Swaine, 1984: 240). While the Lisa line of computers later proved to be a failure, the Macintosh line became the most successful response of the existing personal computer manufacturers to IBM's prospective entry. The Macintosh incorporated a revolutionary user interface modeled on the graphical interface invented at the Xerox PARC research center where Wozniak and Jobs had worked prior to starting Apple. This graphical interface greatly improved the ease of use of the Macintosh relative to any other computer, including the forthcoming IBM PC. The use of a graphic user interface (GUI) operating system provided Apple with a significant advantage for some time, but also generated rapid efforts by competitors to imitate this advantage. In our schema of competences, GUI acted as an SSC, providing a contestable advantage for the Apple configuration, but one which (with Windows, OS/2, etc.) has evolved into an industry standard. However, Apple's originality and keen sense of what constitutes a "user friendly" personal computer can be seen as typical of the organizationally embedded competences which are true FSCs.

The growth and subsequent shakeout in personal computers following the entry of IBM is described in Bauerschmidt and Chrisman (1993) and Atchison and Tallman (1994). They date the genesis of IBM compatible personal computing to 1981. IBM's introduction of its first PC was so successful that is established a de facto standard that served as a base for subsequent industry evolution. The perceived expertise and market power of IBM helped the PC to dominate the market quickly, but its entry was closely followed by a host of imitators, typically small "IBM clone" manufacturers. The "clone problem"—i.e., other manufacturers imitating the IBM standard and undercutting IBM's price structure—dogged IBM in subsequent years and followed naturally from IBM's market entry strategy.

IBM delayed entry into the personal computer industry until it had been proven viable by Apple. In effect, IBM played catch-up to the smaller, upstart firm. In an effort to speed the introduction of its PC, IBM elected to depart from its traditional approach of maintaining direct control over all aspects of system development (Freiberger and Swaine, 1984: 273). For the first time, IBM relied on external suppliers and developers for vital parts of their new PC—without obtaining exclusive rights to the parts. IBM used widely available "off the shelf" components.

While IBM was making this critical decision, another firm, now called Microsoft, was experiencing a turning point of its own. Microsoft chairman Bill Gates had allowed software development in his firm to specialize in programs compatible with Intel microprocessors. Market-leading Apple adopted Motorola microprocessors intentionally so that Microsoft programs could *not* run on Apple's machines. When IBM licensed the Intel family of microprocessors as the "engine" for its new PC (initially the 8088), they contracted with Microsoft to supply the operating system (MS-DOS) and high level programming languages for their new PC system.[2] IBM also contracted out the creation of a variety of application programs, emulating one of the decisions by Apple that led to the ascendance of its computers: the ready availability of a range of applications programs.

In retrospect, it is interesting to recall that many industry observers believed that IBM had blundered badly by adopting Microsoft's new operating system rather than the "industry standard" CP/M (Manes and Andrews, 1993: 193). However, the strategy of contracting out application software soon blossomed, and MS-DOS rapidly displaced CP/M as the preferred personal computing environment and attracted the support of the majority of new hardware makers and applications programmers. The four-way alliance among IBM, Intel, Microsoft, and application suppliers thus opened the door for clone competitors to adopt a non-proprietary micro-computing standard supported by the largest computing firm in the world.

Another departure from the traditional IBM strategy of maintaining total control over its products was the decision to sell the new PC through a non-traditional channel of distribution. Rather than rely on its mainframe sales force, IBM elected to have the PC distributed by an authorized agent—the ComputerLand stores founded by Bill Millard, formerly of IMSAI (Freiberger and Swaine, 1984: 278).

From this situation evolved a dramatic variation in strategies with market leader IBM and the "clone" manufacturers adopting the same MS/DOS standard, while Apple continued to pursue a wholly different approach. IBM's open design strategy established a specific competence requirement for entry into the various IBM-related strategic configurations, but also quickly eliminated any rents to be gained from the open-design technology. IBM and the clones did differ in their strategies and market positions. IBM emphasized total solutions and support for business computing needs, while the clones generally concentrated on economical hardware solutions with limited service support. Further strategic differentiation occurred among the clone manufactures with a minority group adopting strategies based on besting IBM in terms of hardware performance (e.g., Compaq). Of course, Apple survived during this phase with its own unique vision of the market focused on ease of use resulting from their proprietary graphical interface.

Four years after the entry of IBM, the personal computer industry had grown to include 345 firms and had coalesced into six distinct strategic configurations (Bauerschmidt and Chrisman, 1993). The rapid growth of the industry resulted from the low overall density of firms compared with the large demand capacity of the developing market. The limited diversity of strategic configurations was maintained by the effects of adaptation by firms entering the industry as low overhead, low price assemblers, but then moving to copy existing broad strategies which permitted rent accumulation from unique distribution, marketing, and packaging concepts.

One notable event in the growth phase of the industry was the emergence of a software industry as a supporting segment of the overall personal computer industry. This emergence was, in part, a result of advances in processor technology (16-bit processing) coincident with the introduction of the IBM PC. This advance supported the creation of more complex and more useful software (Manes and Andrews, 1993: 191). Bauerschmidt and Chrisman's (1993) analysis suggests that as early as 1985, producers of networking and software products or high end system software had become numerous and distinct enough to have coalesced into strategic configurations of their own. Bauerschmidt and Chrisman further suggest that configurations which in 1985 combined hardware manufacturing with a software emphasis had, by 1989, come to concentrate solely on the software aspect of their business. The combined hardware/software configuration subsequently dropped out of this analysis of hardware manufacturing (Bauerschmidt and Chrisman, 1993). The percentage of personal computer manufacturers that also wrote software declined from 30.4 in 1985 to 14.7 in 1989, while the percentage of full line integrated producers went from 100% to 88.2% (Bauerschmidt and Chrisman, 1993). The clear inference is that, by 1989, network and software programming had become a related but large and distinct industry in its own right, an immense achievement given that it came into existence only nine years earlier.

Another interesting characteristic of the growth stage was that channels of distribution became more important to competitive advantage and became a defining characteristic of strategic configurations as the personal computer became a retail product. Earlier computers had been sold most often through mail order and electronic/hobbyist stores. Apple pioneered the creation of a specialized dealer network of computer stores to provide after-sales support for Apple products. These authorized distributors superseded the hobbyist "computer club" as a source of information on computing. When IBM elected to follow Apple's lead in setting up a network of authorized dealers, possession of this type of distribution system became a competence which clone makers were forced to meet if their products were to be viewed as comparable to IBM PCs. This development instigated competition among computer makers to acquire display space with established computer retail stores. Many of the weaker clone manufacturers were unable to set up adequate dealer networks and were squeezed out of the retail market. Others, such as Compaq, not only competed successfully with IBM for distributors, but often bested IBM in technological performance.

The lack of adequate access to channels of distribution for all clone makers was a contributing factor to a perception of two tiers of quality among IBM compatible computers—with "high quality" products being sold through a trained dealer network and "low quality" systems being available only through other channels such as mail order. However, the rise of quality mail-order firms such as Dell Computers began to blur this distinction by the late 1980's. Mail-order firms were able to offer toll free telephone support, money back guarantees, and on site service as early as 1986. The rise of high quality mail-order computer makers began to increase the competitive pressure on firms using dealer networks and contributed to a major shakeout in the industry. The resulting decrease in perceived quality differentiation undercut the quality image that IBM tried to project through their advertisements touting that "[no information system executive] ever got fired for buying [premium quality] IBM PC's". In this development, competences which a firm developed to serve a specific market need were shown to be contestable, to attract imitators, and to become defining characteristics of configurations rather than rent-generators for a single innovative firm.

By 1985 the rate of industry growth in the microcomputer industry "had begun to slow", both in terms of units sold and total revenues, and the shakeout period had begun (Bauerschmidt and Chrisman, 1993: 64). Bauerschmidt and Chrisman suggest that strategic adaptation had visible effects during the shakeout period. They note that incremental adaptation by firms, evidenced by changes in product lines, continued over the full time period 1985–1989. In their analysis, the number of viable strategic groups identified in the personal computing industry decreased from six in 1985 to four in 1989. Strategic migration, indicated by the movement from one strategic group to another, was also common during the shakeout period, with 44% of the surviving firms adopting radically new strategies. Migration patterns also were consistent, with firms from a given non-viable group tending to move to the same new configuration. The high mortality of the shakeout period is reflected in the fact that of the 345 firms in the personal computer industry in 1985, fewer than one in three was still in existence by 1989 (Bauerschmidt and Chrisman, 1993: 71), the year which is asserted to mark the transition of the industry into maturity.

Bauerschmidt and Chrisman also note that new firms continued to enter the industry during this period (most in the low-price assembler configuration) so that the total number of firms actually was larger in 1989 than in 1985. However, the number of long-term viable competitors was much reduced, and many of the new entrants failed quickly. In general, Bauerschmict and Chrisman found that narrow product scope (possibly implying a lack of co-specialized resources) was associated with failure. The broadest scope firms in each group tended to survive, and to stay with their strategy, while medium product scope firms tended to survive, but to change groups more often. This finding lends clear support to our argument that a higher level of strategy-specific investment reduces mobility. It also suggests that possession of significant industry competences facilitates repositioning to new configurations and thus should be associated with survival.

The Mature Context

As an industry comes out of shakeout, strategists expect consolidation around a few dominant strategies and a move toward price-based competition. In our model of configurational evolution, the transition to maturity suggests the concentration of strategic configurations into a small number of clearly identifiable strategies and less movement between configurations. Consolidation of firms around a small number of "proven" strategies in the mature phase of an industry also implies that the proportion of imitative strategies will increase. This shift also suggests that companies which are more efficient in the application of their resources will begin to dominate. However, efficiency is typically gained by investment in strategy specific competences, reducing the flexibility of a firm by raising the costs for it to change to a new strategy. Thus, the transition to industry maturity is marked by an increase in numbers and intensity of *apparent* mobility barriers.

Anecdotal evidence for maturity in the personal computer industry can be drawn from the recent comments of two of its most influential executives, Louis Gerstner, Chairman of IBM, and Bill Gates of Microsoft. In reply to a reporter's question about his recipe for an IBM comeback, Gerstner replied, "The last thing IBM needs now is a vision," implying that the nuts and bolts of running a business should take precedence over innovation (Lavin, 1993). Likewise Gates commented, "Being a visionary is trivial" (Lavin, 1993). These comments imply that the personal computer industry now has moved beyond the period when innovation confers significant advantage and has entered a period when incremental improvements in efficiency provide any performance advantages accruing to an established strategic configuration.

A technical sign of the increasing maturity in the personal computer indus-try is the continuing improvement of user interfaces. IBM promotes its OS/2 operating system, Microsoft continues to develop Windows, Unix operating systems support X-Windows and Motif, all of which are GUIs resembling the acclaimed Apple user interface (Divorak, 1993). The convergence of user interfaces toward the graphical computing environment suggests that soft-ware strategies centered on the more processor-efficient—but less user-friendly—command line interface has become strategically unviable.

The convergence in user interface also has led to the erosion of Apple's one time FSC—its graphical interface and superior ease of use. The increasing parity in ease of use between Apple and IBM compatible computers is progressively eliminating the premium that computer buyers are willing to pay for Apple's premier line of computers, the Macintosh. In 1990 the popular Mac SE/30 listed at $5569.00 in its standard configuration, "expensive" in the minds of computer journalists (Joch, Yager and Thompson, 1991). By mid 1991 the same computer listed for only $3896.00 (Joch, Yager and Thompson, 1991). While Apple retained a superior GUI in 1991, it was no longer able to ignore advances in IBM compatibles. Advances in their GUI technology and faster development of new Apple machines forced Apple to drop prices much faster than it had done traditionally.

Another notable strategy convergence ongoing in the PC industry is in channels of distribution. While "premium" quality manufactures such as IBM and Compaq resisted the adoption of efficient mail-order distribution strategies for fear of tarnishing their quality images, the intense price competition of other clone makers has forced their hands. The increasing standardization of both hardware and software, in conjunction with the growing knowledgeability of computer users, decreased the customer's perceived value of specialized support services available from authorized dealerships. Direct mail-order sales have become, therefore, a key element of Compaq's strategy to take the lead from a troubled IBM in the 1990's

(Fitzgerald, 1993). By mid-1993 such premium line manufacturers as IBM, Digital, NEC and Compaq advertised mail order service in a wide variety of computer oriented magazines. Apple likewise "dramatically altered its sales and distribution channels" by strengthening corporate sales and moving to mass market retailers as opposed to specialized dealers (Lach, 1993). It appears that "proprietary" channels of distribution may be losing their impact as strategy-specific competences, although the larger firms may be able to retain a level of variety in distribution outlets unavailable to smaller or new-entry firms for some time.

Our model further suggests that efforts at coordinating strategies, the use of joint ventures, and even outright collusion will increase among firms in a mature context. Coordination to reduce competition (Pfeffer and Nowak, 1976) is most likely when competitive interactions are stable and small efficiency gains are the source of gains in performance. In fact, coordination has become an increasingly prominent issue in the PC industry. Networking (connecting many different types of computers) has induced a proliferation of alliances, joint ventures, and industry standard-setting organizations. Apple and IBM have formed an alliance to share networking technology (Apple-IBM..., 1991), while Apple is simultaneously working on improved Apple/Unix interfacing (Bozman, 1993) and mainframe links (Keenan and Li, 1991). Other manufacturers and software suppliers are teaming up to challenge Apple's dominance in desktop publishing (Corcoran, 1993).

Environmental changes in a mature industry (regulation, deregulation, foreign competition, etc.) may result in consistent adjustments by firms within strategic configurations, such that existing configurations remain essentially intact, but adopt some changes in market position, competences, and strategies. Only major, competence-destroying change (Tushman and Anderson, 1986) can destroy the configuration structure, moving the industry back to the fluid structure of the entrepreneurial context. Flamm (1988: 236) notes that in the case of our industry example, "incessant, rapid advance of computer technology was to upset the apparent balance [between competing technologies]" during the growth stage. However, most of these technological advances were incremental in nature, maintaining backward compatibility with the growing user base. Many firms were able to adapt their strategies incrementally, for example, to compensate for technological evolution in processor capacity. As configurations increasingly consolidate today, strategies show no evidence of returning to the fluidity of the 1970s.

As product innovation becomes an issue of refinement rather than revolution, efficiencies in use of time, human skills, and capital investment increasingly become important. While Bauerschmidt and Chrisman's study seems to support the consolidation predicted here at the end of the shakeout period, they do not follow the PC industry beyond 1989. As our discussion shows, technical improvements based on incorporating the latest microprocessors and software capabilities have been important. Small firms which try to incorporate these changes come and go frequently. Among established firms, technical equivalency has become essential, and today's competition increasingly is focused on distribution and service, with the low-cost option of mail-order distribution outpacing computer stores. Brand-dedicated retail outlets are nearly extinct.

Since product differentiation in personal computers is based on widely available chips and software packages, and service support can be handled through widely available toll-free telephone support, the clones can now concentrate on improving their competences in efficiency, reliability, and persuading potential customers of their survivability. Apple maintains its unique systems-based niche but is now seeking compatibility with the IBM world. By holding on to its relatively high prices IBM fell to a much less dominant position. Now IBM, too, is aggressively offering lower-price models. Established firms thus appear now to be trying to compete by being better at a relatively fixed strategy (rather than by changing strategies often), but growing interdependencies in microprocessors and software and increasing needs for cooperation among firms, both within and between configurations, seem to be moving the industry toward further blurring of boundaries and ever greater consolidation of strategic configurations.

CONCLUSIONS

The evolutionary model presented here suggests that strategic groups are indeed real, in the sense that competitive forces will produce a few innovators and many imitators in any industry, thereby creating ad hoc groupings of firms pursuing similar strategic configurations. These groups arise from distinct, but interacting, approaches to an uncertain world and are the unintended consequences of competition under uncertainty. Some collusion, joint venture formation, or networking may well be observed between firms in a group in response to resource dependencies (DiMaggio and Powell, 1983; Pfeffer and Nowak, 1976). However, it is not necessary to conclude from this that industry groups are super-firm organizations with common objectives organized intentionally to compete with other groups. Indeed, competition for resources and rents may well be greater between the similar firms within strategic configurations than across the market and resource gaps between configurations.

The evolutionary model addresses a number of the issues raised by Hatten and Hatten (1987), Thomas and Venkatraman (1988), and Barney and Hoskisson (1990) about the meanings of groups and group studies. Does it also provide improved insight on the three questions raised in the introduction?

Why and How do Groups Form?

Groups form in part as the result of differences in strategic behavior and in endowments of specialized resources. Innovative and imitative strategies move firms to cluster in limited numbers of strategic configurations. Market strategies are reinforced by possession or acquisition of strategy specific resources which make a configuration viable and efficient.

Why do Groups Persist?

The evolutionary model of groups suggests that firms can differ on market position strategy, on their propensity to take risks (innovate) or not (imitate), and in their resource bases at several levels. Investments in SSCs and FSCs build firms which are specialized to a single configuration, enhancing efficiency but reducing flexibility. The considerable differences in potential rents between the specialized strategy and any alternative results in persistence of configurations. Strategy specific investments gradually increase the differences between firms pursuing different strategic configurations—belonging to different groups.

How do Groups Relate to the Success or Failure of Firms?

Success and failure are related to firms' processes for creating strategy, to their market positions, and to the resource investments they make. Success in a particular configuration and context is related to investment in strategy specific resources, whether contestable (group-specific) or sustainable (firm-specific). However, firms face the paradox that overinvestment in efficiency through specialized resources creates the danger of strategic inflexibility in the face of major exogeneous environmental change. So, SSI may generate short-term success but lead to long-term complacency and ultimate failure.

Our extensive case example of the personal computer industry's development over two decades supports the potential value of the conceptual model. We see a new industry populated by a variety of technologies, visions of market niches, and abilities converging into a set of distinct groups in the 1980s. Then, after a market induced shakeout, we see a rapidly maturing industry in the 1990s. Today's PC makers are actively reducing technological barriers while competing on efficiency issues such as distribution and price. Group formation, strategic convergence, and the evolution of resource bases in tandem with market strategies are observable. The reduction of price differentials between firms, even as price competition heats up in the industry suggests that our prediction of the switch of competitive advantage from innovative ideas to efficient execution holds in the PC industry.

The conclusion from these arguments is that an evolutionary perspective on strategic groups provides a rich source of insight on certain of the fundamental questions posed by Rumelt, Schendel, and Teece (1990). While this model can benefit from refinement and empirical testing of predicted outcomes, it does show that strategic groups are a viable construct in a model where competition is directed by managerial decision-making under uncertainty rather than determined by industry conditions.

NOTES

1. Extensive networks of assets, whether plants, distribution networks, or marketing skills, take time to develop.
2. In the software industry, MS-DOS seems to represent a tangible FSC, due to strong copyright protection and strict enforcement and aggressive marketing by Microsoft.

REFERENCES

Apple-IBM Update: Computer Makers Finalize Alliance, Outline Joint Efforts; Apple Introduces Portables, High-End Workstations". *Editor and Publisher*, Vol. 124(44), p. 28, 1991.

Arthur, W. B. "Self-Reinforcing Mechanisms in Economics". In Anderson, Arrow, and Pines, eds., *The Economy as an Evolving Complex System*. New York: Addison-Wesley, 1988.

Atchison, D. L. and Tallman, S. B. "Exploring the Formation and Stability of Strategic Groups: A Synthesis of Population Ecology and Strategy Group Theory. Paper Presented at the 1994 Western Academy of Management Conference, 1994.

Barney, J. B. "Strategic Factor Markets: Expectations, Luck, and Business Strategy". *Management Science,* Vol. 32(10), pp. 1231–1241, 1986.

Barney, J. B. "Firm Resources and Sustained Competitive Advantage". *Journal of Management*, Vol. 17(1), pp. 99–120, 1991.

Barney, J. B. and Hoskisson, R. E. "Strategic Groups: Untested Assertions and Research Proposals". *Managerial and Decision Economics*, Vol. 11, pp. 187–198, 1990.

Bauerschmidt, A. and Chrisman, J. J. "Strategies for Survival in the Microcomputer Industry: 1985–1989". *Journal of Management Inquiry*, Vol. 2(1), pp. 63–82, 1993.

Bozman, J. S. "Mac/Unix Marriage Takes Off". *Computerworld*, Vol. 27(25), p. 51, June 21 1993.

Casson, M. *The Entrepreneur*. Totowa, NJ: Barnes and Noble, 1982.

Caves, R. E. and Porter, M. E. "From Entry Barriers to Mobility Barriers: Conjectural Decisions and Contrived Deterrence to New Competition". *Quarterly Journal of Economics*, Vol. 91, pp. 241–261, 1977.

Cool, K. and Schendel, D. E. "Strategic Group Formation and Performance: U.S. Pharmaceutical Industry, 1963–82". *Management Science*, Vol. 33, pp. 1102–1124, 1987.

Cool, K. and Schendel, D. E. "Performance Differences Amonag Strategic Group Members". *Strategic Management Journal*, Vol. 9, pp. 207–223, 1988.

Corcoran, C. "PC Alliance Challenges Mac for Color Throne". *Infoworld*, Vol. 15(21), p. 37, May 24 1993.

Dierickx, I. and Cool, K. "Asset Stock Accumulation and Competitive Advantage". *Management Science*, Vol. 12, pp. 1504–1511, 1989.

DiMaggio, P. J. and Powell, W. W. "The Iron Cage Revisited: Institutional Isomorphism and Collective Rationality in Organizational Fields". *American Sociological Review*, Vol. 48(2), pp. 147–160, 1983.

Divorak, J. C. "Windows NT: Workstation Killer". *PC Magazine*, Vol. 12(17), October 12 1993.

Feigenbaum, A. and Thomas, H. "Strategic Groups and Performance: The U.S. Insurance Industry, 1970–84". *Strategic Management Journal*, Vol. 11, pp. 197–215, 1990.

Fitzgerald, M. "Compaq Hatches Plan to Loosen IBM's Grip; Aggressive Product Rollouts, Direct Sales Key to Strategy". *Computerworld*, Vol. 27(7), pp. 1–2, February 15 1993.

Flamm, K. *Creating the Computer*. Washington, D.C.: The Brookings Institution, 1988.

Frazier, G. L. and Howell, R. D. "Business Definition and Performance". *Journal of Marketing*, Vol. 47, pp. 59–67, 1983.

Freiberger, P. and Swaine, M. *Fire in the Valley,*. Berkeley, CA: Osborne/McGraw-Hill, 1984.

Galbraith, C. and Schendel, D. E. "An Empirical Analysis of Strategy Types". *Strategic Management Journal*, Vol. 4, pp. 153–173, 1983.

Ghemawat, P. "Sustainable Advantage". *Harvard Business Review*, pp. 53–58, September–October 1986.

Hatten, K. J. and Hatten, M. L. "Strategic Groups, Asymmetrical Mobility Barriers and Contestability". *Strategic Management Journal*, Vol. 8(4), pp. 329–342, 1987.

Hunt, M. S. "Competition in the Major Home Appliance Industry, 1960–1970". Unpublished Doctoral Dissertation, Harvard University, 1972.

Joch, A., Yager, T. and Thompson, T. "Desktop PC's: The Buyers Market Continues". *Byte*, Vol. 16(11), p. 157, October 15 1991.

Johnson, D. "Testing for Industry Infrastructure: Do Strategic Groups Exist?". Paper Presented at the 1993 Academy of Management Conference, 1993.

Johnson, G. and Thomas, H. "The Industry Context of Strategy and Performance: The U.K. Brewing Industry". *Strategic Management Journal*, Vol. 8, pp. 343–361, 1987.

Keenan, V. and Yi, P. "The Invisible Bridge to Mainframe Data". *MacUser*, Vol. 7(1), p. 138, January 1991.

Lach, E. "Resellers Fine-Tune Strategy as Apple Changes Channels". *MacWEEK*, Vol. 7(34), p. 30, August 23 1993.

Lawless, M., Bergh, D. and Wilsted, W. "Performance Variations Among Strategic Group Members: An Examination of Individual Firm Capability". *Journal of Management*, Vol. 5(4), pp. 649–661, 1989.

Lavin, D. "Robert Eaton Thinks 'Vision' is Overrated and He's not Alone". *Wall Street Journal*, Vol. 124(66), p. 1, October 4 1993.

Lewis, P. and Thomas, H. "The Linkage between Strategy, Strategic Groups, and Performance in the U.K. Retail Grocery Industry". *Strategic Managment Journal*, Vol. 11, pp. 385–397, 1990.

Lippman, S. A. and Rumelt, R. P. "Uncertain Imitability: An Analysis of Interfirm Differences in Efficiency Under Competition". *The Bell Journal of Economics*, Vol. 13, pp. 418–438, 1982.

Manes, S. and Andrews, P. *Gates.* New York: Doubleday, 1993.

Mascarenhas, B. and Aaker, D. A. "Mobility Barriers and Strategic Groups". *Strategic Management Journal*, Vol. 10, pp. 475–485, 1989.

McGee, J. and Thomas, H. "Strategic Groups: Theory, Research, and Taxonomy". *Strategic Management Journal*, Vol. 7(2), pp. 141–160, 1986.

Mehra, A. "A Resource Based Theory of Strategic Groups". Paper Presented at the 1991 Academy of Management Conference, 1991.

Miller, D. "Configurations of Strategy and Structure: Towards a Synthesis". *Strategic Management Journal*, Vol. 7, pp. 233–249, 1986.

Miller, D. and Friesen, P. H. *Organizations: A Quantum View*. Englewood Cliffs, NJ: Prentice-Hall, 1984.

Newman, H. H. "Strategic Groups and the Structure-Performance Relationship". *Review of Economics and Statistics*, Vol. 60, pp. 417–427, 1978.

Penrose, E. *The Theory of the Growth of the Firm*. New York: Wiley, 1959.

Pfeffer, J. and Nowak, P. "Joint Ventures and Interorganizational Interdependence". *Administrative Science Quarterly*, Vol. 21, pp. 398–418, 1976.

Porter, M. E. "The Structure Within Industries and Companies' Performance". *Review of Economics and Statistics*, Vol. 61, pp. 214–219, 1979.

Porter, M. E. *Competitive Strategy*. New York: Free Press, 1980.

Reed, R. and DeFillippi, R. J. "Causal Ambiguity, Barriers to Imitation, and Sustainable Competitive Advantage". *Academy of Management Review*, Vol. 15, pp. 88–102, 1990.

Rumelt, R. P. "Towards a Strategic Theory of the Firm". In Lamb, R. B., ed., *Competitive Strategic Management*. Englewood Cliffs, NJ: Prentice-Hall, 1984.

Rumelt, R. P. "Theory, Strategy, and Entrepreneurship". In Teece, D. J., ed., *The Competitive Challenge: Strategies for Industrial Innovation and Renewal*. Cambridge, MA: Ballinger, pp. 137–158, 1987.

Rumelt, R. P., Schendel, D. E. and Teece, D. "Fundamental Issues in Strategy: A Research Agenda for the 1990s". Announcement for the Silverado Conference on Strategy, 1990.

Sanchez, R. "Strategic Flexibility, Firm Organization, and Managerial Work in Dynamic Markets: A Strategic-Options Perspective". In Shrivastava, P., Huff, A. and Dutton, J., *Advances in Strategic Management*. Greenwich, CT: JAI Press, Vol. 9, pp. 251–291, 1993.

Schumpeter, J. A. *The Theory of Economic Development*. Cambridge, MA: Harvard University Press, 1934.

Teece, D. J. "Profiting from Technological Innovation: Implications for Integration, Collaboration, Licensing, and Public Policy". In Teece, D. J., ed., *The Competitive Challenge, Strategies for Industrial Innovation and Renewal*. Cambridge, MA: Ballinger, 1987.

Thomas, H. and Venkatraman, N. "Research on Strategic Groups: Progress and Prognosis". *Journal of Management Studies*, Vol. 25(6), pp. 537–555, 1988.

Tushman, M. and Anderson, P. "Technological Discontinuities and Organizational Environments". *Administrative Science Quarterly*, Vol. 31, pp. 439–465, 1986.

Wernerfelt, B. "A Resource-Based View of the Firm". *Strategic Management Journal*, Vol. 5, pp. 171–180, 1984.

Williamson, O. E. *Markets and Hierarchies*. New York: Free Press, 1975.

16

THE ROLE OF INTERNATIONAL R&D IN THE COMPETENCE-BUILDING STRATEGIES OF JAPANESE PHARMACEUTICAL FIRMS

Tom Roehl

INTRODUCTION

Firms are often faced with external shocks from their environment which render their existing competences less effective (Nelson and Winter, 1982). At the same time, such shocks may offer increased opportunities for changes in competitive position within the industry. The study of firm responses to environmental shocks is an important research challenge for strategy, and one for which the concept of competence-based competition is a natural framework for discussion (Itami, 1987). This paper studies the Japanese pharmaceutical industry, an industry for which there has recently been substantial changes in the external environment. The paper focuses on one important aspect of the competence-building response of these Japanese firms to major environmental change: their use of international research to build new competences to match their new environment.

The paper is organized as follows: in the next section we present a short description of the Japanese pharmaceutical industry and of the environmental changes it recently faced. The third section describes the various competence-building responses of these firms and attempts to identify categories of firms with similar strategies. The fourth section discusses the issues of internal organizational constraints, while the final section comments on what can be learned through the exercise of identifying patterns of competence-building.

THE JAPANESE PHARMACEUTICAL INDUSTRY: FACING ENVIRONMENTAL CHANGE

The Japanese pharmaceutical industry includes firms of various sizes, but the largest firm is less than one half the size of the leading firms in the United States and Europe. The industry has long been focused on its domestic market, with exports now growing but seldom accounting for more than ten percent of sales. Research and development efforts are significant, however, and many firms have R&D to Sales ratios which compare favorably with those of U.S. and European firms. This effort has paid off with an increasing stream of new products developed solely within Japan. In some years in the decade of the 1980's, the Japanese firms as a group produced a larger number of new patents in pharmaceutical products than their U.S. counterparts, although there is some debate about the level of innovation of their patented drugs. One piece of evidence suggesting the increasing sophistication of their drug development efforts is, however, the increasing amount of licensing revenue earned by these firms and the growing incidents of cross-licensing by Japanese pharmaceutical firms. Nevertheless, the overall level of the research and development effort is limited by the relatively small sizes of these firms and by their dependence on sales largely to the local Japanese market.

We have shown elsewhere that Japanese firms find it difficult to reach beyond an average level of research and development intensity, indicating that their relatively small size may indeed limit the rate of growth in research and development. (Mitchell, Roehl and Slattery, 1995). In contrast to the commonly held image of Japanese firms, firms in this industry struggle to compete and to extend or build new competences which can improve their competitive positions.

Like many other industries in the early post-war period, the Japanese pharmaceutical industry was the beneficiary of government policies which created a protected and supportive domestic environment in which to operate (Reich, 1990). Two important classes of changes in the regulatory environment, however, upset their comfortable, isolated market and forced these firms to change: (1): increased pressure for cost reduction from the government's universal medical insurance system; and (2): increased competitive pressure from foreign firms which entered the Japanese market directly as rules for foreign investment changed.

Health System Changes

In the immediate post-war period, the Japanese Ministry of Health and Welfare provided a very favorable environment for the Japanese pharmaceutical firms. Japanese firms enjoyed rather high fixed prices for their pharmaceuticals. They were also legally permitted (within Japan) to copy drugs developed abroad simply by using a different process to make a drug identical to a drug patented outside Japan. These two policies created a rather comfortable environment, giving Japanese pharmaceutical firms both a favorable cost position in R&D (a major cost in the value chain for this product), as well as profitable sales into a controlled market.

Japanese pharmaceutical firms were obliged, however, to share the gains from this cozy system with other members of the health care system, specifically with doctors, doctors who enjoyed an effective monopoly on the sale of prescription drugs. Firms therefore competed to provide information and assistance to doctors, anticipating that the result would be increases in sales of the firm's drug portfolio. Firms were free to sell drugs to doctors at a negotiated discount which could vary by doctor and by product. The result was that pharmaceutical firms felt it necessary to maintain large staffs of medical representatives to promote drugs to doctors, which certainly reduced somewhat the net value of the regulatory protection. Because they wanted to sell as many drugs as possible to each doctor with which they established a relationship, the firms also felt compelled to have a full set of drugs in their portfolio, meaning that they would always try to match the portfolios of other drug firms, even when drugs had to be obtained via licensing from abroad. There was also an incentive to make a stream of incremental changes to drugs to continually provide the marketing department with 'new' drugs (so called 'me-too' drugs) to gain doctor attention and maintain customer loyalty.

The first significant change in the regulatory environment. occurred In 1975, when Japan adjusted its patent system to match those of other developed countries. This change made the chemical composition of a drug—rather than the process used in making the drug—the source of pharmaceutical product protection under Japanese law. Japanese pharmaceutical firms could no longer copy drugs discovered outside Japan by just devising a different production process.

The second important environmental change occurred when Japanese medical costs skyrocketed in the 1970's, at the same time that Japanese government budget deficits put the government under severe pressure to eliminate budget increases for existing programs. The government response was a change in policies that meant that firms could no longer expect to maintain prices which allowed for comfortable margins (Mitchell, Roehl and Campbell, 1996). Government rules were changed in the early 1980's so that both the initial price the government approved, and the rates of price changes it approved, were now less attractive to firms. Under the tougher regulations, the initial price approved by the government is based on the level of increased benefits of the new drug rather than its costs of development. An innovative drug, defined as one which has 'significantly' greater efficacy than existing drugs, gets favorable pricing treatment, while 'me-too' drugs similar to other existing products can expect only a modest price. Further, rather than ministry actions which support the drug price, firms can now expect periodic reevaluations from the Ministry of Health and Welfare which continuously and more rapidly ratchet down the prices of existing drugs. Moreover, the rate of decrease in the approved price for a drug is likely to increase if competitors have started to introduce 'me-too' drugs. Thus the actions of competitors could greatly influence the total returns a firm might receive from its prior investment in drug R&D. Generics are much less necessary under this system of drug reimbursement. Generic drugs enter the market after patent protection lapses, forcing the price of the existing price of the drug coming off patent to drop to a competitive level. In the Japanese system, the government has already forced the price of the drug down substantially, making the generic drug entry less attractive, and unnecessary to encourage competitive drug pricing.

Foreign Investment Rule Changes

Initial postwar rules effectively encouraged foreign firms to license their drugs to Japanese firms for clinical testing and distribution in the local market. In addition to Japanese patent rules which made it easy for Japanese firms to copy new foreign drugs, firms were not allowed to present their drugs for ministry approval in their own name. They had to have a Japanese 'partner' make the formal application. Other rules which made it difficult for all foreign firms to invest in Japan of course applied to foreign pharmaceutical firms as well. The predictable result of these restrictions was marketing alliances which matched the foreign firms with domestic partners.

By the middle of the 1980's, these restrictions had all been dropped. After the change in patent laws in the mid 1970's and the adoption of a more liberal Foreign Exchange Control Law in 1980, there were essentially no formal regulatory barriers to investment. Further, regulatory changes in the 1980's enabled foreign firms to apply for their own drug approvals.

The results of the relaxation of these restrictions were predictable, if somewhat slow to develop. Since 1980, foreign firms have introduced independent marketing units into Japan and have begun to set up or expand R&D facilities in Japan. The weak competences of Japanese firms in drug creation relative to foreign firms was exposed by these environmental changes. Foreign firms could even consider taking over of a poor performer in the Japanese industry (e.g. Merck's purchase of a lagging Banyu in 1983).

For Japanese firms, these environmental changes had several implications for their R&D strategies. Increasing numbers of competitors could only drive down the returns available from the Japanese domestic market. Even more worrisome is that the availability of new pharmaceutical products from abroad for licensing into Japan is likely to diminish, since foreign firms, like any other firms operating in the domestic market, will want to have a full and (if possible) an exclusive line of drugs to offer to doctors.

In the last two decades, all the world's pharmaceutical firms have faced the pressures of escalating research and development expenses. Japanese firms were no different. Yet the two foregoing trends in the *domestic* environment have exacerbated the pressures on Japanese pharmaceutical firms. These firms now face reduced access to their (previously) low cost foreign source of new drugs—i.e., the drug-creation competences of foreign firms—willing to license to Japanese firms. Moreover, they also faced a reduced payoff in profits made by developing incrementally effective drugs which their existing R&D operations had strong competences in developing. Following these momentous environmental changes, Japanese pharmaceutical firms clearly needed to develop new R&D competences to survive in their new competitive environment.

These changes also reduced the effectiveness of the firms' other strong competence, their marketing capability. With more sophisticated products increasingly available in the Japanese market, medical representatives need to become more sophisticated. Large numbers of representatives alone would no longer be as effective. In addition, while it takes foreign firms some time to develop a marketing network of their own, Japanese firms would surely find that increased competition in marketing progressively erodes the value of their current marketing system. It seems inevitable that Japanese pharmaceutical firms would have to develop competences which are capable of creating and marketing new, truly innovative pharmaceuticals.

PATTERNS OF COMPETENCE-BUILDING IN RESPONSE TO ENVIRONMENTAL CHANGE

These changes did not affect all firms in the industry equally. The changes in environment have had, at least for some firms, a *positive* effect, as they search for opportunities to improve their existing competitive positions in the Japanese industry. If a firm had—or could build more quickly or more effectively—the research and development skills needed to succeed in the new environment, it could reasonably expect to change its relative position within the Japanese (and perhaps even the worldwide) pharmaceutical industry. On a relative basis, marketing competences have become less critical, since superior competence in new drug development also should enable a firm either to license drugs or to form an alliance with another firm to market the products it develops. Thus, one can argue that Japanese pharmaceutical firms most likely to benefit from these changes would be those which have a longer experience in doing research, those firms with technologies useful in creating innovative drugs (e.g. fermentation technology), and those with a currently profitable drug portfolio from which to fund an increase in R&D.

The response of Japanese pharmaceutical firms to these environmental changes has been to increase both internally and via contracting and alliances, their efforts to attain domestic and international access to a more innovative stream of pharmaceutical products. A more detailed analysis of the Japanese pharmaceutical firms in this regard is found in another recent paper (Roehl, Mitchell and Slattery, 1995). The focus of this paper is on the *international activities* of the firms, and on how those activities relate to these firm's R&D competences both actual and desired. Five types of competence-building activities are identified, and detailed information about the competence-building activity of one or more exemplar firms is provided to illustrate each observed pattern of competence-building. While the placing of a given firm in a specific category of competence-building can always be debated, the collections of firms included under each category do show evidence of following different trajectories in both the kinds and levels of competences they are apparently striving to achieve.

Much of the information presented below was obtained from public sources, including government reports Data Book, 1991, newspapers, (Economist, 1987) and an increasingly sophisticated set of analyses from securities firms operating in the Tokyo market. In addition, interviews were conducted in the summer of 1992 and the summer of 1993 with managers in the research and development areas of fifteen major Japanese pharmaceutical firms. To protect confidentiality, companies are not identified by name in the discussion which follows.

TYPE ONE: TARGETED COMPETENCE-BUILDING TO SUPPORT INTERNATIONAL HARVESTING

For this group of firms, the main motive for expanding into international research operations is apparently to gain full value for the internally generated pharmaceutical products of the firm, which were developed and commercialized in Japan. These firms recognize that marketing alone is not sufficient to gain worldwide benefits from their drugs. The pattern of competence-building they pursue, therefore, is to invest in overseas clinical development activities which can lead to improving the process of obtaining approvals of their Japanese-developed drugs in other countries.

Firm One

This firm, one of the largest in the industry, has a large portfolio of products, and a large domestic research staff. While they do occasionally contract with outsiders when they do not have the required competence in-house, or when entering into parallel research efforts looks attractive because of the uncertainty of critical outcomes, the major efforts to develop new drugs are internal and in Japan. The firm has had a long history of international operations. It has more than twenty years of foreign sales experience in Triad (U.S. Europe and Japan) markets. Contrary to many other firms, it has always thought that it could make money marketing its products abroad. In the early 1980's, it decided that licensing was not an adequate means of getting full value for its drug portfolio, and it decided to get more involved in the clinical development process abroad. As the first Japanese firm to make this move, it felt that it could not do it alone, and so chose overseas joint venture partners, hoping thereby to develop competences through its joint venture experience. In many cases, partners were available from previous relationships in Japan.

The timing of the firm's move was important, since the firm had some good products to put into overseas clinical trials at that time. The firm realized that its lack of experience would mean that initially the clinical trials costs would be higher in its internal laboratories than if it contracted with local suppliers of the testing. Yet, there were several opportunities to build competences which outweighed the costs. Control over scheduling of the tests necessary for approvals, which is important to the achievement of marketing authority for the drugs in a timely manner, would be in their hands. Information about its drugs could be controlled better as well. There was another important marketing benefit: reputation. The company established new ties to overseas doctors, and as a result was able to do some promotion to some influential players in the health care professions. The result of developing the competence to undertake (successful) clinical trials overseas was the ability to do product development work throughout the Triad. The timing was also fortuitous, since the large number of new chemical entities available to the firm by that time made such a large risk worth taking. By the early 80's, the company also had some experience abroad through its bulk sales operations, so that made it somewhat easier for top management to make the commitment to go overseas. The company is now deepening that commitment by gradually assuming majority control over many of these joint venture operations. In this regard, it is worth noting that the firm follows a pattern more typical of European drug firm operations than American firm operations. Locals typically run the operations, while a small number of Japanese fulfill mostly support and coordination roles.

Firm Two

This firm is a top tier firm in the industry, with a strong organizational commitment to doing basic research domestically. Its international operations are focused on some work in clinical labs and on licensing products to foreign firms. The firm keeps contact with foreign developments through work with overseas universities and by sending ten to twenty scientists to work abroad at any one time. While the firm has bought a foreign operation, the objective in this purchase was primarily to use its marketing channels. The existing clinical development skills of the acquired firm were integrated into the operations of staff in Japan who do similar work, and the firm focused on coordinating clinical activities across organizational borders. Semiannual meetings, common in all the international operations, did not provide sufficient coordination, so it has initiated a six-month exchange of researchers to improve information flows, especially at lower levels in the organization. The firm's move toward foreign clinical development is at an earlier stage than that of firm one, but the objectives are similar—i.e., to build competences to support a marketing effort which has products for which markets are thought to exist abroad.

Firm Three

Not all firms expect that their objectives in competence-building will remain constant as they develop and change the mix of their competences. The third firm is an example of a firm which, while initially developing international operations for clinical development and marketing, is now experimenting with more basic research and development as well. This company is a smaller firm, but still is generally highly rated for its research competence by analysts. It has its own wholly–owned clinical laboratories in Europe and the U.S., but has also acquired firms on both continents which have some limited development capabilities. The firm's overseas labs are important to make sure the firm can take advantage of market opportunities for its drugs. Development overseas therefore usually lags development in Japan. The firm intends to develop the competences of these subsidiaries so that they can take on more responsibility for early clinical testing, and the firm is investing in hiring new R&D personnel to do so.

Recently the firm has started a new small scale research institute in Europe that will look for new chemical entities (categories of chemicals that may lead to future drugs) in an area important to the firm. The researchers will be given substantial independence during a five year period. Researchers from Japan have joined that project for periods of time, but its contacts with Japan will be more limited.

Benefits of Competence-Building to Support International Harvesting

These three companies see their current company strengths as derived from a wide portfolio of pharmaceutical products, a portfolio initially created in Japan and targeted at a domestic Japanese market. Confident of their ability to generate new products within Japan, they see opportunities to gain quick access to all Triad markets as being crucial for their competitive success, and thus for their ability to continue to fund the large internal research activities they are currently undertaking in Japan. Their emphasis on clinical labs, well-integrated with their domestic operations, increases the return on domestic research competences, while limiting management costs and investments.

TYPE TWO: INTERNATIONAL COMPETENCE BUILDERS

Managers in these firms are less sanguine about their firm's ability to develop the research and development competences necessary for the new environment within their own existing domestic organizations. Each feels that by accumulating research experience abroad within their own organization, the firm will be a stronger competitor in the worldwide market and is likely to improve its position in the Japanese market as well. More so than other firms considered here, these firms are skeptical about their ability to gather information and knowledge from abroad without strong organizational control over the research process itself. Thus, in each case we see a conscious effort to build a broad internal capability for research across the Triad. This does not mean that we see none of the activities of the type one firms, but that the basic research effort receives equal or even primary emphasis within the international competence-building activities of the firm.

Firm One

This firm is a smaller but very innovative firm within the pharmaceuticals industry, with a significant presence in both over-the-counter and ethical drugs. The firm's managers believe that it is the creation of innovative drugs that attracts the attention of the drug wholesalers to the firm, so the firm has always put a lot of effort into basic research. Thus, the firm's mix of R&D is more heavily weighted to research than is the case in most Japanese pharmaceutical firms. It has a culture which allows for selection of risky projects, but it does maintain tightly controlled implementation procedures within projects. The current organization of research already gives a great degree of latitude to research directors in the domestic market, so the organization has a research culture which could facilitate independent competence-building international investments.

The company's initial international laboratories were for clinical work, in both the United States and (on a smaller scale) in Europe. Very soon, however, the company added a research institute which took advantage of biotechnology expertise in an American university. In contrast to both its clinical work in foreign labs and its relationships developed with university labs in Japan, the research at this research institute is more basic, and does not have a project focus or a strict time limit. In contrast to the groups in the first group which focus on marketing in the Triad, this company has developed a wider set of foreign activities which includes activities earlier in the value chain.

Firm Two

This firm is a large firm in the industry which is currently growing in sales faster than the industry average. Since the company actually started as a research laboratory many years ago, it is perhaps a more natural extension for this firm than for some others to think about competence-building in research through international operations. With clear top management support for research, the firm could pursue a more risky approach that might eventually lead to the accumulation of new products and knowledge from abroad, rather, than limiting its competence-building to research laboratories in Japan. Here as in other cases, timing also played an important role. The firm had the support of a well-respected bicultural Japanese professor in the U.S. with whom they had previous experience. Had they not previously developed ties with this boundary-spanning advisor, they might not have had the confidence to undertake such an organizationally ambitious undertaking.

Building on that experience of setting up and running this laboratory in the U.S., the firm moved to set up another relationship in a different research area in Europe, using the lessons learned from the United States venture to manage a European relationship in which they had no cultural intermediary.

In both cases, good communication between the top research manager and top management at the firm was a determining factor in the decision to invest. Although senior managers became involved when specific problems arose, the firm managed to avoid many potential problems by establishing formal systems for the exchange of information between management and the foreign researchers. General managers at the firm's Japanese laboratories are given opportunities to be involved in international information exchange, thereby both broadening the knowledge base of the firm and building capabilities in disseminating information from the foreign labs.

In both the U.S. and the European ventures, the firm holds the equity in the lab. Rather than seeking tight integration, these two units are purposely not overlapping in research objectives, and are given independence. Japanese are assigned to the labs primarily to see that coordination takes place with domestic laboratories, and that any new products developed in the labs are smoothly introduced in the downstream development process in Japan.

Firm Three

The final firm in this category is a somewhat more reluctant international resource accumulator. The firm is not one of the largest firms in the industry, but it has been active in developing a number of foreign operations. It has a relationship in the U.S. that started as contract research, but which the Japanese firm bought in the late 1980's. The company thought that biotechnology would reinvigorate a product area, and the foreign firm offered that technology. The firm has sent all its Japanese researchers to the foreign location to obtain critical mass for this research area. Another foreign operation was developed in response to the success of a competitor's drug in the Japanese market. They used capital participation to gain a greater say in the activities of the foreign firm, important because of the rather specific objective of responding to a domestic market challenge. They also do contract research, and in their minds, a good international program will always have a balance between the two approaches. In basic research, they have an ownership stake in a British pharmaceutical lab, but even that was rather passive, since they were introduced to the firm by an investment bank.

In addition to the above-mentioned relationships in the triad, the firm has a joint venture with an Asian firm to do organic synthesis for it. This very labor intensive aspect of the drug discovery process can be speeded up via this collaborative effort, which would have been necessary anyway to gain market access to that country.

Firm Four

The firm is a major player in the Japanese industry. Its international operations indicate that it feels it must develop assets abroad at all levels of the value chain for pharmaceuticals. It has bought firms which will allow it to develop distribution and local production in both Europe and the U.S., and is slowly increasing the amount of clinical work done in house abroad. In addition to these complementary assets to its marketing efforts abroad, however, it has two international laboratories which focus on the more basic end of the research spectrum. These labs, in contrast to the development operations, are given substantial free-dom to develop research plans and to manage local operations. Visits to Japan substitute for substantial Japanese involvement in the laboratories.

Resource Benefit of International: Type Two

The innovations and the market scanning activities of these firms are expected to enhance the domestic position of these firms. If the marketing of the firm is relatively weak, or if the firm expects the current system of marketing to be less potent in the future, then this alternative set of firm resources will have a higher return for this type of firm. Firms often suggested that they expected the relationships to energize the local researchers as well as provide output in its own right. The organizations of these firms seem to be more capable of using a greater variety of input without as much danger to the cohesion of the research organization. If the organization is willing to tolerate more independence within its domestic operations, as some of the firms in this category indicated, then it is not as great a reach for the organization to integrate a foreign research laboratory as well.

TYPE THREE: PARTNER-SEEKING INTERNATIONALIZERS

Many new players have entered the Japanese pharmaceutical industry. Firms with fermentation technology from the foods or beverage industry and firms from the chemical industry predominate. These firms, possessing only one resource necessary for success of the pharmaceuticals industry, and starting from a very low base in human resources, need a wider variety of outside partnerships if they are to develop the resources to move quickly into the industry. At the same time, their skills in process technology are newly important to firms using biotechnology to develop new drugs. This complementarity leads to a distinct pattern of international research and development activity.

Firm One

Biotechnology was selected as one of the diversification moves of this profitable outsider. It seemed a natural extension of its fermentation technology resource base. Choosing a product that at the time seemed difficult to produce, they tried to develop the substance on their own. They felt that a small stable of such innovative products might over time let them gain access to distribution without the huge investment in marketing staff common in the industry. When a foreign firm succeeded in cloning that substance, they made contact to develop a joint venture company. The venture was an effective means for the Japanese firm to gain biotechnology experience quickly, while the foreign firm gained access to the technology for volume production of the drug. The cooperation led to very speedy clinical trials and quick access to the marketplace. Production expertise was even given for the foreign location plant outside the joint venture.

The firm has also made very specific contracts with firms which have basic research programs, with the intent of providing new drugs which can be developed and produced using the firm's core production technologies. Since the clinical development also requires relatively large increases in volume for testing, their resources are valuable at that stage as well. Thus, these 'contracts' are more like joint ventures than many of the other contract research that is funded by Japanese firms. Assets are complementary.

Firm Two

This company is also a new entrant, with pharmaceuticals only a small portion of the total sales, and with its first pharmaceuticals appearing only in the mid 1980's. The firm searches for partners both domestically and internationally. With a main business less profitable than Firm One, it must search for complementary resources outside the firm. The importance of that effort is indicated by a separate department which handles only the international alliances. The firm, with little distribution in Japan, much less abroad, developed ties to strengthen the marketing function, and gain additional assistance in development resources. They depend on their foreign alliance partner for basic research. Another partner was expected to develop their products for the foreign market, with the quid pro quo being development of that foreign firm's products by the Japanese firm for Japan. These activities can be kept separate, making management quite simple.

Resource Benefit of International: Type Three

These partnerships are able to trade process expertise for access to a wider knowledge base in pharmaceuticals. While seemingly quite different from cross licensing, the results are similar, with both sides increasing the value of their resource portfolio. The partners do not, even with the changed and enriched portfolio of assets, directly compete with each other, so the resource accumulation process should be less acrimonious. This is important, since there is a longer period of cooperation required than with more simple product exchanges common in cross licensing, yet no means for control. Had either side had more experience on its own, this ability to accumulate assets in partnership would not have been feasible. Resources are of grater value if they can be used simultaneously (Itami, 1987), so the additional use for the fermentation technology adds value to the domestic resource portfolio of these firms.

TYPE FOUR: DOMESTICALLY-FOCUSED INNOVATORS

Not all firms which choose to deemphasize international research and development do so because they are not capable of generating world-class products. The firms in this group have a good record in developing products, but contrary to the Type One firms, are less interested in developing international distribution channels. Their return is expected to come from out licensing, or the access, via cross licensing, to pharmaceuticals developed abroad. With more faith in the effectiveness of market exchange, the firms feel less inclined to accumulate assets internationally.

Firm One

This company has had basic research laboratories in Japan for over thirty years, and while not among the largest of the Japanese firms, is one of the most profitable. The firm has been very successful in finding multiple uses for an individual drug, attributable to the unique nature of many of their drugs. Licensing is frequently done when a drug is successful and has foreign potential. They will try to trade the drug via cross license, but only when they have gaps in their product line. They limit their foreign activity to very specific funded research of relatively short duration, taking rights to any discovery in exchange. The contracts run the gamut from basic research to computer searching for new chemical entities. A small number of Japanese researchers may be sent to help with information flow, but given the extremely successful domestic research organization, it is costly to do so. The very success of their internal activities reduces their contacts with foreign firms via the licensing process. At this point, they are content to monitor foreign developments via these sponsored research projects. The company has no stated plans to change this method of international operation.

Firm Two

This medium sized firm uses its core resource base of fermentation technology to develop pharmaceuticals. It keeps all its basic research in Japan, and has not been that active in developing an internal organization for clinical testing abroad, establishing the formal organization only in 1992 in the U.S. The organization's function is also much wider, monitoring contacts with universities, dealing with in and out licensing, and generally transmitting information on the technical activity in that area of the Triad. The individual collaboration with institutes is appropriate, this firm believes, given the large amount of research being developed within the firm in Japan. A very significant increase in the research organization size in Japan has taken place at the same time that international research and development has become feasible. The domestic investment has started to generate a lot of promising ideas, and that has forced the firm to limit its activities abroad to individual contracts and collaboration, often with public sector institutes. The personal networks that develop through these transfers of people substitute for the overseas organizations used by other firms. If the firm monitors the clinical trials contracts carefully, it feels it can get effective service even on its clinical testing through contract laboratories.

Resource Benefit of International: Type Four

These firms clearly have demonstrated an interest in and often success in the development of innovative pharmaceutical products. It is the characteristic of this industry that firms are not able to forecast the success of their research organization and the output of development candidates. Firms felt that licensing was a far superior method to get full value for the assets which the firm had accumulated internally. Thus, a firm with a record of *unexpected* strong performance would have to reallocate internal resources, and move to get full value for the opportunities which it had developed. Without an active labor market in research personnel, and with the problems of integration looming with any great increase of staff, it is understandable that the firms see the success as limiting additional initiatives. Alternative domestic paths to resource accumulation dominate, since these newly developed and very firm-specific assets must be exploited quickly or they will lose value. The success might also increase the firm managers' confidence that their domestic internal efforts will be able to generate the necessary resources for competition in the pharmaceutical markets of the 21st century. That also would dictate a weaker effort to develop new organizational resources for research internationally. Note that this approach is more powerful if coupled with a more optimistic view of the markets for information and for licensing products internationally.

TYPE FIVE: INTERNATIONAL SKEPTICS

In many firms, top management has been extremely skeptical about international involvement of any type other than licensing. Given the resource base of the firm, there is less potential for them either to build assets which fit their overall resource building plan, or increase returns on their existing asset base. Firms with both strong and weak positions in ethical drugs fall into this category, but the reasons are somewhat different. Mid-level firms are concentrating on the development of a strong research organization within Japan, and have few resources left to deploy abroad. This contrasts with the previous group whose domestic success leads to a shortage of internationally deployable resources. For some more established firms, the importance of relationships in their current resource base makes the introduction of new partners more difficult than the average firm.

Firm One

This firm has been a strong player in the domestic market, based on an extensive marketing organization, and with a product line weighted toward one type of pharmaceutical. It has filled in its product line with drugs from foreign firms, depending to a large extent on a relationship with one foreign firm. It has maintained ties with its partners for a long period of time and feels that these relationships are an important part of its own resource base, making its research and development system effective. Even in the domestic market, it is hesitant to develop ties with research personnel outside the firm if there is no previous relationships to help smoothly develop and effectively manage the relationships. The firm is trying, within its domestic research organization, to develop a wider range of products, since its source of drugs from foreign firms is now in some doubt as foreign firms enter the marketplace It has few current international activities, concentrating its activities on licensing out its successful products. Remembering the earlier comment about the importance of cross licensing in the new environment as a source of new drugs from abroad, the strategy of the firm to emphasize licensing has another strong justification. With a more concentrated product line in Japan, continued access to foreign products helps smooth the transition to a more broadly based product line.

Foreign operations would by definition decrease the number of drugs the firm could offer in cross-licensing deals. This opportunity cost to its cross-licensing arrangements, in addition to the relationship concerns, make the policies consistent with the firm's overall competence-building strategy.

Firm Two

Not all firms in this category have a strong record in ethical drug research. Firms which are trying to make major improvements in the quality of their domestic research base may also fall into this category of international skeptics. The most important challenge for these firms is to change their position in the domestic market. With little experience to draw on for international activities, these firms allocate few resources to the international arena at this time. This firm is a mid-size player in the pharmaceuticals business, with a very large concentration in over the counter drugs. It uses its strong position in over the counter to add strength in what it sees as a more profitable and faster growing field of ethical drugs. This has meant a significant increase in research personnel, and a major laboratory expansion. While the profitability of the over the counter drugs would have permitted financial support for an overseas research operation, the limits on personnel necessary to staff and coordinate it are lacking. For the time being they are limiting themselves to university contacts and individual research assignments abroad, with the hope that these will provide some of the human resources for future internationalization which they currently lack. The company recognizes that it is likely to require international activities at some point in the future, but does not have a policy yet on timing or on the nature of the process of such 'late internationalization.'

Resource Implications of International: Type Five

The most important implication in this section is the importance of complementary assets to use in building and utilizing the foreign research organization. Compared to other firms in the industry, the firms in this group found that their resource base was more complementary to other domestic alternative resource accumulation paths than for increasing foreign research.

ORGANIZATIONAL ISSUES

The overall research organization and philosophy of the company is an important element in the discussion of each of the five types of international R&D strategies. As Mitchell, Roehl and Slattery (1995), have argued, cohesion is an important element in understanding the path taken by all Japanese firms. With smaller research staffs, the Japanese firms must be able to get all parts of the organization to work together effectively if the firm is to compete with foreign firms with larger research staffs. Internationalization is thus constrained by these internal requirements in all firms.

We have argued above that a resource-based approach to strategy should consider both the constraints and the opportunities which the existing resource base offers to a firm's strategic direction. This section presents some more general comments about the importance of certain firm organizational resources. These are important in explaining why firms use different paths in encouraging a more significant allocation of resource and resource building effort to international.

Role of Top Management

Interviews often made comments on the importance of top management in the increased research and development efforts. If the firm were in transition between top managers, or if a succession of top managers had very different ideas of how internationalization should fit within the wider research organization, then resource building strategies could not be entered into with any confidence. In several cases this lack of continuity paralyzed the organization for a time. International efforts, with its greater levels of uncertainty, suffered more than other parts as firms chose to continue the status quo.

Family ownership remains important in many of the firms in the industry. Many of the firms have long histories as Chinese medicine entrepreneurs dating back centuries. Without the need for consensus decision making that can often limit the flexibility of Japanese firms, such concentrated ownership would seem likely to permit the more radical changes that internationalization might require. We do not find that to be the case, however. Concentrated ownership can just as easily lead to an unwillingness to change direction as it can support a radical transformation, and we find no consistent relationship between the ownership concentration and the international activity of the firm.

What seems more common is the importance of top management knowledge of technology. When managers talked informally about the process of selling top management on increased research and development activity, and international activity in particular, they feel more confident if senior management shows by words and actions a strong interest in research. Since these resource building strategies are not easy to explain, and require a tolerance of rather slow development, management attitudes toward research seem important considerations in choosing among alternative strategies.

When top management must search for new areas to use and develop its current portfolio of resources, the firm seems willing to attempt more innovative types of international strategies. This can come from the very weakness of the firm's current businesses, as with the firms in the chemical industry that are newcomers to pharmaceuticals. Yet it could also stem from a conscious attempt on the part of the firm to develop a domestic strategy which depends for success on a series of rapidly changing products and strategic elements, so that change is the normal organizational environment in the firm.

Profitable operations in Japan, though it might predict increases in research and development, does not necessarily mean that the firm will have a larger international component to its R&D strategy. Profitable operations can make it hard to increase international resource building in some firms, especially when the success is from a single area, or when the success does not provide the complementary human resources necessary to carry out international as opposed to domestic research strategies.

LABELLING A SUCCESSFUL INTERNATIONAL RESEARCH STRATEGY

We are not able to label any one of these five types as necessarily more or less successful within the industry. We could show both successful and unsuccessful firms in most if not all categories. International activities can contribute in a variety of ways to the development of the firm's resource base, while the resource base of the firm does to some extent constrain the potential activities which the firm can undertake. The competence-building strategies can also depend on the pattern of internationalization for the worldwide pharmaceutical industry, as described in Mitchell, Roehl and Slattery (1995). Even if the international strategy matches the current resources and the resource building goals of the firm, trends in the world-wide industry which no one currently can forecast can strongly influence the returns to any decision regarding international resource accumulation (Grabowski, 1990).

No one now can forecast the effectiveness of the current moves toward global marketing. The jury is still out on whether it will be more effective to centralize R&D or spread a worldwide net to catch a variety of ideas from the wider pool. With these uncertainties added, it is not surprising to see the significant differences in resource building strategies identified within the Japanese pharmaceutical industry. That very variety may assure that at least some Japanese firms will be major players in the industry of the 21st century, but it may also assure that the relative fortunes of firms in the industry will ebb and flow as the industry changes and develops.

REFERENCES

"Molecules and Markets: A Survey of Pharmaceuticals". *The Economist*, pp. S3–S14, February 7 1987.

Grabowski, H. "Innovation and International Competitiveness in Pharmaceuticals". In Heertje, A. and Perlman, M., eds, *Evolving Technology and Market*

Structure: Studies in Schumpeterian Economics. Ann Arbor: University of Michigan Press, pp. 167–185, 1990.

Itami, H. and Roehl, T. *Mobilizing Invisible Assets.* Cambridge, MA: Harvard University Press, 1987.

Data Book 1991. Tokyo: Japan Pharmaceutical Manufacturers Association, 1991.

Mitchell, W., Roehl, T. and Slattery, R. "Influence on R&D Growth of Japanese Pharmaceutical Firms, 1975–1990". *Journal of High Technology Management,* Vol. 6, pp. 17–31, Spring 1995.

Mitchell, W., Roehl, T. and Campbell, J. C. "Sales, R&D and Profitability in the Japanese Pharmaceutical Industry, 1981–1992." In Ikegami, N. and Campbell, J. C., eds, *Containing Health Care Costs in Japan.* Ann Arbor: University of Michigan Press, forthcoming, 1996.

Nelson, R. R. and Winter, S. G. *An Evolutionary Theory of Economic Change.* Cambridge, MA: Harvard University Press, 1982.

Reich, M. R. "Why the Japanese Don't Export More Pharmaceuticals: Health Policy as Industrial Policy". *California Management Review,* Vol. 32, pp. 124–150, Winter 1990.

Roehl, T., Mitchell, W. and Slattery, R. "The Growth of R&D Investment and Organizational Changes by Japanese Pharmaceutical Firms, 1975–1993." In Liker, J. K., Ettlie, J. E. and Campbell, J. C., eds, *Engineered in Japan: Japanese Technology Management Practices.* New York: Oxford University Press, pp. 40–69, 1995.

INDEX

Tube Bases (TB) 250
Turin, Jolly Hotels 133

U.K.
  Advanced Audio Ltd. 149–61
  temperature control industry 190–204
uncertainty 336
understandibility, resources 203–4
uniqueness 176–7
U.S.
  AT&T Network Systems 282, 284
  car industry 209–23
  Japanese pharmaceutical industry 380,
    384–5, 387–9, 392
  "quick-connect" technologies 306, 314,
    315
  semiconductor industry 328, 342
  strategic configurations 360–74

strategic goals taxonomy 79

vacuum tube technology 340–1
value-chain "arrow" 114
variance model 231, 238–41, 241
versatility, resources dimension 201–4
vertical quasi-integration 168, 169–71
vertically-constrained industry structure
    165–82
very large scale integrated circuits (VLSI)
    344–6
virtual assembly 309
virtual reality 308
"virtuous circle" 68, 69
vocabulary 6–11
Volkswagen (VW) group 214, 215

"zero-based" strategy making 56